Petrine Studies

Petrine Studies

Support and Ethical Expressions of Petrine Theology

DOUGLAS W. KENNARD

WIPF & STOCK · Eugene, Oregon

PETRINE STUDIES
Support and Ethical Expressions of Petrine Theology

Copyright © 2022 Douglas W. Kennard. All rights reserved. Except for brief quotations in critical publications or reviews, no part of this book may be reproduced in any manner without prior written permission from the publisher. Write: Permissions, Wipf and Stock Publishers, 199 W. 8th Ave., Suite 3, Eugene, OR 97401.

Wipf & Stock
An Imprint of Wipf and Stock Publishers
199 W. 8th Ave., Suite 3
Eugene, OR 97401

www.wipfandstock.com

PAPERBACK ISBN: 978-1-7252-6001-6
HARDCOVER ISBN: 978-1-7252-6002-3
EBOOK ISBN: 978-1-7252-6003-0

10/10/22

This book is dedicated to
Edwin Blum
For whom an earlier version of a part of
this manuscript was prepared decades ago.

Contents

Abbreviations | ix

1. Lost Boy or Foundation for Christian Theology | 1
2. Source Material for Petrine Theology | 11
3. The Recipients of the Petrine Epistles | 36
4. Form in the Epistles of Peter | 47
5. The Man Called Peter | 57
6. Petrine Epistemology of Testimony, Prophecy as Proclamation, and Evidentialism | 86
7. Jewish Traditions and Gentile Conversion | 107
8. Marriage, Not Divorce | 116
9. Mark 10:17–31: Standard and Poor | 124
10. Jesus' Historical Death and Resurrection | 134

Select Bibliography | 151
Suject Index | 189
Author Index | 191
Scripture Index | 197

Abbreviations

ʽAbod. Zar.	Rabbinic ʽAbodah Zarah
Abr.	On the Life of Abraham
Adv. Gent.	Adversus nationes
Adv. Haer.	Against Heresies
Advice	Advice about Keeping Well
Adv. Jud.	Adversus Judaeos
Aem.	Aemilius Paullus
Aen.	Aeneid
Aet.	On the Eternity of the World
AfO	Archiv für Orientforschung
AfOB	Archiv für Orientforschung: Beiheft
Ag.	Against
Ag. Ap.	Josephus, Against Apion
ʼAg. Ber.	ʼAggadot Berešit
Agr.	Agricola
Aj.	Ajax
AJT	American Journal of Theology
Alex.	Alexander
Alex. fort.	De Alexander magni fortuna aut virtute
All.	Allegoriae

Anab.	Anabasis
AnBib	Analecta biblica series
Ancor.	Ancoratus
ANEP	Ancient Near Eastern Pictures Relating to the Old Testament. Edited by James Pritchard.
ANET	Ancient Near Eastern Texts Relating to the Old Testament. Edited by James Pritchard.
Ann.	Annales
ANRW	Aufstieg und Niedergang der römischen Welt: Geschichte und Kultur Rom sim Spiegel der neueren Forschung. Edited by H. Temporini and W. Haase. Berlin.
Ant.	Antiquities as in Josephus, Jewish history or Sophicles, history
Ant. rom.	Antiquitates romanae
Apoc.	Apolalypse
Apoc. El.	Apocalypse of Elijah in Hebrew and Coptic
Apocr. Jn.	Apocryphon of John
Apol.	Apology, as for Plato, Apology of Socrates or Justin Martyr, numbered Apology
Apos.	Apostles as in pseudepigrapha Epistle to the Apostles
ʿArak.	Rabbinic ʿArakin
Arist.	Aristites
ARN	ʾAbot de Rabbi Nathan
ARW	Archiv für Religionwissenschaft
Ascen. Isa.	Ascension of Isaiah
As. Mos.	Assumption of Moses
ASTI	Annual of the Swedish Theological Institute
ATJ	Ashland Theological Journal
Att.	Epistular ad Atticum
Aul. Gel.	Aulus Gellius
B. or b.	Babylonian Talmud

BA	*The Biblical Archaeologist*
BAG	Bauer, W., W. E. Arndt, and F. W. Gingrich. *Greek-English Lexicon of the New Testament and Other Early Literature*. Chicago, 1957.
Bapt.	*Baptism*
Bar	Apocrypha Baruch with number 1 or 2 before
BAR	*Biblical Archaeology Review*
Barn.	*Barnabas*
BASOR	*Bulletin of the American Schools of Oriental Research*
Bat.	Rabbinic *Baba Batra*
BBR	*Bulletin for Biblical Research*
BDB	Francis Brown, S. D. Driver, and Charles Briggs, eds. *A Hebrew and English Lexicon of the Old Testament*. Oxford: Clarendon, 1907.
BECNT	Baker Exegetical Commentary on the New Testament
Bell. Cat.	*Bellum catalinae*
Bell Civ.	*Civil War*
Ben. Is. Jac.	*De benedictionibus Isaaci et Jacobi*
Ber.	Rabbinic *Berorot*
BEvT	Beiträge zur evangelischen Theologie
BHT	Beiträge zur historischen Theologie
Bib	*Biblica*
BJRL	*Bulletin of the John Rylands University Library of Manchester*
BMAP	*The Brooklyn Museum Aramaic Papyri*. Edited by E. G. Kraeling.
BN	*Biblische Notizen*
BR	*Biblical Research*
Bride	*Advice to Bride and Groom*
Brut.	*Brutus* or *De claris oratoribus*

BSac	*Bibliotheca sacra*
BTB	*Biblical Theology Bulletin*
BTZ	*Berliner Theologische Zeitschrift*
BV	*Biblical Viewpoint*
BZ	*Biblische Zeitschrift*
BZAW	*Beihefte zur Zeitschrift für die alttestamentliche Wissenschaft*
C. Ap.	Josephus, *Contra Apionem*
C. Ar.	*Orations against the Arians*
Carn. Chr.	*The Flesh of Christ*
Cat.	*Catechetical Lecture*
CBQ	*Catholic Biblical Quarterly*
CD	Damascus Document also found at Qumran
Cels.	*Against Celsus*
Cherubim	Philo, *On the Cherubim*
Chron.	*Chronicle*
CIJ	*Corpus inscriptionum judaicarum.* Edited by J. B. Frey, Rome, 1936–52.
Cim.	*Cimon*
Claud.	*Claudius*
Clem.	*Clement*, 1 or 2 or a pseudo-Clement manuscript
Cod.	*Codex*
Col. In omnes B. Pauli epist.	*Collection of Commentaries of Pauline Epistles*
Comm. Isa.	*Commentarii in Isaiam*
Comm. Jo.	*Commentarii in evangelium Joannis*
Comm. Rom.	*Commentarii in Romanos*
ConB	Coniectanea Biblica: New Testament Seires
Conf.	*On the Confusion of Tongues*
Consol. Phil.	*Consolation of Philosophy*
Controv.	Seneca the Elder's *Controversiae*

CPJ	*Corpus papyrorum judaicarum*. Edited by V. Tcherikover, Cambridge, 1957–64.
CSEL	*Corpus Scriptorum Ecclesiasticorum Latinorum*. Edited by Filium.
CTJ	*Calvin Theological Journal*
CTM	*Concordia Theological Monthly*
CTQ	*Concordia Theological Quarterly*
Cult. Fem.	*The Apparel of Women*
CurTM	*Currents in Theology and Mission*
C.W.	*On the Civil War*
Cyr.	*Cyropaedia*
DBS	*Dictionnaire de la Bible*: Supplement. Edited by L. Pirot and A. Robert.
Decl.	*Declamations*
Def. Or.	*Defense of Oratory*
Def. orc.	*De defectu oraculorum*
De lib. arb.	*De Libertate Arbitrii*
Dem. ev.	*Demonstration of the Gospel*
Demon.	*Ad Demonicum*
Deus	*That God Is Unchangeable*
Dial.	*Dialogue*
Dial. D.	*Dialogue of the Dead*
Diatr.	*Diatribe (Dissertationes)*
Did.	*Didache*
Diogn.	*Diognetus*
Doctr. chr.	*De doctrina christiana*
Down. J.	*Downward Journey*
DSD	*Dead Sea Discoveries*
Eb.	*Ebionites*
Ebr.	*On Drunkenness*
'Ed.	Rabbinic *'Eduyyot*
Eleem.	*Works and Almsgiving*

Eloc.	*Style*
En.	*Enoch* with number 1 or 2 or 3 before
Ep.	*Epistle*
Eph.	*To the Ephesians*
Eph. Tale	*Ephesian Tale* by Xenophon of Ephesus
Epid.	*Epidemics* or Irenaeus, *Demonstration of the Apostolic Preaching*
Epigr.	*Epigrams*
Ep. More.	*Epistulae morales*
'Erub.	Rabbinic *'Erubin*
Esar	Esarhaddon Treaty
Esd	Apocrypha Esadras with number 1 or 2 before
Esth.	*Esther*
Eth. nic.	*Ethica nicomachea*
EvQ	*Evangelical Quarterly*
EvT	*Evangelische Theologie*
ExAud	*Ex auditu*
Exh. Cast.	*Exhortation to Chastity*
Expl. Dan.	*Explanatio in Danielem*
Exp. S. Pauli epist. Ad Rom.	*Exposition of Saint Paul Epistle of Romans*
ExpTim	*Expository Times*
Fac. Dict.	*Factorum ac dictorum memorabilium libri* or *Memorable Deeds and Sayings*
Fid. Grat.	*De fide ad Gratianum*
Fin.	*De finibus*
Fiod. op.	*De fide et operibus*
Flaccus	*Against Flaccus*
Frag.	*Fragment*
Frat. Amor	*De fraterno amore*
Fug.	*De fuga et inventione*
GELNT	*Greek English Lexicon of the New Testament*

Geogr.	*Geographica*
Giṭ.	*Giṭṭin*
Good Person	Philo, *That Every Good Person Is Free*
Gos.	*Gospel* as in pseudepigrapha *Gospel of Peter* or others
Hab. Virg.	*The Dress of Virgins*
Haer.	*Against Heresies*
Ḥag.	Rabbinic *Ḥagigah*
Hall	*The Hall*
HAT	Handbuch zum Alten Testament
Heb.	*Hebrews* as in *Gospel of the Hebrews*
Heir	*Who Is the Heir?*
Her.	*Quis rerum divinarum heres sit*
Herm. Mand.	*Shepherd of Hermas, Mandates*
Herm. Sim.	*Shepherd of Hermas, Similitudes*
Herm. Vis.	*Shepherd of Hermas, Visions*
Hist.	*History*
Hist. Consc.	*How to write History*
Hist. eccl.	*Histora ecclesiastica* or *Ecclesiastical History*
Hist. plant.	*Historia plantarum*
Hom.	*Homily*
HTR	*Harvard Theological Review*
HUCA	Hebrew Union College Annual Int *Interpretation*
Ḥul.	*Ḥullin*
Hypoth.	*Hypothetica*
ICC	International Critical Commentary
Inst.	*Institutes* as: Lactantius, *The Divine Institutes* or Quintilian, *Institutio oratorio*
Int	*Interpretation*
Inv.	*De invention rhetorica*
Ioh.	A work on *John*

IRT	Issues in Religion and Theology
Is. Os.	*Isis and Osiris*
JAAR	*Journal of the American Academy of Religion*
JAC	*Jahrbuch für Antike und Christentum*
JAOS	*Journal of the American Oriental Society*
JBL	*Journal of Biblical Literature*
JBTh	*Jahrbuch für biblische Theologie* (Neukirchener)
Jdt	Apocrypha Judith
JETS	*Journal of the Evangelical Theological Society*
JJS	*Journal of Jewish Studies*
JLW	*Journal of Luther's Works*
JNES	*Journal of Near Eastern Studies*
Jos.	*On the Life of Joseph*
Jos. Asen.	*Joseph and Aseneth*
Josh.	*Joshua*
Jov.	*Adversus Jovinianum libri II*
JRT	*Journal of Religious Thought*
JSJ	*Journal for the Study of Judaism in the Persian, Hellenistic, and Roman Periods*
JSNT	*Journal for the Study of the New Testament*
JSNTSup	*Journal for the Study of the New Testament: Supplement Series*
JSOT	*Journal for the Study of the Old Testament*
JSOTSup	*Journal for the Study of the Old Testament: Supplement Series*
JSP	*Journal for the Study of the Pseudepigrapha*
JTS	*Journal of Theological Studies*
JTSA	*Journal of Theology for Southern Africa*
Jub.	*Jubilees*
Kel.	Rabbinic *Kelim*
Ketab.	Rabbinic *Ketubbot*

Kgdms	Kingdoms in LXX (reflects Hebrew of 1–2 Kgs) preceded by 3 or 4
KTU	*Keilalphabetische Texte aus Ugarit*. Edited by Manfried Dietrich et al.
L.A.B.	*Liber antiquitatum biblicarum Pseudo-Philo*
Lac.	*Respublica Lacedaemoniorum*
L.A.E.	*Life of Adam and Eve*
Lam.	*Lamentations*
LCL	Loeb Classical Library
Leg.	*Leges* or *Laws*: Cicero, *De legibus* or Philo, *Allegorical Interpretation*
Life	Josephus, *The Life*, or Philstratus, *The Life of Apollonius*
LQ	*Lutheran Quarterly*
Luc.	*Luke* or *Lucan*
Lucil.	*Ad Lucilium*
LW	*Living Word*
LXX	Septuagint
Lyc.	*Lycurgus*
m. or *M.*	*Mishnah*
Macc	Apocrypha Maccabees with number 1 or 2 or 3 or 4 before
Magn.	*To the Magnesians*
Mak.	Rabbinic *Makkot*
Marc.	*Against Marcion* or Seneca, *Ad Marciam de consolatione*
Mart.	*To the Martyrs*
Mart. Pal.	*The Martyrdom of Palestine*
Mart. Pol.	*Martyrdom of Polycarp*
Matt.	*Matthew*
Meg.	Rabbinic *Megillah*
Mek.	Rabbinic *Mekilta*

Mem.	*Memorabilia*
Menaḥ.	Rabbinic *Menaḥot*
Mes.	Rabbinic *Metzi'a*
Midr.	Rabbinic *Midrash*
Migr.	*On the Migration of Abraham*
Mil.	*Pro Milone*
MM	Moulton, J. H., and G. Milligan, *The Vocabulary of the Greek Testament.* London, 1930.
Mor.	*Moralia*
Mort.	*The Deaths of the Persecutors*
Mos.	*Moses*
Moses	*On the Life of Moses*
MSJ	*The Master's Seminary Journal*
MT	Hebrew Masoretic Text, reflected in *Biblica Hebraica Stuttgartensia.* Edited by Funditus Renovata et al., 1977.
NAC	New American Commentary
Names	*On the Change of Names*
Narr.	*Narration*
Nat.	*Naturalis historia* of Pliny the Elder
Nat. d.	*De natura deorum*
Naz.	Rabbinic *Nazir*
NCB	New Century Bible
Ned.	Rabbinic *Nedarim*
Neot	*Neotestamentica*
NICNT	New International Commentary on the New Testament
Nid.	Rabbinic *Niddah*
NIDNTT	*The New International Dictionary of New Testament Theology.* Edited by Colin Brown.

NIDOTTE	*New International Dictionary of Old Testament Theology & Exegesis.* Edited by Willem VanGemeren.
NIGTC	New International Greek Testament Commentary
Noc. att.	*Attic Nights*
NovT	*Novum Testamentum*
NovTSup	Supplements to Novum Testamentum
NT	New Testament
NTOA	Novum testamentum et orbis antiquus
NTS	*New Testament Studies*
Num.	*Numa*
Od.	*Odyssey*
Odes Sol.	*Odes of Solomon*
Oec.	*Economics*
Oed. frag.	*Oedipus* fragment
Off.	*De officiis*
'Ohal.	Rabbinic *'Ohalot*
Ol.	*Olympian Odes*
Oneir.	*Oneirocritica*
Op.	*Works and Days*
Or.	*Prayer*
Orat.	*Orations*
OT	Old Testament
Paed.	*Christ the Educator*
Pan.	*Refutation of All Heresies*
Part. or	*Partitiones oratoriae*
Pelag.	*Adversus Pelaganos dialog III*
Pesaḥ.	Rabbinic *Pesaḥim*
Pesiq. Rab Kah.	*Pesiqta de Rab Kahana*
Pet.	*Peter* as in *Apocalypse of Peter* or *Acts of Peter*

PG	*Patrologia graeca.* Edited by J.-P. Migne. 161 vols.
Phil.	Ignatius or Polycarp, *To the Philadelphians*
Philops.	*The Lover of Lies*
Phoen.	*Phoenician Maidens*
PL	*Patrologiae cursus completus: Series Latina.* Edited by J.-P. Migne. 221 vols.
Plant.	*On Planting*
P.Lond.	*Greek Papyri in the British Museum.* Edited by F. G. Kenyon et al,. London, 1893.
P.Mich	Greek Papyri in University of Michigan.
Pol.	Ignatius, *To Polycarp* or Aristotle and Martial, *Politics*
Post.	*On the Posterity of Caini*
P.Oxy.	*The Oxyrhynchus Papyri.* London, 1898–2010.
Pr Azar	Apocrypha Prayer of Azariah
Praed.	*The Predestination of the Saints*
Praem.	*De praemiis et poenis*
Praep. ev.	*Preparation for the Gospel*
Praescr.	*Prescription against Heretics*
Princ.	*First Principles*
Pr Man	Apocrypha Prayer of Manasseh
Prog.	Theon's *Progymnasmata* in James Butts' translation and treatises on it
Ps.-Arist.	Pseudo-Aristides
Ps.-Jon.	*Targum Pseudo-Jonathan*
Ps.-Phoc.	Pseudo-Phocylides
Pss. Sol.	*Psalms of Solomon*
Pun.	*Punica*
Q	within Qumran manuscript (e.g., 11Q132.2 is read as cave#Qdocument numbers #chapter.#verse)

QE	*Quaestiones et solutions in Exodum*
Qidd.	Rabbinic *Qiddušin*
Quint. Fratr.	*Epistulae ad Quintum fratrem*
Rab.	*Rabbah* often with a biblical book, such as Leviticus (Lev)
RB	*Revue biblique*
RBL	*Review of Biblical Literature*
Res.	*Resurrection of the Flesh*
Resp.	*Republic*
Rev.	*On Revelation*
RevExp	*Review and Expositor*
RHA	*Revue Hittite et asianique*
RHE	*Revue d'histoire ecclésiastique*
Rhet.	*Rhetoric*
R. N.	*De rerum natura*
rom.	*Romanae* as in Dionysis, *Ant. rom.*
Roš Haš.	Rabbinic *Roš Haššanah*
RQ	*Römische Quartalschrift für christliche Altertumskunde und Kirchengeschichte*
RTR	*Reformed Theological Review*
Rust.	*De re rustica*
Šabb.	Rabbinic document *Šabbat*
Sacr.	*De sacrificiis Abelis et Caini*
Sanh.	Rabbinic document *Sanhedrin*
SANT	Studien zum Alten und Neuen Testaments
Sat.	*Satirae*
SB	*Sammelbuch griechisher Urkunden aus Aegypten.* Edited by F. Preisigke et al.
SBL	Society of Biblical Literature
SBLDS	Society of Biblical Literature Dissertations Series

SBLMS	Society of Biblical Literature Monograph Series
SBLSP	Society of Biblical Literature Seminar Papers
Scap.	*To Scapula*
Scorp.	*Antidote for the Scorpion's Sting*
SCS	*Society of Christian Scholars* series (Scholars Press)
Šeb.	Rabbinic *Šebiʿit*
Šebu.	Rabbinic *Šebuʿot*
Sedr.	*Sedrach*
Sem.	Rabbinic *Semaḥot*
Šeqal.	Rabbinic *Šeqalim*
Serm.	*Sermon*
Sib. Or.	*Sibyline Oracles*
Sir	Apocrypha Hebrew Sirach/LXX Ecclesiasticus
Smyrn.	*To the Smyrnaens*
SNTSMS	Society for New Testament Monograph Series
Sobr.	*On Sobriety*
Sol.	*Solomon*
Somn.	*On Dreams*
Spec. Laws	*On the Special Laws*
Speech	*Speech in Character*
Str-B	Strack and Billerbeck, *Kommentar zum Neuen Testament*
Strom.	*Miscellanies*
StudBib	*Studia Biblica*
Sull.	*Sulla*
SwJT	*Southwestern Journal of Theology*
Symp.	*Symposium*
t. or *T.*	*Tosefta*

T. 12 Patr.	Testaments of the Twelve Patriarchs
T. Abr.	Testament of Abraham
T. Benj.	Testament of Benjamin
T. Dan.	Testament of Daniel
T. Hez.	Testament of Hezekiah
T. Hos.	Testament of Hosea
T. Isaac	Testament of Isaac
T. Iss.	Testament of Issachar
T. Job	Testament of Job
T. Jud.	Testament of Judah
T. Levi	Testament of Levi
T. Mos.	Testament of Moses
T. Naph.	Testament of Naphtali
T. Sim.	Testament of Simeon
Ṭ. Yom	Rabbinic Ṭebul Yom
T. Zeb.	Testament of Zebulum
Taʿan.	Rabbinic Taʿanit
Tan.	Rabbinic Tanḥuma
TB	*Theologische Bücherei*: Neudrucke und Berichte aus dem 20. Jahrhundert.
TDNT	*Theological Dictionary of the New Testament*. Edited by Gerhard Kittel and Gerhard Friedrich.
TDOT	*Theological Dictionary of the Old Testament*. Edited by G. Johannes Botterweck and Helmer Ringgren.
Test.	*To Quirinius: Testomonies against the Jews*
Tg.	Targum
Tg. 1 Chr.	Targum of 1 Chronicles
Tg. Isa.	*Targum Isaiah* as an Early Jewish commentary on Isaiah
Tg. Jon.	Targum Jonathan

Tg. Neof.	*Targum Neofiti*
Tg. Ps.-J.	*Targum Pseudo-Jonathan*
Ṭhar.	Rabbinic *Ṭhearot*
Them.	*Themistocles*
Theoph.	*Divine Manifestation*
Thom.	*Thomas* as in *Gospel of Thomas*
Tim.	Plato's *Timaeus* or Aeschines' *In Timarchum*
TNTC	Tyndale New Testament Commentaries
Tob	Apocrypha Tobit
Top.	*Topica*
TQ	*Theologische Quartalschrift*
Trall.	*To the Trallians*
Tranq. an.	*De tranquillitate animi*
TRev	*Theologische Revue*
Trin.	*Trinity* or in Latin, *Trinitate*
TrinJ	*Trinity Journal*
TRu	*Theologische Rundschau*
TS	*Theological Studies*
TSK	*Theologische Studien und Kritiken*
TU	Texte und Untersuchungen
TWOT	*Theological Wordbook of the Old Testament.* Edited by R. Laird Harris et al.
TynBul	*Tyndale Bulletin*
USQR	*Union Seminary Quarterly Review*
Val. Max.	*Valerius Maximus*
VC	*Vigilae christianae*
Verr.	*In Verrem*
Vesp.	*Vespasianus*
Vir. ill.	*De viris illustribus*
Virt.	*De virtutibus*
Vis. Isa.	*Ascension of Isaiah*

VT	*Vetus Testamentum*
VTE	*Succession Treaty of Esarhaddon*
VTSup	Supplements to *Vetus Testamentum*
War	Josephus, *Jewish War*
WBC	Word Biblical Commentary
Wis	Apocrypha Wisdom of Solomon
Worse	Philo, *That the Worse Attacks the Better*
WTJ	*Westminster Theological Journal*
WUNT	Wissenschaftliche Untersuchungen zum Neuen Testament
Y. or y.	Jerusalem Talmud
Yad.	Rabbinic *Yadayim*
Yebam.	Rabbinic *Yebamot*
ZA	*Zeitschrift für Assyriologie*
ZAW	*Zeitschrift für die alttestamentliche Wissenschaft*
ZNW	*Zeitschrift für die neutestamentliche Wissenschaft und die Kunde der ältern Kirche*
ZRGG	*Zeitschrift für Religions und Geistesgeschichte*
ZST	*Zeitschrift für systematische Theologie*
ZTK	*Zeitschrift für Theologie und Kirchee*

1

Lost Boy or Foundation for Christian Theology

THE EARLY CHURCH CONSIDERED Peter to be the foundation for apostolic Christian tradition. Stating this, J. N. D. Kelley identified, "St. Peter is the starting point of apostolic tradition and the symbol of unity" for the church.[1] For example, the Gospels always list Peter as first apostle (Matt 10:2–4 even uses πρῶτος "first" to refer to Peter; Mark 3:13–19; Luke 6:13–16; Acts 1:13). The Gospels, Acts, and the early church declare Peter to be repeatedly the spokesman for the apostles (Matt 14:28; 15:15; 16:16–19; 18:21; 26:35, 40; Mark 8:29; 9:5; 10:28; John 6:68; Acts 1:15; 2:14; 3:4, 12; 4:8; 5:3, 8; 8:20; 10:9—11:18; 15:7)[2] and one of three within the core disciple band (Matt 17:1; 26:37; Mark 5:37; 9:2; 13:3: Luke 9:28). Paul and Clement of Rome declared Peter to be one of the pillars of the church, along with Jesus' brother James and John Zebedee (Gal 2:9).[3] On the basis of Jesus' commission of Peter in Matt 16 and the record of the book of Acts, much of the early church declared Peter to be the foundation for the church.[4] The Orthodox Church considers Peter as foundation for the church, undergirding apostolic tradition and patriarchy of

---

1. Kelly, *Early Christian Doctrines*, 205.

2. John Chrysostom, *Hom. 2 Tim* 3:1 4; Cyril of Alexandria, *In Ioh.* 1:42; *De trin. dial.* 4; Theodoret, *Quaest In Gen. interp.* 110; *In Ps.* 2.

3. Clement of Rome, *1 Cor* 5.

4. Cyril of Alexandria, *In Ioh.* 1:42; *In Luc* 22:32; Epiphanius, *Ancor.* 9; Maximus the Confessor, *Vita accert* 24; Cyprian, *Ep. Of Cyprian* 54.7; 70.3; 72.11; 74.16; *Treatise of Cyprian* 1.2.

Syria and Rome.[5] This is the starting point that later gets spun in the Roman Catholic Church grounding Peter as the first pope, possessing the keys of the kingdom with Jesus Christ as the foundation, but before that doctrine emerges, many in the church considered Peter to be the foundation. Either way, Peter certainly laid the foundation for the church universal as Ignatius claimed.[6] Didymus declared Peter to be the leader and chief among the apostles.[7] Philip Schaff summarized this sentiment of Peter being the church's chief actor to ground the apostolic tradition, "Peter was the chief actor in the first stage of apostolic Christianity and fulfilled the prophecy of his name in laying the foundation of the church among the Jews and the Gentiles."[8] Mature scholarly biographers of Peter, such as Pheme Perkins concur, "Peter is the universal 'foundation' for all the churches. . . . There is no figure who compasses more of that diversity than Peter."[9] F. J. Foakes-Jackson concluded, "the very fact that Peter was singled out by the unanimous voice of the writers of the N.T. for pre-eminence is sufficient reason why he should demand our serious attention."[10] From this foundational bridge position, Martin Hengel begins to make integrated attempts toward a Petrine theology.[11] Martin Hengel and Larry Hurtado conclude that Peter has a "particular theological competence" to contribute to the field of biblical theology.[12] This book brings together a theological construction to reflect the biblical claims from biblical and early patristic sources expressing Peter's voice.

In later patristics, the historical Peter became less the focus and traditional appropriation of a "Peter of faith" moved to the fore to ground Roman Catholic doctrines, such as the papacy retaining Peter's leadership for the church. With Protestantism taking up Paul as their patron apostle, Peter gets lost behind Roman Catholic tradition. An example is that Martin Luther shifts from loving Peter's spiritual contributions "as the noblest books of the New Testament" to that of hating the Roman Catholic use

---

5. Photius, *PG* 120.800B; Palamas, *Trials* 2.1.38; Meyendorff et al., *Primacy of Peter*.

6. Ign. *Magn.* 10:9.

7. Didymus, *De trin.* 1.30.

8. Schaff, *History of Christian Church*, 1:96.

9. Perkins, *Peter*, 184; Hengel, *Saint Peter*, 79–80, 102; Helyer, *Life and Witness of Peter*.

10. Foakes-Jackson, *Peter*, xii.

11. Hengel, *Saint Peter*, 86–87.

12. Hengel, *Saint Peter*, 35; see Hurtado, "Apostle Peter in Protestant Scholarship," 8.

of a tradition of Peter to support the papacy.¹³ To reflect this transition, Gene Green used a metaphor from J. M. Barrie's novel *Peter Pan* to declare Peter as one of the "lost boys" of Christian theology.¹⁴ For example, NT theologies often exclude Petrine theology altogether, namely: Rudolf Bultmann, Udo Schnelle, Adolf Schlatter, and Greg Beale.¹⁵ This neglect of Peter to "neverland" became a motive for Green to try to put together part of a theology for Peter.

With the rise of later biblical criticism, Petrine theology fragmented, and viewed within those fragments it has become viewed as "warmed-over Paulinist," and thus both irretrievable and largely irrelevant. For example, Francis Beare analyzed parallels among Peter and Paul's contributions and concluded that 1 Pet "is strongly marked by the impress of Pauline theological ideas, and in language the dependance on St. Paul is undeniably great. All through the Epistle we have the impression that we are reading the work of a man who is steeped in the Pauline letters."¹⁶ In contrast, Goppelt made a similar analysis and concluded that many of these shared themes actually were from paraenetic sections sharing wisdom that Jesus' teachings or Jewish wisdom, such that he concluded concerning a relationship between Peter and Paul, "there can be no mention of any literary dependence."¹⁷ It is probably better to view Petrine theology as providing a bridge from Jesus' ministry to that of Paul's.

Peter Davids, making major contributions to Petrine theology, mostly described the separate theologies of 1 Pet and 2 Pet, summarizing that many major Pauline themes are missing from 1 Pet:

> Many of the major Pauline themes are missing from 1 Peter. Faith, justification, and works are not an issue for 1 Peter, much less specific "works of the law" such as circumcision and Jewish festivals, which are so important for Paul. First Peter does not use *ekklesia* (ἐκκλησία, "church"), which is also important for Paul. While both Paul and 1 Peter discuss election, the discussion in 1 Pet 2:4–10 is much different than that in Rom

---

13. Luther, "Preface to the New Testament," quoted by Elliott, *1 Peter*, 5; *Luther's Works*, 35.361–62; *Table Talk* (1533) WATR 1:194, no. 445 (*Luther's Works* 54:72).

14. Green, *Vox Petri*, 1; using "lost boys" as those children who fall out of the baby carriages when the nanny is looking the other way. Elliott described this as an "exegetical step-child" (*1 Peter*, 3)

15. Bultmann, *Theology of the New Testament*; Schnelle, *Theology of the New Testament*; Schlatter, *New Testament Theology*; Beale, *New Testament Biblical Theology*.

16. Beare, *First Epistle of Peter*, 44.

17. Goppelt, *1 Petrusbrief*, 4,9 with fuller discussion on 48–51.

11:26–29, nor does Paul ever cite Exod 19:6, which is central to 1 Peter's discussion. When Paul talks about gifts, he associates them with the Spirit, but Peter makes no mention of the Spirit in his discussion about gifts. Finally, the list of terms and ideas that are important to 1 Peter and not found in Paul or important to Paul and not found in 1 Peter is significant.[18]

This provides a warning so that an interpreter should not read Paul onto the text, but rather understand meaning within Peter's context.

Furthermore, splintering Petrine theology fosters so many biblical theologies discussing Petrine attributed works divided into theologies of 1 Pet and of 2 Pet, separated by different vocabulary and expression. Additionally, often one of these sources is considered to not be from Peter, and thus removed from consideration. Rarely is the broad patristic claim considered for Mark within the Petrine corpus which won this Gospel's canonicity. Recently Gene Green has made a valiant case for Mark's inclusion while separating Peter's theology into: 1 Pet, Mark, and Peter imbedded in Gospels and Acts. Green leaves 2 Pet excluded from Petrine theology, though he acknowledged that Peter likely wrote that epistle that claims him as author, that the majority of the global church considers Peter wrote the epistle, and there is not sufficient warrant to reject Peter as author.[19] Additionally, Ralph Martin indicated that, "probably no document in the N.T. is so theological as 1 Peter, if 'theological' is taken in the strict sense of teaching about God."[20] Joel Green extends this thought with "1 Peter is about God and the ramifications of orienting life wholly around him."[21] Occasionally, the Petrine statements from the book of Acts and the Gospels are folded in to inform a theology of Peter, but this approach is more common among those exploring the early history of the church than those who explore biblical theology.

Ferdinand C. Baur and the Tübingen school followed G. W. F. Hegel's concept of evolving religion dividing Christianity into thesis-Peter's Jewish Christianity in Acts, countered by antithesis-Paul's gentile Christianity that becomes synthesized in second-century traditional Christianity (including Petrine epistles seen through Pauline interpretations). My previous critique of Hegel presented Hegel's thesis, antithesis, and synthesis as contradictory and thus unable to be fused into a meaningful

---

18. Davids, *Theology of James, Peter, and Jude*, 111; Elliott, *1 Peter*, 38–39.
19. Green, *Jude, 2 Peter*, 172, 144–45; *Vox Petri*, 97.
20. Helyer, *Life and Witness of Peter*, 105.
21. Helyer, *Life and Witness of Peter*, 105.

synthesis.[22] When the Tübingen school followed Baur's lead to develop that Christianity developed from Judaism before it universalized under Paul, early Christianity ended up not following Hegel into the early church tradition, but returning to its Protestant bias for Pauline theology, and cutting adrift selective aspects of Peter for Roman Catholics to prooftext their claims. Peter and Paul were not oppositional in their ministries as Baur developed from Gal 2:7. Thus, when Protestant scholars read 1 Pet they tend to read it through a "warmed-over Paulinist" lens, and Jewish forms of Christianity got lost as an echo of Paul. Of course, Peter is far more complex than Jewish Christianity,[23] since he wins the first gentiles to Christ and writes 1 and 2 Pet primarily to gentile Christians.

Lutz Doering documents recovery of Petrine studies from this anti-Pauline restrictive "bumbler" and from "warmed-over Paulism" to a bridge figure and symbol of unity.[24] For example, James Dunn celebrated, "Peter was probably in fact and effect the bridge-man (pontifex maximus!) who did more than any other to hold together the diversity of first-century Christianity."[25] Peter serves as the outstanding bridge from the oral apostolic witness to that of the foundational written witness.

The Gospels and Acts were witness expressed through an oral phase, more authoritative than written texts. Perhaps recognizing that the disciples were called to be this oral-witnesses (Luke 24:48; Acts 1:8, μάρτυρες). Such a role of witness is one of memory and testimony from personal experience. As such, the subject matter to which a witness testifies is not likely to be submitted to empirical investigation because the events and statement of views occurred previously as testimony (Matt 8:4; 18:16).[26] In a Hebrew trial setting multiple oral witnesses were involved to strengthen credibility (Deut 17:6; 19:15). If the witnesses prove to be contradicted credibly then they were considered a false witness and could suffer the same judgment that they were trying to obtain for the one accused (Deut 5:20; 19:16–18). In the Greco-Roman legal system, a

---

22. Kennard, *Critical Realist's Theological Method*, 70–72.

23. Baur, *Kritische Untersuchungen*; modernized by Goulder, *St. Paul versus St. Peter*, 1–7; but defeated by the complex pictures shown by Grappe, *Images de Pierre* and Bockmuehl, *Remembered Peter*.

24. Doering, "Schwerpunkte und Tendenzen," 203–23.

25. Dunn, "Has the Canon a Continuing Function?," 577; similarly, *Unity and Diversity in the New Testament*, 385–86.

26. Aristotle, *Rhet.* 1.15; Plato, *Leg.* 12; Josephus, *Ant.* 6.66; 1QS 5.24–26.1; Philo, *Spec. Laws* 4.30, 41–44, 59–61; *Jos.* 242; *m. Mak.* 1.6; *m. Roš Haš.* 1.8; *Sifre* on Deut 19:19; *Šeb.* 30a; *Gem. Mak.* 5B; Trites, *New Testament Concept of Witness*.

witness needed to be an adult free male Roman citizen with honorable reputation and not operating for personal gain.[27] Such a witness would make appropriate comments in court as eyewitness testimony he had actually experienced.[28] With legal imagery encouraging the credibility of the role of a witness, Papias found the collective memory of Christian eyewitness testimony to be more valuable than the written texts being produced for as long as available eyewitnesses testified about Jesus' ministry and the early church.

> I shall not hesitate also to put into properly ordered form for you everything I learned carefully in the past from the elders and noted down well, for the truth of which I vouch. For unlike most people I did not enjoy those who have a great deal to say, but those who teach the truth. Nor did I enjoy those who recall someone else's commandments, but those who remember the commandments given by the Lord to the faith and proceeding from the truth itself. And if by chance anyone who had been in attendance on the elders should come my way, I inquired about the words of the elders—[that is] what [according to the elders] Andrew or Peter said, or Philip, or Thomas or James, or John or Matthew or any other of the Lord's disciples, and whatever Ariston and the elder John, the Lord's disciples were saying. For I did not think that information from books would profit me as much as information from a living and surviving voice.[29]

In the second century both Irenaeus and Papias recount that their early memories of the eyewitness testimony took great prominence and were in full accord with the written texts of Scripture.[30] Similar claims for accurate vivid early memories framing later perception were made by Seneca the elder.[31] When such testimony occurred in Christian contexts a corporate memory of tradition could be specifically identified and the

---

27. Pindar, *Ol.* 1.54; Plato, *Apol.* 31c; *Gorgias*, 27–31, 41E–5E; Demosthenes 58.4; Plutarch, *de Amicorum Multitudine* 2.2.93e; TDNT 4:479.

28. Plato, *Symp.* 179b; Heraclitus, *All.* 34; Sophocles, *Ant.* 515.

29. Eusebius, *Hist. eccl.* 3.39.3–4; Arthur Dewey develops an argument from Rom 10 that the written *torah* supported the authoritative and transformative oral gospel testimony ("Re-Hearing of Romans 10:1–15," 109–27); Bauckham, *Jesus and the Eyewitnesses*, 293–94; Kelber, "Generative Force of Memory," 15–22.

30. Papias recounted in Eusebius, *Hist. eccl.* 5.20.4–7; Irenaeus, *Letter to Florinus*; Bauckham, *Jesus and the Eyewitnesses*, 295.

31. Seneca, *Controversiae*, preface 3–4; Bauckham, *Jesus and the Eyewitnesses*, 295–96; Mackay, *Signs of Orality*; Horsley et al., *Performing the Gospel*; Cooper, *Politics of Orality*; Horsley, *Oral Performance*.

others of the group would provide a resilience to reinforce the accuracy of their corporate memory.[32] Such a pattern mirrors the corporate memory of rabbinic Judaism that began to establish written accounts of their oral discussions beginning around AD 200 with the *Mishnah* and then the two corroborating written accounts of the *Talmud* later around 450 and AD 600. Such Jewish oral tradition and written oral tradition shows very little shift of account except the addition of more recent rabbinic voices.[33] Also, in Judaism there was liturgical retelling of narrative in *rabbah* texts composed during the second to fourth centuries, which resiliently re-tell the biblical narratives for liturgical purposes. The resilience and consistency in the agreement of these written accounts of oral *Torah* or narrative re-telling provide a pattern for how local Jewish-Christian corporate eyewitness memory could be corporately preserved into written texts of Gospels and Acts.

From such eyewitness testimony, Markus Bockmuehl develops *The Remembered Peter* as "arguably the only major player to feature in the ministries of both Jesus and Paul; and on any reckoning he provides a vital personal continuity between them both."[34] Bockmuehl encouraged use of techniques of the Jewish affirming side of the third quest for the historical Jesus and that of the dialog around the new perspective concerning Paul. Bockmuehl anticipated that reflection on Peter will provide significant benefit in understanding the transition from Jesus' exclusive mission to Israel (Matt 10:5–6) to Paul's mission to the gentiles (Acts 9:15; 22:21; 26:17). As such, Petrine theology becomes another planet

---

32. Examples of such claims include: Clement of Alexandria, *Strom.* 7.106.4; Eusebius, *Hist. eccl.* 2.1.4; similar claims were made at Qumran (1QS 6.6–8) and by gnostic *2 Apoc. of James* 36.15–25; Halbwachs, *On Collective Memory*; Assmann, *Das kulturelle Gedächtnis*; Kelber, "Case of the Gospels," 65; "Generative Force of Memory," 15–22; Dunn, *Jesus Remembered*, 239–43; Ricoeur, *Memory, History, Forgetting*; Bauckham, *Jesus and the Eyewitnesses*, 296, 310–57; "Gospel of John," 659; Silberman, *Orality, Aurality and Biblical Narrative*; Dewey, *Orality and Textuality in Literature*; Draper, *Orality, Literacy, and Colonialism*; Kirk, "Social and Cultural Memory," 14–15; Thatcher, "Why John Wrote a Gospel," 82–85; Thatcher, *Jesus, the Voice, and the Text*; Kelber and Byrsog, *Jesus in Memory*.

33. Gerhardsson, *Gospel Tradition*; *Memory and Manuscript*; Bailey, "Informal Controlled Oral Tradition," 34–54; "Middle Eastern Oral Tradition," 363–67; Boomershine, "Jesus of Nazareth," 7–11, 16–17; Jaffee, "Oral-Cultural Context," 27–73; Dunn, *Jesus Remembered*, 197–254; Bauckham, *Jesus and the Eyewitnesses*; Walton and Sandy, *Lost World of Scripture*, 97–101, 105–8, 110, 152–66.

34. Bockmuehl, *Remembered Peter*, 31; Perkins, *Peter*, 13 presents Schillebeeckx as saying the same point.

between Jesus[35] and Pauline[36] studies, with lesser moons such as a theology of James,[37] Heb,[38] and Luke[39] circling.

Though Petrine theology has gone through an era of neglect,[40] Peter has theological expression that both fits his time and makes significant contributions to the field of biblical theology. For example, Martin Hengel declared Peter to be the "Underestimated Apostle."[41] It is time for Peter's voice to be heard.

Most Petrine theology treats the contributing units as independent of each other: a theology of 1 Pet, a theology of 2 Pet, sometimes contributions from Peter in Mark or Acts. However, the field of biblical theology is admitting more honestly to a methodology construct from a point of view.[42] Rarely have these glimpses of Petrine theology been integrated into a unified construct, as the current work before you will attempt to accomplish. Separating Peter into a theology of his sources fragments his theology and diminishes the integrated depth of theology that Peter contributes. Gene Green grants that Peter's voice is contained within Mark and allows the Gospel to continue to contribute to a composite of Peter's theology.[43] However, Green's theology of Peter does not interact with 2 Pet, even though he inclines to accept Petrine authorship, because he considered his engagement to be a large enough task already and the academic disagreement over authorship.[44] Green concluded his synthesis of Peter by recognizing that his unified construct "only skims the surface of the apostle's thought as it has come down to us in the various Petrine

---

35. Dunn, *Jesus Remembered*; Wright, *Jesus and Victory of God*; Kennard, *Messiah Jesus*.

36. Dunn, *Theology of Paul*; Wright, *Paul and Faithfulness of God*; Kennard, "Covenant Pneumaticism," 30–161; Moo, *Biblical Theology of Paul*.

37. Eisenman, *James the Brother of Jesus*; Davids, "James," 31–91.

38. Kennard, *Biblical Theology of Hebrews*.

39. Bock, *Theology of Luke and Acts*.

40. Elliott, "Rehabilitation of an Exegetical Step-Child," 243–54; Howe conclude, "No longer 'an exegetical step-child,' 1 Peter has not only been adopted by the biblical studies guild; it continues to receive the attention and recognition it deserves" in her "Review of *Reading First Peter with New Eyes*."

41. Hengel, *Saint Peter*.

42. Johnson, *Constructing Paul*; Boring, "Narrative Dynamics in First Peter," and Bauman-Martin and Webb, "Reading First Peter with New Eyes," 1–40; Petrine sources are justified in Kennard, *Petrine Studies*, chapter on Sources.

43. Green, *Vox Petri*, 32–45, 126–233.

44. Green, *Vox Petri*, 97–98; though I suspect his previous commentary (Green, *Jude, 2 Peter*, which does not have a section engaging theology satisfied his personal study.

sources."[45] Larry Helyer extends the synthesis a bit further in recognizing the "heart" focuses on Peter's two epistles as the primary content, but interacting with the leading theme of 1 Pet as it appears in the Gospel of Mark and Peter's speeches in the book of Acts.[46] Helyer added 2 Pet to his Petrine theology, even though he acknowledged many scholars consider it written by someone other than the author of 1 Pet. In both Green's and Helyer's approach the separate epistles, Gospel of Mark, and Peter's speeches contribute separate gems for their collage of theologies of Peter,[47] thus creating a theology of Petrine sources. The construct of the present volume attempts to go further by providing a more detailed engagement integrating each source to unify a Petrine theology as well as interacting with depth and complexity rather than merely skimming the sources.

Kennard's *Petrine Theology* has the basic integrated chapters to reflect the standard biblical theological discussion of Peter's theology, with its many contributions: Peter's Jewish heritage, compatible sovereignty and free will, high Christology, missional Trinity, Hebraic anthropology, Jewish atonement, redemption and new exodus, Gospel as allegiance to Christ, contextual sociological ecclesiology, suffering and spiritual warfare in a narrow virtuous exodus way to kingdom, and nuanced consistent eschatology. However, due to the size of the study, a companion book, *Petrine Studies*, was also composed to discuss: foundational issues (which sources can be demonstrated to be Petrine, and recipients and form of Peter's letters), a brief biography of Peter, Peter's communal revelational testimony and empirical evidentialist epistemology, Markan sociological issues to extend Peter's concept of the church into relevant life concerns (such as tradition, inclusion of gentiles, divorce and wealth), and Markan historical issues concerning Jesus' death and resurrection. Narrative theology contributions are especially provided by chapters developing Peter's biography, the Markan section of "Exodus Following Jesus to Kingdom Virtues," and "Jesus' Historical Death and Resurrection." Originally, both books were composed to reflect a fully integrated Petrine theology, supporting and playing off each other. However, for the reader's ease the work was divided into integrated companion volumes: *Petrine Theology* and *Petrine Studies*. The topic of a Petrine theology entails both volumes, though *Petrine Theology* contains the primary trajectory, with

---

45. Green, *Vox Petri*, 417.
46. Helyer, *Life and Witness of Peter*, 16–17.
47. These sources are justified in Kennard, *Petrine Studies*, chapter on Sources.

Petrine Studies providing important support material to complete a Petrine theology project.

Green expressed the value of such an integrated Petrine theology. For example, he summarized Peter's theology as the grounding for the early church.

> Peter's theology is, in the end very much the theology of the early church. At various points we encounter unique contributions to early Christian theologizing, such as the apostle's discussion of Christian theologizing, such as the apostle's discussion of Christ's proclamation to the spirits in prison (1 Pet 3:18–22) and his affirmation that if Israel repents, "times of refreshing" will arrive "from the presence of the Lord," and then God will "send the Messiah appointed for you, that is Jesus" (Acts 3:19–20).[48]

Green continues to encourage Petrine theology to be valued in prime place.

> Peter stands at the very beginning of Christian theology. May the "lost boy" of Christian theology find his rightful place at the table once again. But if we look closely, we will see that he has been seated at the head of the table all along.[49]

---

48. Green, *Vox Petri*, 417.
49. Green, *Vox Petri*, 418.

2

Source Material for Petrine Theology

THE PURPOSE OF THIS chapter is to develop the extent of the source material which will be utilized for this statement of Petrine theology. This will include treatments of the authorship of 1 and 2 Pet, the relationship of Jude and Mark to Petrine theology, the legitimacy of Petrine statements in the Gospels and Acts, and the exclusion of pseudepigraphal works with Peter's name attached.

1 PETER AS A PRIMARY SOURCE

There continues to be much debate concerning who wrote 1 Pet. The decision as to whether 1 Pet is Petrine determines whether it should be included as contributing to Petrine theology.

Claims of Authorship

The letter claims Peter as its author and identifies Peter as the one who was an apostle of Jesus Christ (1 Pet 1:1). Within this, the author claims that he is a witness of Christ's sufferings (1 Pet 5:1). Peter claims to have written the letter probably from Rome, called "Babylon,"[1] and sent it through Silvanus carrying the letter (1 Pet 5:12).[2]

---

1. While Qumran blended "Babylon" as northern opposition Babylon/Assyria (4Q163 frag. 4 7.2.1–4, frag. 8 10.1; 4Q385a; 4Q554 frag. 3 3.14–22), but early Christian texts identify Rome with "Babylon" around the Jewish wars (1 Pet 5:13; Rev 14:8; 16:19; 17–18; 2 Bar 11.1; 67.7; *Sib. Or.* 5.143, 159–60, 168–70; *4 Ezra* 3.1, 28, 31; 15.46–48). Elliott, *1 Peter*, 134–48; Bockmuehl, *Simon Peter in Scripture and Memory*, 128.

2. Berkowitz et al., *Thesaurus Linguae Graecae*; Richards, "Silvanus Was Not Peter's

The author of 1 Pet knows early Christians personally. He knows Silvanus (1 Pet 5:12). He also knows John Mark intimately, like a son (1 Pet 5:13). The author of 1 Pet should be viewed as a Christian of the middle first century unless compelling evidence indicates otherwise.[3]

Petrine authorship was broadly granted until nineteenth century criticism began to call this authorship into question.[4] Craig Keener sides with Raymond Brown, James Dunn, and Rinedhard Feldmeier in recognizing that the evidence scholars cite is not conclusive against Petrine authorship and that this evidence more likely supports authorship by Peter.[5] Craig Keener also claimed that the wording of *1 Clem.* 5 argues for acceptance of the book composed by Peter in the sixties before his death under Nero.[6] Keener also supplied quotes of 1 Pet from Polycarp where he follows Kenneth Berding in positioning 1 Pet as authored by the same person as the Acts 2 speech.[7]

Literary Style

It is generally agreed by most scholars that the literary style of 1 Pet is of high quality. This claim is used by some as an argument against the authorship of Peter. Beare marvels that "If this man was a Jew, he emancipated himself from his own religious inheritance to a degree that was never possible to Paul."[8] However, Spicq and Charue concluded that the Greek in 1 Pet was stylistically not as good as classical writers Polybius and Josephus, so neither the best nor the worst Greek of the New

---

Secretary," 417–32; Davids, *Theology of James, Peter, and Jude*, 108.

3. *First Clement* cites 1 and 2 Pet around AD 96 (*1 Clem.* 1.1–2; 4.8; 5.4; 7.1–6; 9.4; 16.3–4, 17; 31.2; 22.1–7; 23.3; 30.2; 36.2; 37.3; 38.1; 49.5; 57.1; 59.2; 61.1–3; 64; 65; *2 Clem.* 11.2; 16.3; also *Barn.* 1.5; 4.12, 19; 5.1, 6; 6.2; 7.2; 14.6; 16.8–10; *Herm. Vis.* 3.5, 11; 4.2.4–5; 4.3.4; *Herm. Sim.* 9.16.5, 28; *Did.*; Ignatius, *Pol.*; *Phil.*; *Mart. Pol.*; Justin Martyr, *1 Apol.*; *Dial.*; Melito, *Peri Pascha*). Other patristics cite Peter by name (Irenaeus, *Haer.* 4.9.2; 4.16.5; 4.34.2; 5.7.2; Eusebius, *Hist. eccl.* 2.3.2; 3.3.4; 3.4.2; 3.25.2; 3.39.17 [Papias]; 6.25.8; 13.13.84 [Origen]; Tertullian, *Scorp.* 12; *Mart.* 4.13; *Or.* 15). Pliny (*Ep.* 10.96) identifies an apostasy in Pontus around AD 92 that Peter does not mention, so Peter writes before this.

4. Keener, *1 Peter*, 24.

5. Brown and Meier, *Antioch and Rome*, 129–30; Dunn, *Christianity in the Making*, 1148–53; Feldmeier, *1 Peter*, 38; Keener, *1 Peter*, 13.

6. Keener, *1 Peter*, 25.

7. Berding, *Polycarp and Paul*, 13–24, 40, 50, 78, 95–96, 102; Keener, *1 Peter*, 17–19, especially 1 Pet 1:8, 12 and Polycarp, *Phil* 1:3.

8. Beare, *1 Peter*, 27.

Testament.⁹ For example, within the book there is a nice balance in Greek with μὲν followed by δὲ (1 Pet 1:20; 2:4, 14; 3:18; 4:6, 14). There is a command of the article which in a few passages allows its removal a long distance from the word it modifies (1 Pet 3:1, 3, 20; 4:14; 5:1, 4). Also, the use of the optative mood for hopes and prayers indicates some familiarity with literary Greek (1 Pet 1:2; 3:14, 17), only found elsewhere in the NT within Luke and Paul.

The author repeatedly uses Jewish concepts. Frequent Hebraism are found in the letter including "children of obedience (1 Pet 1:14), "loins of understanding" (1 Pet 1:13), "word of the Lord" (1 Pet 1:25), and "people for a possession" (1 Pet 2:9). At least thirty-one Old Testament quotations are present in the letter, with many more alluded passages.¹⁰ Most of these references are from the Septuagint, so he is working with the authoritative text of Jewish dispersion. Sixty-two words are present in 1 Pet that occur nowhere else in the NT, but thirty-four of these can be found in the LXX.¹¹ This is an average number for a NT epistle of this size. Many of these theological concepts are Jewish or are developed from Jewish themes.

As a Galilean Jew, Peter could have produced such a letter, for Galilee even in Isaiah's time was described as thoroughly colored by foreigner influence (Isa 9:1). There is ample evidence to indicate that Galilee was a bilingual area significantly affected by Hellenism.¹² Peter's brother, Andrew, has a Greek name. There are other references to Greek names among the Gospels. The statements of sponsorship for columns and city streets are all in Greek for the Galilean public to read and acknowledge the patron. Additionally, the reference to ἀγράμματοι in Acts 4:13 Sanhedrin context probably means "lacking expertise concerning the Law,"¹³ so not a student of established rabbinic schools. Likewise, Peter was a partner in a dragnet fishing enterprise with father Zebedee (Matt 4:21; Mark 1:19–20; Luke 5:10). Such an individual could have developed a facility in the use of the Greek language. Furthermore, at least thirty years had elapsed between the time when Peter left his life as a fisherman to travel as a missionary across the Roman empire before he finally wrote this letter.¹⁴ Much of this time, Peter had spent traveling in a predominantly

---

9. Spicq, L'Epitre aux Hebreux, 1:2; Charue, Les Epitres Catholiques, 441.
10. Ebright, Petrine Epistles, 75–78.
11. See Ebright, Petrine Epistles, 70–75 for a list of these.
12. Guthrie, New Testament Introduction, 778.
13. BAG, "ἀγράμματος," 13.
14. Guthrie, New Testament Introduction, 778.

Greek-speaking world and would have developed an ability to speak and write in Greek.

First Peter and Pauline letters reflect a common faith in Jesus. Similar theological comparisons with the other apostles demonstrate this common ground rather than any specific dependance.[15] In fact, while similarities exist, so do significant distinctions that demonstrate the unlikeliness of dependence and the high probability of merely a common ground. For example, Peter never develops Pauline doctrines as justification, law, the new Adam, the flesh, and a fully-developed ministry of the Spirit.

Peter wrote to provinces of Pontus, Galatia, Cappadocia, Asia, and Bithynia (1 Pet 1:1), maybe because he traveled the Roman road that laced these provinces together,[16] which would have been a more northern road than we know Paul traveled (Acts 13–14; 16:1–10). Additionally, there were Jewish folk from Cappadocia, Pontus, and Asia at Peter's Pentecost sermon announcing the gospel of Christ in Acts 2, and some of these likely have returned to their homes.[17] Of these provinces, Paul only ministered in Galatia and Asia. Guthrie considered that the other provinces were likely evangelized by Peter or the converts of Peter and Paul.[18]

Streeter's claim that the author identifying himself as an elder (1 Pet 5:1) and thus not apostle Peter, does not hold up, because he could be both, since he identified himself as both (1 Pet 1:1; 5:1).[19] To identify with one's readers as a fellow elder does not diminish his apostleship, for apostle John does the same identification as well (2 John 1; 3 John 1).

Possibility of a Pseudonymous Letter

Some scholars propose that 1 Pet was composed later by a disciple of Peter, making it a pseudonymous letter. For example, the Tübingen school saw it as a later celebration of the union between rival Pauline and Petrine parties, thus accounting for the Pauline theological elements within a Petrine pseudonymous letter.[20] Others think that Silvanus composed

---

15. Bigg, *Epistles of Peter and Jude*, 21–24; Blenkin, *1 Peter*, liii–lx, lxviii–lxix; Kelly, *Epistles of Peter and Jude*, 11–12; Wand, *Peter and Jude*, 24–29; Tenney, "Some Possible Parallels," 370–77.

16. See "Hippolytus on the Twelve Apostles," a fragment in Roberts and Donaldson, *Ante-Nicene Christian Library*, 2.2:130; Jerome, *Vir. ill.* 116; *Ep.*47.3.

17. Jobes, *1 Peter*, 27.

18. Guthrie, *New Testament Introduction*, 784.

19. Guthrie, *New Testament Introduction*, 784.

20. Von Harnack, *Die Chronologie der altchristlichen Literatur*, 1:456.

the letter under Peter's name to encourage Christian suffering under the Domitian persecutions.[21] This view understands 1 Pet 5:1 as a reference to Peter's own martyrdom, which would require this pseudonymity to be rejected as a late forgery.[22] Knopf and Beare reject this view because there is no reason why Silvanus would not write in his own name.[23] A third view claims that the unknown author intimately knowing Paul's theology wrote in Peter's name to give the work extra authority.[24] This view falls under extreme complexity. Why not write under Paul's name, since the mention of Mark and Silvanus are within his circle as well.[25] Furthermore, Hebrews wrote without the need for including an apostolic author's name and it was recognized to be authoritative. Finally, there is significant research to demonstrate that pseudonymity was not a harmless literary device and should be rejected.[26]

Persecution

If the persecution in 1 Pet can be identified then it has bearing on whether Peter could have written the letter. There are five possible persecutions under which the letter has been claimed to have been written: Trajan's persecution during AD 112, Domitian's during AD 95, Vespasian's around AD 75, Neroian AD 64–67, and general scattered persecutions usually before Nero.

The suffering in 1 Pet was suffering undertaken because the persecuted were Christians (1 Pet 4:14, 16). This could mean that the official offense was holding to Christianity or that the condition of suffering is as in everything, that one is a Christian in whatever one does. However, none of the normal charges against Christians (atheism, nonconformist, infanticide, cannibalism, or inappropriate love)[27] are mentioned as the

21. Soden, *Die Brief des Petrus, Jakobus, Judas*, 117.
22. McNeile and Williams, *Introduction to the Study of the New Testament*, 219.
23. Beare, *1 Peter*, 29; Knopf, *Die Briefe Petri und Juda*, 18.
24. Julicher, *Einleitung*, 199–200.
25. Luke records Silas as a messenger accompanying Paul, including time in Thessalonica and Corinth (Acts 15:22, 27, 32, 40; 16:19, 25, 29; 17:4, 10, 14–15; 18:5). When Paul writes to Thessalonica and Corinth, Silvanus and Timothy are co-authors (2 Cor 1:19; 1 Thess 1:1; 2 Thess 1:1). Thus, it is reasonable to assume Silas and Silvanus are the same person.
26. Guthrie, "Tertullian and Pseudonymity," 341; "Development of the Idea," 14–39; Lea, "Early Christian View," 65–75.
27. Keener, *1 Peter*, 29.

reason for this suffering. For example, Polycarp was martyred for obstinacy in refusing to offer sacrifice to the national deities and emperor.[28] Clearly, his faith in Christ prevented him from doing these offerings, even though Christianity was not mentioned in the charge against him. The early church in Acts, including Peter, does many things in the name of Jesus Christ, including: preaching (Acts 4:17; 9:27), healing (Acts 3:6; 4:30), obtaining salvation (Acts 4:12), forgiving sins (Acts 10:43), praying (Acts 9:21; 22:16), baptizing (Acts 2:38; 10:48), and suffering persecution (Acts 5:41; 9:14, 16; 21:13).[29] Prior to E. G. Selwyn, most commentators assumed that the addressees of 1 Pet were suffering because of the Roman imperial persecution of Christians under Nero or a later Caesar but Selwyn led the way to describe the suffering as sporadic and localized slander and discrimination on the basis of Peter's descriptions in 1 Pet 2:12; 3:9, 16; 4:4, 14, rather than an official Roman policy.[30] In the wake of such a socio-historical context, John Elliott applied a social-scientific perspective to argue that actual resident aliens were in social estrangement in a foreign land and thus prone to be taken advantage of in persecution and suffering.[31] In this wake, it is better to view such suffering as occurring to a Christian not officially because one is a Christian, but rather as mostly occasional local and sporadic persecutions.[32]

The suffering seen in 1 Pet is better viewed as that of a general kind instead of political martyrdom. For example, 1 Pet 1:6–7; 3:13–17 describe potential general suffering. Furthermore, "trial" (πειρασμὸν) would be a peculiar term for persecution (1 Pet 1:6; 4:12). Likewise, in 1 Pet 3:15 there is an indication that the Christian needs to be ready to give a defense at any time for any kind of persecution. The fact that legal penalties might be applied from the state upon evildoers or thieves shows that generally these sufferers were not being persecuted for these state crimes (1 Pet 2:12; 4:15–16). Such state judgments would usually end in death, but Peter expected the suffering not to end in that manner as he encourages his readers to continue to do good (1 Pet 4:19). The

---

28. Best, *1 Peter*, 37.
29. Best, *1 Peter*, 37–38.
30. Selwyn, *1 Peter*, 47–56.
31. Elliott, *Home for the Homeless*, 48 provides a nice summary; *1 Peter*, 101–3, 312–16, 457–62, 476–83.
32. Van Unnik, "Teaching of Good Works in 1 Peter," 95–109; Elliott, *Home for the Homeless*, 78–82; Achtemeier, *1 Peter*, 33–36; Harland, *Associations, Synagogues, and Congregations*, 188–89.

only suffering in the letter that clearly involves death is that of Christ's crucifixion suffering (1 Pet 2:23–24). Other suffering described by Peter entails abuse of a slave (1 Pet 2:19–20) and dishonor (1 Pet 4:14). The use of "fiery" (πυρώσει) probably indicates that the suffering experienced was emotionally difficult and perhaps morally refining rather than incendiary (1 Pet 4:12 with 1:7). The phrase, "to the degree that you share in the sufferings of Christ" makes martyrdom possible but contextually it is explained by reproach rather than loss of life (1 Pet 4:13–14). The suffering which occurred in 1 Pet is thus general persecution not limited to a set time (1 Pet 5:9–10). For example, the apostles and their followers suffer under the hands of Jewish religious leaders (Acts 5:40; 6:8—8:3), rulers (Acts 12:1–6; 16:19–24), and mobs (Acts 9:23–25; 14:5, 19; 19:23–41; 23:11–21). Additionally, three of the mob persecutions of Acts occur in regions to which Peter writes.[33] Furthermore, a combination of Jewish and mob persecution fostered the banishment of Jews and Christians from Rome over the issue of Chrestus.[34] Perhaps the scattering of Christians that 1 Pet addresses may have been recently caused by this eviction from Rome or by the death of James (ca. AD 62).[35] Keener also argues from Tacitus that Christians were already suspect and beginning to be persecuted under Nero before the fire in Rome.[36] General suffering would also be the conclusion if Keener's claim that the wording of *1 Clem.* 5 argues for acceptance of the book composed by Peter in the sixties before his death under Nero.[37]

External Attestation

If 2 Pet is attributed to Peter as it claims (2 Pet 1:1), it would seem most reasonable to accept 1 Pet as the first letter of Peter which is implied by

---

33. Selwyn, "Problem of the Authorship of 1 Peter," 257–58; van Unnik, "Christianity According to Peter," 79–83.

34. Suetonius, *Claud.* 25.4; *Nero* 16; Tacitus, *Ann.* 15.44; Justin, *1 Apol.* 4; Tertullian, *Apol.* 3; Lactantius, *Inst.* 4.7.

35. Guthrie, *New Testament Introduction*, 761, 796; Schürer, *Jewish People*, 2:186; Mayor, *James*, xxxix–xl.

36. Keener, *1 Peter*, 30; Tacitus, *Ann.* 15.44, especially 15.44.2; Suetonius, *Nero* 16.2; Pliny, *Ep.* 10.96; agreeing with Feldmeier, *1 Peter*, 2–5; Lund, "Zur Verbrennung der sogenanten *Chrestiani*," 253–61; Harrison, "Persecution of Christians," 266–300.

37. Keener, *1 Peter*, 25.

the claim of a second letter (2 Pet 3:1). Some see this reference as to a lost epistle, but this is largely an assumption without evidence.

Bigg and Elliott produce an extensive list of possible evidence among the Church fathers of a knowledge of 1 Pet.[38] For example, Polycarp in his *Epistle to Philippians* cites 1 Pet as Scripture.[39] John Elliott and Craig Keener identified that Clement of Rome around AD 95 cites shorter phrases that reflect knowledge of 1 Pet.[40] Irenaeus cites Peter by name as he quotes from 1 Pet around AD 180.[41] Eusebius of Caesarea cites 1 Pet as Scripture accepted by the whole church.[42] Eusebius also mentions that Papias also quotes from 1 Pet.[43]

Summary

It is best to view 1 Pet as authored by apostle Peter around AD 62–64. Thus 1 Pet is primary source material for a Petrine theology.

2 PET IS A PRIMARY SOURCE

For the extent of the recorded history of the church there has been a debate concerning the authorship of 2 Pet. Determination of the authorship is an important step for considering 2 Pet as primary source material.

Claims of Authorship

The letter claims Simon Peter is its author as a servant and apostle of Jesus Christ (2 Pet 1:1). The inclusion of "Simon" or the alternative reading "Symeon" is unusual and would argue for it being genuine, connecting with the Gospels and Acts. If the book was trying to pass as pseudepigraphal then the name on the second letter (2 Pet 3:1) would be the same as on 1 Pet 1:1. This claim was regularly disputed among the patristics and

---

38. Bigg, *Peter and Jude*, 7–15; Elliott, *1 Peter*, 142–49.

39. Polycarp, *Epist. Phil.* salutation = 1 Pet 1:2; 1.3 = 1 Pet 1:18; 2.1 = 1 Pet 1:13, 21; 2.2 = 1 Pet 3:9; 5.3 = 1 Pet 2:11; 7.2 = 1 Pet 4:7; 8.1–2 = 1 Pet 2:21, 24; 10.1 = 1 Pet 2:17; 10.2 = 1 Pet 2:12.

40. Elliott, *1 Peter*, 138–40; Keener, *1 Peter*, 21–23.

41. Irenaeus, *Haer.* 4.9.2; 4.16.5; 5.7.2.

42. Eusebius, *Hist. eccl.* 3.25.2.

43. Eusebius, *Hist. eccl.* 3.39.17.

contemporary critics. For example, Origen authoritatively quotes from 2 Pet but identifies it as a disputed work.[44] The book finally began to gain acceptance into the canon with Athanasius Easter letter (AD 367) and the synod of Carthage (AD 397). Gene Green concluded for accepting 2 Pet as authentic from the apostle Peter,[45] however Green sets 2 Pet aside, without including any contributions to Petrine theology. Consistency would both accept 2 Pet as authentic and contributing to Petrine theology.

The author claims that his death is close and approaching swiftly[46] indicating he is likely writing around AD 64–66 (2 Pet 1:14). Those who oppose Petrine authorship generally propose that this is an allusion to John 21:18–19, indicating literary dependence.[47] Because Jesus' statement was said to Peter, there is no need for literary dependance, and doesn't just mean that Peter is old and on death's door, but Peter adds a statement about his death coming swiftly. This additional information either indicates revelation or the process of a trial ending with an impending death sentence. Such information adds to the authenticity of the letter as being authored by Peter.

In 2 Pet 1:15, this thought continues with perhaps an indication of a literary work about to be sent out, "I will be diligent that at any time after my departure you may be able to call these things to mind." Some surmise that this statement may refer to the Gospel of Mark,[48] but there is no evidence for this in the context. It is better to understand "these things" (τούτων) of verse 15 as referring to the "these things" (τούτων) of verse twelve, namely, an exhortation to press on toward salvation (2 Pet 1:1–11). There is no basis for claiming this expression as a pseudepigraphal tool to present the past in order to set out prophecy for the future;[49] both history and prophecy are interspersed throughout the letter.

The claim for being an eyewitness to Jesus' transfiguration fits Petrine authorship especially since unique information is expressed from the experience (2 Pet 1:16–18). Some claim that this is a forced intrusion considered pseudepigraphal[50] because there are few other events men-

44. Origen, *Comm. Jo.* 5.3.
45. Green, *Vox Petri*, 97; *Jude, 2 Peter*, 172, 144–45.
46. ταχινὴν cannot mean "soon" but rather "swiftly" as in 2 Pet 2:1.
47. Moffatt, *Introduction to the Literature*, 366.
48. Ebright, *Petrine Epistles*, 132–33; Mayor, *Jude and 2 Peter*, cxlii.
49. Munck compares 2 Pet with a farewell discourse in Jewish apocalyptic ("Discours d'adieu dans le Nouveau Testament," 155–70.
50. Guthrie, *New Testament Introduction*, 822; Ebright, *The Petrine Epistles*, 132.

tioned from Jesus' life, but the transfiguration contributes to the plot of the letter in ways other Jesus events might not to set up the authority of prophecy and the anticipation of kingdom. Peter chose the one event from Jesus' life where Christ's greatest glory was visible. Specific details are unique when compared to the synoptic tradition. There is no mention of Moses and Elijah; the word order has been changed; the synoptic "hear him" is omitted; an emphatic ἐγώ is added to the parallel 2 Pet 1:17 (compared to Matt 17:5). Additionally, the idea of a holy mount is not a reference to a late veneration of a place, but "the appreciation of the sanctity of an impressive occasion in which the writer himself shared."[51]

In 2 Pet 3:1 there is a claim of a previous letter having been written to this audience by Peter, and that this letter extends the previous encouragement. Some reject 1 Pet as this previous letter because it was written to a gentile audience, but Peter also preaches to a gentile audience at times (Acts 10). Furthermore, 1 Pet 1:12 identifies that Peter's ministry reiterating what the prophets said joined others among the gentiles receiving 1 Pet.

Peter claims to be aware of Pauline letters and views them as Scripture, though containing some concepts that are hard to understand (2 Pet 2:15–16). There is no claim for awareness of the full Pauline corpus, merely an assessment that "all" the Pauline letters Peter is aware of fit this description. The apostates are heading for destruction because they disregard such writings from God (2 Pet 3:16 contrasted with 1:21 and 2:1).

Literary Style

Stylistic differences between 1 Pet and 2 Pet were noticed early and commented upon by Jerome.[52] The vocabulary in 1 Pet is dignified while the language of 2 Pet is grandiose, ambitious, and somewhat pedantic.[53] Many of the common words and connecting particles of 1 Pet are absent in 2 Pet. A few places in 2 Pet 2:1–4 even have an iambic rhythm, which can be seen elsewhere in Hellenistic Judaism.[54] These stylistic elements

---

51. Guthrie, *New Testament Introduction*, 831.

52. Jerome, *Scriptorium Ecclesiastricorum* 11 and *Ep.* 120.11, letter to Hedibia; Guthrie, *Introduction to the New Testament*, 826; Bigg, *Peter and Jude*, 199.

53. Green, *2 Peter Reconsidered*, 11.

54. Bigg, *Peter and Jude*, 227; Green, *2 Peter Reconsidered*, 11.

have motivated some to claim that the author attempted to write "in a style which is beyond his literary power."[55]

There is some recognition that 2 Pet might have been written in "a definite Asiatic style of writing, with florid, verbose type of diction verging on the bizarre which was a far cry from the canons of classical simplicity."[56] The different style could have been specifically chosen to accomplish two different tasks. The simpler style of 1 Pet could be a more calculating attempt to inform and encourage the recipients to hope in God and to live properly. The more grandiose Asiatic style could be chosen to write a few last urgent exhortations to remain faithful, pressing the recipients on a full salvation. Two contexts and the degree of urgency could significantly effect the style and contents.[57]

Though these differences are significant, there are no less significant similarities. Hebraisms appear in both letters such that neither should be considered too Hellenistic for Peter. For example, the habit of verbal repetition is common in both letters.[58] Additionally, there are parallels of common language to both, such as the use of τιμὴν (1 Pet 1:7, 19; 2 Pet 1:1, 4) or the salutation (1 Pet 1:2; 2 Pet 1:2). Even a rare NT word, ἀρετὰς is used similarly (1 Pet 2:9; 2 Pet 1:3). Forms of ἐπόπται are used in both (1 Pet 2:11; 2 Pet 1:16). Redemption (ἀγοράσαντα) is used similarly in both (1 Pet 1:18; 2 Pet 2:1, 19–22). Many other similarities could be listed.[59]

Linguistic statistics demonstrate similar balance between each epistle:[60]

---

55. Chase, "2 Peter," 3:809.

56. Green, *2 Peter and Jude*, 18; first-century descriptions of this Asiatic style are made by Quintilion, *Inst.* 12.10.16 and Cicero, *Brut.* 13.51; 95.325; two first-century examples are: "The Decree of Stratonicae" in Caria, Asia Minor in Böckh and Franz, *Corpus Inscriptionarum Graecarum*, 2:2715 with Deissmann commenting in *Bible Studies*, 360, and "Inscription of Antiochus the First of Commagene" in Central Asia Minor commented upon in Norden, *Die antike Kunstprosa*, 126–52 and Waldis, *Sprache und stil der grossen Griechischen Inschrift*, 57–59.

57. Green, *2 Peter Reconsidered*, 14–32; Guthrie, *New Testament Introduction*, 839–45.

58. Bigg, *Peter and Jude*, 226–27.

59. Green, *2 Peter Reconsidered*, 12–13; Boobyer, "Indebtedness of 2 Peter," 34–38.

60. Green, *2 Peter Reconsidered*, 12.

	1 Pet	% 1 Pet	% 2 Pet	2 Pet
Total Words	543	–	–	399
Hapax Legomena	63	12	14	57
Words Only in Later Ecclesiastical Authors	9	1.6	1.2	5
Words Not Found in Any Classical Author	27	5	6	24

Furthermore, with regard to the use of the article, these two epistles are closer than any other NT book.[61] Edwin Blum concluded that computer analysis of various data from both letters rendered them "linguistically indistinguishable."[62] However, with only two letters and a small word count there is no way to conclusively identify whether 1 and 2 Pet are from the same author because one would need about ten thousand words from each source to definitely demonstrate whether 1 and 2 Pet are from the same author.[63]

Historical Issues

Some have argued that 2 Pet 3:4, "since the fathers fell asleep" requires a second or third generation of Christians after the apostles die.[64] However, the "fathers" could refer to the Jewish OT fathers as the term does elsewhere in Petrine use (Acts 3:13) and the rest of the Bible (John 6:31; Rom 9:5; Heb 1:1).[65] Such Jewish fathers is whom is repeatedly referred in 2 Pet 3:4 context, namely: Abraham and Lot (2 Pet 2:6–7), the exodus (2 Pet 2:15), and Noah (2 Pet 3:6).

In the same verse these mockers question the delay of the παρουσίαν. It is argued that this is a second-century problem after the apostles die off. This completely disregards the abundance of NT teaching addressing this very issue of eschatological delay among both Christ's and early

---

61. Green, *2 Peter Reconsidered*, 12.
62. Blum, "2 Peter," 12:258–59.
63. Green, *2 Peter Reconsidered*, 12.
64. Mayor, *Jude and 2 Peter*, 126, dating 2 Pet to AD 90–125.
65. Blum, "2 Peter," 12:285.

apostolic ministry (Matt 25:1–13; John 21:20–23; Acts 1:6–11; 2 Thess 2:1–4; Heb 9:28).

Accepting Petrine authorship would date the composition of 2 Pet to just prior to Peter's impending death (AD 64–67; 2 Pet 1:14). Furthermore, pseudonymity was not acceptable among mainstream Christianity because the presbyter who pseudonymously wrote the apocryphal *Acts of Paul and Theclas* was deposed.[66]

Early quotes of 2 Pet are done anonymously.[67] However, Origen recognized this second letter from Peter but acknowledged that the difference of style meant 2 Pet was contested in his day.[68] The third-century Bodmer papyrus P72 claims 2 Pet, 1 Pet, and Jude are all sacred Scripture, but it favors 2 Pet more,[69] whereas Eusebius affirms both Petrine epistles acknowledging 2 Pet was disputed.

> As to the writings of Peter, one of his epistles, called the First, is acknowledged as genuine. For this was anciently received by the ancient fathers in their writings as an undoubted work of the apostle. But that which is called the Second we have not indeed understood to be embodied in the sacred books, yet as it appeared useful to many, it was studiously read with the other Scriptures.[70]

Jerome also attests to 2 Pet as authoritative but because of stylistic differences with 1 Pet, he attributes each to different amanuensis.[71] The small church council at Laodicea (AD 366) was the first council to consider the books of 1 and 2 Pet as canonical.[72] Athanasius' Easter letter (AD 367) listed all twenty-seven NT books as canonical and the third Council of Carthage (AD 397) confirmed a similar list, which included both 1 and 2 Pet. The letter 2 Pet remained virtually unquestioned until the time of the Reformation.

---

66. Guthrie, *New Testament Introduction*, 671–84; Walls, "Canon of the New Testament," 1:638.

67. *1 Clem.* 1.2; 7.6; 63.1; *Barn.* 15, *Apoc. Pet.*; Eusebius, *Eccl. Hist.* 6.14.1; Photius, *Codices* 109.

68. Origen, *Hom. Josh.* 7.1; *Comm. Jo.* 5.3.

69. Gundry, *Survey of the New Testament*, 353.

70. Eusebius, *Hist. eccl.* 3.25.3–4.

71. Jerome, *Scriptorium Ecclesiasticorum* 1; and *Ep.* 120.111, "Letter to Hidibia."

72. Smith, "Laodicea, Canons of," 578; sixteen articles recognized all the NT books as canonical, except Revelation. The 59th article forbids the use of any other books in the liturgy of the church.

Summary

Second Peter will be viewed as authored by the apostle Peter, sometime around AD 64–67, close before Peter's martyrdom (2 Pet 1:14). Second Peter will be a primary source for this construction of Petrine theology.

JUDE IS NOT A PRIMARY SOURCE FOR PETRINE THEOLOGY

Jude and 2 Pet begin with some similarities. Both identify their authors are a servant (δοῦλος) of Jesus Christ and bless with peace (εἰρήνη). They both intend to write about the common salvation but only 2 Pet does this, maybe indicating Jude might be using 2 Pet as a source (2 Pet 1:3–11; Jude 3). Both letters discuss false teachers, though 2 Pet used examples that set out two alternatives illustrating the two ways of salvation and judgment, and Jude uses triads of mixed metaphors. Second Peter predicts (with future tense; 2 Pet 2:1) that these false teachers will arise, while Jude describes the false teachers as a present reality (aorist tense; Jude 4), possibly indicating 2 Pet predictions help Jude to address his present reality, though we do not know where Jude sends his letter and false teachers could be present there and about to enter 2 Pet's Asia Minor without reference to priority of a letter. These similarities will prompt comments on the Jude text when they cover similar material to that of 2 Pet but may indicate that Jude is not a source for 2 Pet. Scholars claim each may be the source for the other and include the possibility of some unknown common source for both, but no side has conclusive evidence, and each side can raise doubts about the other point of view. If one examines the parallel passages comprising 2 Pet 1:2, 12; 2:1–4, 6, 11–12, 15–18; 3:2–3 and Jude 2, 4–13, and 17–18, the former contains 297 words, the latter contains 256 words, with only seventy-eight words shared. If 2 Pet borrowed from Jude then 2 Pet changed 75 percent of the words, thus showing substantial autonomy. If Jude borrowed from 2 Pet, then the percent change is even higher, with a reduction of quality. Additionally, neither author is more concise than the other; out of twelve parallel sections, Jude's text is verbally longer than 2 Pet on five occasions. The only passages with extended verbal agreement are 2 Pet 2:12 with Jude 10 (fourteen words) and 2 Pet 3:2–3 with Jude 17–18 (sixteen words), but between these texts the passages diverge. Joseph Mayor compared the theology of both epistles and concluded that while there are significant similarities between the two, there are also significant differences on all topics he compared.[73] These similarities and differences will be commented on in the notes.

PETER'S SPEECHES IN ACTS ARE SECONDARY PETRINE SOURCE

A. T. Robertson, J. de Zwaan, C. H. Dodd, and C. K. Barrett agree that Peter's speeches in the book of Acts are full of Aramaisms appropriate to a Galilean Jewish speaker.[74] That is, the writer, Luke, has composed abbreviated speeches both reflective of what Peter said and using the characteristic language "of the speaker, using language appropriate to the speaker's education, social class, values, and even regional characteristics."[75] Furthermore, Jonathan Lo analyzed the Acts Petrine speeches for Petrine titles of Jesus and for a disciple's description of Jesus' life and concluded that the Acts descriptions fit a Galilean description of Jesus.

> The speeches frequently refer to Jesus "of Nazareth" (2:22; 3:6; 4:10; 10:38) and tend to emphasize details from the earthly ministry of Jesus, a focus mostly absent outside the Gospel narratives. Peter's speeches mention the baptism of John (10:37; 11:16), Jesus being anointed by the Holy Spirit (10:38), the Progression of his ministry from Galilee to Jerusalem (10:37, 39), and Jesus' ministries of healing and exorcism (10:38). Furthermore, Jesus is described as a "man" appointed by God (2:22), whom God "made Lord and Christ (2:36).[76]

Jonathan Lo further defended the Petrine nature of the speeches by identifying the conservative consensus of a high Christology in earlier and later apostolic traditions consistent with Peter's high Christology (1 Pet 2:6–8; 2 Pet 1:1–2).[77]

---

73. Mayor, *Jude and 2 Peter*, xvi–xxv.

74. Robertson, *Grammar of the New Testament*, 105; Zzaan, "Use of the Greek Language in Acts," 2:30–65; Dodd, *Apostolic Preaching*, 20; Barrett, *Acts*, 1:521; Lo, "Did Peter Really Say That?," 69–70.

75. Lo, "Did Peter Really Say That?," 70; Keener, *Acts*, 1:284–86; Hurtado, "Christology in Acts," In *Issues in Luke-Acts*. edited by Adams and Pahl, 217–37.

76. Lo, "Did Peter Really Say That?," 72.

77. Lo, "Did Peter Really Say That?," 72–73; Keener, *Acts*, 1:312; Hurtado, *Lord Jesus Christ*, 650; Kennard, *Petrine Theology*, chapters on Christology and Trinity.

Jesus' statements in the Gospels and Peter's sermons in the book of Acts are all summaries. Each sermon can be read in three to fifteen minutes, and likely the speaker talked longer than that. So the important feature of classical historical accounts recording speeches was to provide teaching consistent with the narrative hero's character and speech patterns.[78] Partly this is because Aristotle argued that ancient witnesses are known broadly by many humans, so that uncharacteristic speech would render accounts less credible.[79] Such speeches are quite significant within the Gospels because Jesus occupies a rabbinic role and Peter becomes his supreme follower and early leader within the developing tradition of Christianity.

Likely an author included the sermonic material only once in a representative form to cover for the repetitive sermons (Mark 4:1–34; 10:2–13; Acts 2–4; 10:23—11:18). These sermons are imbedded within the stated purpose of recording salvation history and thus repeatedly telling of the gospel message. Narrative asides and summaries were utilized to provide interpretive guidance among the narrator's account as a framework (Mark 1:1, 15; 4:11; Acts 2:47; 6:7; 9:31; 12:24; 16:5; 19:20; 28:31).[80] Such material helps to organize the thrust of the narrative and to show important overarching concerns. These summaries by Mark and Luke emphasize salvation history and the continued development of the Church into new regions. Furthermore, if the same speaker is recorded to be speaking the same Gospel at different locations in the same written account, as Peter does, then those similar sermons subsequently are shortened. However, the essence of the sermon, the contextual engagement, and the characteristic language of Peter is retained throughout the sermons.

The Lukan material in Acts shows some of the consistent language of Peter's writing[81] even though the gospel speeches in Acts accomplish a different purpose than their written epistles attempt. For example, Kistemaker finds convoluted Greek in Peter's sermons (Acts 3:16; 10:36–37) similar to 1 Pet 4:11 and 2 Pet 3:5–6.[82] Additionally, characteristic phrases are utilized by Peter, such as "God's foreknowledge" (Acts 2:23; 1 Pet 1:2,

---

78. *Rhetorica ad Herennium* 4.52.65; Quintilian, *Inst.* 3.8.51; Thucydides, 1.22.1; Dionysius of Halicarnassus, *Ant. rom.* 7.66.2–3; 11.1.3–4.

79. Aristotle, *Rhet.* 1.15.13, 15.

80. Irenaeus, *Haer.* 3.1.1; 3.14.1; Eusebius, *Hist. eccl.* 3.4.7; Rood, "Thucydides," 123; Sheeley, *Narrative Asides in Luke-Acts*, 40–96.

81. Peter's consistency: Selwyn, *1 Peter*, 33–36; Williams, *Acts*, 11.

82. Kistemaker, *Acts*, 9–11.

20) and "judge of the living and the dead" (Acts 10:42; 1 Pet 4:5), identify that Luke has authentically recorded Peter.

Additionally, there are also unique accounts in Acts that Peter experienced alone as the only witness, such as: his vision in Joppa (Acts 10:9–20) and his escape from prison (Acts 12:3–11, 18–19). In many other events, Peter plays a part in the narrative of the Gospels and Acts and is likely one of the witnesses that are drawn upon, and these narratives inform the chapter on Peter's life.

Peter's speeches in Acts inform a Petrine theology as a secondary source, filtered through the expression of Luke. So, the context and Lukan purposes of salvation history need to be considered to explain meaning in any one speech. Marianne Bonz analyzed Luke-Acts from the lens of ancient epic and concluded that the narrative center was the speeches, especially Acts 2 that places Petrine theology as an emphasis of the book of Acts.[83] Inducing "a Petrine theology from the speeches must also consider the function of the speeches in the literary and theological structure of Acts."[84] The same could be said about Peter's brief comments in the Gospels as well.

THE GOSPEL OF MARK IS SECONDARILY A PETRINE SOURCE

If the Gospel of Mark recorded Peter's gospel messages or his reminiscences of Christ, then the theology of Mark contributes to a theology of Peter. Such a historical assessment would compare Mark among the multiple testimony continuing among the Gospels and highlight Mark's unique elements.[85] However, an additional factor of continuity with other Petrine literature (1 and 2 Pet) and the unique contributions of their discontinuity should also be considered.

---

83. Bonz, *Past as Legacy*, 95; using epics such as Virgil's *Aeneid*.

84. Lo, "Did Peter Really Say That?," 73, reflective of Ridderbos, *Speeches of Peter in Acts*, 5.

85. Kennard, *Messiah Jesus*, 6.

Early Tradition

The tradition, that Mark records Peter's description of Jesus from sermons, originates in Eusebius from a lost exposition of the Lord's sayings written around AD 115–40 by Papias, Bishop of Hierapolis.

> Mark, who became Peter's interpreter, wrote accurately, though not in order, all that he remembered of the things said and done by the Lord. For he had neither heard the Lord nor been one of his followers, but afterwards as I said, he had followed Peter, who used to compose his discourses with a view to the needs (of his hearers) but not as if he were composing a systematic account of the Lord's sayings. So Mark did nothing blameworthy in thus writing some things just as he remembered them; for he was careful to make no untrue statement therein.[86]

The statement that Mark was Peter's "right-hand man" and missionary traveling companion identifies Mark's appropriateness for recording Peter's testimony of Jesus. Eusebius' statement preceding the quote gives the testimony of an older contemporary of Papias, perhaps John who discipled Papias, who has just been quoted by Eusebius prior to this statement. Eusebius also indicated Mark wrote in Rome what Peter had been empowered by the Holy Spirit to give witness.[87]

Papias' primary interest is to demonstrate the apostolic authority of Peter is conveyed through the Gospel of Mark.[88] Papias utilizes similar language to that of Luke 1:2–3 to root his claim. Based upon this evidence, Ralph Martin summarized that "this striking agreement in terminology and tendenz invites the suggestion that Papias is thereby consciously paying tribute to Mark as a Gospel writer who, in spite of well-known deficiencies, could lay claim to an authority which matched that of Luke."[89] Martin concluded that Papias' point is "to show Mark's Gospel faithfully contains Peter's original deposit of witness and thus it is an accurate source of apostolic teaching."[90]

---

86. Eusebius, *Hist. eccl.* 3.39.14–15.

87. Eusebius, *Hist. eccl.* 2.15; 25.5–8; 4.14.5–7 records Clement of Alexandria saying the same; *Paed.* 6.25.3 has Origen claiming the same and that based on 1 Pet 5:13 that Peter and Mark were close; Ignatius, *Rom.* 4.3 and Irenaeus, *Haer.* 3.1.1–3 further confirm these statements.

88. Walls, "Papias and Oral Tradition," 137–40; Farrar, *Study in Mark*, 15–17.

89. Martin, *Mark, Evangelist and Theologian*, 31.

90. Martin, *Mark, Evangelist and Theologian*, 82.

Peter's contribution to the book of Mark was either through chreia-forms or ad hoc. The cheria-forms are brief statements, too unconnected to form the story narrative or a compendium of teaching.[91] However, there is no evidence that Peter wrote a series of brief notes, such as Q or the *Gospel of Thomas*. Furthermore, the Gospel of Mark primarily recounts events of healing and interactions in Jesus' life, rather than extended teaching from Jesus, as one can find in Matthew, Luke, and John. However, if Mark records Peter's speaking ad hoc, there would be narrative storylines to which appeals could be made to tailor the account to his audience, thus the narrative story line would also be attributive to Peter. Thus, unique features, such as the ending to the Gospel of Mark 16:8, shows that this Petrine-Markan account is creating its own narrative without dependance upon other Gospel accounts.[92]

Other apostolic fathers echo Papias' assertion that Mark was an accurate source of Peter's teaching. For example, around AD 160, "the Anti-Marcionite Prologue" to Mark declared that stump-fingered Mark wrote down Peter's testimony of Jesus in Italy.[93] Such multiple attestation supports the essence of Peter's testimony while providing discontinuity with unique features or slight differences.[94] Gene Green concluded that Mark wrote his Gospel to the Roman church utilizing Peter's sermons, "The association between Peter and Mark—and between them, the city of Rome—enjoys very strong testimonial support. Mark therefore was most likely written to the Roman church, the same community which had encouraged him to pen the memoir of Peter."[95] This tradition clearly connects Mark with Peter as a friend, disciple, and a kind of interpreter, who composed the Gospel of Mark from Peter's sermons. Mark's use of Peter's preaching provides eyewitness accuracy and apostolic authority. Green concluded that "the consensus of the church fathers is that Mark was not produced by an author who worked up multiple sources or simply crafted

---

91. See the ground-breaking discussion of chreia-forms by Taylor, *Groundwork of the Gospels*, 75–90; Green, *Vox Petri*, 102–3.

92. Magness, *Sense and Absence*; Ferda, "Ending of Mark and the Faithfulness of God," 36–52, esp. 40.

93. Cranfield, *Mark*, 4; Huck, *Synopsis of the First Three Gospels*, viii, statement in Latin.

94. France, *Mark*, 37n72; Green, *Vox Petri*, 32.

95. Green, *Vox Petri*, 109.

his unique telling of the story according to his own reader's interests. Rather the book is a redaction of Peter's gospel story."[96]

Other Proposed Evidence

Several additional points are cited by scholars to show that Peter was the source for Mark.[97] Peter comes to Mark's house in Jerusalem (Acts 12:12). Mark is with Peter in Rome as a son at the time of the writing of 1 Pet (1 Pet 5:13).

Peter has been claimed to be the only apostle present in several texts but the only one experience that fits this is Peter's denials (Mark 14:66–72). Several of the other claimed events have the Zebedee brothers also present to provide testimony (Mark 1:29–39; 9:2–13; 14:32–42). The only Gospel which has Simon Cyrene carrying the cross is Mark 15:21 but Peter is not mentioned, so Mark does not specifically identify the witness to this event.

Some claim that Peter is singled out more in Mark than in other Gospels, but Matthew and Luke single out Peter more (Matt 16:17–19; Luke 5:1–11). Mark puts more emphasis upon the intimate core group of the disciples which included Peter and the Zebedee brothers (Mark 1:16–20; 5:37; 9:2; 13:3).

Another argument for Peter as the source of Mark is that of the structural similarity of the Gospel of Mark when compared to each of Peter's gospel sermons. Part of the similarity is that each is focused on Jesus' life and ministry, and that similar chronology and theological emphasis structures the concept of gospel. Similar titles are used in Mark as in Acts, though Peter's sermons in Acts include more variety. Similar structural features and language are shown on the chart.

---

96. Green, *Vox Petri*, 105.
97. Good examples are: Anderson, *Mark*, 17 and Green, *Vox Petri*, 31–45, 101–26.

SOURCE MATERIAL FOR PETRINE THEOLOGY

Mark	Acts 2:14–39	Acts 3:11–26	Acts 10:34–43
Beginning of gospel of Jesus as Lord (1:1)	Tongues explained by Joel (2:14–21)	Healing in Christ (3:11–12)	Universal blessing (10:34–37)
Jesus empowered by Spirit at baptism (1:10)	Giving of Spirit (2:4, 17)	God glorified Jesus to heal (3:13; 4:10)	Spirit anointed Jesus, (10:38)
Jesus heals sick (1:21–34; 2:1–12; 3:7–12; 5:1–43; 6:53—7:37; 8:22–26; 9:14–29; 10:46–52)	Jesus attested by God with miracles (2:22)	3:11–12; also 4:9–10	Jesus heals (10:38)
Jesus preached kingdom (1:14–45; 4:11–34; 8:35–38; 10:17–27; 12:28–34)	Kingdom (1:6–8)	Kingdom restoration (3:21)	Preached peace (10:37)
Peter confessed Jesus is Christ (8:27–30)	Jesus is Christ (2:34–36)	Prince of Life (3:15)	Jesus is Christ (10:36)
Jesus glorified as God's Son in kingdom (9:1–10)	Glorified in resurrection and ascension (2:33)	Glorified in resurrection (3:13)	
Jesus' triumphal entry into Jerusalem (11:1–11)			
Jewish leaders oppose Jesus and he condemned them (2:1—3:6, 20, 35; 7:1–23; 8:10–13; 10:1–12; 12:13–34)	Jesus condemns Jewish leaders (2:23)	Denied Jesus to death (3:14–15)	Jews killed Jesus (10:39)
Angel informed women of Resurrection (16:1–8)	God raised Jesus as was prophesied (2:24–31), and we are witnesses (2:32)	God raised Jesus and we are witnesses (3:15)	God raised Jesus and we are witnesses (10:40–41)
	Jesus exalted to God's right hand as Lord and Christ (2:33, 36)	Glorified in Resurrection (3:13)	
Faith receives forgiveness (2:5)	Repent and be baptized (38; 2:39)	Repent for restoration (3:19–26)	Believe for forgiveness (10:43)

Schleiermacher was the first to conjecture that Mark used a "proto-Mark" source, which Wrede identified as providing a "messianic secret" without calling Jesus as "Christ" and "Son of God."[98] However, Mark does call Jesus: "Christ" and "Son of God" (Mark 1:1, 11; 3:11; 8:29; 12:35; 15:39). Johannes Weiss claimed that the Gospel of Mark was a coherent reconstruction of Peter's reminiscences (an oral "proto-Mark" source) that retained real historical value.[99] Hermann von Soden, E. Wendling, and Eduard Meyer affirmed this Petrine source as interspersed with a twelve source.[100] J. M. C. Crum attempted to distinguish the Petrine stratum (with an assumed lower Christology) from the other by noting where the Greek of the LXX shows through in Mark and where the Christology is high.[101] However, Crum's method is merely assumed because Petrine Christology elsewhere in Acts and epistles is high, affirming him as Christ and God. A conservative consensus defends a high Christology in Petrine speeches and the Gospel of Mark consistent with Peter's high Christology (1 Pet 2:6–8; 2 Pet 1:1–2).[102]

B. Rigaux concluded that no objective criterion could be found to distinguish the Petrine strata from any other source.[103] Returning to a patristic post-critical assessment, Gene Green concluded that Peter's preaching stands behind the Gospel of Mark and that the book of Acts recording a number of Peter's speeches.[104] However, since Mark presents itself as a narrative or biography, the interpreter and biblical theologian should approach Mark's contributions through an appropriate narrative criticism that tries to assess how each pericope fits within the narrative arc, or as Jeannine Brown concluded, the Markan narrative theology features intentional highlights in tension with the rest of the narrative to present a whole picture of Jesus with his disciple band and suffering under Jewish religious leadership.[105] In these narrative genres there will be an attempt to corroborate the narrative historically with other gospels

---

98. Schleiermacher, "Uber die Zeugnisse des Papias"; Wrede, *Messianic Secret*.

99. Weiss, *Das Alteste Evangelium*.

100. Soden, *Urchristliche Literaturgeschichte*, 71–73; Wendling, *Ur-Marcus*; Meyer, *Ursprung und Anfänge des Christentums*, 1:121–60.

101. Crum, *Mark*, 13.

102. Lo, "Did Peter Really Say That?," 72–73; Keener, *Acts*, 1:312; Hurtado, *Lord Jesus Christ*, 650.

103. Rigaux, *Testimony of St. Mark*, 68.

104. Green, *Vox Petri*, 98.

105. Brown, *Gospel as Stories*, 148.

and noncanonical sources, especially in the notes. Such an approach realizes Jeanne Brown's goal, "story informed by history leads us to theology and theologizing."[106]

PSEUDEPIGRAPHAL WORKS ARE EXCLUDED FROM SOURCING PETRINE THEOLOGY

Because of Peter's prominence in the early church, many pseudepigraphal works are credited to Peter but they all are clearly produced by later unknown authors.[107] For example, the *Gospel of Peter* was found in 1886, but no ancient, nor modern scholar views it as authentic from Peter even though it can confirm features about historical Jesus' death.[108] The *Fayûm Fragment* contains six lines of a version of the cock-crow story from Mark 14:26–30, but otherwise only contributes a novel abbreviation of Peter's name as πετ.[109] Other Nag Hamadi gospels, such as the *Gospel of Thomas*, have Peter doubting female salvation and present Jesus advocating Gnosticism as well as strange things like transforming Mary Magdalene into a man in order to get her saved.[110] Furthermore, the *Acts of Peter* is a rejected second-century description of fantastic events such as healing his daughter, resurrecting her and a dried fish, more confronting of Simon Magus, and a talking dog, though there is a confirming account for Peter's crucifixion being upside down. The rejected *Slavonic Acts of Peter* supplement the *Acts of Peter* with additional stories, such as a vision compelling Peter to travel to Rome to have a nobleman buy a child that turns out to be Jesus, who confounds counselors and causes the nails to fall out of Peter's cross so that Peter can die praying on his knees. The *Passion of Peter* is a sixth-century Latin expansion of martyrdom of Peter from the *Acts of Peter*. The *Acts of Peter and Paul* elaborates further on their martyrdom. The *Acts of Peter and Andrew* recounts stories of them returning from the city of the man-eaters to do miracles such as ripening a crop so bread can be made and making a camel pass through the eye of a needle. The Nag Hammadi *Acts of Peter and the*

---

106. Brown, *Gospel as Stories*, 184.

107. Hennecke, *New Testament Apocrypha*, 1:179; 2:573–74, 576; a thorough analysis of these books for unique contributions, corroborative contributions and limitations on authority is made by Lapham, *Peter*, 1–116, 172–253.

108. Eusebius, *Hist. eccl.* 3.3.2; 3.25; 6.12.2, quoting Serapion.

109. Foster, "Peter in Noncanonical Tradition," 225–27.

110. *Gos. Thom.* 114.

Twelve Apostles shows evidence of Christianizing gnostic teaching. The *Preaching of Peter* is quoted by Origen (citing Clement of Alexander) but questions its spurious potential, and Eusebius rejects it as not authentic.[111] The Syriac *Preaching of Peter* is a later work possibly related to the *Acts of Peter* but also rejected along with the *Kerygmata Petrou*.[112] Furthermore, Origen also rejects the *Doctrine of Peter*.[113] The *Epistle of Peter to Philip* provides a gnostic-tainted framework for the Olivet discourse and Philips response.[114] The *Apocalypse of Peter* and a longer Ethiopic version develop an abbreviated Olivet sermon that transforms into a transfiguration account and has some verbal similarities to 2 Pet, but is rejected by Eusebius as spurious.[115]

Andrew Alls summarized this rejection of pseudepigraphy.

> Deliberate pseudepigraphy was not, as is often stated, an established and acceptable convention. To this day, though hundreds of writings of a pseudepigraphic nature from the early Christian centuries have survived, the overwhelming majority of them are more or less affected by Gnostic or other tendentious influences, and many were clearly written to propagate such views. Most of the rest of them are works of what one might call "popular religion"—cheap devotional literature, not intentionally deviant in theology but using expressions theologians would abhor and concentrating on the miraculous and the bizarre. The contrast with the works in the emergent canon is unmistakable.[116]

Paul Foster examined each of these pseudepigraphic writings and concluded that the Peter presented in them is an invented figure to fit whatever their "authors wanted or needed him to be."[117]

---

111. Origen, *Comm. Jo.* 13.17; Eusebius, *Hist. eccl.* 3.3.2.

112. Also called the *Epistle of Peter to James*, which is rejected along with the pseudo-Clementine homilies; Novenson, "Why Are There Some Petrine Epistles?," 151.

113. Origen, *Princ.* 8.

114. Novenson, "Why Are There Some Petrine Epistles?," 151–53.

115. Eusebius, *Hist. eccl.* 3.3, 25; Foster, "Peter in Noncanonical Tradition," 258, concurs.

116. Walls, "Canon of the New Testament," 1:638–39.

117. Foster, "Peter in Noncanonical Tradition," 262.

CONCLUSION

The primary sources for Petrine theology are 1 and 2 Pet. The Gospel of Mark as a whole, and Petrine comments in the canonical Gospels and Acts, are secondarily a source for Petrine theology. No other source has a credible claim to inform Petrine theology except on the level of background or corroborative support.

3

The Recipients of the Petrine Epistles

BIBLICAL THEOLOGY IS BASED upon proper exegesis. Proper exegesis requires understanding the social and religious context of the readers of the two letters to the extent that they are accessible.

SCATTERED ALIENS OF ASIA MINOR

First Peter is written to "those who reside as aliens, scattered throughout Pontus, Galatia, Cappadocia, Asia, and Bithynia" who are believers in Christ (1 Pet 1:1). Second Peter is written presumably to the same audience since this is now a second letter from Peter to his audience (2 Pet 3:1). The Gospel of Mark and Acts are written to a Mediterranean gentile audience.

All agree that the area described in 1 Pet 1:1 is part of Asia Minor, though there are two possible ways of determining which part. Some advocate that they are Roman provinces, while others advocate the older national areas from which the Romans created their provincial system. Both approaches include the northern two thirds of Turkey, the section North of the Taurus mountains. The debate has to do with boundaries and whether Pontus and Bithynia formed one Roman province. Though there are documents that unite these into one province, Pontus and Bithynia are sometimes separated when a messenger's route is implied.[1] Elliott's view of the route of a messenger, probably Silvanus (1 Pet 5:12),[2] might mean a

1. Elliott, *Home for the Homeless*, 60 and 90 include inscriptions that separate these provinces.

2. Berkowitz et al., *Thesaurus Linguae Graecae Canon*; Richards, "Silvanus Was Not Peter's Secretary," 417–32; Davids, *Theology of James, Peter, and Jude*, 108.

circuit back to his starting point. Also, the older national area of Phrygia, not mentioned, was included within the Roman province of Galatia. The southern coastal areas of Lycia and Pamphilia are not mentioned, probably because they had natural relations with the south and east.

Pontus and Bithynia formed the northern coastal province of Asia Minor. As a senatorial province, it was an interior province of the Roman empire, able to be maintained by a few cohorts of soldiers.[3] The area was rich in natural resources and produced great wealth for a few, but the masses were kept on subsistence levels. Roman administrators tried to remedy the worst abuses but membership in the local councils required ownership of property, so the oppressed had no means of having their grievances heard.

Galatia was the province including most of the central plateau of Asia Minor from the foothills of the Taurus mountains in the south to the rugged area of Paphlagonia in the north. The interior pastures of this province produced considerable wool. Coming from the coasts, Greco-Roman culture had penetrated most areas of Galatia. However, Christianity made inroads as Paul established some Christian churches in this province on his first missionary journey (Acts 13:13—14:24; Gal 1:2).

Cappadocia became a province in AD 17.[4] Beare described, "the territory of Cappadocia was a wild and inaccessible country of heavy forests and deep gorges, lying to the east of Galatia, between the mountains of Armenia and the headwaters of the Euphrates."[5] Cappadocia maintained its native language and customs without much change.[6] It was on the Roman frontier, with legions of troops nearby to protect and to expand the Roman frontier.

Asia was one of the wealthiest and most populous regions of the empire. It included the Phrygia interior highlands to the western coastal region and adjacent islands. The rich island seaports of the past centuries (Rhodes and Lesbos) and the great seaports of that day (Ephesus and Miletus) were in this province. There were also important inland towns, such as Sardis, Pergamum, and Colossians. Under the ministry of Paul and others, Christianity had rooted well and was raising up many leaders.

Generally, there were great extremes of wealth. In rural areas, feudal conditions existed with a few wealthy landowners and many slaves. In

3. Beare, *1 Peter*, 20.
4. Bigg, *Peter and Jude*, 68.
5. Beare, *1 Peter*, 21.
6. Best, *1 Peter*, 16–17.

the cities, a few wealthy merchants employed large numbers of slaves, including craftsmen and household slaves.

Mixed among this population were temporary resident aliens (παρεπιδήμους, παροίκους, διασπορᾶς, 1 Pet 1:1, 17; 2:11). John Elliott pioneered the sociological study of these individuals and concepts within the recipient section of 1 Pet.[7] Unfortunately, most commentators have not embraced his groundbreaking study but instead treat these geographic-socio-political descriptions as metaphors to support Christians as citizens of heaven.[8] However, there is real value in treating the recipients of the letter as describing real socio-political conditions for the readers of the letter (1 Pet 1:1), especially in understanding their suffering, eschatological hope, and their sense of belonging provided by the church community.

The word παρεπιδήμους is a general term, meaning "temporary resident," "a sojourner," a non-permanent settler in the land (1 Pet 1:1; 2:11).[9] The word emphasizes transitoriness of the sojourner's stay in a place; the issue of citizenship is excluded. The idea is seen in Gen 23:4 where Abraham speaks of himself as a resident alien and a temporary resident (LXX: πάροικος καὶ παρεπίδημος), who by virtue of this role does not own land where he lives. Grieving Abraham needed land to bury Sarah who has recently died. Genesis developed the literal sociological concept of sojourning Abraham, though the concept can stand as a metonymy of adjunct communicating the transitoriness of life because it is identified with the temporary (Ps 39:12). When the term is used as a metaphor for temporariness, the context clearly identifies that it is operating as a figure of speech. For example, the writer of Hebrews identifies the temporary resident status of Abraham, Isaac, Jacob, and Sarah as dwelling in a foreign land with tents and seeking a divinely made city (Heb 11:8–13). In this instance, the inheritance had to do with the land of promise, a divinely produced reward to be realized by Abraham on the earth in kingdom. However, Peter identifies that his readers are literal temporary residents in Pontus, Galatia, Cappadocia, Asia, and Bithynia (1 Pet 1:1). The literal places to which he referred indicated that the readers are socio-political temporary residents, with limited rights, and thus vulnerable.

The second literal description is that of those "scattered outside one's homeland" (διασπορᾶς, 1 Pet 1:1).[10] LXX Deuteronomy 28:25 and

7. Elliott, *Home for the Homeless*, 1–84; *1 Peter*, 94–103.
8. Jobes, *1 Peter*, 24–25.
9. Beare, *1 Peter*, 49.
10. Schmidt, "διασπορα," TDNT 2:102, 104.

30:4 describes Israel in covenant curse as being scattered outside their homeland (διασπορᾶς). There are other kinds of scatterings in LXX but the NT retains this sense of scattered outside one's homeland. For example, John records some Jews wondering if Jesus would depart to the Greek speaking dispersion (John 7:35 διασπορᾶς). James 1:1 joins 1 Pet 1:1 in describing Christians literally living outside their homeland, to whom these letters have been sent. Furthermore, Luke using this word recounts the geographic scattering of Christians resulting from persecution (Acts 8:4; 11:19, διασπαρέντες).

The word παροίκους (1 Pet 1:17, 2:11) is a political and legal term meaning "the state, position or fate of a resident alien 'dwelling abroad' without civil or native rights."[11] In sociological studies, such "resident aliens" are ranked below full citizens and above transient strangers, freedman, and slaves. John Elliott identified that inclusion among this group could occur primarily through two means: a transient stranger could set up his residence in a place and stay a sufficient length of time or the state might grant this right to a lesser class to secure their loyalty.[12] Even though an individual gains this social status, the barriers of language, custom, and religion might brand one as a nouveau resident alien, despised by some longstanding resident aliens.

The word πάροικος is used in LXX as referring to a resident alien living in a temporary arrangement with respect to land, which is echoed in the Lukan NT. For example, Abraham admits to being a resident alien without owning land, and thus in need of a place to bury Sarah (Gen 23:14; Ps 105:12). God predicted that Abraham's descendants would be resident aliens in a strange land (Gen 15:13). This prophecy was fulfilled in Israel's temporary residence and slavery in Egypt (Exod 2:22; Deut 23:7; Acts 7:6; 13:17). Likewise, Moses lived with his father-in-law as a resident alien in Midian (Exod 2:15, 22; 18:3; Acts 7:29). When armies live outside the land in tents, they live as temporary residents (1 Chr 5:10). The Mosaic law permitted certain cities and practices for resident alien occupancy in the land (Deut 14:21). Resident aliens cannot live where they please in Israel, there are restrictions (Num 35:15). The resident alien is likened to a hired servant, poor countryman, and a traveler (Exod 12:45; Lev 22:10; 25:6, 35, 40, 45, 47; Jer 14:8). Sometimes the condition resulted in oppression of the resident alien (Exod 2:22).

---

11. Schmidt, "πάροικος," TDNT 5:842.
12. Elliott, *Home for the Homeless*, 25.

This sociological concept is understood four times in LXX as a resident alien before God. First, since the land is God's possession and Israel is only a temporary resident on the land, the land cannot be sold permanently (Lev 25:23). Thus, Israel is a tenant on the land before God (1 Chr 29:15). Third, πάροικος functions as a metaphor for "temporary" as a metonymy of adjunct with παρεπιδήμους (Ps 39:12). Finally, this condition of resident alien whether actual or metaphorical motivates the psalmist to pray for God to make his commandments known (Ps 119:19). Each of these references extend beyond the socio-political to include resident alien condition before God, but unless the context makes it clear that a metaphor for fleeting of life is in view, the geographical-sociological-political condition is maintained in Peter's discussion. While this metaphorical sense of temporary resident before God extends beyond Peter's use, it eventually enters use in Paul.

Paul uses πάροικος as the opposite to being in God's household (Eph 2:19). Here the gentile stranger becomes a fellow citizen with the saints since the metaphor of the Jewish temple barrier wall between Jews and gentiles is broken down in Christ. The gentile described here leaves this negative resident alien status when he enters the household of God.

In the late second century, the *Epistle of Diognetus*, defending Christians, turns the negative metaphorical resident alien condition into a positive metaphorical distinctive holy life with engagement in Hellenistic society which had not been realized yet in Peter's day, even though many of the assimilated practices were occurring in Peter's day.

> Christians are not distinguished from the rest of humanity by country, language, or custom. For nowhere do they live in cities of their own, nor do they speak some unusual dialect, nor do they practice eccentric lifestyle. . . . But while they live in both Greek and barbarian cities, as each one's lot was cast, and follow the local customs in dress and food and other aspects of life, at the same time they demonstrate the remarkable and admittedly unusual character of their own citizenship. They live in their own homelands, but only as aliens (πάροικοι); they participate in everything as citizens, and endure everything as foreigners. Every foreign country is their homeland, and every homeland is foreign.[13]

---

13. *Ep. Diognetus* 5.1–5; discussed by Harland, *Associations, Synagogues, and Congregations*, 251.

Within this metaphorical description there is some degree of Hellenistic connection and assimilation. Such a condition was facilitated for Christianity by living several generations in the region, but in Peter's day Christianity was pioneering into this region, unlike Judaism which had been established for centuries. Martin Marger identified that, "the more recent a group's entry into the society, the more resistance there is [both on the part of the group and of society], to its assimilation."[14] Longstanding involvement in a location removes the foreignness of the other and provides opportunities of common practices and being perceived as good citizens. For example, Jewish participation in trade guilds was evident when the leader of an Ephesian synagogue was also a member of the physician's trade guild, and the head of the goldsmiths guild at Korykos, Cilicia was a Jewish person named Moses,[15] while the only record of Christian trade guild participation in the first century is Paul as a tentmaker doing so with other Christians, Aquila and Priscilla (Acts 18:1–2), or maybe Lydia, a dyer of fabric from Asian Thyatira, living in Macedonian Philippi (Acts 16:14). Jewish epigraphic evidence etched in reserved seating at Miletos shows participation in theater going alongside other emperor-loving trade guilds, and there is no record of Christians joining this practice in the first century.[16] There is also some evidence that of Jewish inclusion of trade guilds in some funerals and on graves,[17] but there is no record of Christians doing this in the first century. Josephus identified that Jews honored members of the imperial family by offering sacrifices for them in the Jerusalem temple and by praying for them in synagogue.[18] Whereas at the beginning of the third century, Origen identified that Christians still avoided temples and were perceived as a secret association.[19] However, part of Tertullian's defense is that Christians also prayed for the emperors.[20] By the middle of the second and continuing into the fourth century, Christianity had joined with Judaism in making the case

---

14. Marger, *Race and Ethnic Relations*, 127; Harland, *Associations, Synagogues, and Congregations*, 199.

15. Harland, *Associations, Synagogues, and Congregations*, 206.

16. Harland, *Associations, Synagogues, and Congregations*, 110, 201.

17. Harland, *Associations, Synagogues, and Congregations*, 206–7, 228.

18. Josephus, *Ag. Ap.* 2.68–78; *War* 2.195–98, 409–16.

19. Origen, *Cels.* 1.1; 3.23; 8.17.

20. Tertullian, *Apol.* 32.1; 30.4–5; such a prayer for emperor health and peace is contained in 1 Tim 2:1–2 and *1 Clem.* 60.4—61.3.

that both religions were fitting in Hellenistic culture,[21] which probably means that there was still a problem if Christians are making an apology addressing broad cultural perception in the second to fourth centuries. Peter's descriptions reflect that his audience is mainly the underclasses of society and these do not have the same connections and influence, so Christians must be on their best behavior (1 Pet 2:11—3:13).

Luke and Peter maintain a literal sociological meaning of πάροικος that excludes the figurative meanings. Unlike Paul's figurative meaning of πάροικος describing unbelieving gentiles who leave this status to become part of the household of God, Luke and Peter use πάροικος as the people of God's household who are literally socio-political resident aliens (1 Pet 1:17; 2:5, 11; 4:17; Acts 7:6, 29; 13:17). Peter combines the literal sociological concept of παρεπιδήμους with its synonym πάροικος to facilitate a command to abstain from fleshly lusts (1 Pet 2:11). The details of social alienation, confrontation, and conflict presented in 1 Pet accurately picture the cultural reality of this class. Because Peter does not use these words as a figure for "transitoriness," the socio-political context will contribute to Peter's theology of church, suffering, and ethics.[22] This impact is further supported by the contextual development of God as judge (1 Pet 2:17–20; 3:4, 9–12; 4:5–6, 17–19) and the role of fear as a motivation to prevent such judgment (1 Pet 2:17–18; 3:6, 14–15).

Resident alien along with freedmen and slaves made up the working class who produced the goods which the wealthy and the army consumed.[23] The chief industry that a resident alien would be involved in is agriculture, often as a tenant farmer. Other occupations for resident aliens included harvesting natural resources (timber, gold, silver, iron, emeralds, and marble), producing textiles (wool, linen, dyeing, leather goods, and parchment), fishing, baking, metallurgy, gem- and glass-making, stone cutting, pottery and terra-cotta production, ship building, and general contracting. Many of these professions have classical textual support that participants were involved with trade guilds including weavers, fabric workers, dyers, bakers, potters, metalsmiths, builders, bankers, physicians, performers, and athletes.[24] For example, when Paul travels

---

21. Comparing Philo (*Contempl.*; *Spec. Laws* 2.145–46; *Embassy to Gains* 312–13; *Virt.* 33.178) in the first century with Tertullian, *Apol.* 38–39 and Eusebius, *Hist eccl.* 10.1.8, and in 4.26.7–9 contains Melito of Sardis' apology to Marcus Aurelius.

22. Elliott, *Home for the Homeless*, 42–43.

23. Elliott, *Home for the Homeless*, 68.

24. Harland, *Associations, Synagogues, and Congregations*, lists of professions, with

to Corinth, he connects up with temporary resident Aquila of Pontus, and works with this fellow tentmaker, recently evicted from Rome by Claudius decree[25] (Acts 18:2). In many of these occupations, the resident alien lived in a city or village within another's house or rented land.[26]

The plight of the resident alien was partially the plight of the small rental farmer or semi-free agricultural laborer. Their situation was made more difficult by compulsory services, famines and drought, exorbitant prices due to monopolization of the grain for Rome and the army, and the difficulties of transportation.

The plight of the resident alien in a household economy is that one must fit within the houseowner's agenda. Ecclesiasticus 29:21–28 points to the benefit of having one's own "house" (οἶκος) instead of being a "resident alien" (πάροικος).

> The essentials for life are water and bread and clothing and a house to cover one's nakedness. Better is the life of a beggar under the shelter of his roof than sumptuous food in another man's house. Be content with little or much and you will not hear reproach of your alien residence. It is a miserable life to go from house to house; and where you reside as an alien you may not open your mouth. You will play the host and provide drink without being thanked, and besides this you will hear bitter words: "Come here, alien, prepare the table, and if you have anything at hand, let me have it to eat." "Give place, alien to an honored person; my brother has come to stay with me; I need my house." These things are hard to bear for a man who has feeling: scolding about lodging and the reproach of the moneylender.

The resident alien's plight is further heightened by his legal standing. Adolf Berger discussed the legal plight under the equivalent Latin term "*peregrinus.*"

> [The *peregrinus* is] a foreigner, a stranger, a citizen of a state other than Rome. A great majority of the population of Rome were *peregrines*, subject of Rome after the conquest of their country by Rome. With the increase of the Roman state, the number of *peregrines* grew constantly without being compensated by the number of new citizens to whom Roman citizenship was granted. Within Roman territory the *peregrines* enjoyed the rights

---

textual support: 39–40, 144.

25. Suetonius, *Claud.* 25.4.
26. Elliott, *Home for the Homeless*, 26–27.

of free persons unless a treaty between Rome and their native country granted them specific rights. Generally, the legislation under the Republic, both statutes and status *consulta*, applied to *peregrines* only when a particular provision extended their validity to them. *Peregrines* had no political rights, they could not participate in the popular assemblies and were excluded from military service. A *peregrines* might conclude a valid marriage (*iustae nuptiae*) only when he had the *ius conubii* . . . either granted to him personally or acquired through his citizenship in a *civitas* which obtained this right from Rome. A *peregrine* could not make a testament in the forms reserved for Roman citizens nor act as a witness thereto. He could not be instituted an heir of a Roman citizen nor receive a legacy (*legatum*) except in a testament of a soldier. He was able to conclude a commercial transaction with a Roman citizen if he had the *ius commercii*, which was granted in the same ways as *ius conubii*. Though excluded from the proceedings by *legis action*, a *peregrine* had the benefit of protection in Roman courts, in particular before the *praetor* who had jurisdiction inter *peregrines*. . . . [But usually] foreigners from the same state concluded transactions in accordance with the laws of that state and litigation among them were settled according to their own laws.[27]

The condition of the working class encouraged an apocalyptic mood. Without a permanent alleviation of the problems, the promise of a new age of righteousness in which God feeds the hungry and exalts the downtrodden could easily gain a hearing.[28]

JEWISH AND PAGAN BACKGROUND

The general religious condition of Asia Minor included diverse religious cults. The philosophical worldviews of Stoicism and Epicureanism competed with mystery cults. Cappadocia had the primitive moon goddess, Ma. Greek polytheism, including Artemis and Jupiter, was also prevalent. The worship of the emperor as an established religion began in Asia and Bithynia. No doubt, these cults mixed with each other and with Judaism to form a syncretistic hybrid.

---

27. See *"Peregrinus"* in Berger, *Encyclopedic Dictionary of Roman Law*, 2:626–27; Clerc, *De la condition des étrangers*; Francotte, "De la condition des étrangers," 350–88.

28. Elliott, *Home for the Homeless*, 71–72.

Against this background, Judaism was deeply imbedded in the provinces, especially the cities. The morals and imperial acceptance attracted many proselytes, though there is no evidence of evangelism from the synagogues. In synagogues, the Jews maintained many of the forms of worship, but the proselytes probably rejected many of the ceremonial and ritual demands.[29] This imperial favor guaranteed the Jews domiciliary rights such as legal jurisdiction over their own members and the ability to raise their own funds. Provided Christianity was considered by city officials and synagogues as a sect of Judaism, the Christian churches retained these same rights. However, in local settings where Christianity was no longer viewed as a sect of Judaism, persecutions ensued (Acts 13:50; 14:19; 17:13).

The group to which Peter writes is a mixture of both Jews and gentiles. Jewish converts from the region appear early. At Pentecost, Jews and proselytes are present in Jerusalem from Cappadocia, Pontus, and Asia, and some believed in Christ (Acts 2:9). The Jewish character of author Peter is seen in his use of Old Testament quotes and allusions. This may imply the audience had a Jewish synagogue background but clearly portrays Peter's intimate awareness of Judaism. Such a picture fits with the descriptions of the churches founded by Paul, having the core founding from evangelizing local Jewish synagogues and then expanding into gentile god-fearers and pagans (Acts 13:13—14:20; 15:41—16:8; 18:23–41). In these contexts, many Jews resisted and funded opposition to the ambassadors of the gospel, though Jewish-Christians remained faithful (Acts 13:50–51; 14:4–6, 19–20).

Gentile believers in Christ emerged around the Jews who embraced Christ (Acts 13:43, 48–49). First Peter describes the readership as having departed from their former lusts which they maintained in ignorance (1 Pet 1:14). A Jew might fall into these lusts but they would not do it in ignorance. These desires are further characterized as gentile vices (1 Pet 4:3) and those gentiles still practicing them are surprised that these believers do not continue to practice these vices with them (1 Pet 4:4). Jews can practice gentile vices but no gentile would be surprised if a Jew abstained, therefore the believers are not Jews alone. The readers had a futile way of living inherited from their forefathers (1 Pet 1:18). Peter probably would not describe Jews as having inherited this futility, since he describes the fathers of Israel (Abraham, Isaac, Jacob, Moses, Samuel,

---

29. Selwyn, *1 Peter*, 50–51; Best, *1 Peter*, 17.

David, and the prophets) as looking to God and expecting a messiah to come with salvation (Acts 2:25–31; 3:13, 21–26). In 1 Pet 2:10 the quote of Hosea 1:6, 9–10 best develops a people who never were the people of God and now are included among the people of God, much like Paul uses the quote (Rom 9:25–26).

The gospel was heard in the region through many avenues. Initially, some brought the gospel back from hearing it in Jerusalem at Pentecost (Acts 2:9). Paul and his teams ministered to Jews and gentiles in Galatian cities (Act 13:13—14:20; 16:1–10; 18:23) and in Asia (Acts 18:19–21, 24–41; 20:6—21:1). Peter likely traveled from Antioch on across to Laodicea[30] in Asia, probably ministering to Jewish and gentile Christian. If 2 Pet is a second letter to the same region as 1 Pet (2 Pet 3:1; 1 Pet 1:1), Peter includes personal information as "I am reminding you" and includes himself among the "we" who made kingdom salvation and the transfiguration known to his audience (2 Pet 1:12–16). It is reasonable to conclude that Peter traveled through these Roman provinces ministering both to Jewish and gentile Christians, to whom he writes (1 Pet 1:1).[31]

---

30. *Pseudo-Clementine Recognitions* 7.25.3; 7.36.1; 9.38; *Homiline* 13.1.1; 13.11.2; Hengel, *Saint Peter*, 125–27.

31. See "Hippolytus on the Twelve Apostles," a fragment in Roberts and Donaldson, *Ante-Nicene Christian Library*, 2.2:130; Jerome, *Vir. Ill.*; *Epist.* 47.3.

4

Form in the Epistles of Peter

THE FORM OF A literary piece and its *sitz im leben* bring a significant contribution to the interpretation of literature considered. This is even true if the literary piece is an aggregate of sub-forms. In that case, each smaller unit contributes its context and thus may add an element to the theological thrust of the letter. Determining formal material for 1 and 2 Pet is an important step to develop Petrine theology. In the chapter on source material, the Gospel of Mark was already developed as Mark's retelling Peter's gospel sermons in the form of a biography of Jesus, so those formal issues do not need to be repeated here. Likewise, comments drawn from the other Gospels and Acts were also developed in the source material chapter. The goal of this chapter is to work through the critical issues in order to arrive at a post-critical engagement of Petrine theology from his letters.

FIRST PETER IS A LETTER

First Peter was characteristically acknowledged through the centuries as a letter, written by Peter with the intention of strengthening the Christian communities of Asia Minor. From the time of Adolf von Harnack, scholars have sought more radical solutions.

Harnack first proposed that by deleting the first two verses and the last three, the letter showed that it had been a baptismal homily which eventually got sent out as a letter.[1] Perdelwitz developed the theory for 1

---

1. Von Harnack, *Die Chronologie der altchristlichen literatur*, 451.

Pet 1:3—4:11 to be the baptism homily with the addition of short warnings and encouragement added.² Philip Carrington proposed a common pattern for Ephesians, Colossians, James, and 1 Pet as a baptism catechism including calls to put off lusts (1 Pet 2:1, 11), to humility and submission (1 Pet 2:12—3:9), to watch and pray (1 Pet 4:7; 5:8), and resist the devil (1 Pet 5:8–9).³ The highly selective approach, leaving large portions unexplained, was rehabilitated by Martin Dibelius as a baptismal liturgy.⁴ Frank Cross connected this liturgy to the particular *sitz im leben* of an Easter eve service by assuming words must have similar meaning in different contexts, such as the exodus.⁵ The fundamental difficulty with these approaches is that there are no repeatable criteria for definitely distinguishing such conjectured genre. Additionally, while baptism gets a mention in the book, it is not a dominant theme, so it should not control the letter.

Rudolf Bultmann selectively lifted fragments of the book to be highly concentrated theological hymns, such as 1 Pet 2:1–10, 21–23; and 3:18–22.⁶ Following this approach, Boismard developed four composite hymns, such as his second one splicing together 1 Pet 1:20; 3:18, 22; 4:6; and the fourth only remaining in a paraphrase echo in 1 Pet 5:5–9, which he admits would make this hymn indistinguishable from a letter.⁷ Using the same concentrated strategy, Hans Leitzmann proposed that 1 Pet 3:18–22 was a baptism creedal formula, and Bultmann proposed the same for 1 Pet 2:20–25 but admits that the redaction has left these sections indistinguishable from the rest of the letter.⁸ John Elliott, Ralph Martin, and Ernest

---

2. Perdelwitz, *Die Mysterienreligion und das Problem*, 1–28, 95–97; Bornemann, "Der erste Petrusbrief–eine Taufrede?," 143–65; Streeter, *Primitive Church*, 129–34; Hauck, *Die Katholischen Briefe*, 35–36; Beare, *1 Peter*, 6–9.

3. Carrington, *Primitive Christian Catechism*.

4. Dibelius, *Fresh Approach to the New Testament*, 187.

5. Cross, *1 Peter* (compared with Melito of Sardis, *Homily on the Passover*), 46; Hippolytus, *Homeless Pascales* 1.49, followed by Deterding, "Exodus Motifs in First Peter," 62, and Leaney, "1 Peter and the Passover," 238–51; an approach challenged by Thornton, "1 Peter, a Pascal Liturgy?," 17–20.

6. Bultmann, "Bekenntris-und Lied fragmente," 12–13; *Theologie des Neuen Testaments*, 532; followed by Windisch and Preisker, *Die katholische Briefe*, 6–8, 158, and Selwyn, *1 Peter*, 276.

7. Boismard, "Une liturgie baptismale"; *Quatre Hymns baptismales dans la Première Epître de Pierre* develops the view but on p. 14 he admits such a paraphrase technique renders this hymn as indistinguishable.

8. Leitzmann, "Die Anfange des Glaubensbekenntnisses," 3:163–81; Bultmann, "Bekenntnis und Lied fragment," 1–14.

Best conclude that the normal characteristics of primitive hymns or early Christian hymns are absent from the Petrine text.[9]

Harris, Windisch, Preisker, and Dodd proposed that the early church collected a body of OT quotes as proof texts for apologetic purposes to fund section such as 1 Pet 2:6–8, though Dodd concluded that 1 Pet 2:21–25 was probably free quotations from Isaiah directly.[10] This view obtained some impetus with the finding of 4QTestimonia at Qumran but this text concentrates on Deuteronomy, Numbers, and perhaps Joshua messianic texts, so there is no overlap with Petrine quotes.[11] However, the oral community of disciples copying Jesus' post-resurrection statements could easily explain the use of these texts, especially since no testimony text has the specific texts used by Peter and Paul.[12] Ernest Best engaged the OT quotes as interspersed with explanatory comments in 1 Pet and that changes in the LXX text adapt the text to the argument that Peter makes.[13] These are all marks indicating direct quotation, with modifications rather than a use of an imaginary testimony.

Coults proposed that 1 Pet 1:3–12 was a liturgical prayer like Eph 1:3–14,[14] but there is no difference from this being a long blessing within an epistle. Likewise, Preisker proposed 1 Pet 4:7b–11 to be a closing prayer, serving as a final blessing,[15] but here this section contains more of an exhortation than prayer.

Lauri Thurén analyzed the whole document of 1 Pet from the vantage of Hellenistic rhetoric to establish meaning of phrases within a speech-act theory,[16] although Peter never had such Hellenistic rhetorical training (Acts 4:13), and instead grew up in a Jewish Galilean

---

9. Elliott, *Elect and the Holy*, 133–35; Martin, "Aspects of Worship," 17–18; Best, "1 Peter II 4–10," 270.

10. 4QTestimonia described in Milik, *Ten Years of Discovery*, 61–64; genre applied to 1 Pet: Harris, *Testimonies*; Windisch and Preisker, *Die katholische Briefe*, 60–61; Dodd, *According to the Scriptures*, 26–27, 43 with free quotation discussed on 94.

11. 4Q175 cites Deut 5:28–29; 18:18–19; 33:8–11; Num 24:15–17; *Apocryphal Joshua* 92 containing frag. 22, col. 2, which includes Josh 6:26.

12. Best, "1 Peter II 4–10," 270.

13. Best, "1 Peter II 4–10," 270–93.

14. Coults, "Ephesians 1:3–14 and 1 Peter 1:3–12," 115–27.

15. Windisch and Preisker, *Die katholische Briefe*, 60–61.

16. Thurén, *Rhetorical Strategy of 1 Peter* and *Argument and Theology in 1 Peter* following Hellenistic rhetoric: Aristotle, *Rhetoric* 1.3.3–4; 1.4–10; 3.14–19; Cicero, *Inv.* 1.1–13; *Part. or.* 27; *Att.* 8.19.1; 9.10.1; 12.53; Demetrius, *Eloc.* 226, 228–29, 231, 234; within a strategy of Austin, *How To Do Things with Words*, and Searle, *Speech Acts*.

culture.[17] This approach reads 1 Pet through a Hellenistic lens reading Greek conjunctions from Hellenistic sources to facilitate the argument, biasing good works to be a Hellenistic contribution and concluding for a kingdom salvation as already and not yet.[18] This strategy assumes that the readership would pick up on subtle relationships of conjunctions to Hellenistic rhetorical function but the described underclasses in the book have not had such rhetorical training, nor likely developed such Hellenistic rhetorical subtlety to acknowledged ambiguous expressions.[19] As mentioned, Thurén diminishes the Jewish authorial context that reflects a rabbinic use of *pesher* to move the argument forward in the letter. Barth Campbell joined Thurén in Hellenistic rhetorical criticism through 1 Pet, with a particular honor/shame emphasis as a Christianized version of the argument from *Rhetorica ad Herennium*, in which the audience has been slandered as outcasts, but will receive vindication.[20] Such regaining of honor, in a context of shame and suffering, is present in 1 Pet but citations from the OT in a Jewish *pesher* approach permeate the whole book, delineating what is happening in 1 Pet as substantially different than Latin rhetoric. In contrast, Danielle Ellul presented a modest strategy of rhetorical criticism concluding that 1 Pet alternated between exhortative and proclamatory blocks of material (a similar strategy to *pesher*), connecting earlier material as parallel with later material around a central passage of 1 Pet 2:21–25.[21] Ellul's attempts at parallel connections and the claim for a central passage are strained,[22] rather discussions launch from *pesher* quotes of OT. Troy Martin claimed these quotes set up metaphor clusters that utilize the ontological status of the readers to supply the basis for exhortations, following John Elliott's sociological analysis of the readers.[23] Martin concludes that there is no evidence of epideictic speech for baptismal ceremony and he urges restraint for placing 1 Pet into categories of

---

17. Kennard, *Epistemology and Logic*, 121–27, 132–33.

18. Thurén, *Argument and Theology in 1 Peter*, 68–85, 192–93, 202; however, these gains can be obtained from a Jewish perspective (Pate and Kennard, *Deliverance Now and Not Yet*).

19. Campbell, *Honor, Shame, and the Rhetoric*, 23–24.

20. Campbell, *Honor, Shame, and the Rhetoric*, 26; *Rhetorica ad Herennium*.

21. Ellul, "Un exemple de cheminement rhétorique," 33–34; Selwyn, *1 Peter* has a similar alternation within an epistolary framework.

22. Campbell, *Honor, Shame, and the Rhetoric*, 18.

23. Martin, *Metaphor and Composition in 1 Peter*, 270.

classical rhetorical criticism.[24] Martin admits that analyzing 1 Pet through classical categories is an imposition of foreign rhetorical genres upon 1 Pet's paraenetic nature.[25] Whereas, Robert Webb, following Vernon Robbins, embraced a new category of "apocalyptic rhetorolect" to position 1 Pet as a letter describing how God will destroy all evil and gather the righteous into divine presence.[26] Webb considered this to be a helpful starting point but not providing much engagement of a genre, since these themes are present broadly. John Elliott concludes that such rhetorical criticism provides modest gains.

> This rhetorical criticism may help show relations within the body of the letter but that 1 Peter is essentially a letter and should be analyzed as a letter, which from the perspective of Hellenistic rhetoricians they were different. Furthermore, Peter never trained in Hellenistic schools of rhetoric (Acts 4:13) and utilizing more of a rabbinic strategy of quotations from the O.T. and depending upon a *pesher* extension of prophecy, the analysis of rhetorical criticism is a foreign imposition upon 1 Peter as a letter.[27]

It has been widely acknowledged that the final form of 1 Pet is that of a letter. Some have seen a sermon or liturgy pressed into this letter form. Based on repetition, Moule proposed that it was two letters copied together, but he recognized that this repetition could also be for emphasis.[28] So, 1 Pet 4:12—5:11 could be restating and emphasizing important elements for application rather than a second letter dealing with a different persecution.

Letter form provides the following structure for 1 Pet and 2 Pet:

- Author described (1 Pet 1:1a; the next section will develop 2 Pet as a letter 2 Pet 1:1).
- Recipients described (1 Pet 1:1b–2a; 2 Pet 1:1).
- Short blessing as a prayer (1 Pet 1:1b; 2 Pet 1:2).
- Doxological blessing (1 Pet 1:3–12; absent in 2 Pet).

24. Martin, "Rehabilitation of a Rhetorical Step-Child," 48–49.

25. Martin, "Rehabilitation of a Rhetorical Step-Child," 43.

26. Webb, "Intertexture and Rhetorical Strategy," 72–75; Robbins, *Exploring the Texture of Texts* and *Tapestry of Early Christian Discourse*.

27. Elliott, *1 Peter*, 81–82.

28. Moule, "1 Peter," 7–11; on p. 10 Christ is seen as an example in 1 Pet 2:21 and 3:18.

- Main body of the letter (1 Pet 1:13—5:11; 2 Pet 1:3—3:13).
- Silvanus coming with letter (1 Pet 5:12a),[29] and the Lord is coming (2 Pet 3:10).
- Final exhortation (1 Pet 5:12b; 2 Pet 3:14–18a).
- Greetings (1 Pet 5:13–14a; absent in 2 Pet but there is a personal reminder in 2 Pet 1:12–14).
- Final blessing (1 Pet 5:14b; 2 Pet 3:18b).

Letter form primarily gives meaning to the beginning and end of the letter. A few theological contributions are worth mentioning here. First the recipients are socio-politically in the condition of a temporary resident outside their homeland (1 Pet 1:1). This is not an exhortation for them to be pilgrims in their Christianity. Secondly, the recipient description and the doxological blessing restate the trinity twice (1 Pet 1:2, 3–12), making Peter's missional trinity a significant contribution to NT theology.[30] Third, the short blessing is rather standardized in form, so not the primary message,[31] but in 1 Pet grace and peace are intertwined throughout the letter as significant ingredients in its message.[32] Grace refers to the greatness of God's saving program that he is providing to humans, and also provides a greeting. The doxological blessing and early exhortations emphasize God's grace (1 Pet 1:3—2:10) but mentions peace (1 Pet 1:22). Peace refers to a harmonious order wrought with God and fellow humans because of this salvation. The following exhortations emphasize peaceful relationships (1 Pet 2:11—5:11) but mention grace throughout (1 Pet 3:7; 4:10; 5:5, 10). The closing exhortation is based on the whole letter being the true grace of God (1 Pet 5:12b). The letter ends with a ringing closing blessing "Peace be to you all who are in Christ" (1 Pet 5:14).

The letter form is a personal communication device as Adolf Deissmann explained.

---

29. Berkowitz et al., *Thesaurus Linguae Graecae Canon*; Richards, "Silvanus Was Not Peter's Secretary," 417–32; Davids, *Theology of James, Peter, and Jude*, 108.

30. Michaels, *1 Peter*, 4, 13 develops this Trinitarian view from 1 Pet 1:2; Kennard, "Doctrine of God in Petrine Theology," presented a fuller missional Trinitarian view; 1 Pet 1:2 draws a brief mention of Trinity by the following: Kistemaker, *Peter and Jude*, 12; Jobes, *1 Peter*, 45, 68.

31. Michaels, *1 Peter*, 13; Tite, "Compositional Function of the Petrine Prescript," 53, grace and peace present in 2 Pet; Pauline letters; 2 John; Rev; *1 Clem*. while mercy and peace are present in Jude; Polycarp, *Phil*.; and *Mart. Pol*.

32. Hillyer, *1 and 2 Peter, Jude*, 27.

A letter is something non-literary, a means of communication between persons who are separated from each other. Confidential and personal in its nature, it is intended only for the person or persons to whom it is addressed, and not at all for the public or any kind of publicity.[33]

Greeting from "she who is in Babylon" (ἡ ἐν Βαβυλῶνι), presumably referencing the grammatical feminine "church" (ἐκκλησία, not Peter's wife as claimed by Bigg[34]) in Rome as identified by early Christians.[35] The fact that Peter refers to his interpreter Mark, as his son, makes it more likely these greetings are not from biological family members, even though Peter treats them as metaphorical family members.[36] Furthermore, the use of a "kiss of love" (φιλήματι ἀγάπης) treats his readership as metaphorically family relationship, and removes any erotic allusion.[37] Peter writes to a group whom God has chosen, developing them as family and friends (1 Pet 2:11; 4:12). The personal and practical nature of the letter adds personal relationship within Petrine theology.

2 PET IS A LETTER

Second Peter has been characteristically acknowledged through the centuries as a letter, as claimed by 2 Pet 3:1. The grammatical structure around "Jesus" in the recipients and short blessing contribute to the two divine powers view, developed in the chapter on trinity. Second Peter begins with a similar short blessing (of grace and peace) but adds the personal Aramaic "Simon" as a slave in Christ (2 Pet 1:1). Peter's humility is evident in his acknowledging the equality of his recipients' faith (2 Pet 1:1), with his compassionate reminder to them (2 Pet 1:16). The Jewish flavor continues through the letter with the perspective of exodus salvation and eschatological kingdom intertwined, and a multitude of biblical examples. The recipients are not named but their description serves as

---

33. Deissmann, *Light from the Ancient East*, 218.

34. Bigg, *Peter and Jude*, 197.

35. While Qumran blended "Babylon" as northern opposition Babylon/Assyria (4Q163 frag. 4 7.2.1–4, frag. 8 10.1; 4Q385a; 4Q554 frag. 3 3.14–22), early Christian texts identify Rome with "Babylon" (Rev 14:8; 16:19; 17–18; *Sib. Or.* 5.159–60, 168–70; *4 Ezra* 15.46–48; Bockmuehl, *Simon Peter in Scripture and Memory*, 128.

36. Jobes, *1 Peter*, 322; Eusebius, *Hist. eccl.* 3.39.15.

37. Davids, *1 Peter*, 204–5; A similar practice is urged by Paul, Rom 16:16; 1 Cor 16:20; 2 Cor 13:12; 1 Thess 5:26.

the basis for magnificent blessings and exhortations with which the letter begins. These blessings are grounded upon the knowledge of Jesus as God and Lord (2 Pet 1:2). This knowledge is part of the means whereby God provides saving blessings. Knowledge is one resultant quality of being abundantly saved. As such, Peter desires to stir up their memory of this knowledge of kingdom because it is grounded on revelation and empirically witnessed to by Peter at the transfiguration. A standard epistle disclosure formula is used to revelationarily ground this kingdom point.[38] False teachers reject this knowledge. Believers remember this kingdom knowledge in view of eschatological judgment.

The letter concludes with final exhortations (2 Pet 3:14–18a) and final blessings (2 Pet 3:18b). There is no plan to come, since Peter will die quickly (2 Pet 1:12–14), but the Lord is coming (2 Pet 3:10). There is no greeting, but Peter adds a personal touch with a personal reminder in 2 Pet 1:12–14 and calls them friends (2 Pet 3:1, 17), having written to them before (2 Pet 3:1).

Some propose this letter to be a testament from the OT pattern of a farewell speech like Gen 47–49; Deut; 1 Sam 12; and early Jewish testaments.[39] Farewell speeches continue into the NT in John 13–17; Acts 20:17–38; and 2 Timothy (which is also a letter). Second Peter contains testament features such as a description of Peter's imminent death (2 Pet 1:14–15) and exhortation to survivors (2 Pet 2:1–22; 3:3–4). However, this exhortation is grounded elsewhere than Peter's death, so with only one characteristic of testament, this is not a dominant trait in the letter.

Danker proposed 2 Pet was a decree, as a solemn call to faithful allegiance to Christ.[40] However, his proof-texting to make 2 Pet fit a Hellenistic decree pattern leaves his claim vulnerable. He admits that such decrees make clear distinctions between benefactor and recipient but he recognized that in 2 Pet 1 these are "blurred and even seem to interchange."[41] Since 1 Pet 1 is the primary area in the letter where de-

---

38. Porter, "τοῦτο πρῶτον γινώσκοντες ὅτι in 2 Peter 1:20," 156–71.

39. *T. 12 Patr.*; *T. Mos.*; *T. Job*; *1 En.* 91–104; Tob 14.3-11; 2 Esd 14.27-36; 2 Bar 77.86; Jub 21–22; 35; 36:1–18; *L.A.B.* 19.1–5; 24.1–5; 28.3–10; 33; *L.A.E.* 25–29; Josephus, *Ant.* 4.7.45–47; 4.309–19; *Acts Pet.* 36–39; *Acts John* 106–7; *Acts Thom.* 159–60; Baltzer, *Covenant Formulary in the Old Testament*, 41–63; Knopf, *Die Briefe Petri und Judas*, 274; Reicke, *James, Peter and Jude*, 146; Kolenkow, "Genre Testament and Forecasts of the Future," 57–71; Bauckham, *Jude, 2 Peter*, 131–35; Richards and Boyle, "Did Ancients Know?," 403–23.

40. Danker, "2 Peter 1," 65–72.

41. Danker, "2 Peter 1," 65.

cree is proposed and he admits the main characteristic is "blurred," this proposed genre does not help much.

Jerome Neyrey compared Plutarch's *De Sera Numinis Vindicta* argument against epicureanism with 2 Pet to conclude they were both theodical polemics.[42] The similarities are that both books contain an argument against evil by granting providence, fulfillment of prophecy, and God judging the wicked and rewarding the righteous. However, Plutarch argued these within a Hellenistic polytheism to defend change is driven by human agency and freedom. Plutarch maintained that there was no delay in punishment because there is a constant consciousness of guilt and fear. Instead, 2 Pet quotes and alludes to OT events within sovereign Jewish monotheism's urging a prophetic narrow way of salvation to kingdom rather than departing to a broad way to eventually be judged because God has judged the world before. Furthermore, Ernest Kasemann argued that the polemical character of 2 Pet is present to defend against the delay of judgment; judgment will come.[43] Likewise, 2 Pet argued against false teachers departing from Christianity denying judgment rather than against epicureanism. So, the similarities are superficial, and 2 Pet retains the form of a letter.

D. E. Watson attempted to fully analyze 2 Pet through patterns of Hellenistic rhetoric and concluded the prescript was that of an epistle (2 Pet 1:1–2), there is no narration, and the exordium was irrelevant to Peter's argument (2 Pet 1:3–15).[44] To dismiss most of chapter 1 is to exclude the positive common salvation and Peter's personal biographical comments to focus primarily upon judgment. Furthermore, 2 Pet presents itself as coming from the apostle Peter, who never had such Hellenistic rhetorical training (Acts 4:13), and instead grew up in Jewish Galilean culture.[45] So, a use of Jewish *pesher* and OT allusions contribute more to understanding 2 Pet than Hellenistic rhetoric. Gene Green analyzed this rhetorical approach and concluded that, "Significant adjustments in the understanding of the structure of rhetorical discourse need to be made to fit 2 Pet into this schema."[46] As such, Green cautions fitting 2 Pet into such a rhetorical

---

42. Neyrey, "Form and Background of the Polemic," 407–31.

43. Kasemann, "Apologia for Primitive Christian Eschatology," 169–95.

44. Watson, *Invention, Arrangement, and Style*, 143, 96, following Hellenistic rhetoric: Aristotle, *Rhetoric* 1.3.3–4; 1.4–10; 3.14–19; Cicero, *Inv.* 1.1–13; *Part. or.* 27.

45. Kennard, *Epistemology and Logic in the New Testament*, 121–27, 132–33.

46. Green, *Jude, 2 Peter*, 164.

strategy because 2 Pet is a letter, and letters and Hellenistic rhetoric of public speaking were considered very different.[47]

CONCLUSION

First and Second Peter are letters personally communicating to their recipients. This personal communication and family relationship is a gain in viewing them through their letter form. Also, epistle form accentuates the divinity of Christ and missional Trinitarianism, making significant contributions to theology.[48]

---

47. Green, *Jude, 2 Peter*, 164; following Cicero, *Att.* 8.19.1; 9.10.1; 12.53; Demetrius, *Eloc.* 226, 228–29, 231, 234.

48. Shown in Kennard, *Petrine Theology*, chapters on Christology and Trinity.

5

The Man Called Peter

To APPRECIATE A PERSON's theological persuasions, one benefits by understanding something of the context from which the person emerges. However, much of this brief biography of Peter is intertwined with theological and relational descriptions about Jesus, so it contributes as a Petrine narrative theology.

Simon or Symeon was Peter's personal name. It was perhaps the most common name used in Israel of his day. The Semitic form of the name, "Symeon" is reflected in the Greek text (2 Pet 1:1; Acts 15:14). His name is more commonly called Simon. Jesus addressed him in this manner, "Simon son of John" (Σίμων ὁ υἱὸς Ἰωάννου, John 1:42). The form "Simon bar-Jona" (Σίμων Βαριωνᾶ) in Matt 16:17 is not an abbreviation of "John" (Hebrew: *yehohonan*), for that would be *yoḥai*[1] but may refer to Peter being perceptive enough to understand the sign of Jonah before Jesus' resurrection occurs (Matt 16:4, 17).

Jesus starts his ministry during the fifteenth year of Tiberias' reign, or likely AD 28 (Luke 3:1–2).[2] Peter is likely called near the beginning of Jesus' ministry (John 1:34–42; Mark 1:14–20).

Sometimes fanciful sixth-century Antioch chronicler wrote of Peter's mature appearance, which may indicate something of his earlier appearance as well.

---

1. Williams, "From Shimon to Petros," 34 countering Bruce, *Peter, Stephen, James, and John*, 16 who claims it as an abbreviation, and Eisler, *Messiah Jesus and John the Baptist*, 252–54, who advocates that this is an Akkadian loan word for "terrorists."

2. Tacitus, *Ann.* 1.

St. Peter was an old man, in stature of average height with receding short hair, both hair and beard completely grey, fair but rather sallow skin, wine-colored eyes, a good beard, a long nose, eyebrows that met, upright in posture; he was sensible, swift to anger, changeable, humorous; he spoke through the Holy Spirit and was a miracle worker.[3]

Simon was a member of the "people of the land," which means that he is a common person who has not been educated with rabbinic or scribal training beyond what synagogues provided. Perhaps, he was exposed to the Pharisaic study of the Scriptures provided through a synagogue for boys from age five to twelve, to train them in basic Jewish understanding and worship practice.[4] Jesus praised God that his kingdom program was revealed to babes, such as these common people and hid from the learned (Matt 11:25). Shammai scribes and pharisees accused the disciples of not fulfilling a basic rule of washing hands before eating (Mark 7:2), but while the practice was widespread in second through fourth centuries it was not widespread before AD 70 and not embraced among Hillel pharisees.[5] The Sadducees and priests later contemptibly observed Peter and John as uneducated in advanced Jewish instruction, but marveled at the dramatic healing of a lame man, recognizing they reproduced the traits that identified them as having been with Jesus (Acts 4:13).

Simon Peter was a simple Galilean fisherman with an average home life. John Lightfoot described Galileans as generally warm-hearted, impulsive, and generous people.[6] They were more concerned for sincere practical piety and honor than either speculation, or strictness to pharisaical traditions, or the getting of money. He probably grew up in Bethsaida (John 1:44)[7] though he had moved to Capernaum by the time of Jesus' ministry (Mark 1:29; Luke 9:31–38).

---

3. Maklas, *Chron.* 10.266; Bockmuehl, *Simon Peter in Scripture and Memory*, 41.

4. M. *'Abot* 5.21; Moore, "Am Ha-ares," 1:439.

5. M. *Hag.* 2.5–6; b. *Šabb.* 13b–14a; 62b; y. *Šabb.* 1.3d; b. *Yoma* 87b; T. *Ber.* 5.13; TB *Ber.* 8.2; 60b; TB *Soṭah* 4b. Especially m. *'Ed.* 5.6 places hand washing in the category of heresy. Booth argues that the practice was not widespread before AD 70 (Jdt 12.7; Ep. Arist. 305–6; Sib. Or. 3.591–93; Booth, *Jesus and the Laws of Purity*, 159–60; Dunn, "Pharisees, Sinners, and Jesus," 61–88; Klawans, *Impurity and Sin in Ancient Judaism*, 146–50, and Davies and Allison, *Matthew*, 2:521–22; Gundry, *Mark*, 358–71; Finkel, *Pharisees & the Teacher of Nazareth*, 140–41, 152–56).

6. Lightfoot, *Commentary on the New Testament*, 1:168–69; Eidersheim, *Sketches of Jewish Social Life*, 39–40.

7. Bockmuehl, "Simon Peter and Bethsaida," 53–91.

Simon's occupation was fishing, a profession of low status.[8] He was a successful fisherman in partnership with father Zebedee, which team had more than one boat at their disposal (Luke 5:7, 10). This probably indicates that Peter and Andrew are of father Zebedee's generation as partners (thirtysomethings), while the Zebedee sons may be teenagers. Probably father Zebedee's boat was a large (thirty something feet), fast rowing boat designed to operate a dragnet, since it included hired men (Mark 1:20; Matt 13:47). Such equipment constituted the more expensive fishing outfit of the day, requiring a large crew to work it but also a second smaller boat to align the net. They would work through the night, sometimes returning with meager catch (Luke 5:5). In warmer weather, they would strip to fish only in a diaper wrap (John 21:7). Storms could descend quickly upon the sea of Galilee endangering their lives (John 6:16–21). However, the partnership was successful, obtaining substantial profits (Luke 5:7–10).[9] Which helps one appreciate Peter's commitment to Christ, "We have left everything and followed you" (Mark 10:28).

Simon owned a house in Capernaum, probably not far from the synagogue (Mark 1:21, 29; Matt 8:14; Luke 4:38). Archeological digging of the traditional site of Simon's house has uncovered a ten-foot-square house among others off a small courtyard, all made of black basalt stones surrounding a beaten earth floor.[10] The only shaped stones are in the door frame and threshold. The roof was probably made of tree branches covered with a mixture of mud and straw, though roof tiles have been found at the synagogue porch roof (so tiles are a possibility with Luke 5:19 comment). During Constantine's era, a small octagonal church was constructed over the small house and pilgrims left graffiti scratched on its red plastered walls.[11] In Peter's generosity, his house probably became a home base for Jesus' ministry when in Capernaum (Mark 1:21, 29; 2:1). Probably during one such stay, some men lowered a paralytic through the roof, so Jesus could heal him (Mark 2:1–12).

Those who lived with Peter were his wife, mother-in-law, and his brother Andrew. Andrew brought Jesus to Simon, hailing Jesus as Messiah

---

8. Plautus, *Rud.* 290–305; Athenaeus, *Deipn.* 6.226a, e; 6.228c; 7.309d; Green, *Saint Peter*, 56; Helyer, *Life and Witness of Peter*, 28.

9. Oliver, "Fisherman as Expositor," 230.

10. Tzaferis, "Capernaum," 1:292.

11. Peter the Deacon, *De locus sanctis* 5.2 discussed the graffiti on church plaster wall; Strange and Shanks, "House Where Jesus Stayed," 30–32; Corbo, "House at Capernaum," 23–27.

(John 1:40–42). Simon's mother-in-law was healed by Jesus in the house early in Jesus' ministry (Mark 1:29–31; Matt 8:14–15; Luke 4:38–39).[12] Grateful, she began to minister to their needs and to serve them a meal. Little is said of Simon's wife except that she traveled with Peter on his missionary journeys (1 Cor 9:5). Stories of a daughter named Petronilla lack evidence of validity.

The calling of Simon and his companions to be Jesus' disciples emerges from a general account of Jesus' preaching. The crowds physically pressed around Jesus as he spoke. To enable all to hear, Jesus got into Simon's boat and asked him to steady it just offshore. Adopting the seated posture of a Jewish teacher, Jesus taught the crowd, including the captive audience in the boat (Luke 5:3).

When Jesus had finished his teaching, Jesus commanded Simon to put out into deep water where the men were to lower the nets for a catch. Simon respected Jesus' authority, calling him "master" (Ἐπιστάτα),[13] but was skeptical since they had spent the night without catching fish and daytime fishing in deep water did not offer much likelihood for a catch. Simon willingly obeyed with the realization that Jesus' word was not to be ignored on any subject.[14] Submissive Simon was amazed at the large size of the catch, with the nets in danger of bursting and the boats so full they almost sank.[15] Simon impulsively reacted falling to his knees and humbly calling Jesus "lord" (κύριε) with such dramatic revelation of Jesus' divine power and the realization of his own sinfulness (Luke 5:7–9).

Jesus addressed Simon and his partners with "do not fear" and called Simon to follow Jesus into discipleship so that he would henceforth be fishing for men (Mark 1:17; Matt 4:19; Luke 5:10). Simon responded by following Jesus and reprogramming his life after Jesus' pattern. John 3:22 describes that Jesus was baptizing his disciples, as John the Baptist had done. Perhaps to defend Peter's lead apostolic role, Clement of Alexandria and Eusebius claim that Jesus baptized Peter and then Peter baptized his brother Andrew.[16]

---

12. Multiple attestation supports the authenticity of this miracle. The miracle is also pictured in the third-century AD church in Dura Europa (Flusser, *Jesus' Jerusalem*, 65).

13. Marshall, *Luke*, 203; Ellis, *Luke*, 102.

14. Morris, *Luke*, 112–13.

15. Creed, *Luke*, 73–74 and Leaney, *Luke*, 54–57 argue that this is the same event as John 21 but Dodd claims that this event does not have resurrection context (Nineham, *Studies in the Gospels*, 35; Marshall, *Luke*, 200–201, 204).

16. Clement of Alexandria, *Hyp.* 5 cited in Eusebius, *Hist. eccl.* 20.

Jesus made his home base in Capernaum (Mark 1:29; 2:1–12; Matt 9:2–8; Luke 5:18–26), and in a synagogue, on the sabbath, Jesus healed a man with a withered hand (Mark 3:1–5; Matt 12:9–13; Luke 6:6–10). Some Jews tried to shame Jesus, questioning Jesus about the propriety of healing on the sabbath, but he responded with compassion, and that the sabbath is the appropriate release day to experience the benefits of kingdom salvation by stretching out the man's infirmed withered hand (Mark 3:4; Luke 6:9).[17] Knowing Jesus was being watched by religious leaders as to whether he would violate the Sabbath, Jesus asked them, "Is it lawful to heal on the Sabbath?" and responded to their silence by taking hold of a man with dropsy and healing him (Mark 3:1–6; Luke 14:1–6). Such a condition of swelling of limbs and tissues, accompanied by distention, rendered him unclean (Lev 15:1–12).[18] As Jesus touched the man, the infirmed man was healed and cleansed.

On Jesus' way to heal a synagogue official's daughter, a woman with a twelve-year uterine hemorrhage came and touched Jesus' Jewish tassel (κράσπεδα)[19] and she was healed (Mark 5:25–34; Matt 9:20–22; Luke 8:43–48).[20] This condition of uterine hemorrhage left her in a perpetually unclean condition (Lev 15:19–31).[21] This meant that anyone who touched her would also become unclean (Lev 15:27). She had become impoverished at the hands of many physicians, but she only grew worse. She thought if I only touch Jesus' garment tassel, I shall get well.[22] When she touched Jesus, her hemorrhage stopped. Jesus was aware that a healing had taken place because he had felt power go from him. He insisted that someone had touched him, which Peter and the disciples dismissed in lieu of the crowds pressing all around him. She and Jesus realized that she would not make Jesus unclean, for instead Jesus' kingship banished

17. Jeroboam was healed of his withered hand by a prophet (1 Kgs 13:1–10) and Simeon prays for such restoration of his own withered hand (*T. Sim.* 2.11–14).

18. Condition described by Fitzmyer, *Luke* 2:1041. Dropsy rendered one unclean (SB 2.203). Herod was said to have suffered from dropsy (Josephus, *Ant.* 17.6.5). Early Judaism thought dropsy was caused by either a sexual offense (*b. Šabb.* 33a) or from intentionally failing to have bowel movements (*b. Ber.* 25a).

19. Compare MT and LXX in Num. 15:38–41 and Deut. 22:12.

20. Multiple attestation supports the authenticity of this miracle; also corroborated by a picture on third-century AD Roman catacomb in Flusser, *Jesus*, 116.

21. There is Jewish repugnance for menstruous women (Ezek 36:17; CD 4.12—15.17; 11QTemple 48.15–17; Josephus, *War* 5.227; *C. Ap.* 2.103–4; *m. Nidda*; and *m. Zabim* 2.4; 4.1; 5.7).

22. There is some basis for the representative nature of clothes to accomplish miracles (Mark 6:56; Acts 19:12; Josephus, *Ant.* 8.353–54).

her uncleanness as she was healed. With Jesus' insistence that someone had touched him, she came forward trembling and confessed her intention and her healing. Turning to her, Jesus said, "Daughter, take courage; your faith has made you well; go in peace, and be healed of your affliction." And at once the flow of blood in her body was dried up and she was made well. Such healing is within kingdom salvation (σέσωκέν; Mark 5:28, 34; Matt 9:21–22). Her condition of peace identifies her with those called "children of peace," those who respond to the kingdom message (Mark 5:34; Luke 1:79; 2:14, 29; 7:50; 10:5–6; 19:38, 42; 24:36; John 14:27; 16:33; 20:19–26; Acts 10:36).

Jarius[23] asked for Jesus to heal his daughter but with her dying, Jesus raised Jarius' twelve-year-old daughter from the dead (Mark 5:22–24, 35–43; Matt 9:18–19, 23–26; Luke 8:41–42, 49–56).[24] Matthew recounts that the synagogue ruler, Jarius, bowed down before Jesus and said that his only daughter had just died, but Mark and Luke report that she is on the verge of death when Jarius came to Jesus. Mark develops Jarius' hope that she would get well or be saved (σωθῇ) and live. Jesus followed Jarius and in the process the woman suffering from the hemorrhage discussed above was healed. As the hemorrhaging woman's healing was being realized, some came from Jarius' house and announced that "Your daughter had died; do not trouble the Teacher anymore." But Jesus responded, "Do not be afraid, only believe, and she shall be made well [σωθήσεται]." Coming to the house, Jesus saw the flute and clarinet players and the crowd in noisy weeping and wailing disorder. He urged them to depart, claiming that she was asleep,[25] at which they laughed. With the crowd put out of the house and only Peter, John, James, and the girl's father and mother accompanying Jesus into the house, Jesus took the girl by the hand, which would render others unclean (Num 19:11), but instead Jesus dispelled her uncleanness of death with her resurrection. Jesus calls out "Child, arise!" and the little girl's spirit returned to her body[26] and she got up

---

23. Jarius name may be read as "he will enlighten" (Num 32:41; Judg 10:3–4; Esth 2:5) or "he will awaken" (1 Chr 20:5), but none of the authors make an issue about his name.

24. Multiple attestation supports the authenticity of this miracle.

25. Sometimes death is referred to as "sleep," especially "slept with his fathers" (Gen 47:30; 1 Kgs 1:21; 2:10; 11:21, 43; 1 Chr 17:11; 2 Chr 9:31; 16:13; 21:1; 26:2, 23; 27:9; 28:27; 32:33; 33:20; 36:8; Dan 12:2; 2 Macc 12.45; *1 En.* 49.3; Matt 27:52; 1 Cor 15:6; Eph 5:14; 2 Pet 3:4; *1 Clem.* 44.2). Additionally, the rabbinic *dĕmak* means both "to sleep" and "to lie in the grave."

26. Upon death the NT writers consider that the spirit leaves the body (Matt 27:50; Luke 8:55; 23:46; Acts 7:59; similarly Acts 20:10 "soul still in him"). Peter refers to the

and began to walk. Immediately, they were all completely astonished, and Jesus gave strict orders to tell no one of this. Jesus also urged them to give her something to eat.

Responding to John the Baptist's martyrdom, Jesus withdrew but when the crowd found him on the Northeast shore of the Sea of Galilee,[27] he had compassion on them, healing their sick, and then in late afternoon he fed five thousand men and their families that had gathered (Mark 6:34-44; Matt 14:14-21; Luke 9:12-17; John 6:5-13).[28] This is reminiscent of the exodus "manna" (meaning "whats it") in the wilderness (Exod 16:14-22).[29] Jesus saw the people as sheep without a shepherd and had compassion on them. Jesus urges the disciples to do a miracle for the crowd, but they admit that they only have five loaves and two fish and the disciples only thought in natural means, like going to the nearest village to spend 200 days wages on food.[30] Jesus urged the disciples to bring them near and to recline on the green grass in groups of hundreds and fifties. Jesus looked up to heaven,[31] blessed the food, and began to break[32] the loaves until an abundance had been given out and everyone was satisfied. Such creative miracles of food are reminiscent of the prophetic miracles of Elijah and Elisha, even using some similar phrases (1 Kgs 17:8-16; 4:1-7, 42-44; 2 Kgs 4:42-44). The abundance was so great that there were even twelve full stiff cane baskets[33] of broken pieces left over. Such miraculous abundance of food fits with the eschatological expectations of

---

martyrdom experience of Christ and Christians to be followed by a divine vindication of making their spirit alive in resurrection (1 Pet 3:18; 4:6).

27. "Bethsaida" means "a place of hunting," indicating some distance to towns.

28. Multiple attestation supports the authenticity of this miracle.

29. There are also a few early Jewish accounts that God created food to help his servants (b. Ta'an. 24b-25a; T. Zeb. 6.6; b. Yoma 39a; PG 1.103-4).

30. According to m. Pe'a 8.7, this much money would buy about 2400 loaves, seven inches in diameter and one-half inch thick or about a half day ration for 5000 men.

31. The normal posture of Jewish prayer (LXX of Deut. 4:19; Job 22:26; Josephus, Ant. 11.5.6; 1 En 13.5; b. Yebam. 105b; Gen. Rab. 33.3 on Gen 8:1).

32. There is no direct allusion to the Lord's supper; the breaking of bread here is merely stylistic for having a meal.

33. κοφίνους is a stiff cane basket of variable size and found in the feeding of the five thousand, whereas σπυρίδας is the variable sized flexible mat-basket from the feeding of the four thousand and its shortened form (σπυρίς) is used in Acts 9:25 as the basket in which Paul was lowered over the city wall (Juvenal, Sat. 3.14; 6.542; Hort, "Note on the Words κοφίνους, σπυρίς, sarganh"). κοφίνους are not implying a particular Jewish basket only (contra Juvenal, Sat. 3.14; 6.542), since Josephus describes them among the load of a Roman soldier (War 3.5.5). Likewise, the point is not an allegory to the twelve tribes of Israel or disciples.

the bounty God provides in kingdom (Jer 31:12; Hos 2:22; Joel 2:19).[34] It may even prefigure the messianic feast into kingdom (Luke 14:15; 22:16; Rev 19:9).[35] Part of the multitude's motivation is that some Jewish traditions emphasized that the final redeemer would bring down manna like Moses did.[36] Jesus withdrew from the increasing crowd because they recognized him to be this eschatological messianic prophet after Moses' manna providing pattern.[37] The disciples gained no lasting insight from the feeding of the 5000 because their hearts were hardened (Mark 6:52).

Then on the Southeast shore of the Sea of Galilee, in the Decapolis region, four thousand men and their families had stayed with Jesus for three days of healing and teaching, and Jesus compassionately fed them (Mark 8:1–9; Matt 15:32–39).[38] Motivated out of compassion, Jesus wished to send the people away but not in a fasting condition lest they faint on the way, since the availability of food was not near. The disciples were at a loss as to where they could get food since they admit that they are a desolate place. Again, this is reminiscent of the manna in the wilderness. Jesus asked what the disciples had. This time the disciples had seven loaves and a few small fish. Jesus had them direct the multitude to sit on the ground.[39] Jesus gave thanks and then began to break the bread and continued to give it out as the disciples carried it to the people. The whole multitude ate and was satisfied, and the scraps filled seven large flexible mat-baskets.[40]

The Pharisees and Sadducees came out asking Jesus for a sign from heaven when Jesus had just met people's needs with wilderness feeding signs (Mark 8:1–21; Matt 16:1–12). Jesus answered that they can read the weather, but that they cannot read the signs of the times. "An evil and adulterous generation seeks after a sign, and no sign will be given it except the sign of Jonah," which he mentioned as an enigmatic allusion to

---

34. *Sib. Or.* 3.622–23.

35. 2 *Bar* 29.3–8; 4 *Ezra* 6.52.

36. Early Amoraic tradition in *Pesiq. Rab Kah.* 5.8; *Num. Rab.* 11.2; *Ruth Rab.* 5.6; *Eccl. Rab.* 1.9; and a revivified Moses as eschatological leader of Israel (John 6:14–15; *Ex. Rab.* 2.6; *Deut. Rab.* 9.9).

37. Such Mosaic leaders drew large crowds (Josephus, *War* 2.261–63; *Ant.* 20.169–71).

38. Multiple attestation supports the authenticity of this miracle.

39. Perhaps it is a different season or different place than the feeding of the five thousand which has them sit on much green grass (Mark 6:39; John 6:10).

40. σπυρίδας are flexible mat-baskets, which are different from the stiff cane baskets of the feeding of the five thousand (κοφίνους).

his own resurrection. Jesus left the religious leaders and went away. Jesus warned the disciples, "Watch out [βλέπετε] and beware of the leaven of the Pharisees and Sadducees." However, the disciples misunderstood him and started talking about the fact that they had no bread with them in the boat. Jesus then berated the disciples: "Are you so dense as to not see [βλέπετε] and believe?" Jesus clarified that we don't need bread with us— "When I broke the five loaves for the five thousand, how many stiff cane baskets full of broken pieces did you pick up?" They answered, "Twelve." Jesus responded, "When I broke the seven loaves for the four thousand, how many flexible mat-baskets of broken pieces did you pick up?" The disciples answered, "Seven." Jesus then clarified, "Do you not yet understand that I was not talking about bread but warning you concerning the leaven of the Pharisees and Sadducees?" Then the disciples understood that Jesus had been warning them to beware of the teaching of the Pharisees and Sadducees. Mark illustrates these disciples coming to see while the religious leaders remain blind by retaining "seeing" imagery within this account (Mark 8:15, 18) and by immediately following it by the blind man healed by Jesus in stages of seeing men as trees walking, then clearly (Mark 8:22–26; βλέπεις, βλέπω, διέβλεψεν). Jesus heals the blind man by spitting in his eyes and then laying his hands upon him (Mark 8:23, 25).[41] Such clear sight connects with the following account of Peter, the son of Jonah[42] announcing that Jesus is the Davidic king (Mark 8:27–30; Matt 16:16–17). The hazy sight transition of the blind man might metaphorically picture the incomplete understanding of those who claimed Jesus to be a prophet, further implying that those who didn't understand (such as the religious leaders) remained blind.[43]

One night, Jesus got into a boat with his disciples and fell asleep in the stern upon the cushion until the experienced fishermen disciples woke him and Jesus stilled the storm (Mark 4:35–41; Matt 8:18, 23–27;

---

41. The technique of healing by spit also occurs by Vespasian in Egypt (Suetonius, *Vesp.* 7; Dio Cassius, *Hist.* 65.8.1; Tacitus, *Hist.* 4.81) and in Jewish culture (*y. Šabb.* 14d; 17f; *y. Sanh.* 101a), a pattern for which Jesus is accused of magic (Origen, *Cels.* 8.9; 1.38, 68; *b. Sanh* 43a; Lactantius, *Ep.* 45) but Jesus' name is a power word to reflect his authority to heal not dependent upon spells (*PG* 3.420; 4.1233; 4.3020); Ayayo, "Magical Exectations," 379–91.

42. This might be a wordplay off the sign of Jonah (Matt 16:4, 17). There is no evidence that the heavenly sign is "bread from heaven," as claimed by de Campos, "'Sign from Heaven,'" 234–56.

43. Lightfoot, *History and Interpretation in the Gospels*, 90–91; Garland, *Mark*, 313; France, *Mark*, 301.

Luke 8:22–25).[44] A fierce gale wind churned up a great shaking[45] storm that caused these experienced seamen to fear for their lives. The boat was swamping in the waves. The disciples woke Jesus, crying out, "Save us, master;[46] we are perishing!" Jesus responded to them, "Why are you timid, you men of little faith?" Then Jesus arose and rebuked the winds and the sea; and it became perfectly calm. The disciples fearfully marveled, saying, "What kind of man is this, that even the winds and the sea obey Him?" Such reflection goes beyond that of a prophet, like Jonah,[47] since he was dominated by the elements and the sovereign merciful God who controlled them. Here Jesus takes on the sovereign role of Yahweh, controlling the storm to silence wind (Ps 107:25–30; Prov 30:4; Job 38:25; Amos 4:13) and subdue waves (Pss 33:7; 65:7; 77:16; 88:26; 89:8–9, 25; 93:3–4; 106:8–9; 107:23–32; Isa 51:9–10).[48]

In a later instance after the feeding of the five thousand, Jesus sent the disciples to the other side of the Sea of Galilee to Capernaum without him and he came to them in the midst of another storm walking on water (Mark 6:45–52; Matt 14:24–33; John 6:16–21).[49] Jesus sent the multitude away, who wished to make him king as they recognized a Mosaic quality about him unto kingdom, then Jesus departed to the mountain top to pray. When it was dark Jesus saw that the boat was in the middle of

44. Multiple attestation supports the authenticity of this as a real miracle, not an allegory of the persecution tossed church (contra Tertullian, *Bapt.* 12). A stern seat developed in the passages is discussed by archeologist Wachsman, "Galilee Boat," 18–33.

45. The word σεισμὸς indicates the shaking as in an earthquake.

46. "Master" (ἐπιστάτα) is a unique Lukan term parallel to "lord" (κύριος) and "teacher" (διδάσκαλε), but especially shows his authority and their submission to him (Luke 5:5; 8:24, 45; 9:33, 49; 17:13).

47. Davies and Allison, *Matthew*, 2:70 draws parallels with the Jonah account. Antiochus IV Epiphanes claimed that the sea would obey him but never demonstrated this ability like Jesus did here (2 Macc 9:8). A couple of early Jewish accounts and Greek narratives describe how storms were eased by prayer (*y. Ber.* 9.1; *b. B. Mes.* 59b; Homer, *Hymns* 33.12; Aristides, *Hymn to Serapis* 33), which shows the disciples culpability for lack of faith in praying about the storm. Likewise, *b. B. Bat.* 73a indicates a tradition that clubs engraved with "I am that I am, Yah, the Lord of Hosts, Amen, Amen Selah" will subdue waves that would otherwise sink a ship. Such rescues are the work of the deity, thus implying Jesus is God.

48. 2 Macc 9.8; 4Q381; Isa 51 describes Yahweh as the one who controls the sea; Ortlund, "Significance of Jesus Walking," 325–26; Ps 88:26 describes that God is the one whose "hand is set against the sea;" Kirk and Young, "'I Will Set His Hand,'" 333–40.

49. Multiple attestation biblically and *Odes Sol.* 39.8–13 supports the authenticity of this miracle. Also, the Dura Europa third-century AD Christian chapel pictures Peter in this miracle walking on water (Bockmuehl, *Simon Peter in Scripture and Memory*, 40, 72).

the sea (about three or four miles out), being battered by waves and the disciples strained on the oars against a contrary wind. In the fourth watch of the night (3–6 a.m.), Jesus walking on the water, intending to walk past them, but his disciples saw him walking on the sea, frightened, they cried out in fear, "It's a ghost!" Immediately Jesus spoke to them, "Take courage, it is I;[50] do not be afraid." Jewish tradition had it that God was the one who walked on water (Job 9:8 LXX), and Jesus was identifying himself with that divine role.[51] Peter blurted out, "Lord if it is you, command me to come to you on the water." When Jesus said "Come," Peter got out of the boat and walked on the water toward Jesus. However, when Peter saw the wind, he became afraid and began to sink, calling out, "Lord save me!" Immediately Jesus grabbed him, saying, "You[52] of little faith, why did you doubt?" In Jewish tradition it is God alone who can rescue from the sea (Exod 14:10—15:21; Ps 107:23–32; Jonah 1:1–16).[53] When they got into the boat, the wind stopped, and they were greatly astonished. They were then immediately on the other side. Those who were in the boat worshipped Jesus, saying, "You are certainly God's Son!"

Simon exampled the disciple's commitment confessing Jesus as the Christ (Mark 8:27–29; Matt 16:16–20; Luke 9:20). Jesus asked who the people thought the Son of Man was and the disciples responded with revivified prophets like John the Baptist, Elijah, or Jeremiah. However, Peter identified that Jesus was the anointed one to be king, the son of the living God.[54] In Simon's statement of Jesus' lordship, Peter became a symbol of the personal commitment of a disciple. Jesus called Simon blessed as a son of Jonah, perhaps because he could see the messianic outcome after the Jonah sign miracle would occur (Matt 16:4, 17). Simon is blessed with a personal beatitude[55] in that this insight defines him here

---

50. Jesus' statement, "It is I" (ἐγώ εἰμι) is how the LXX Exod 3:14 describes "I am who I am" (אֶהְיֶה אֲשֶׁר אֶהְיֶה), so possibly another hint at divinity.

51. Also Job 38:16; Ortlund, "Significance of Jesus Walking," 319–37, especially 325–26; Kirk and Young, "'I Will Set His Hand,'" 335; also there is no parallel Greco-Roman mythology for walking on water, even though Poseidon and Xerxes are reported to fly in a chariot over water (McPhee, "Walk, Don't Run," 763–77).

52. These "you" statements are grammatically singular referring to Peter doubting.

53. Wis 14.2–4; 1QH 6.22–25; *T. Naph.* 6.1–10.

54. Schweizer affirms such Christological commitments and confession is the core of discipleship (*Lordship and Discipleship*).

55. Other personal beatitudes toward recipients include: Matt 13:16 = Luke 10:23; John 20:29; *4 Ezra* 10.57 and *Jos. Asen.* 16.14.

as informed from the Father, rather than his own human agency.[56] Simon and his insight[57] becomes foundational and thus Jesus changes Simon's name to Peter (Πέτρος) and explains that it is he with his insightful confession that will become foundational rock (ταύτῃ πέτρᾳ) upon which Jesus will build his church. Other disciples following Jesus should likewise affirm Jesus as the messiah. This assembly (ἐκκλησίαν) of people already begun and being built up by Jesus is probably the disciple band, which will universally grow as Jesus' church. This very group (ἐκκλησίαν) will take the aggressive charge of attacking the gates of Hades (the place of the dead; Isa 38:10; Pss 9:13; 107:18; Job 38:17 LXX "gatekeepers").[58] Hades gates will fall, so that the dead will be rescued from Hades' clutches by the church. With the Jonah resurrection sign in view, this aggressive rescue from Hades extends beyond evangelism and kingdom miracles to resurrections from Hades, which Jesus leads the way and Peter's insight shows the way to resurrect unto kingdom. Peter becomes a scribe of kingdom, complete with the scribal sign of keys to the kingdom. Thus, from this insight of Jesus' kingship, Peter is here granted a scribal role that the whole disciple band, as church, is later also granted (Matt 16:19; 18:18; John 20:23). If Peter and the disciples "bind" a practice or a person as excluded from kingdom, it is excluded with reference to heavenly salvation and practice.[59] Whereas, if Peter and the disciples "loose" a practice as permitted or a person as included in kingdom, then it is included with

---

56. "Flesh and blood" reflect the rabbinic sense of human agency (Davies and Allison, *Matthew*, 2:623).

57. Peter's *declaration* is likely included within the feminine foundation rock (πέτρᾳ) because it is referred to as "this rock" with the feminine pronoun (ταύτῃ), rather than second-person singular masculine "you" referring to Peter, who was described as rock in the masculine (Πέτρος), or first-person masculine "me" referring to Christ (Matt 16:18), who is not in this context described as a rock but is only elsewhere described as a rock (which in those other contexts makes good sense) without reference to this text. Caragounis, *Peter and the Rock*, 119. John 1:42 recounts Simon being called the Aramaic "Cephas" ("rock") from early in his discipleship.

58. Wis 16.13; 3 Macc 5.51; *Pss. Sol.* 16.2; Cullmann, *Peter*, 208.

59. These verses can grammatically be treated as future perfect paraphrastics (what you bind shall have been bound) but the contexts' emphasis on privilege and responsibility makes it more natural to read it as indicating real scribal privilege and responsibility of issuing authoritative *halakah* (teaching), as I have indicated above and this is the early Jewish pattern elsewhere (CD 5.24–25; 1QS 5.24–25; 4Q477 frag. 2.1–2; *m. Naz.* 5.1–4; *y. Jom. Tobb* 60.1; 61.1; *y. Oriah* 61.2; *y. Šabb.* 4.1; 6.1; 16.2, 4; *b. Ḥag.* 10a; *b. Meg.* 26.7; *b. Avodah Zarah* 7.1; 39.2; *b. Ber.* 23.1; *b. Sanh.* 100.1; *Tosaphata in Jevam.* cap. 1; *Pesachim*, cap. 4 hal. 5; *Mamrim*, cap. 1, cap 2; Lightfoot, *Commentary on the New Testament*, 2:237–40; Bornkamm, "Authority to 'Bind' and 'Loose,'" 83–97).

reference to heavenly salvation. If these scribal actions entail forgiving, then as the disciples forgive, divine forgiveness will be meted out unto kingdom. With the disciple's realization that Jesus is the messiah, Jesus begins to predict his coming death and resurrection. Peter responds with a comment that rejects Jesus' predictions so much so that he becomes emblematic of Satan's interests and puts Jesus at risk for damnation, with Peter as a stumbling block (σκάνδαλον; Matt 16:23).[60] Such a context raises the cost of discipleship. With the risk of Jesus impending death, the cost of discipleship stiffens. Jesus began to instruct the disciples that he was going to be killed and that would put their own lives at risk through mimetic or imitative atonement (Matt 16:15-28; Mark 8:33-38; Luke 9:20-27, 57-58).

One week[61] later, Jesus took his inner circle of Peter and the Zebedee brothers to a high mountain and Jesus was transfigured before them as a momentary glimpse into Jesus' kingdom (2 Pet 1:11, 16-18; Mark 9:1-10; Matt 16:28—17:9; Luke 9:27-36). Jesus' face and clothes shone as the sun, enabling these disciples to be eyewitnesses of Jesus' majesty. Moses and Elijah appeared talking with Jesus. Luke identified that the topic of their conversation is Jesus' "exodus" (Luke 9:31 ἔξοδον).[62] Such an exodus reference is quite appropriate to prefigure kingdom (Isa 40:3-5; Mark 1:2-3). Out of fear, Peter blurted out that it was good for them to be there and that if Jesus wished, they could make three tabernacles, one each for Jesus, Moses, and Elijah. Perhaps Peter was thinking that the Feast of Tabernacles might be appropriate as kingdom is initiated, since as a festival, it will be celebrated in kingdom (Zech 14:16), and perhaps it was that time of year. Instead, a bright cloud overshadowed them and the

---

60. At places like this exemplar of Satan, and Peter's denials, Gundry argued that Peter was an exemplar of false discipleship and apostate (*Peter: False Disciple and Apostate*; similarly, Stock, "Is Matthew's Presentation of Peter Ironic?," 64-69). However, as a whole it is better to see Peter as both an exemplar of discipleship as well as a warning of potential apostasy (continuing discussion: Ridlehoover, "Matthean Peter," 729-44).

61. Matt 17:1 identified the transfiguration as occurring six days after Peter pronounced Jesus was the Christ (Matt 16:16), whereas Luke records this span of time to be about eight days (Luke 9:20, 28). This can be harmonized because Matthew used Hebrew time and Peter could confess Jesus is the Christ in the beginning of the Hebrew day after sunset, while Luke used Roman time (Acts 2:15), which would mean that Peter's statement would occur toward the end of the first day. With the days breaking at different points, the transfiguration could be six days later according to Matthew (on the seventh day), which would be Luke's eighth day.

62. Philo and Josephus often take ἔξοδον as the exodus rather than merely a departure.

bath qol,[63] the voice of God (the Excellent Glory) spoke from the cloud, saying, "This is My beloved Son, in whom I am well pleased. Hear Him!" In sampling a taste of the kingdom, this voice reassured the disciples that the prophecies of Christ's kingdom will be confirmed further (2 Pet 1:11, 16–19; Mark 9:7).[64] Then Jesus came alone and touched the disciples, asking them to rise and not be afraid but "Tell the vision to no one until the Son of Man is risen from the dead." The disciples kept quiet about what they had seen until later, but they questioned Jesus what rising from the dead meant.

When Jesus and the disciples came back to Capernaum, Jesus orchestrated money in a fish's mouth to pay the two-drachma temple tax to support the sacrificial system (Matt 17:24–27; Exod 30:11–16). According to the Mishnah, the temple tax was to be paid annually, in the month of Adar (February-March).[65] Those collecting the two-drachma[66] tax did so near the place where a person considers his residence so the Capernaum tax collectors asked Peter if Jesus pays the temple tax. Peter answered, "yes." Later when Jesus caught Peter indoors, Jesus asked him, "From whom do kings of the earth collect customs or poll-tax, from their sons or from strangers?" Peter responded, "From strangers." Jesus said to him, "Consequently the sons are exempt." That is, Peter had answered incorrectly. Jesus went on to explain, "But lest we give them offense, go to the sea, and throw in a hook, and take the first fish that comes up; and when you open its mouth, you will find a stater (a Greek silver coin worth

---

63. On the concept and instance of *bath qol*: Dan. 4:31; Josephus, *Ant.* 13.282–83; *Song Rab.* 8.9.3; *b. 'Abot* 6.2; *B. Bat.* 73b; 85b; *Mak.* 23b; *'Erub.* 54b; *Šabb.* 33b; 88a; *Soṭah* 33a; *p. Sota* 7.5.5; *Pesiq. Rab Kah.* 11.16; 15.5; *Lev. Rab.* 19.5–6; *Deut. Rab.* 11.10; *Lam. Rab. Proem* 2, 23; *Lam. Rab.* 1.16.50; *Ruth Rab.* 6.4; *Qoh. Rab.* 7.12.1; *Sib. Or.* 1.127, 267, 275; Artapanus in Eusebius, *Praep. ev.* 9.27.36; Arrian, *Alexander* 3.3.5; Lucian, *C.W.* 1.569–70; Plutarch, *Is. Os.* 12; *Mor.* 355E; *Mart. Pol.* 9. The *bath qol* was present in Israel before the spirit of prophecy departed (*b. Pesaḥ.* 94a; *Ḥag.* 13a; *Sanh.* 39b) and a few sources give it future ramifications as well (*Lev. Rab.* 27.2; *Pesiq. Rab Kah.* 17.5).

64. The statement does not require a claim for Jesus' divinity, so it does not preview deification contra Burkett, "Transfiguration of Jesus," 413–32.

65. Josephus, *War* 6.281; *m. Šeqal.* 1.1–3.

66. Temple tax amounted to two drachmas or didrachmon (Josephus, *Ant.* 18.312; *War* 7.218). The Essenes, who held that this tax need only be paid once in one's lifetime, considered that they were complying with Moses (4QOrdinances). Likewise, priests were held to not need to pay the tax (*m. Šeqal.* 1.4; *Mek. on Ex.* 19:1; *b. Menaḥ* 65a).

four drachmas).⁶⁷ Take that and give it to them for you and me."⁶⁸ There is no discussion of this miracle working out but Matthew's inclusion in his account leaves the impression of yet another odd creation miracle accomplished by Jesus. John Meier calls this miracle that of the "fiscally philanthropic fish."⁶⁹

Jesus took his disciples up to Jerusalem for Passover celebrations and turned them into a new covenant memorial for kingdom (Mark 14:22–25). As they left for the Mount of Olives, Jesus stunned the whole disciple band with a claim that they would all fall away based on Zech 13:7, "I will strike the shepherd and the sheep of the flock shall be scattered" in impending apostasy (Mark 14:26–31; Matt 26:31–32). Peter responded that others may fall but he will not. Jesus repeatedly called "Simon, Simon," perhaps to downplay the rock metaphor. Mark 14:29–31 joins Luke 22:31–34 in identifying Peter himself will deny Jesus, as they all claim loyalty to Jesus. However, Luke 22:31–34 frames the temptation by Satan's sifting to occur to the whole disciple band (plural "you," ὑμᾶς)⁷⁰ who are reclining at table, "Satan has demanded to sift 'you all' (ὑμᾶς) like wheat; but I have prayed for "you" (individual "you," σοῦ) Peter, that your (σου) faith may not fail and you (σύ), after you (σοῦ) have turned again, strengthen your (σου) brothers" and that before a rooster crow you (σοι) Peter will deny me three times (Mark 14:29–31; Luke 22:31–34). Prayed for Peter will recover and have the ministry of strengthening the disciple band. Grieved, Peter and all the disciples focus on their impending failure and insist on their loyalty.

While Jesus prayed in the olive grove on the mount, all the prayerless disciples fell asleep and Jesus was captured by the Sanhedrin guard. As the disciples jumped to their feet, Peter desperately swung his sword to kill one who had come against them, but, missing his target, he merely cut off the ear of a slave (John 18:26). Jesus halted this action by healing the ear of the high priest's slave and rebuking his disciples with statements

---

67. There are accounts of fish that when caught return coins, keys or jewelry (*b. Šabb.* 119a; Herodotus 3.39–42). *The Epistle of the Apostles* 5 recounts a similar story, probably reflecting dependence upon this text in Matthew.

68. These four clauses have a nice form, each with a participle and aorist imperative (Matt 17:24–27) and Clement of Alexandria, *Quis Div Salv* 21 recounting event provides specific instruction from Jesus on paying of the temple tax (Smith, *Petrine Controversies in Early Christianity*, 207), rather than the *Acts of Thom.* 143 descriptions that Jesus paid tax for himself and his disciples.

69. Meier, *Marginal Jew*, 2:884.

70. Bourke, "Peter in the Gospel of Luke," 120–21.

of: the certainty of death for any disciple who tries to use force, that Jesus has legions of angels at his disposal if defense was in order, and that Jesus' death fulfilled Scripture. The guards took Jesus away to be tried before Sanhedrin and Roman rulers for a death sentence. The disciples scatter, except Peter, who followed at a distance into the high priest's courtyard and warmed himself at a charcoal fire.

While Jesus was silent before his accusers (1 Pet 2:23; Mark 14:61), eventually, the high priest put Jesus under oath to clarify if he was the Christ, and Jesus clarified by quoting that he is Daniel's prophesied "Son of Man," who will come on the clouds (Mark 14:61–62; Dan 7:13). In contrast, Peter denied being Jesus' disciple, even as a servant girl asked him (Mark 14:66–72; Matt 26:69–75; Luke 22:55–72; John 18:25–27).[71] Peter's previous weakness and prayerlessness had come to a head in denying Jesus.[72] Peter left the fire and made his way to the gate to escape but others accused him there, indicating that Peter's accent identified him to be a Galilean because he had difficulty pronouncing gutterals by dropping the *H* sound in the standard Galilean manner (Mark 14:70; Matt 26:73; Luke 22:59).[73] After about an hour another accused Peter and he denied it with an oath (Mark 14:71).[74] Immediately, a rooster crowed, Jesus looked at Peter, and Peter went out and wept bitterly (Mark 14:72; Luke 22:61–62). Sliding into apostasy, Peter could probably recall Jesus' words, "Whoever shall deny me before men, I shall deny him before my Father who is in heaven" (Matt 10:33).[75]

Jesus was rejected, sentenced, and crucified with the charge that he was the king of the Jews (Mark 15). Jesus' trial and death under Pilate

---

71. At places like this denial and when Peter is exemplar of Satan in Matt 16:22–23, Gundry argued that Peter was an exemplar of false discipleship and apostate (*Peter: False Disciple and Apostate*; similarly, Stock, "Is Matthew's Presentation of Peter Ironic?," *BTB* 17.2[1987] 64–69). However, as a whole it is better to see Peter as both an exemplar of discipleship as well as a warning of potential apostasy (continuing discussion: Ridlehoover, "The Matthean Peter: as Archetype and Antitype," *JETS* 64.4[2021] 729–44).

72. Borrell, *The Good News of Peter's Denial*, 124–25, 203–5.

73. B. ʿErub. 53b "A certain Galilean went around saying to people, 'Who has *amar*?' They said to him, 'You Galilean fool: do you mean an ass (*ḥāmār*) for riding, or wine (*ḥamar*) for drinking, or wool (*ʿamar*) for clothing or a lamb (*ʾimmar*) for slaughtering?'"; Lightfoot, *A Commentary on the New Testament*, 1:170–72; Vermes, *Jesus the Jew*, 52–53.

74. Peter's oath could have been the oath phrase, "I neither know nor understand what you are saying" (*m. Šebu.* 8.3, 6).

75. Lanzinger, "Petrus und der Sigende Hahn," *ZNW* 109:1(2018) 32–50 develops this as a pattern for Neroian persecution.

occurs near Passover on a year between AD 30 and 34.[76] After identifying the father of two of his friends, Simon Cyrene carried Jesus' cross (Mark 15:21), Mark presents Jesus' death as a "desolate scene" with no family or disciples to observe it, unlike other Gospels which include women or John being present.[77] Under a darkened sky at midday and upon Jesus' death, an earthquake occurred tearing the visible temple curtain to the outer sanctuary from the top to the bottom, to which a centurion claimed "Truly this man was a son of God"[78] (Mark 15:38–39; Matt 27:51–54). Joseph of Arimathea, from the Sanhedrin, arranged with Pilate to bury Jesus' body in his own tomb before sundown began Passover, and several women noticed in which tomb Jesus was lain (Mark 15:42–47; Matt 27:57–66; Luke 23:50–56).

Pilate gave the priests a guard to seal the tomb but early on the first day of the week the women found the stone rolled away, leaving the tomb open (Mark 16:1–8; Matt 28:1–17; Luke 24:1–11; John 20:1–18).[79] Two angels (looking like men) announced to the women at the grave that Jesus had arisen, but that they should not be afraid. The angel showed the women where Jesus had been laid. An angel told Mary Magdalene, Joanna, Mary the mother of James, and other women to tell Peter and the disciples. The women departed quickly with fear and great joy to tell the disciples. The disciples did not believe the women at first. John outran Peter to the tomb but did not go in. Simon Peter arrived and went into the tomb and beheld the linen wrappings lying there and face cloth rolled up by itself.[80] The view of the wrappings in the tomb was compelling for

76. Jesus' ministry is at least two years long based on the mention of a Passover early in his ministry (John 2:13, 23), a Passover close to the feeding of the 5000 (John 6:4), and a Passover as the Last Supper (Mark 14:12–25; Matt 26:17; Luke 22:7). So, the earliest the Last Supper could be is AD 30. There are no other Passovers mentioned during Jesus' ministry but neither does any account claim that all festivals are mentioned. Historically, Jesus was crucified between AD 30–34 because after that date Pilate became too entangled with a rebellion in Samaria and then was removed by the Roman Senate (Josephus, *Ant.* 18.85).

77. Dawsey, *Peter's Last Sermon*.

78. This statement could either mean a divinely empowered individual, or a king, perhaps the messiah.

79. While the canonical Gospels report Jesus resurrection as having occurred without observers except the guards, *Gos. Pet.* 34–39 presents a crowd of observers watching angels role the stone away in compliance to a divine voice. Perhaps the Nazareth stone also hints at resurrection in banning moving of bodies from one grave to another.

80. The description of the linen wrappings in John 20:6–7 probably does not give credence to the view that Jesus in His resurrection passed through the burial clothes, leaving them undisturbed. He may have, but if He had, one would expect the face cloth

John to believe. No one would have taken the body and left the wrappings; Jesus must have resurrected! Jesus then met women and reassured them not to be afraid (John 20:11–18).[81] Jesus urged Mary Magdalene to not keep clinging to him because he had not ascended to the Father. Then Jesus urged the women to tell the brethren that he would meet them in Galilee. The women worshipped Jesus.

Jesus appeared to some disciples, including Simon, on the Emmaus Road. Was this Simon Peter who Paul records as seeing the risen Christ before the twelve (1 Cor 15:5)[82] or is this Simon the Zealot, and Cephas had another resurrection appearance? There is not enough said here to answer this question. The two walking to Emmaus were sad because they viewed Jesus as a prophet empowered by God to bring in the kingdom, but their hopes for this were dashed with Jesus' death (Luke 24:13–35). Then they recounted that they were troubled earlier in the day by the testimony of some women that that tomb was empty, and Jesus was alive. On the road to Emmaus, Jesus explained to this group from the Scriptures why the anointed king must suffer these things before entering glory.[83] Then Jesus vanished from their sight. Jesus' miraculous appearing and disappearing through walls may reflect that he is divine rather than being normative for resurrection bodies. This group of disciples with

---

to be lying where the head had been. In fact, it was rolled up in a place by itself. The one thing that can be certainly said is that it was extremely unlikely that someone had taken the body and left all these wrappings. Brown, *John*, 1007–8.

81. The author cannot agree with Cullmann (*Peter*, 59, 64) that Peter was the first to see the risen Christ (presumably based on 1 Cor 15:5) and thus authenticated a greater position for himself. If anyone can be said to have seen the risen Christ first, it is Mary Magdalene (John 20:11–18; corroborated by Byzantine textual addition Mark 16:9).

82. Origen claims that Simon Peter was one of the two Emmaus disciples (*Cels.* 2.62, 68; *Hom. Jer.* 20), but this claim goes further than Luke and 1 Cor.

83. This claim is justifiable from the perspective of early Jewish targum evidence and the NT quotes of OT texts concerning resurrection Bock, (*Proclamation from Prophecy and Pattern*) develops OT quotes are used by Luke for their "proclamation value" in Peter's sermons (another way of saying *pesher*); Marshall (*Acts*, 77–78) claims that like Ps 132 and 2 Sam 7:10–16 (present in Acts 2:30) were interpreted by 4Q Florilegium as Messianic, so to Peter understands Ps 16 as referring to the messiah. Additionally, the scriptural rationale for why Jesus' resurrection is predicted to occur on the third day must be seen through the slight targum evidence interpreting the scriptures as describing the general resurrection of the elect occurring on the third day (*T. Hos.* 6:2 interprets this text to be resurrection whereas the text speaks of the reviving of Israel on the third day; *Tg. Jon. on Isa.* 27:12f. describes salvation as being accomplished on the third day, implying a resurrection); there is also mention of third day resurrection in *Midrash Rab.* on Gen 22:4; 42:18; Exod 19:16; Josh 2:16; Jonah 2:1; Ezra 8:32; Wright, *Resurrection*, 321–22; Thiselton, *1 Corinthians*, 1196–97.

Jesus at Emmaus quickly returned to Jerusalem and told the other disciples of these things.

Then, Jesus appeared in their midst, saying, "Peace be with you." The disciples were startled and frightened thinking they were seeing a spirit (Luke 24:36–46; John 20:11–23). Jesus urged them to not be troubled but to touch him because a spirit does not have flesh and bones as Jesus has. While they were marveling, Jesus asked for some broiled fish, and he ate before them. Jesus opened the disciples' minds to understand that he had predicted his death and resurrection, and so had Moses, the prophets and the Psalms, which all must be fulfilled (Luke 24:44; 1 Cor 15:4).[84] Jesus then reminded them that he will send them to preach repentance and remission of sins in Christ's name, as the Father had sent him (Luke 24:47–49; Acts 1:8). Jesus probably appeared to the disciples more than once in Jerusalem with further empirical demonstration (John 20:24–31).

Jesus then met the disciples in Galilee, by the Sea of Tiberias (Luke 24:36–46; John 21:1–25). Peter and the fishermen had gone fishing but had caught nothing. Jesus urged them to cast their net on the right side of the boat, which probably meant for them to fish the very water that they had cast their net in from the left side. The catch was too great to haul into the boat with one hundred and fifty-three fish (John 21:3–6, 11).[85] At that point John recognized that it was Jesus who had made the request, so Peter jumped overboard and swam the hundred yards to shore. The rest rowed the catch in behind the boat. When they got ashore, Jesus had a charcoal fire with some fish on it and some bread, but he requested some more fish from them. So, Peter drew the net into shore and John remembered the count of the number of the fish. Jesus fed them breakfast.

After breakfast Jesus questioned Peter to help him articulate his supreme love (John 21:15–17). Jesus repeated Simon's name in a very formal pattern reiterating that what followed was significant. The question was aimed at discerning Peter's supreme loyalty.[86] This question was asked

---

84. This claim is justifiable from the perspective of early Jewish targum evidence, and the NT quotes of OT texts as developed in previous note. Ignatius, *Smyrn*. 3 identified Peter saw the resurrected Christ.

85. This account has specific eye-witness evidence.

86. The question "Do you love Me more than these?" has three possible meanings. Perhaps, because Peter had previously professed a greater loyalty than the others (Mark 14:29; Matt 26:33; John 13:37; 15:12), Jesus asked are you more loyal than they. Maybe Jesus asked if Peter loved Jesus more than he loved these other disciples. That is, Peter had remained with his friends when they all forsook Christ. Perhaps, Jesus asked Peter if he was more loyal to Jesus than to these things of fishing (his old occupation). The text

three times. Each time Peter answered in the affirmative. Jesus responded to each answer with a command reiterating Peter's responsibility to care for the flock owned by Jesus, the Great Shepherd.[87] Jesus did not give the flock over to Peter but he delegated to Peter the task of shepherding Jesus' flock. With the third question, Peter is grieved perhaps because the repetition called to mind Peter's three denials (John 18:17–18, 25–27). With each of these questions there was a reminder that Peter had a significant leadership role in shepherding Christ's flock. Jesus also went further than reiterating Peter as a leader among the disciples. With Peter's loyalty firmly declared again and in a dramatic way his three denials undone, Jesus prophesies of Peter that he will be called upon to be a martyr he previously claimed he could be. The imagery of stretching forth the hands and having them girded or bound picks up on the same kind of conditions that Jesus was in during his arrest (John 18:12, 24; 21:18). The binding comes before the leading in directions where Peter does not want to go, the process of Peter's death.[88] Maybe Jesus indicated it but certainly John concluded that in his death Peter would glorify God. Jesus attempted to end the conversation with the pointed exhortation ringing in Peter's ears, "Follow me!" In this context this exhortation calls for a commitment of loyalty to Christ all the way to death, with Christ being Peter's example. Peter tried to relieve the pressure with, "What about this other disciple?"

---

appears to be ambiguous in discerning between these, but the commonality between them all is a discernment of Peter's supreme loyalty for Christ. Morris, *John*, 870–71.

87. The different ways of speaking in this passage are probably not significant. For example, Jesus asks whether Peter loves him with ἀγαπᾷς the first two times and φιλεῖς the third time. To each of the questions Peter answered "Yes" and then added that he loved (φιλῶ) Jesus. The result of this is that Peter loves Jesus with both ἀγαπαω and φιλενω. Likewise, the reiteration of "feed" or "tend" and "lambs" or "sheep" is also not significant except that Peter is given the shepherding responsibility over Jesus' whole flock. Brown, *John*, 1102–6.

88. There are many ideas of what stretching forth the hands and binding means including crucifixion or prayer. Prayer seems to be a rather odd way to die and is not attested to in any early accounts. If it meant crucifixion the order appears to be wrong; the binding occurs before the being led where he does not want to go. Bauer tried to solve this problem by proposing that the stretching out of hands is not the actual crucifixion but the extending of the prisoner's hands to be tied to the crossbeam that had to be carried to the place of execution. This explanation fits with many first-century crucifixions. However, tradition has it that Peter was crucified upside down on a unique cross, so a readymade crossbeam would not fit a stationary upright in that novel manner (see "Hippolytus on the Twelve Apostles," a fragment in Roberts and Donaldson, *Ante-Nicene Christian Library*, 2.2:130; Eusebius, *Theoph.* 5.31; *Dem. ev.* 3.5.65; *Hist. eccl.* 2.25.5). In the author's opinion it is far simpler to refer to the visual binding involved in the procedure of arrest (John 18:12, 24; Acts 21:11–12). Brown, *John*, 1107–8.

Perhaps Peter wondered why he was being singled out or was groping for encouragement that he would not be the only martyr. Jesus does not relieve the pressure—"If I want him to remain until I come what is that to you? You follow Me!" (John 21:22).

These Galilee resurrection appearances continued to occur because in one instance only seven were present, while another instance may have had the eleven, and another which Paul indicates had five hundred at one time (Matt 28:7–20; John 20:24–26; 21:2; Acts 1:2–13; 1 Cor 15:6). Eventually, the whole of the new twelve saw Jesus raised including Mathias (Acts 1:22–23), as well as Justus (1 Cor 15:5). Was this another instance or part of the five hundred? Jesus confirmed his resurrection to them by his appearance, eating fish, and by explaining from the Scriptures why the anointed king must suffer and rise again from the dead on the third day (Luke 24:36–46). Jesus claimed all authority in heaven and earth, commissioning the disciples with Spirit empowerment to be witnesses proclaiming the kingdom message of repentance for forgiveness of sins to all nations beginning in Jerusalem and to make disciples of all people groups baptizing and teaching them to observe all that Jesus commanded them (Matt 28:18–20; Luke 24:47–53; Acts 1:5–8). After reassuring them that he would be with them until the end of the age Jesus lifted his hands to bless them and then bodily ascended into heaven (Acts 1:9–11). Two angels told the disciples that Jesus would return in the same manner as you have watched him go. They returned to Jerusalem with great joy and continued to praise God in the temple. Jesus appeared to more than five hundred brethren at one time, most of whom remained alive for decades so that they could be asked about it (1 Cor 15:6).

After Christ ascended, the disciples gathered in the upper room and devoted themselves to prayer (Acts 1:12–15). About one hundred and twenty were there. They were waiting expectantly for power so that they could be Christ's witnesses. As they waited, their minds turned to preparatory matters such as completing the number of apostles.

Peter addressed the group concerning Judas' fulfillment of Davidic scripture, specifically two imprecatory Psalm statements (Acts 1:16; Pss 69:22–28; 109:6–29). Judas forfeited his place and ministry among the twelve apostles, and another should take his office (Acts 1:17, 20; Ps 109:8). Since Jesus chose the original twelve, the apostles sought Jesus to indicate by lot Judas' replacement. The Lord Jesus choose Matthias (Acts 1:26).

With the arrival of the Jewish Feast of Weeks (Pentecost), came the arrival of Jews and proselytes from all over the empire streamed into

Jerusalem. What had been a feast to celebrate God's generosity of firstfruits of the harvest had been transformed in early Judaism to celebrate the giving of the law as ground of life, fifty days after Passover (Exod 12:3; 19:1). Peter's Pentecost sermon celebrates the giving of the Spirit so that as witnesses Peter announces Jesus is king, and all humans must align with him unto kingdom. More on the specifics of gospel within the chapter of Peter's gospel.

Peter's most emphasized feature in his gospel sermons is that Jesus' narratives of his death and resurrection identified that Jesus is king (Acts 2:24–36).[89] The fact that Jesus is already king identifies that he will judge and rule all forever, when he returns on the clouds. Prior to then he shows his kingdom greatness by leaving a pattern of service for all disciples to follow epitomized by his martyrdom. Jesus' resurrection and ascension vindicates Jesus as king and identifies him with the authority to commission and empower the disciples to 1) be witnesses of these things, 2) proclaim the kingdom message, and 3) make disciples. Peter's gospel proclamations record that the disciples have seen the risen Lord (Acts 1:22; 2:32; 3:15; 4:10; 10:41).

Thousands of persons repented and were baptized. All the believers continued to devote themselves to Christ's teaching, and the sharing of meals, goods, and themselves (Acts 2:42–47). Within this generous voluntary socialism to meet each other's needs, even land and houses were sold and distributed so that their needs could be met (Acts 4:32–37). Barnabus demonstrated this level of generosity before Peter, whereas Ananias and Sapphira embezzled their gift to receive greater honor than warranted (Acts 5:1–11). Peter confronted each in turn and God executed Ananias and Sapphira in judgment of trying to lie to God, and they died. The method of judgment is not described but near the beginning of new divine programs there is more likely to be swift and severe judgments for rebellion, and this fits that pattern (Judg 7:19–26). Young men[90] carried their bodies out and buried them. The swift judgment upon these apostates fosters great fear on all who heard, for deception and personal gain have no place among the Christians.

---

89. Künneth (*Theology of the Resurrection*, 114–15) even claims that through the resurrection his divinity was conferred upon him. However, Christ's pre-incarnate divinity indicates that resurrection would not be conferral but possibly could be a recognition of his divinity.

90. "Younger men" (Acts 5:6 νεώτεροι and 10 νεανίσκοι) are not an official office, contra Raackam, *Acts*, 67. The multiplicity of descriptions argues against a fixed title and office (Neil, *Acts*, 95).

God's generous healings continued to attract people to the apostle band to be healed and have their needs met. Some instances gathered crowds and provided further opportunities to evangelize the people and the Sanhedrin (Acts 3–4), while other situations provided odd opportunities, such as Peter's shadow falling on people so that they might be healed (Acts 5:12, 15–16). In Lydda, Peter also resurrected generous disciple Tabitha, resulting in many believing the Lord throughout Joppa (Acts 9:32–42).

Generous meeting of needs by the apostles became burdensome, so they had to find ways to make sure all needs were going to be met without the apostles being distracted from their proclamation of the word of God and prayer (Acts 6:1–7). The apostles had the congregation choose Spirit-filled wise men, with good reputation, who would serve the community food distribution. Because the neglect was especially felt among Hellenistic Jews, the men chosen all had Greek names, probably indicating their Hellenistic background.

When the apostles in Jerusalem heard that Samaria had received the word of God, they sent Peter and John to welcome them (Acts 8:14–25). Apostles Peter and John laid their hands upon the new converts, and they all received the Holy Spirit. Recently coming to faith, Simon the magician was amazed at their ability and offered money to obtain the ability to bestow this power. Peter responded with a curse designed to inform Simon that he was apostatizing, "To hell with you and your money" (Acts 8:20).[91] Peter explains that one cannot obtain the gift of God with money and that Simon has no share in this ministry because his heart is not right before God. Peter called Simon to repent of this wickedness by praying for the Lord to be merciful and forgive. Peter gave Simon a final warning, Simon is involved in unrighteousness, which produces bitter results and bondage (Acts 8:20–23). Pheme Perkins explains Simon Magnus' entrapment.

> The "gall of bitterness" and "bond of iniquity" have hold of Simon Magnus. The "gall" refers to the wrath with which the Lord will punish those who commit idolatry (Deut 29:17–19 LXX), the "bondage" to the "bonds of wickedness" (Isa 58:6) which Jesus came to break (Acts 10:38).[92]

Simon apparently repented and urged Peter to also pray that these judgments would not overtake him (Acts 8:24). The book of Acts leaves

91. Marshall, *Acts*, 159.
92. Perkins, *Peter*, 92.

Peter and Simon Magnus' conflict here with the outcome unclear, but the early church unconvincingly continues to trace this conflict to Rome and Simon being killed in a gnostic attempt to defeat apostle Peter, who is more empowered by God.[93]

Clement of Alexandria and Eusebius claim that Peter did not seek the bishopric of Jerusalem even though he was preferred by the Lord Jesus, so Peter and the Zebedee brothers were involved in humbly choosing James, Jesus' brother to occupy that role.[94] This opinion is likely reading a more advanced later ecclesiological structure upon the emerging church, but James performs a Jerusalem leadership role (Acts 15:13–21; Gal 1:19).

The persecutor of Christians, Saul joined the disciples in proclaiming Jesus Christ. Three years after his conversion, he came up to Jerusalem to get to know Peter. After Barnabus gained him access, he stayed for fifteen days, talking primarily to Peter, but also James (Acts 9:26–30, 27 plural "apostles"; Gal 1:18–24, 19 includes James).

The persecution of Peter arose from his persistent clear proclamation of good news and kingdom. In response to Peter and John healing a lame man in the temple and preaching Christ, the Sanhedrin locked them up, called a hearing and warned them to stop talking about Jesus. Filled by the Spirit, Peter identified that the healing and salvation is only through Jesus Christ (Acts 4:8–12). The Sanhedrin was split but this first hearing ended with a warning. Peter responded that they could not comply with Sanhedrin demands and subsequent trials because they had to obey God and give testimony of what they have seen and heard (Acts 4:19; 5:29–32). The Sanhedrin was furious with the apostles' insubordination and flogged them, but the apostles continued to preach Jesus in obedience to God (Acts 5:33–42). The persecution ramped up killing Stephen and James Zebedee, with Christians beginning to scatter. During his reign as king of Israel (AD 41–44), Herod Agrippa had Peter imprisoned but Peter was miraculously rescued by an angel and set free late in Herod's reign (Acts 12:1–11). Just after the celebration of the founding of Caesarea on March 5, Herod dies in AD 44 eaten by worms (Acts 12:20–23).[95] Peter gave testimony to the divine rescue and then moved

---

93. Justin, *1 Apol.* 26; 56; *2 Apol.* 15; *Dial.* 120.6; Irenaeus, *Haer.* 1.23.1–4; Hippolytus, *Haer.* 4.51.3–14; 6.7–20; 10.12.

94. Clement of Alexandria, *Inst.* 6, cited by Eusebius, *Hist. eccl.* 2.1.3.

95. Josephus, *Ant.* 19.343–50; Eusebius, *Mart. Pal.* 11.30, though it could be a festival instituted by Agrippa to honor Claudius birthday on the previous Aug 5 (Suetonius, *Claud.* 2.1) or an unnamed celebration joined by representatives from Tyre and Sidon.

further afield preaching the gospel as he went (Acts 8:25; 9:32; 10; 1 Cor 9:5; Gal 2:11).

Peter traveled to Joppa and stayed with Simon the tanner, where he saw a vision of animals let down from heaven, like the sheets above the roof draped over the animal skins to slow the drying process, and Peter heard an angel voice encouraging Peter to kill and eat, because such food should not be considered as unclean, an implication for a gentile audience that Jesus had previously developed (Acts 9:43; 10:9–17; Mark 7:19). While Peter was reflecting on the vision, the Spirit commanded Peter to travel with three men at the gate that were looking for him because god-fearing Cornelius had also seen a vision prompting him to send for Peter. When Peter arrived at Cornelius' house, Cornelius tried to worship Peter, but Peter would not permit it.[96] While Jews do not associate with and eat with gentiles, Peter explained that beyond the vision, God had showed him that he should not consider any person unclean (Acts 10:28–29). Peter preached the gospel to Cornelius' household and the Spirit fell upon them and they began to praise God and were baptized. When Peter got back to Jerusalem some circumcised believers took issue with him but he defended that God initiated the acceptance of gentile Christians with the same evidence that had come upon the apostolic band (Acts 11:1–18). In this way, Peter becomes the founder of the gentile mission obeying the command of Christ (Matt 28:19; Luke 24:47; Acts 1:8).[97] To reflect this, Bockmuehl describes Peter like Paul as a pioneer evangelist, missionary, prophet, and healer.[98]

Peter traveled to Antioch, where he followed Barnabus and Saul in encouraging the gentile and Jewish Christians, eating and fellowshiping with them (Acts 11:21–26; Gal 2:11). With the church established before Peter arrived (Acts 11:19–22), Peter is not the founder, nor first bishop in Antioch as Ignatius and Origen claim.[99] Though it is possible that Peter

---

96. Not an anti-imperial dominance metaphor (as claimed by Kochenash, "Cornelius's Obeisance to Peter," 627–40), just that Jewish worship should not be done toward any other than God.

97. Also the Byzantine textual addition of Mark 16:15; Stobel, "Das Aposteldekratt als Folge," 81–104.

98. Bockmuehl, *Simon Peter in Scripture and Memory*, 28.

99. Contra: Ignatius within Origen, *Hom. On St. Ignatius* 5; *Hom. Luc.* 6; Jerome, *Vir. Ill.* 16; Bauer, *Orthodoxy and Heresy in Earliest Christianity*, 117; Cullmann, *Peter*, 231; supported by Parvis, "When Did Peter Become Bishop?," 264; Bockmuehl, *Simon Peter in Scripture and Memory*, 40.

spent seven years of ministry in Antioch as Gregory the Great claimed,[100] so he may have consecrated Ignatius as bishop in Antioch.[101] Ferdinand Baur's claim that Peter ministered to Jews to win them to Christ while Paul ministered to gentiles (Gal 2:7)[102] was overplayed Hegelianism. It is better to view the statement in Gal 2:7 as an earlier assessment before Peter had begun to travel and contemplating Paul's future ministry told him by Jesus being realized in his missionary travels (Acts 9:15, 27–30; 26:17–18). Indeed, Peter had been instrumental in winning the first recorded gentiles, that of Cornelius household to Christ and was in Gal 2 confirming the gentile Christian ministry in Antioch. Likewise, Paul's preaching begins in proclaiming Christ to Jews in synagogue and then expands to reach out to gentiles as well (Acts 13:14–46; 14:1–4; 16:13–15; 17:1–4). So, Peter and Paul have a more unified ministry, trying to bring both Jewish and gentiles to Christ. With most of the church in Antioch being gentile Christian, Peter ate and lived as a gentile to express authentic Christianity among them (Gal 2:12, 14).[103] He did not insist upon circumcision, nor obedience to the law. When some Jewish Christians came from James, he once withdrew to eat kosher with the Jewish Christians and thereby showed his inconsistency of previously fully accepting all believers. At this instance, Paul confronted him concerning his inconsistency, since God and Peter previously had fully accepted the gentile believers (Gal 2:11–21).[104] Peter repented and tried to live consistently thereafter.

At the Jerusalem council (AD 50), a more extreme form of the Jewish Christianity comes to a head by certain Pharisaic Christians claiming that gentile Christians had to become Jews (circumcised and obeying the law) for them to become authentic Christians. Peter stood against this claim by testifying how God accepted Cornelius household as gentiles, "God made no distinction between us and them, cleansing their hearts by faith, now therefore why do you put God to the test by placing upon the neck of the disciples a yoke which neither our fathers nor we have been able to bear? But we believe that we are saved through the grace of the Lord Jesus, in the same way as they are" (Acts 15:7–11). Paul and Barnabas followed with their testimony of similar Spirit-empowering gentile ministry. The church

---

100. Gregory the Great, *Ep.* 7.40; *PL* 77.899.

101. Origen, *Hom. On St. Ignatius* 5; *Hom. Luc.* 6; Jerome, *Vir. Ill.* 16.

102. Baur, *Kritische Untersuchungen*; modernized by Goulder, *St. Paul versus St. Peter*; but defeated by Grappe, *Images de Pierre*; Bockmuehl, *Remembered Peter*.

103. Hengel, *Saint Peter*.

104. Brown, Donfried, and Reumann, *Peter in the New Testament*, 50–52.

leadership pronounced by James, Jesus' brother, that neither circumcision nor the law were required for gentile conversion, while requiring a few proselyte preliminaries to help facilitate a unified church. Luke emphasized that the leadership of the church was of one mind concerning the acceptability of gentile Christians without becoming Jews.[105]

In Corinth, factionalisms developed associated with Peter, Paul, and Apollos (1 Cor 1:12–13; 3:4–6, 22). F. C. Baur developed that this evidenced a factionalism between Peter's Jewish-Christians against Paul's gentile-Christians before a Hegelian synthesis could be arrived at within early Christianity.[106] However, in Paul's Corinthian correspondence there is no evidence that these individuals are themselves at odds with each other, as F. C. Baur claims. The issue in Corinth is not theological difference (such as Jewish-Christianity against budding Marcionism) but hero appreciation prompted by oratory skill (Acts 18:24; 1 Cor 1:12—2:16, with special emphasis on 2:1–5). Apollos' followers are the more prominent foil fragmenting the Christians in Corinth from Paul and Peter. Additionally, Apollos is presented as an ally for whom Paul encourages financial support (Acts 18:24; 19:1; 1 Cor 4:6; 16:12; Titus 3:13). Furthermore for Paul, Peter is not an opponent funding factionalism but an apostolic pattern by which Paul justifies his own behavior, and Luke vindicates Paul in comparisons to this Petrine pattern (1 Cor 9:5; Acts 1–12; cf. Acts 9; 13–28).[107] Instead, Paul's solution to this factionalism is to call the Corinthian church to unity around Christ (1 Cor 1:12–17; 3:1–23), the very thing that Peter also does as well (1 Pet 2; Acts 2–4; 10; 15:7–11).

Peter likely traveled from Antioch on across Asia. If 2 Pet is a second letter to the same region as 1 Pet (2 Pet 3:1; 1 Pet 1:1), Peter includes personal information as "I am reminding you" and includes himself among the "we" who made kingdom salvation and the transfiguration known to his audience (2 Pet 1:12–16). There is also some support for Peter to have traveled to Laodicea,[108] which probably also includes coastal Ephesus to sail to the next destination, maybe Corinth. Additionally, it is likely that Peter traveled to the Roman provinces to which he writes as Hippolytus

105. Brown et al., *Peter in the New Testament*, 50–52; Hanneken, "Moses Has His Interpreters," 686–706; Varma, "Jews and Gentiles Together," 153–74.

106. Baur, "Die Chrisuspartei."

107. Baur's simplistic view is defeated by the complex pictures shown by Grappe, *Images de Pierre*; Bockmuehl, *Remembered Peter*; Doering, "Schwerpunkte und Tendenzen," 203–23.

108. *Pseudo-Clementine Recognitions* 7.25.3; 7.36.1; 9.38; *Homiline* 13.1.1; 13.11.2; Hengel, *Saint Peter*, 125–27.

and Jerome claim,[109] namely, the Roman provinces Pontus, Galatia, Cappadocia, Asia, and Bithynia (1 Pet 1:1). Perhaps Peter traveled through these provinces on a Roman road closer to the Black Sea than Paul, thus traveling through Pontus, Bithynia, and Cappadocia. Perhaps Peter traveled through inland Asia more than Paul, to likely approach coastal Ephesus from Laodicea. Additionally, the fact that Paul discussed Peter in his letter to Galatians likely means that Peter visited some of the cities in this province as well (Gal 1:18—2:21), maybe on north roads between Pontus and Cappadocia, or maybe the Roman road through south Galatia, that Paul traveled, or maybe both (especially if Peter had traveled the route in the order in which he lists the Roman provinces in 1 Pet 1:1).

Peter likely traveled to Corinth because Paul alludes to Peter's travel in a manner that indicates the Corinthians were aware of his travels (1 Cor 1:12; 3:22; 9:5).[110] However, it is unlikely for Peter to have founded the church in Corinth as Dionysius, bishop of Corinth claims (1 Cor 3:10–15, 4:15)[111] for Paul identified that he fathered the Corinthian church by laying the foundation for the Corinthian church and that others (Apollos and likely Peter) were building upon that foundation (1 Cor 3:10–15; 4:15). This identifies that the church in Corinth especially began in the wake of Jews and Christians (such as Aquila and Priscilla) being expelled from Rome during Claudius' reign (AD 44–53, with the favorite date being AD 49; Acts 18:1–11).[112] This means that Peter is likely in Corinth before Paul writes 1 Corinthians in the mid-fifties AD to make his allusions to Peter in 1 Cor 1:12; 3:22; 9:5.

Peter traveled these missionary journeys with his wife and probably also their children (1 Cor 9:5).[113] Clement of Alexandria presents Peter and his wife as an example of blessed Christian marriage, each collaborating on the mission, controlling their feelings even in deeply emotional settings, such as martyrdom.[114] Ignatius and Clement of Alexandria discussed that during Peter's travels, Peter's wife was led to

---

109. See "Hippolytus on the Twelve Apostles," a fragment in Roberts and Donaldson, *Ante-Nicene Christian Library*, 2.2:130; Jerome, *Vir. ill.*; *Ep.* 47.3.

110. Eusebius, *Hist. eccl.* 4.23.1–13.

111. Eusebius, *Hist. eccl.* 2.25.8.

112. Suetonius, *Claudius* 25.4; Cassius Dio, *Hist.* 60.6.6–7; Paulus Orosius, *Hist.* 7.6.15–16.

113. Clement of Alexandria, *Strom.* 3.52.1–2, 4; 3.52.5 = Eusebius, *Hist. eccl.* 3.30.1; *Acts of Peter* 7; *Acts of Philip*; *Pseudo-Clementine Recognitions* 7.25.3; 7.36.1; 9.38; *Homilies* 13.1.1; 13.11.2; Hengel, *Saint Peter*, 125–27.

114. Clement of Alexandria, *Strom.* 3.53.3; 7.11; Hengel, *Saint Peter*, 125–27.

martyrdom, so that Peter encouraged her to resign to her martyrdom and anticipate kingdom.[115]

Peter ministered in Rome, though Papias claims Peter gets there after Paul had gone to Spain, while Dionysius of Corinth claimed that Peter and Paul ministered in Rome together.[116] Peter is in Rome with Silas and Mark, when Paul is absent (for greetings in 1 Pet 5:12–13 to not include Paul). Critics challenge claims for Peter in Rome.[117] However, ministry in Rome is likely but the church in Rome is founded before either Peter or Paul arrive, countering Irenaeus' and Hippolytus' claim that they together founded the church in Rome (Rom 1:10–15; 15:22–29).[118]

Nero crucified Peter upside down in Rome during a persecution of Christians within AD 64–67 window.[119] Peter died in the same persecution that had Paul decapitated by sword.[120]

The tomb under the Vatican claimed for Peter by third-century presbyter Gaius has been evaluated by Markus Bockmuehl and others to "not inspire confidence" and that "it seems right to join the majority of scholars in being cautious about Pope Paul VI claim in 1968 that these are indeed the bones of Peter."[121] The tomb contains part of a skeleton of a sixty-year-old of about five feet five inches, with fragmentary graffiti from the Constantine era claiming "Peter inside." The location of this tomb is where Nero would have had his circus,[122] so at best it might be a possible area where Peter might have died, rather than his resting place.

---

115. Ignatius, *Phil.* 4; Clement of Alexandria, *Strom.* 7.11.

116. Papias in Eusebius, *Hist. eccl.* 2.15.2; 2.25.8 for Dionysius of Corinth; Gregory Thaumaturgus, *Sectional Confession of Faith*, sec. "Elucidation", 47, agrees with Papias.

117. Baur, "Die Chrisuspartei," 137–39.

118. Irenaeus, *Haer.* 3.3.3; Hippolytus in Eusebius, *Hist. eccl.* 3.2.1; Cyprian, *Epis.* 74 in *Corpus Scriptorium Latinorum* 3:799; countered by Lightfoot, *Apostolic Fathers*, 1.1:73, 351–52; von Harnack, *Die Chronologie der altchristlichen Literatur*, 1:244n2; Duchesne, *Histire ancienne de l'Englise*, 55, 61; Hengel, *Saint Peter*, 71–74.

119. Ign. *Tars.* 3; *Apocalypse of Peter* 14.4–6; *Martyrdom Isa.* 4.3; Tertullian, *Scap.* 15; *Apol.* 5; *Praescr.* 36; *Muratorium Canon*, line 37; Lactantius, *Mort.* 2; Eusebius, *Theoph.* 5.31; *Dem. ev.* 3.5.65; *Hist. eccl.* 2.25.5; 3.1.2; *Acts of Pet.* 9.37.8–38.9; Bauckham, "Martyrdom of Peter," 539–95.

120. Tertullian, *Scap.* 15; *Apol.* 5; *Praescr.* 36.

121. Gaius' initial claim quoted by Eusebius, *Hist. eccl.* 2.25.6–7; Bockmuehl, *Simon Peter in Scripture and Memory*, 148–49 interacts with Guarducci, *La tomba di San Pietro* and Hurtado affirms Bockmuehl's conclusions in "Apostle Peter in Protestant Scholarship," 14, as Hurtado also interacts with Snyder, "Survey and 'New' Thesis," and O'Conner, "Peter in Rome."

122. Tacitus, *Ann.* 15.44.4–5.

6

Petrine Epistemology of Testimony, Prophecy as Proclamation, and Evidentialism[1]

PETER IS ONE OF the most significant speakers of the first-century Christian church.[2] Canonically, apart from Acts, Peter has two small epistles where in mid-century he writes from Rome to the northern two-thirds of Turkey concerning salvation and to encourage the churches in their suffering (1 Pet 1:1; 2 Pet 1:1). Additionally, 2 Pet is presented as Peter's farewell letter shortly before he is crucified (2 Pet 1:1, 12–14). The inclusion of Mark along with several chapters in Acts as a record of Peter's sermons adds Peter's testimony of Jesus statements and events, much like Peter's testimony of Jesus' transfiguration in 2 Pet 1:16–19.

Peter used a multitude of words to communicate the idea of knowing (γινώσις, words intensified by ἐπι-, and οἶδὰ). All these words include the field of knowing, understanding, perceiving, acknowledging, and recognizing (1 Pet 1:13; Luke 1:51; Acts 20:3; 28:22; 1 Cor 1:10; 7:25, 40; 13:11; Eph 1:18; Heb 4:12; 1 John 5:20; Rev 17:13, 17).[3] Peter used μνησθῆναι and ἀνεμνήσθη to indicate remembering previous information (2 Pet 3:2; Mark 14:72). Sober diligence with insight and purpose

---

1. Adding Markan descusion to Kennard, *Epistemology and Logic*, 121–27.

2. Peter is principal speaker in first half of Acts; 1 and 2 Pet; some attribute additional texts to Peter: *Gos. Pet.*; *Acts Pet.*; *Acts of Pet. and Twelve Apos.*; *Pseudo-Clem.*; *Apoc. Pet.*; *Coptic Apoc. Pet.*; Lapham, *Peter*.

3. BAG 159–62, 290–91, 558–59; Gilchrist and Wilson, TWOT, 1:366, 2:580; Dunn, *Theology of Paul the Apostle*, 73–74; Goetzmann, NIDNTT, 2:616–20; McDonald, *Christian View of Man*, 24–25.

are described by ἔννοιαν (1 Pet 4:1). Believers are to be of "one mind" or "harmonious" (ὁμόφρονες, 1 Pet 3:8). When a demoniac is made well, he returned to a "sound mind" (σωφρονοῦντα, Mark 5:15).

Peter used οἶδα more broadly than any other word for knowledge. It is used for the recall of facts and events like the ministry and signs of Jesus (Acts 2:22; 3:17; 10:37). This approach is an externalism of a practical realistic non-foundational empiricism similar to Thomas Reid's common sense realism.[4] However, such a common-sense realism underwent a communal transformation with Alvin Plantinga's concept of basic belief as he shifted from an individual basic belief to a communal basic belief.[5] Even more oriental than Plantinga's communal basic belief, Joel Green identified that this knowledge was communal understanding shared by the community, rather than the individualism of modern epistemology.[6] When miracles are involved, such knowledge evidences authority in the context of Lockean supernatural evidence of kingdom (Acts 10:44–47; 11:15; 15:8 with 2:4, 17–21; and 3:11 and 4:8–10 with 3:7–9; Mark 1:25–34, 40–42; 2:4–12; 3:5–15, 22–30; 5; 6:53–56; 7:24–37; 9:14–29).[7] Within this communal knowing, believers can individually provide testimony that one knows that they were not redeemed with perishable things (1 Pet 1:18).[8] Such knowledge extends beyond the cognitive to that of filial knowledge of God and fellow believers as family, and the life change wherein God transforms the believer's experience.[9] Such filial knowledge has been noticed to characterize discipleship by using the family quality of "house" (οἶκος; Mark 3:25; 10:29; 1 Pet 2:5).[10] Stephen Barton says, "The language of kinship functions as a way of expressing fundamental

---

4. Reid, *Thomas Reid*; Abraham, "Epistemology of Jesus," 158–59; Brueggemann, *Pathway of Interpretation*, 115.

5. Plantinga argued for individual basic belief in "Reason and Basic Belief in God," 16–93 and then changed to a communal basic belief in *Warrant and Proper Function* and *Knowledge and Christian Belief*.

6. Green, "Embodying the Gospel," 11–21.

7. Locke, *Concerning Human Understanding* 1.1.15; 2.11.8–9; 2.32.6; 3.3.6–8; "Discourse of Miracles," 9:256–65; "Reasonableness of Christianity"; premodern empiricism is apparent in Lactantius, *Workmanship of God* 9–10; Keener, *Miracles*, 1:35–208; "Miracle Reports," 475–95.

8. Ricoeur, "Hermeneutics of Testimony," cited in Ford, "Paul Ricoeur," 190.

9. Moser, *Elusive God*, 46–47, 98, 113–23; Locke, *Concerning Human Understanding* 1.1.15; 2.11.8–9; 2.32.6; 3.3.6–8; "Discourse of Miracles," 9:256–65; "Reasonableness of Christianity"; Keener, *Miracles*, 1:35–208; "Miracle Reports," 475–95.

10. Best, *Following Jesus*, 226–29 expresses this idea from Mark more tentatively than does the study from Matt by Crosby, *House of Disciples*.

allegiances and commitments and the transfer from one set of allegiances, beliefs and society to another."[11] Jesus considered his primary family to be whoever does the will of his father in heaven, namely the disciple band (Mark 3:33–35; Matt 12:48–50; Luke 8:21).[12] Joel Green developed that such filial knowledge has a practical element consistent with cognition.[13] Peter reminds and commands believers to fully know and thus practice what they already have (2 Pet 1:1–6, 12). Such knowledge is both a blessing that they have already begun to experience and an obligation which they can continue to grow within for the rest of the believer's life.

Peter used the word γινωσκω to indicate knowledge that extends beyond facts to include an assertion of faith. Initiating this knowledge, Peter's statement of the gospel message calls a person to align with Jesus as Lord and Christ (Acts 2:36). Through a *pesher* rabbinic approach, Acts 2 develops that Peter knows Jesus is the Davidic king promised (Acts 2:30 quoting 2 Sam 7:12–13) announced as the anointed one to be king by God (Acts 2:36), and functioning in this exalted Messianic role as illustrated by Christ receiving and giving the Holy Spirit (Acts 2:33).[14] While in this context "Lord" (κύριος) stands for Davidic King and Deity, as a term it was also appropriated by the Caesars (Augustus, Tiberius, Caligula, Nero and Domitian) and the Jewish rulers (Herod the Great, Agrippa I and Agrippa II), thus the statement "Jesus is Christ" challenges their sovereignty.[15] Contrary to these others, Acts 2 demonstrates Peter knows Jesus is the Lord (Davidic king and God). The concept of "Lord" in Acts 2:36 reference is elevated by the quote from Ps 110:1 in Acts 2:34 which replaces the אדֹנִי /

---

11. Barton, *Discipleship and Family*, 32; Philo, *Her.* 276–83; Santos, "New Family of Jesus," 542–601.

12. Similar subsuming of biological family to those aligned with God's plan occurs in early Judaism description of their heros (Philo, *Her.* 276–83; *Moses* 1.150; 2.142; *Virt.* 53–65; *Spec. Laws* 4.70; Josephus, *Ant.* 1.222–25, 234; 5.263–66; Barton, *Discipleship and Family*, 23–47).

13. Green, "Embodying the Gospel," 11–21.

14. Lim, *Pesharim*, 44–53; Bock, *Proclamation from Prophecy and Pattern*; Josephus, *Ant.* 13.171–73, 297; 18.12–15; *War* 2.119, 162–63; 4 Macc 5:16–27; Philo, *Dreams* 1.124–25; *m. Yad.* 4.6–8; *B. Qidd.* 66a; Resurrection: 2 Macc 7.9–14, 22–23; 14.43–46; 1 En. 22; 58.3; 62.14–16; 91.10; 92.2; 104; 108.11–14; *Jub.* 5.10; 10.17; 22.22; L.A.B.; CD 3.11–16, 20–21; 7.5, 9; 13.11; 20.17–20, 25–27; 1QH 11.19–23 [3.18–22]; 19.10–14 [11.7–11]; 1QS 3.7–12; 4.7; 4Q228 frag. 1 1.9; 4Q266, frag. 11; 4Q385 2; 4Q386 1–2; 4QMMT C; 4Q521 2.2.12; 5.2.5–6; 2 Bar [Syriac] 30.1–5; 49–51; 4 Macc 7.19; 16.25; 4 Ezra 7.26–44; *Sib. Or.* 4.180; *T. Benj.* 10.6–8; *T. Levi* 18; *T. Jud.* 24.

15. See Bietenhard, NIDNTT, 2:511; Cullmann, *Christology of the New Testament*, 197–99; Suetonius, *De Vita Caesarum* 13.2; the title was also used to describe gods (1 Cor. 8:5); Deissmann, *Light from the Ancient East*, 352–53.

Adonai as Lord (κύριος) in referring to Christ. However, since in Acts 2:34 κύριος also translates יְהֹוָה /*Yahweh* in Ps 110:1, this repetition of κύριος draws Jesus' divinity within a Jewish monotheism as an essential part of the gospel as well. Such knowledge of God and Christ express allegiance to them as Lord (2 Pet 2:20; 3:18). The one who has the knowledge identifies themselves within the bounds of present salvation benefits.

Much of this knowledge is revealed knowledge through prophecy and promises, expressed by Peter in a *pesher* application to the new context's agenda.[16] God made known to the psalmist the revelational ways of life (Acts 2:28). Prophets (sensitive to the inspiration of the Holy Spirit and themselves investigating thoroughly) sought to know this Christ and the events which they were predicting (1 Pet 1:11).[17] These statements from Scripture (whether law, psalm, prophet, or apostolic testimony or letter) take on the authority of divine prophetic statement.[18] Peter's quoting these statements of revelation fit them into his agenda for knowing Christ.[19] However, there are limited options to properly interpret the meaning of such statements since the revelation process expresses itself in performative statements of promise (2 Pet 1:20).[20] Peter urged his readership to know God through the promises that God has made available (2 Pet 1:2, 4). In such situations, any interpreter such as Peter must embrace the performative meaning that the Spirit revealed if they wish to understand God's revelational communication.

Through such knowledge, Jesus' disciple must resist temptation as Jesus has done (Mark 1:12–13; 14:32–41). A prime epistemic example of Jesus proclaiming the kingdom of God to resist temptation is expressed in the parable of the Sower (or the parable of the soils, since that is the issue on which it focuses; Mark 4:3–20; Matt 13:1–9, 18–23; Luke 8:5–15).[21]

---

16. Schutter, "1 Peter 4.17," 276–84; *Hermeneutic and Composition,* 100–110, 122; Ps 2 is utilized by Peter in Acts 4 similar to *Ps. Sol.* 17.21–46; Marcus, *Way of the Lord,* 59–61, and in 120–22 Marcus develops *pesher* of Ps 118:22 in 1 Pet 2:7 similar to 1QS 8.4; 1QH 6.25–29; 7.8–9; Chilton et al., *Missing Jesus*; Fernadez, "Rabbinic Text," 95–120.

17. These patristics also support the same epistemic concern of the prophets for their era of concern (Ignatius, *Magn.* 8.2; *Barn.* 5.6; *Herm. Sim.* 9.12.1–2; 2 *Clem.* 17.4; Justin Martyr, *1 Apol.* 31–53; 62.4; *Dial.* 56–57; Irenaeus, *Haer.* 4.20.4). Hines, "Peter and the Prophetic Word," 227–41; Hiebert, "Prophetic Foundation," 166.

18. Grindheim, "Biblical Authority," 791–803.

19. Bock, *Proclamation from Prophecy and Pattern*; Elliott, *1 Peter,* 407.

20. Austin, *How to Do Things with Words*.

21. Similar parables are told in: *m. 'Abot* 5.10–15 (especially verse 12 which describes four kinds of hearers: 1) slow to hear and swift to lose, 2) slow to hear and slow

Jesus addressed the multitude and then interpreted the parable later to his disciples, who asked what it meant. Part of the disciple's epistemic gain is that they interact and ask Jesus for more knowledge. This approach of public discourse followed by private explanation is a common Jewish method enabling the disciples to epistemically go further and grow.[22] In the parable, the sower is unidentified. The seed is the message of the kingdom, which should be understood as largely defined by Jesus' previous kingdom teaching. There are some who hear the word of the kingdom but they do not understand it, and the evil one takes the word away.[23] Even though these may contemplate the kingdom message ("in his heart"), the kingdom message is no longer epistemically accessible to them. There are others who hear the word and receive it with joy but because it gained no root in its rocky environment, when persecution came the outcome was stumbling (σκανδαλίζεται), which in Mark's and Jesus' terminology is damnation in everlasting hell (Mark 9:42–49; Matt 11:6; 13:41–42; 18:7–9). There are others caught up in the worry of the world and the deceitfulness or pleasures of riches. The message of the kingdom is not received but gets choked out by these cares so that the message remains "unfruitful" (ἄκαρπος). This imagery of unfruitfulness remains ambiguous in not defining where the person is between those of a clearer life of good or bad fruit, who can clearly be delineated as included or excluded from Jesus' kingdom (Matt 7:17–18). Luke may imply further ambiguity by the description that the fruit "does not bring about maturity" (τελεσφοροῦσιν; Luke 8:14). This ambiguity raises a lack of clarity about whether these will make it to the kingdom or not. The final soil is good in that this man hears the word of the kingdom, understands it and the person himself epitomizes this message so that he (not merely the word) brings forth the abundant fruitfulness,[24] which clearly identifies these people with the kingdom. Jesus concludes the parable with the exhortation for his audience to understand, and thus to join the last

---

to lose, 3) swift to hear and swift to lose, and 4) swift to hear and slow to lose); *Pesikta Rab.* 11.2; ARNa 40.9; Davies and Allison, *Matthew*, 2:386; but *Gos. Thom.* 9 does not add an interpretation like the biblical texts; Justin, *Dial.* 125.1; *1 Clem.* 24.5.

22. This is a similar pattern to that of first-century teacher Johanan ben Zacchai; Daube, "Public Pronouncement," 175–77.

23. Jesus' identification of the birds with Satan (Matt 13:19) comports with Jewish tradition that reflects Azazel manifesting himself as an unclean bird (*Apoc. Abr.* 13; *Jub.* 11.11).

24. Varro, *Rust.* 1.42.2 claims that seed in Syria could yield a hundredfold: *Sib. Or.* 3.263–64; Theophrastus, *Hist. plant.* 8.7.4; Strabo 15.3.11; Pliny, *Nat.* 18.21.94–95.

group of kingdom-responsive people. That role of being a fruitful disciple has been given them by the Father (Mark 4:11). The Lukan and Markan context spins the parable of the soils into the parable of the lamp (Mark 4:21–25; Luke 8:16–18). Oil lamps lit are used to shine light to their environment, not to be under a basket (Matt 5:14–15; Mark 4:21; Luke 8:16; 11:33).[25] Mark used the parable more as a warning that anything secret will become known. This use further pressed the exhortation of the parable of the soils to be careful to listen and apply the kingdom message because whoever possesses the kingdom benefits will have more given to them. In contrast to the one who does not have, even what he thinks he has will be taken away from him.[26] In this way, then, the parable of the Sower comes to function as an apologetic, even a sort of theodicy, explaining the evil of agnosticism and covenant curse that has befallen Israel (Mark 4:12).[27] Those unwilling to recognize Jesus' authority and become disciples are sovereignly excluded by keeping the unresponsive listeners merely entertained in their blindness by Jesus' parables, not prompted to know, repent, and be forgiven (Mark 4:11–12; Luke 8:10; while the fuller quote of Isa 6:9–10 within Matt 13:13–16 is more explicit for sovereign exclusion).[28]

Unfortunately, false teachers, untaught, and unstable twist such knowledge of these statements to their own destruction by interpreting them in ways that do not fit the textually clear performative meaning (2 Pet 3:16–17). So humans have a responsible role in positioning themselves and are thus accountable for the outcome.

Peter even claims to be surer of coming reality of the kingdom than the prophecies provide because he experienced a moment of the kingdom through the experience of Jesus' transfiguration (2 Pet 1:16–19). This transfiguration experience serves as a pragmatic verification of the future coming reality of the kingdom (2 Pet 1:19).[29] Such an approach couples with a Pharisaic authoritative "daughter of a voice" (*bath qol*) for

---

25. The same point is made in *Gos. Thom.* 33b.

26. The same point is made in *4 Ezra* 7.25; *Gos. Thom.* 41; *b. B. Qam.* 92a.

27. Concealment of kingdom to the outsider as blind and deaf (4Q416 2.3.18; 1QS 4.11; 11.8–7; Davies and Allison, *Matthew*, 2:375).

28. Tyson, "Blindness of the Disciples," 261–68; Marcus, "Mark 4:10–12 and Marcan Epistemology," 557–74; Fay, "Introduction to Incomprehension," 65–81; de Campos, "Markan Epistemology," 74–66; Blakley, "Incomprehension or Resistance?"; Johnson, "Error and Epistemological Process."

29. Alston, *Perceiving God*, 14–35; Pierce, *Collected Papers*, vol. 5, para. 9; "Fixation of Belief," 1–15; "How to Make Our Ideas Clear," 286–302.

Peter to know and provide testimony for the coming future kingdom he has already begun to experience (2 Pet 1:17).³⁰ These epistemic verifications reassure Peter that he was not following myth (μύθοις) as Bultmann claimed.³¹ Rather Peter claims to be giving eyewitness testimony: seeing and hearing the evidence directly (2 Pet 1:16, 18).³² Similar eyewitness claims provided greater credibility in Greco-Roman writings.³³ Not just in Peter's writing but also in Peter's statement of the gospel orally communicated eyewitness claims strongly testify to historical events (Acts 2:14–39; 3:12–26; 4:8–12; 10:34–43).

One repeated Lockian evidential support for the reliability of Jesus as Lord is that Peter and others saw that God raised Jesus from the dead (Acts 2:31–32; 3:15; 10:41–42; 1 Pet 1:3–4, 3:18).³⁴ In such miraculous accounts, an epistemic dualism is implied by having communal and eyewitness experience confirm Peter's perception, when some of his audience disagrees with Peter's understanding. Furthermore, Peter's testimony helps to support³⁵ that Jesus is the Lord that his audience will need to respond to when Christ comes in his kingdom.

With the emphasis of the one who knows being identified as the one who has faith within salvation (2 Pet 1:1–3, 5–6), Peter develops that the one without knowledge is the one who does not have faith and salvation. The person is ignorant who has not initially come to a salvation experience with Christ (1 Pet 1:14, ἀγνοίᾳ). For example, the killing of Christ by the Jewish leaders was a sin of ignorance (Acts 3:17). Further, the governmental leaders who persecuted believers demonstrate that they were

---

30. B. 'Abot 6.2; B. Bat. 73b, 85b; Mak. 23b; 'Erub. 54b; Šabb. 33b; 88a; Soṭah 33a; p. Soṭah 7.5, sec. 5; Pesiq. Rab Kah. 15.5; Lev. Rab. 19.5–6; Deut. Rab. 11.10; Lam. Rab. Proem 2, 23; Lam. Rab. 1.16 sec. 50; Ruth Rab. 6.4; Qoh. Rab. 7.12, sec. 1; Pesq. Rab Kah. 11.16.

31. Bultmann, *Jesus Christ and Mythology*, 18, 36, 39; Bultmann et al., *Kerygma and Myth*; Miegge, *Gospel and Myth*, 8, 91.

32. Paul also rejects "myths" as a strategy for faith (1 Tim 1:4); Papias recounted in Eusebius, *Hist. eccl.* 5.20.4–7; Irenaeus, *Letter to Florinus*; Bauckham, *Jesus and the Eyewitnesses*, 295; Elliott, *1 Peter*, 309–10.

33. Seneca, *Controversiae*, preface 3–4; Clement of Alexandria, *Strom.* 7.106.4; Eusebius, *Hist. eccl.* 2.1.4; Halbwachs, *Les cadres sociaux de la mémoire*; Kelber, "Case of the Gospels," 65; Dunn, *Jesus Remembered*, 239–43; Ricoeur, *Memory, History, Forgetting*; Bauckham, *Jesus and the Eyewitnesses*, 295–96, 310–57.

34. Locke, *Concerning Human Understanding* 1.1.15; 2.11.8–9; 2.32.6; 3.3.6–8; "Discourse of Miracles," 9:256–65; "Reasonableness of Christianity"; Keener, *Miracles*, 1:35–208; "Miracle Reports," 475–95.

35. Ricoeur, "Hermeneutics of Testimony," cited in Ford, "Paul Ricoeur," 190.

ignorant foolish men (1 Pet 2:15). However, they are culpable in their ignorance and destined for condemnation by God.

However, there is another form of ignorant life which has come to know (ἐπεγνωκέναι) the way of righteousness and after experiencing (ἐπιγνοῦσιν) this way with Christ, the false teacher rejects it and departs to apostasy (2 Pet 2:21). This rejection of knowledge has plunged these apostates into a situation where they act without knowledge (2 Pet 2:12, ἀγνοοῦσιν). These ignorant apostates stand justly condemned by God in their rejection of Christ. This point spotlights the deadly ramifications of denying Christ that Peter had briefly experienced (2 Pet 2:2; Matt 26:69–75). That is, when Peter claimed to not know Jesus, he was apostatizing and departing from the sphere of knowledge which surround salvation (Matt 26:70, 72, 74; Mark 14:68, 71; Luke 22:34, 57, 60). However, Peter returned to openly proclaim Christ. Those who do not return continue in their denial and ignorance. God caused these deniers of Christ to be forgetful concerning these things (2 Pet 1:9, λήθην λαβών where λαβών means received from another in Peter's use 1 Pet 4:10; 2 Pet 1:17; Acts 1:20, 25; 2:33, 38; 10:43, 47). These deficient ones receive forgetfulness from God which renders them doubly blind (2 Pet 1:9). Such individuals are bound to remain in their divinely imposed ignorance. God then condemns them in their ignorance (2 Pet 2:1, 4–9).

Peter and his readers know that their redemption by Christ was through Jesus' valued life to bring about a life transformation from a life of futility to that of a meaningful life of resurrection hope (1 Pet 1:3–4, 18). As such Christ's atonement grounds a kingdom virtue ethic that surrounds the process of knowing.[36] This virtue ethic incorporates faith given (λαχοῦσιν) by God and Christ (2 Pet 1:1)[37] which supplies a divinely fostered basic belief of filial loyalty to God and Christ.[38] This epistemic faith is supplemented with knowledge grounded by God's promises (2 Pet 1:2–4). Together these virtues join other kingdom virtues, such as diligence, moral excellence, self-control, perseverance, godliness, brotherly kindness, and love choosing to benefit others (2 Pet 1:5–7). So, if a

---

36. Other virtue lists with faith, knowledge and virtue: Gal 5:22; Phil 4:8; 1 Cor 8:7; 2 Cor 6:6; 8:7; 1 Tim 4:12; 6:11; 2 Tim 2:22; 3:10; Titus 2:2; Rev 2:19; *1 Clem.* 1.2; 62.2; 64.1; *2 Clem.* 10.1; *Herm. Vis.* 3.8.7; *Herm. Mand.* 1.2; 6.1.1; 6.2.3; 8.9; 12.3.1; *Herm. Sim.* 6.1.4; 6.2.3; 8.10.3; 9.15.2; *Act. Ver.* 2; *Barn.* 2.2–3; *Acts John* 29; *Acts Paul and Thecla* 17; Wood, *Epistemology*; Roberts and Wood, *Intellectual Virtues*.

37. After the pattern Peter uses in Acts 1:17; BAG, 463.

38. Plantinga, *Knowledge and Christian Belief*, 57–79; Moser, *Elusive God*, 46–47, 98, 113–23.

believer wishes to pragmatically reassure herself that God has elected her unto kingdom then she needs to cultivate these virtues in Christ (2 Pet 1:10–11).[39] Such a passionate commitment in a virtue epistemology and narrow way salvation is reassured that it will never stumble but will be abundantly supplied in kingdom.

Cultivating these virtues in the midst of the crucible of suffering and difficulty provides common sense evidence of God's authentic election of these believers as possessing authentic faith within the true knowledge of Christ (1 Pet 1:7; 2 Pet 1:8, 10).[40] It is as though gold is being refined in a crucible over a hot fire, and the refiner scrapes the dross away leaving a purer "tested faith" coming through the heat of suffering and persecution. Such a refining process fosters an ever-greater total commitment and love for Christ (1 Pet 1:7–8).[41] Such a matrix and growth of these virtues demonstrates that the believer will be eschatologically saved into kingdom and that they are in good standing on the exodus way toward kingdom (1 Pet 1:7; 2 Pet 1:11).[42] Likewise, vices demonstrate that the rebellious denier is damned (2 Pet 1:9; 2:1–17).[43]

Consistency of life reflecting a commitment to Christ as Lord provides the best apologetic to others of authentic knowledge and faith in Christ (1 Pet 3:15–16). Maintaining a consistent good conscience of life is the best positioning for one's life to convince others that one's faith and knowledge of Christ is authentic. Though the conscience is a person's fallible personal assessment of herself, in a new covenant relationship the conscience can be good affirming the believer in proper helpful choices and acts. This good conscience is maintained by doing practical good deeds (1 Pet 2:12, 15, 18, 21–22; 3:1, 4, 13, 16). With some others wooed and won by good deeds (1 Pet 2:12, 15; 3:1), an apologetic door is open to explain the Christian hope with gentleness and reverence (1 Pet 3:15).

---

39. Peirce, *Collected Papers*, vol. 5, para. 9; "Fixation of Belief," 1–15; "How to Make Our Ideas Clear," 286–302.

40. Wis 3.4–6; Sir 2.1–9; Seneca, *Prov.* 5.10; Elliott, *1 Peter*, 340–41; Reid, *Thomas Reid*; Abraham, "Epistemology of Jesus," 158–59; Brueggemann, *Pathway of Interpretation*, 115.

41. Kierkegaard, *Fear and Trembling*, 40–41; Adams, "Problem of Total Devotion," 94; Nygren, *Agape and Eros*, 216; Wainwright, "Obedience and Responsibility," 68.

42. Virtues identify authentic belonging: Wood, *Epistemology*; Roberts and Wood, *Intellectual Virtues*; Westphal, "Taking St. Paul Seriously," 201, like Judaism (Deut 6:4–9; Wis 12–15; 1QS 3–4) and Stoicism (Seneca, *Ep.* 20.1).

43. Virtue lists provide vice lists as contrast heading to the opposite outcome, like Judaism (Deut 6:4–9; Wis 12–15; 1QS 3–4) and Stoicism (Seneca, *Ep.* 20.1).

When one adds the Gospel of Mark to this Petrine epistemology, testimony of a narrative performs the function of retelling a story.[44] The Gospels develop Jesus in a narrative context that communicates character and displays his epistemology is consistent with the previous teachings.[45] As such Jesus becomes a moral exemplar for disciples to imitate consistent with Jesus' teachings.[46] However, Jesus does not present this narrative, the Gospel authors do, so historical studies frame an account drawing on eyewitness testimony and the weaving together credible testimony from sources. The Gospelers, such as the Gospel of Mark and Peter's sermons, attempted to recover and communicate what can be historically known of Jesus, which is especially appropriate in light of the biblical claims for historicity (Luke 1:1–4; Acts 1:1; 2 Pet 1:16–17; 1 John 1:1). They show awareness of specific events that further evidence an empirical commitment to historical precision.

There was an oral phase of Peter's testimony and others repeating Peter's sermons which was seen as more authoritative than written texts. Perhaps recognizing that the disciples were called to be witnesses (Luke 24:48; Acts 1:8, μάρτυρες). Such a role of a witness is one of memory and testimony from personal experience. As such, the subject matter to which a witness testifies is not likely to be submitted to empirical investigation because the events and statement of views occurred previously to the testimony (Matt 8:4; 18:16).[47] However, witnesses are included in the testimony, so that motivated individuals could ask the witnesses for their corroborating testimony. For example, in a Hebrew trial setting multiple witnesses were involved to strengthen credibility (Deut 17:6; 19:15). If the witnesses prove to be contradicted credibly then they were considered a false witness and could suffer the same judgment that they were trying to obtain for the one he accused (Deut 5:20; 19:16–18). In

---

44. Grice, "Meaning," 377–88; "Utterer's Meaning and Intentions," 147–77; "Utterer's Meaning, Sentence-Meaning," 54–70; Austin, *How to Do Things with Words*; Ricoeur, *Oneself as Another*, 44; Kennard, *Relationship Between Epistemology*, 56, 62–65; *Critical Realist's Theological Method*, 232.

45. Ricoeur, *Oneself as Another*, 113, 119, 140; Johnson, "Jesus of the Gospels," 70–71; a similar role is urged upon any teacher by Seneca, *Moral Ep.* 20.1.

46. Johnson, "Jesus of the Gospels," 68–69; a similar role is provided by the father in Pseudo-Isocrates, *Demonicus* and the teacher in Lucian of Samosata, *Demonax* and *Nigrinus*.

47. Aristotle, *Rhet.* 1.15; Plato, *Leg.* 12; Josephus, *Ant.* 6.66; 1QS 5.24—26.1; Philo, *Spec. Laws* 4.30, 41–44, 59–61; *Jos.* 242; *m. Mak.* 1.6; *m. Rosh Hash.* 1.8; *Sifre* on Deut 19:19; *Šeb.* 30a; *Gem. Mak.* 5B; Trites, *New Testament Concept of Witness*.

Jewish, Greek, and Roman legal systems, a witness needed to be an adult free male Roman citizen with honorable reputation and not operating for personal gain.[48] Such a witness would make appropriate comments in court as eyewitness testimony he had actually experienced.[49] With legal imagery encouraging the credibility of the role of a witness, Papias found the collective memory of Christian eyewitness testimony to be more valuable than the written texts being produced for as long as available eyewitnesses testified about Jesus' ministry and the early church.

> I shall not hesitate also to put into properly ordered form for you everything I learned carefully in the past from the elders and noted down well, for the truth of which I vouch. For unlike most people I did not enjoy those who have a great deal to say, but those who teach the truth. Nor did I enjoy those who recall someone else's commandments, but those who remember the commandments given by the Lord to the faith and proceeding from the truth itself. And if by chance anyone who had been in attendance on the elders should come my way, I inquired about the words of the elders—[that is] what [according to the elders] Andrew or Peter said, or Philip, or Thomas or James, or John or Matthew or any other of the Lord's disciples, and whatever Ariston and the elder John, the Lord's disciples were saying. For I did not think that information from books would profit me as much as information from a living and surviving voice.[50]

In the second century both Irenaeus and Papias recount that their early memories of the eyewitness testimony took great prominence and were in full accord with the written texts of Scripture.[51] Similar claims for accurate vivid early memories framing later perception were made by Seneca the elder.[52] When such testimony occurred in Christian contexts a corporate memory of tradition could be specifically identified and the

---

48. Pindar *Ol.* 1.54; Plato, *Apol.* 31c; Gorgias, 27–31, 41E–5E; Demosthenes 58.4; Plutarch, *de Amicorum Multitudine* 2.2.93e; TDNT 4:479.

49. Plato, *Symp.* 179b; Heraclitus, *All.* 34; Soph. *Ant.* 515.

50. Eusebius, *Hist. eccl.* 3.39.3–4; Dewey develops an argument from Rom 10 that the written *torah* supported the authoritative and transformative oral gospel testimony ("Re-Hearing of Romans 10:1–15," 109–27); Bauckham, *Jesus and the Eyewitnesses*, 293–94; Kelber, "Generative Force of Memory," 15–22.

51. Papias recounted in Eusebius, *Hist. eccl.* 5.20.4–7; Irenaeus, *Ep. Florinus*; Bauckham, *Jesus and the Eyewitnesses*, 295.

52. Seneca, *Controversiae*, preface 3–4; Bauckham, *Jesus and the Eyewitnesses*, 295–96; Mackay, *Signs of Orality*; Horsley et al., *Performing the Gospel*; Cooper, *Politics of Orality*; Horsley, *Oral Performance*.

others of the group would provide a resilience to reinforce the accuracy of their corporate memory.[53] Such a pattern mirrors the corporate memory of rabbinic Judaism that began to establish written accounts of their oral discussions beginning around AD 200 with the *Mishnah* and then the two corroborating written accounts of the *Talmud* later around AD 450 and AD 600. Such Jewish oral tradition and written oral tradition shows very little shift of account except the addition of more recent rabbinic voices.[54] Also in Judaism there was liturgical retelling of narrative in *rabbah* texts composed during the second to fourth centuries, which resiliently retell the biblical narratives for liturgical purposes. The resilience and consistency in the agreement of these written accounts of oral *Torah* or narrative re-telling provide a pattern for how local Jewish-Christian corporate eyewitness memory could be corporately preserved into written texts as well.

As the eyewitnesses began to die off in the second half of the first century, the written testimony took a more prominent role. The eyewitnesses had lived consistently recounting the specifics that they had included in their written Gospels so that their written Gospels gained in prominence as the living eyewitnesses were no longer accessible in the second century. The pattern of authority is somewhat reminiscent of the prosecutions of corrupt politicians by Marcus Cicero. The repeated court speeches Cicero laid down a noble consistency as a witness and a prosecutor, such that when these trial speeches were written into book length critiques of corrupt politicians, his written testimony took on the same weight even out of court. Corrupt politicians such as Sicily governor Gaius Verres fled into

---

53. Examples of such claims include: Clement of Alexandria, *Strom.* 7.106.4; Eusebius, *Hist. eccl.* 2.1.4; similar claims were made at Qumran (1QS 6.6–8) and by gnostic 2 *Apoc. of James* 36.15–25; Halbwachs, *Les cadres sociaux de la mémoire*, translated as *On Collective Memory*; Assmann, *Das kulturelle Gedächtnis*; Kelber, "Case of the Gospels," 65; "Generative Force of Memory"; Dunn, *Jesus Remembered*, 239–43; "Q as Oral Tradition," 45–69; Hengel, "Eye-Witness Memory," 70–96, esp. 78 and 80; Ricoeur, *Memory, History, Forgetting*; "Toward a Hermeneutic," 73–118; Bauckham, *Jesus and the Eyewitnesses*, 296, 310–57; "Gospel of John," 659; Silberman, *Orality, Aurality and Biblical Narrative*; Dewey, *Orality and Textuality*; Draper, *Orality, Literacy, and Colonialism*; Kirk, "Social and Cultural Memory"; Thatcher, "Why John Wrote a Gospel," 14–15, 82–85; Thatcher, *Jesus, the Voice, and the Text*; Kelber and Byrsog, *Jesus in Memory*.

54. Gerhardsson, *Gospel Tradition*; *Memory and Manuscript*; Bailey, "Informal Controlled Oral Tradition," 34–54; "Middle Eastern Oral Tradition," 363–67; Boomershine, "Jesus of Nazareth," 7–11, 16–17; Jaffee, "Oral-Cultural Context," 27–73; Dunn, *Jesus Remembered*, 197–254; Bauckham, *Jesus and the Eyewitnesses*; Walton and Sandy, *Lost World of Scripture*, 97–101, 105–8, 110, 152–66.

exile when the literate population recognized from Cicero's written text the authority of Cicero's charges against Verres' corruption.[55]

The biblical Gospels were known products which the early patristics recognized were from specific people. For example, Luke was understood to write to a patron who knew who he was even though we must reconstruct that Luke is the author by noticing the book of Acts, written by the same individual, has "we" sections when Luke is with Paul (Acts 16:10–17; 20:5—21:18; 27:1—28:16; Col 4:14, "beloved physician"; Phlm 24; 2 Tim 4:11) and the abundant medical terms (Acts 1:3; 3:7; 9:18, 33; 13:11; 28:1–10). In fact, the normal patron arrangement would probably have had Theophilus providing the materials for Luke to compose the accounts in the first place. However, a more extensive record of the Gospel authors is provided within source material section from patristic testimony which recognized who wrote which witness and gave them credit for this writing in their own letters. This patristic witness agrees who wrote which Gospel, so the Gospels are not anonymous, but the patristics identified that the Gospels were composed by known authors.[56]

Patristics recognize that each presentation of Jesus shows unique authorial coloring and strategic vision of what the narrative author tried to portray. For example, in broad brushstrokes the Gospel produced by Matthew is written by the early sixties AD for a Jewish audience, strongly affirming the Messiah as a faithful teacher of the Mosaic law through a new covenant perspective, and for at least some time limiting the disciple's ministry to that of Israel.[57] Matthew as an eyewitness tells of Jesus calling him to conversion and discipleship (Matt 9:9–10; 10:3). The Gospels produced by Luke and Mark are identified by patristics as written by the mid-sixties AD for a gentile audience.[58] Tradition has it that Mark reflects Peter's gospel to Italy, and Luke reflects Paul's gospel to Achaia, and that John wrote last of all from Ephesus.[59] By fusing the sermons together, Mark records an authoritative Christ who heals all in need. Even though

---

55. Cicero, *Verr.*

56. Bauckham, *Jesus and the Eyewitnesses*, 300–305.

57. Irenaeus, *Haer.* 3.1.1–2; Ignatius, *Smyrn* 1.1.1–2; John Chrysostom, *Hom. Matt.* 1.7.

58. Mark: Justin, *Dial.* 106; Eusebius, *Anti-Marcionite Prologue*; *Hist. eccl.* 2.15.1–2; 3.39.14–15; 6.14.5–7; John Chrysostom, *Hom. Matt.* 1.7; Luke: Justin, *Dial.* 103.19; Tertullian, *Praescr.* 4.2.1; 4.5.3; Acts 28:30–31 with 24:27 occurring in AD 59 or AD 60; 1 Tim 5:17 quoting Luke 10:7.

59. Eusebius, *Hist. eccl.* 6.14.6–7; Irenaeus, *Haer.* 3.1.1; Origen, *Frag. En. com. in Mt.* 1.1–20; Gregory of Nazianzus, *Carmida dogmatica* 1.12.6–9.

Mark reflects Peter's testimony, it may also reflect a unique eyewitness account of naked Mark fleeing into the night when Jesus is captured (Mark 14:51–52). Luke-Acts show the extension of Christianity to gentiles and the law-free resolution for gentiles at the Jerusalem council. Such an approach of transitioning from Jesus' Jewish ministry to Peter pioneering gentile ministry and then Paul regularly proclaiming gospel to gentiles has been termed a salvation history approach, which each Gospel contributes toward.[60] Luke also especially encourages the poor and women as having significant inclusion as a part of the audience to which their voice is especially sensitive. All the Gospels contain ample miracles. However, Mark's primary focus on Jesus' miracles meeting real needs presents an authoritative Jesus in all contexts. While the other Gospels include many of the same miracles, their inclusion of sermonic material adds distinctive character to their voice. For example, Matthew includes a series of long sermons which lay out Jesus' kingdom agenda for his disciples. Luke contains much of the same sermonic material presented on alternative occasions and often in Jesus' response to questions. As such, Luke presents a more interactive and responsive Jesus when compared to that of the other Synoptics. The Gospel produced by John retains similar eyewitness interactivity in those conversations which Jesus has with individuals and groups. Additionally, John is focused on Jesus' Judean ministry in contrast to the Synoptics' focus on the Galilean ministry, thus reserving Jerusalem to set up Jesus' martyrdom.

Classical historical writing often includes the author in third or first person as the author claims to be eyewitness to part of the story (Luke 1:2; Mark 1:21; 2 Pet 1:16; "we" Acts 16:10–17; 20:5—21:18; 27:1—28:16; claims to be with Jesus from the beginning of Jesus' ministry [John 15:26–27; Acts 1:21–22]).[61] Such a context of eyewitness is dependent upon the memory of those who give testimony to these events (1 Cor 11:25).[62]

60. Keener, *Acts*, 1:437–41; Conzelmann, *Theology of St. Luke*, 137–206; Noland, "Salvation-History and Eschatology," 63–82; Stegman, "'Spirit of Wisdom and Understanding,'" 90–91, 94.

61. Support the claim for eyewitness account: Eusebius, *Hist. eccl.* 3.39.3–4; 5.20.6; Irenaeus, *Haer.* 3.1.2; Byrskog, *Story as History-History as Story*; Bauckham, *Jesus and the Eyewitnesses*; standard "eyewitness from the beginning" phrase for eyewitness: Josephus, *C. Ap.* 1.55; *Vita* 366; Polybius 3.4.3; Standard third-person pattern: Thucydides, 1.1.1; 2.70.4; 4.104.4; Xenophon, *Anab.* 1.8.15; *Cyr.* 2.2, 10; 3.3.59; 4.5; 6.16, 17; 7.1; 8.1.40; 8.2; 8.8.2, 27; *Symp.* 1.1; Plutarch, *Aem.* 1.5–8; *Alex.* 4.3–4; 69.8; *Cim.* 1.8; *Them.* 32.6; *Sull.* 34.4; Lucian, *Hist. Conscr.* 47; 1 and 2 Macc; Philo, *Moses*; *Abraham*; *Flaccus*; Josephus, *Ant.*; *J. W.*; *Ag. Ap.* 1.45–47 Ps-Philo.

62. Eusebius, *Hist. eccl.* 3.39.14–15 consistent to Socrates' comment in *Memorabilia*

Herodotus and Thucydides function as standards of historiography in their day so they and others will be compared to authenticate high historiography and style of the Lukan material, and by parallel testimony of the Gospel of Mark.[63] In each, the author selects historical source material and writes with historical sensitivity[64] (Luke 1:1–2; Acts 16:10) for particular purposes to tell the biography emphasizing outstanding character features of the hero in view. Mark's or Luke's approach gathers empirical observations from a communal application and testimony of Thomas Reid's or Alvin Plantinga's empiricism rather than Reid's individual common sense realism,[65] Mark presents his perspective similarly to this accurate chronological historical writing so that his readership would have the exact truth of Jesus' and the apostles' deeds and teaching.

Such corroborated historical writing also stands against the Bultmannian hermeneutic that considered that those accounts were substantially constructed from Hellenistic mythology.[66] Greco-Roman historical narrative did not permit the use of mythology.[67] Furthermore, the biblical authors specifically rejected the use of mythology in narrative accounts (1 Tim 1:4; 2 Pet 1:16). With both Christian and Greco-Roman canons of historical writing rejecting a place for mythology, it is better to see Mark's accounts and Luke's record of Peter's sermons as historically accurate accounts.

Narrative asides and summaries were utilized to provide interpretive guidance among the narrator's account (Mark 1:1, 15; 4:11; Acts 2:47;

1.3.1.

63. Theon, *Prog.* 66 cites Herodotus, 1.31; 5.71 and Thucydides, 1.126; 2.68 as best examples of "factual" narratives. They are also often quoted in *progymnasmata* and rhetorical handbooks (Theon, *Prog.* 84–85; 91–92; 118–19; Ps.-Herm., *Prog.* 4, 22; John of Sardis, *Prog.* 17; Quintilian, *Inst.* 10.1.31–34; Lucian, *Hist. Conscr.* 5, 15, 18–19, 26, 38–39, 42, 54, 57; Gibson, "Learning Greek History," 103–29, esp. 117; Myers, *Characterizing Jesus*, 31).

64. Josephus, *Ant.* 20.156–57; *C. Ap.* 1.49–50; Aristotle, *Poetics* 9.2–3, 1451b; Tacitus, *Ann.* 4.53; 5.9; Silius Italicus, *Punica* 9.66–177; Diodorus Sicily, *Hist.* 21.17.1; Dionysius of Halicarnassus, *De Veterum Censura* 1.1.2–4; 1.2.1; 1.4.2; 5.

65. Reid, *Thomas Reid*; Kirk and Thatcher, "Jesus Tradition as Social Memory," 28; Abraham, "Epistemology of Jesus," 158–59; Brueggemann, *Pathway of Interpretation*, 115; Lackey and Sosa, *Epistemology of Testimony*; Plantinga, *Warrant and Proper Function* and *Knowledge and Christian Belief*.

66. Bultmann, *Jesus Christ and Mythology*, 18, 36, 39; Bultmann et al., *Kerygma and Myth*; Miegge, *Gospel and Myth*, 8, 91; MacDonald, "Synoptic Problem and Literary Mimesis" (which is too slight a parallel to Euripides' *Hercules Furens*), 509–21.

67. Dionysius, *Thucydides*, 45–47.

6:7; 9:31; 12:24; 16:5; 19:20; 28:31).[68] Such material helps to organize the thrust of the narrative and to show important overarching concerns. These summaries by Mark and Luke emphasize salvation history and the continued development of the church into new regions. Additionally, repeated aspects bring a certain degree of emphasis by the author to show virtues like unity and the voluntary socialism that generously met all needs within the community (Acts 2:42–47; 4:32–37; 5:42—6:7). Furthermore, divine providence was often important in developing the narrative direction of historical texts[69] (Acts 2:23; 4:24–30; 6:7). One expression of divine involvement was a supernatural element of miracle in the account that would also play a corroborative role for the message especially while eyewitnesses remained alive[70] (Luke 8:49—9:9; John 11:43–47; 1 Cor 15:5–7). As such, Greco-Roman historical accounts utilized supernatural miracles as an apologetic role demonstrating the hero's superiority[71] (Luke 20:9–47).

At times biographic works were also referred to as "good news" or "gospel." For example, the *Priene Inscription* 2.81–82 used the word "good news" (εὐαγγελίου) twice identifying a narrative describing Augustus life up until the time when he began to rule as Caesar. The Gospel of Mark utilized the term in the same biographical manner (Mark 1:1), which in the context identifies the good news of the narrative of Jesus Christ and his kingdom message (Mark 1:14–15; 8:35; 13:10; 14:9; 16:15; Matt 4:23; 9:35) which is repeatedly proclaimed by the apostles (Matt 24:14; 26:13; Mark 16:15).

Often biography intentionally has virtues for the reader to imitate[72] (Luke 6:20–23; Acts 4:32–37). For example, Quintilian folds qualities of

68. Irenaeus, *Haer.* 3.1.1; 3.14.1; Eusebius, *Hist. eccl.* 3.4.7; Rood, "Thucydides," 123; Sheeley, *Narrative Asides in Luke-Acts*, 40–96.

69. Diodorus Sicily, *Hist.* 1.1.3.

70. Josephus, *Life* 359–66; *Ag. Ap.* 1.50.

71. Josephus, *Ant.*; Aristotle, *Rhet.* 1.9.39; Theon, *Prog.* 108–9; Ps. Herm., *Prog.* 12; Aphthonius, *Prog.* 17R; Nicolaus, *Prog.* 42–47; Quintilian, *Inst.* 5.10.72–73; 11.22–26; *Rhetorica ad Herennium* 2.14.21–22; 2.30.49; Cicero, *Top.* 23.68–71; *Part. or.* 55; Aristotle, *Rhet.* 1.9.38–41.

72. Philo, *Moses* 1.158; Josephus, *War* 1.4-8, 13–16; *Ant.* 1.1–2; Plutarch, *Aem.* 1.1, 5; Tacitus, *Agr.* 1; Dionysius, *Ant. rom.* 8.56.1; Kurz, "Narrative Models for Imitation," 171–89; Fiore, *Function of Personal Example*, esp. chapter 3, "Example in Rhetorical Theory, Education, and Literature," 26–44; de Boer, *Imitation of Paul*; Crouzel, "L'imitation et la 'suite,'" 7–41, esp. 7–30; Cothenet, "Imitation du Christ," 7:1536–1601; Gutierrez, *La Paternité*; Pate and Kennard, *Deliverance Now and Not Yet*, 369–72; Trompf, *Idea of Historical Recurrence*, 97–101; Talbert makes from "Biographies of Philosophers and Rulers," 1643; Fornara, *Nature of History in Ancient Greece and Rome*, 104–20.

the person in the narrative to be illustrated by the person's works[73] (Luke 1:1; Acts 1:1). Often the ancestry and origins indicate who the person will be like.[74] For example, Jesus is predicted to be the Messiah to bring in the new exodus announced by God's prophet John the Baptist (Mark 1:1–4). Jesus exemplifies the virtues of the narrow way unto kingdom that Jesus' sermons call his disciples to embrace.

Jesus' statements in the Gospels and the sermons in the book of Acts are all summaries. Each sermon can be read in three to fifteen minutes, and likely the speaker talked longer than that. So, the important feature of classical historical accounts recording speeches was to provide teaching consistent with the narrative hero's character and speech patterns.[75] Partly this is because Aristotle argued that ancient witnesses are known broadly by many humans, so that uncharacteristic speech would render accounts less credible.[76] Such speeches are quite significant within the Gospels because Jesus occupies a rabbinic role in developing a tradition for Christians.

Any good itinerant speaker will say the same content in different locations. Thus, the similarity of Jesus' Sermon on the Mount (Matt 5–7) with his Sermon on the Plain (Luke 6) is easily understandable without forcing them onto the same location. So likely the author will include that sermonic material only once in a representative form to cover for the repetitive sermons. Whereas the book of Acts has the stated purpose of recording salvation history and thus repeated telling of the gospel message. If the same speaker is recorded to be speaking the same gospel at different locations in the same written account, as Peter does, then those similar sermons subsequently are shortened. However, the contextual engagement and the characteristic language of Peter are retained throughout the sermons.

The Lukan material in Acts shows some of the consistent language of Peter's writing[77] even though the gospel speeches in Acts accomplish a different purpose than their written epistles attempt. For example, Kistemaker finds convoluted Greek in Peter's sermons (Acts 3:16; 10:36–37) like 1 Pet 4:11 and 2 Pet 3:5–6.[78] Additionally, characteristic phrases are

73. Quintilian, *Inst.* 3.7.10–22; 5.10.24–31.

74. Quintilian, *Inst.* 3.7.12; Pseudo-Hermogenes, *Prog.* 15–17.

75. *Rhetorica ad Herennium* 4.52.65; Quintilian, *Inst.* 3.8.51; Thucydides, 1.22.1; Dionysius of Halicarnassus, *Rom. ant.* 7.66.2–3; 11.1.3–4.

76. Aristotle, *Rhet.* 1.15.13, 15.

77. Peter's consistency: Selwyn, *1 Peter*, 33–36; Williams, *Acts*, 11.

78. Kistemaker, *Acts*, 9–11.

utilized by Peter, such as "God's foreknowledge" (Acts 2:23; 1 Pet 1:2, 20) and "judge of the living and the dead" (Acts 10:42; 1 Pet 4:5).

In the biblical presentation of narrative *haggadah* Jesus contributes in at least three ways. First, Jesus re-envisions the communal knowledge of the Passover enactment among community commemorating God's redemption of Israel into the meal which initiates the new covenant with his disciples so that they will continue to communally re-enact the new covenant in *eucharist*.[79] The performance is part of its meaning in the context in which such practice has meaning. As such, eucharist becomes performative language and practice in initiating and renewing the disciples place within the new covenant.[80] Jesus final Passover and upper room discourse provides a level of relationship between Jesus and the disciples that indicates the Master is allowing his disciples to be intimately included (Matt 26:20–29; Mark 14:17–31; Luke 22:14–34; John 13:1—16:33; 1 Cor 11:23–26). Jesus told his disciples that he earnestly desired to eat this Passover with his disciples. While they were eating,[81] Jesus took some bread, blessed it, broke it, and gave it to his disciples saying "Take, eat this is my body."[82] Jesus then took the fourth cup (or a second third cup) of the Passover.[83] Jesus gave thanks and gave it to his disciples to drink saying, "This cup is the new covenant in my blood, shed on behalf of many for forgiveness of sins." Each Gospel is enigmatic but when these statements are combined, they add to this covenantal atonement model: Luke adds "the new covenant," Mark adds "for the many," and Matthew "for the forgiveness of sins." The statement of "covenant in blood" is reminiscent of

79. Green, "Embodying the Gospel," 11–21.

80. Barton, "Memory and Remembrance in Paul," 333–34; Foley, "Indigenous Poems, Colonialist Texts," 28–31; Austin, *How To Do Things with Words*.

81. Passover had four cups (*m. Pesah.* 10; Marshall, *Luke*, 797–98; Bahr, "Seder of Passover," 181–202). The third cup would be preceded by the paschal lamb and discussion of the exodus events recounted, then after the third cup, there would be dessert of bread and sometimes salty items, which was open to tailor the conversation to particulars like this novel appropriation by Jesus.

82. Most accounts have bread first then cup, but Luke 22:17–20 has the meal begin with a cup, bread then cup again, which 1 Cor 10:16 and *Did.* 9:1–4 takes as the order of cup then bread. Historically, the likely order is the bread then cup, which is a second third cup, or a fourth cup (Luke 22:20 "after dining") with the kind of blessings of the third cup.

83. After this cup he does not drink again, so likely the fourth cup (Luke 22:19 mentions "after eating") or a second third cup, based on the blessing (Luke 22:18) and the parallel of vows in Luke 22:15 and 17; Plummer, *Luke*, 495; Bock, *Luke*, 2:1722. The use of a common cup is unusual for Passover but not unprecedented (*t. Ber.* 5.9; *m. Ber.* 8.8; Jeremias, *Eucharistic Words of Jesus*, 69; SB 4:58–59, 62).

Exod 24:8 (especially in Matt and Mark, commemorated in discussions from especially the second until the third cup). Luke provides the lens of the new covenant of Jer 31:31 (Luke 22:20), with its forgiveness (themes common to the fourth cup, which sometimes looks toward the kingdom), and perhaps a hint of Isa 53:12 death "for many." Jesus then identified that he would not drink wine again until he did so in the kingdom of God, which would likely be the final (or fourth) cup of the Passover, unless he left Passover unfinished. The subsequent repetition of the meal performs the function of retelling the story which defines the new community.

Second, Joel Green reminds of the mutual community practice in 1 Pet 5:12 and 14, the holy kiss greeting those within the household could understand as a language game of filial knowledge.[84]

> The kissing Peter mentions was mutual ("greet each other"), allowing for no markers of elevated status or heightened honor; and it was inclusive of all within the household of faith. Indeed, Peter qualifies this greeting as a "kiss of love," underscoring his understanding of this simple practice as an apt summary of the whole of his teaching concerning relations within the family of Christ-followers. From his first chapter to the last, he has promoted "love" as a defining characteristic of the life within the community of believers—signifying a group ethos of solidarity and loyalty, an essential pattern of mind favoring others in the community and a commitment to oneness within the group: "Love each other deeply and earnestly" (1 Pet 1:22); "Love the family of believers" (2:17); "Be of one mind, sympathetic, lovers of your fellow believers, compassionate" (3:8); "Show sincere love to each other" (4:8); and now, "Greet each other with the kiss of love" (5:14). This emphasis on the nature of household patterns of life among believers is furthered by familial terms that surface here and there in Peter's letter, together with metaphors of new birth, newborn babies, and the converted as children comprising a family for whom God is Father. Familial love denotes a strong sense of identity as a kin group (see [1 Pet] 1:22; 2:17; 3:8; 5:9) that would stand in sharp contrast to cancerous experiences of marginalization, scoffing, and other forms of distress arising from their status as strangers within their own communities (1 Pet 1:1, 17; 2:11).[85]

---

84. Green, "Embodying the Gospel," 11–21; Klassen, "Sacred Kiss," 122–35; similar pattern to Paul (Rom 16:16; 1 Cor 16:20; 2 Cor 13:12; 1 Thess 5:26).

85. Green, "Embodying the Gospel," 19–20.

Green also develops that such a kiss of love is performative embodied communication that "generates identity and relationships."[86] "As ritual, the "kiss of love" renews, strengthens, and recreates those patterns of believing, thinking, and feeling determined by merciful initiative of the God who brings liberation in Christ and creates a household structured around his grace.[87]

Third, Jesus tells parables as meaningful stories to flesh out and concretize his teachings (Mark 4:2–34), like how they were used among rabbinic writing. This development could be considered as an ancient Jewish sage.[88] As parables their meaning is polyvalent until the context roots its meaning and the *nimshal* (after statement) directs the meaning to address specific issues in a specific manner, thus focusing a particular meaning.[89] For example, the parable of the lost sheep was told six times in three centuries with a different meaning in each context. In Matthew 18:12–13, Jesus urges his disciples as shepherds to humbly look out for the everlasting welfare of all the church, especially any who are vulnerable. This meaning is especially confirmed by the discussion of church discipline and recovery that immediately follows. In Luke 15:2–7 the parable addresses grumbling Pharisees and scribes to urge them to rejoice when sinners are found by Jesus as the shepherd. This meaning is evident by the shepherd's statement in the parable, "Rejoice with me for I have found my sheep which was lost!" (Luke 15:6). This meaning is further confirmed by Jesus' *nimshal* (after-statement), "I tell you in the same way that there will be more joy in heaven over one sinner who repents, than the ninety-nine righteous persons who need no repentance" (Luke 15:7). This message for grumblers to get to joy is further echoed through the passage with the subsequent parables (Luke 15:7, 9–10, 24, 29, 32). The *Gospel of Thomas* 107 records that Jesus will rescue the largest and most

---

86. Green, "Embodying the Gospel," 20.

87. Green, "Embodying the Gospel," 20–21.

88. Johnson, "Jesus of the Gospels and Philosophy," 63; in Kennard, *Messiah Jesus*, 211–42, I argue for parable contextual meaning and connect them with similar rabbinic parables; McArthur and Johnston, *They Also Taught in Parables* nicely collects many of the rabbinic parables; so there is no need to position parables into Aristotilian rhetoric such as Anderson does (*Glossary of Greek Rhetorical Terms*, 86–87; Aristotle, *Rhet.* 2.20).

89. Meier, *Marginal Jew*, 5:193–94; Levine, *Short Stories by Jesus*, 29, 42–45; Gregerman, "Critique of *Short Stories by Jesus*"; Johnson, "Critique of *Short Stories by Jesus*"; Sandmel, "Critique of *Short Stories by Jesus*"; Snodgrass, "From Allegorizing to Allegorizing," 248–68.

loved sheep who strayed, which seems odd when compared to Jesus' character as portrayed by the Synoptics. *The Gospel of Truth* presents Jesus as the shepherd seeking a lost sheep to be found and when it is found the Father provides interior gnostic knowledge fostering perpetual light.[90] *Genesis Rabbah* 86.4 encourages rabbinic Jews to rescue fellow Jews who stray into gentile areas and practices. *Exodus Rabbah* 2.2 identifies that Moses is the appropriate leader of Israel because he went after straying sheep. The point is that Jesus and rabbinic writing are utilizing a similar method, which cross fertilized each. As Jesus and the rabbinic writers addressed similar Jewish communities, one can recognize the application of this method. Thus, *the context of the ones addressed, and the after statement identify the meaning of a parable in a specific context*. The epistemic value of each parable is to evoke the meaning which the after-statement declares in ways that first provoke alienation and then provide a clear route of decision to resolve the alienation for kingdom purposes.[91] Since I have already discussed this at length and connected the biblical parables with similar ones among the rabbinics[92] I will not repeat that here.

Peter uses a divinely given faith and knowledge epistemically to inform and confirm a Pharisaic supernatural realism grounded in his eyewitness experience with Christ. Such an epistemic commitment fosters believers in a growing total communal commitment evident through virtues which foster good deeds. Such a virtue epistemology and revelational eyewitness testimony further pragmatically confirm the believer will be saved and cultivates God's family for kingdom.

---

90. Ehrman, *Lost Scriptures*, 50.
91. Boomershine, "Jesus of Nazareth," 24–29.
92. Kennard, *Messiah Jesus*, 211–42.

7

Jewish Traditions and Gentile Conversion[1]

ONE OF THE RARE texts that is longer in Mark than either Matthew or Luke is the account of the Pharisees and scribes taking issue with Jesus concerning his compliance with the tradition of ritually washing hands before eating (Mark 7:1–23; Matt 15:1–20; Luke 11:37–41).

Such Pharisaic tradition had a controversial status before AD 70, but it was a significant emphasis with 67 percent of the textual discussion between Hillel and Shammai consisting in such ritual purity concerns.[2] The pre-Pharisaic "washing of hands" was necessary before handling holy objects,[3] but it was being extended to the handling of food. Shammai insisted on washing the hands before filling the cup.[4] However, the view of Hillel won out: "Washing hands before a meal is a matter of choice, abolution after a meal is obligatory."[5] The politically connected Sadducees repudiated all this washing before meals and saw that these

---

1. This chapter has been reworked and added to from Kennard, *Messiah Jesus*, 153–55, and *Biblical Covenantalism*, 2:214–20.

2. This tradition was widespread during the second to fourth centuries AD (*m. Hag.* 2.5–6; *b. Šabb.* 13b–14a; 62b; *y. Šabb.* 1.3d; *b. Yoma* 87b; *TB Ber.* 8.2; 60b; *TB Soṭah* 4b). Especially *m. 'Ed.* 5.6 places hand-washing in the category of heresy. R. P. Booth argued that the practice was not widespread before AD 70 (Jdt 12.7; *Ep. Arist.* 305–6; *Sib. Orac.* 3.591–93; Booth, *Jesus and the Laws of Purity*, 159–60; Dunn, "Pharisees, Sinners, and Jesus," 61–88; Klawans, *Impurity and Sin*, 146–50; Davies and Allison, *Matthew*, 2:521–22; Gundry, *Mark*, 358–71).

3. *Šabb.* 14b.

4. Finkel, *Pharisees & the Teacher of Nazareth*, 140–41, 152–56.

5. *T. Ber.* 5.13.

purity laws applied only to those who were entering temple.[6] Likewise, the sectarian Qumran community also repudiated them, but with regard to washing before meals, they required total immersion before meals.[7] With the destruction of the Jewish temple and the success of the Pharisaic synagogue movement, these Pharisaic traditions became codified in the *Mishnah*. Jesus' positions tend to be closer to Hillel Pharisaism but not identical to them.

Within this context, Matthew presents this text as a matter of fact to an informed Jewish reader, whereas Mark adds explanation for a gentile reader who is not so well informed. This is an important distinction because it shows that Mark follows Peter presenting Jesus for a gentile audience and thus shows the applicability of Jesus' teachings for that audience. This is especially apparent by comparing the additions that Mark includes over Matthew's parallel account. Additionally, the gentile agenda of Mark is also enabled by the immediately following account of the healing faith of the Canaanite woman, specifically designated by Mark as a gentile (Mark 7:26). On this issue of Pharisaic washing tradition, Luke does not have a parallel, but he raises the issue in another setting.

Shammai Pharisees and scribes raised the issue with Jesus: "Why do your disciples eat with unwashed hands?"[8] Mark points out an explanation (from this Jewish traditional perspective) that meant the disciples were rendering themselves impure by eating with impure hands (Mark 7:2). That is, the washing concerns ceremonial defilement and ritual impurity (Exod 30:17-21; Lev 15:11). Mark also points out a parenthetic comment about the Jewish tradition.

> For the Pharisees and all the Jews do not eat unless they carefully wash their hands, observing the traditions of the elders; and when they come from the market, they do not eat unless they cleanse themselves; and there are many other things which they have received in order to observe, such as the washing of cups and pitchers and copper pots. (Mark 7:3-4)

---

6. Josephus, *Ant.* 13.297; 17.41.

7. 1QH 4.14-15 identifies their rejection of the traditions. Immersion before meals is supported by: Josephus, *War* 2.129, 138; 1QS 3.8-9; 5:13; CD 10.10-13; Newton, *Concept of Purity at Qumran*, 26-40.

8. Luke records a parallel account in which the Pharisees take issue with Jesus for not washing before he ate a meal (Luke 11:37-41). Jesus responded to this critic by calling him a fool for emphasizing external cleansing while they neglected internal robbery and wickedness. Jesus' solution was to call him to internal "charity, and then all things are clean for you" (Luke 11:41).

This Markan explanation helps the gentile readership to enter this Jewish traditional issue. I even add a little more explanation to help the contemporary reader understand that while the washing at issue was that of hands before eating, part of the tradition included the washing of pots after use. The tradition permits a pot to be externally unclean without defiling the inside of the pot, but if it is defiled on the inside then the whole pot is unclean.[9] When the question is asked a second time in Mark, Jesus responded that Isaiah rightly prophesied that these Jewish hypocrites will be condemned to captivity and dispersion, which Israel continues to suffer, "This people honors me with their lips, but their heart is far away from me. But in vain do they worship me, teaching as doctrines the precepts of men" (Isa 29:13 quoted in Mark 7:6–7; Matt 15:8–9).[10] In Mark, Jesus summarized the Jews problem twice as "neglecting the commandment of God, you hold to the tradition of men" (Mark 7:8–9).[11] After summarizing the issue of rebellion, Mark quoted from the Decalogue concerning honor due parents (Exod 20:12; Deut 5:16; Mark 7:10; Matt 15:4). In Matthew when the question is asked, Jesus responded with this summary in question form and then addressed the Mosaic law concern first, and then only after that addressed this Isaiah citation (Matt 15:3–10). For Mark the issue is that the Jews prefer their tradition over the Mosaic law, in contrast to Matthew's development, which by order could be summarized that the Jews are violators of the Mosaic law favoring tradition. So perhaps Matthew is showing the law's binding nature more than Mark presents it. Furthermore, Matthew prefaced this quote of the honor due parents by "for God said" still giving some credence for its applicability to his Jewish-Christian readership, while Mark phrased the applicability to the Jewish leaders as "for Moses said," thus potentially distancing his gentile readership from implications of the Mosaic law. However, both agree that the main issue being worked here is an unrighteous illustration of how Jewish leadership permit Jews to not honor their parents by rendering their material goods inaccessible for meeting family needs (Matt 15:6; Mark 7:9, 12–13). Mark named the process as *"corban"*

---

9. *m. Kelim* 25.6; however, utensils used as holy things in the temple have no division between inside or outside, for if one is unclean then the whole vessel is unclean (*Tosefta Kelim Baba Batra* 3.12; *Sifra* 114.1.6; Matt 23:25–26).

10. This is like the description of the Jews in the *As. Mos.* 7.9–10, "their hands and hearts are all corrupt, and their mouths are full of boasting."

11. Also an accusation echoed by *T. Levi* 16.2.

and then explains for his gentile readers that this means "given to God" (Mark 7:11).[12]

Jesus then taught the multitude that what defiles a person, is not something that goes into him but that which comes from out of the person's heart (Matt 15:11–20; Mark 7:15–23).[13] That is, Jesus and Peter are not maintaining a priestly distinction of clean on meal cleansing (in contrast to Jesus cleansing unclean lepers through healing: Mark 1:40, 44; Matt 8:2–3; 10:8; 11:5; Luke 5:12; 7:22; 17:14, 17), but Jesus subsumed meal cleansing within the prophetic moral program of sin and righteousness (Lev 16:30; Isa 1:16; 6:5; Jer 33:8; Ezek 36:33; Hos 5:3; 6:10; Ps 51:2, 7, 11; Prov 20:9; Eccl 7:20),[14] identifying that things from outside do not defile a person because it passes through them and then out as waste.[15] Whereas, what proceeds out from a person's heart is what defiles them: "evil thoughts and fornication, thefts, murders, adulteries, deeds of coveting, wickedness, deceit, sensuality, envy, slander, pride, foolishness. All these evil things proceed from within and defile the man" (Mark 7:21–23). Davies and Alison consider this vice list concentrates on the Noahic commandments (Mark 7:21–22; Matt 15:19),[16] but it is broader than that, developing one's whole moral life with others, as early Judaism emphasized (Lev 18:20, 24; Num 35:33–34; Lam 4:14–15).[17] These lists reflect Jesus' new covenant internalizing for Jewish obedience and an internalized uncleanness. To extend this more directly to a gentile audience, idolatry would be eschewed (Lev 19:31; 20:1–3; 2 Chr 23:19; 36:14; Isa 66:17: Jer 2:23; 7:30; 32:34; Ezek 5:11; 9:7; 20:7, 18, 30–31; 22:3, 12–17, 24; 23:7, 13, 30, 38; 36:18; 37:23; 43:6–9; Mal 1:11–12).[18] This issue of

---

12. Throughout the LXX, is rendered by קָרְבָּנוּ δῶρον, or "given." Josephus, *C. Ap.* 1.167; and in *m. Ned.* 3.11; 4.7–8; 5.6; 9.1 it means sacrifice and vow. The issue of depriving relatives by a vow is acknowledged in *m. Ned.* 5.6 and Philo, *Spec.* 2.16–17; Fitzmyer, "Aramaic Qorban Inscription," 60–65; Evans, "Fishing Boat, a House," 212.

13. Mark 7:16 is not the earliest and best manuscripts, so I do not consider it Scripture.

14. Sir 21.28; 51.5; *Jub.* 22.14; 34.19; *Pss. Sol.* 9.6; 18.5; 2 Bar 21.19; 39.6; 50.38; 60.2; 2 *En.* 10.4; in Qumran community moral impurity and ritual impurity are equated (Newton, *Concept of Purity at Qumran*, ch. 2; Martínez and Barrera, *People of the Dead Sea Scrolls*, 139–57; Bauckham, "James, Peter, and the Gentiles," 93; Kennard, *Biblical Covenantalism*, 1:268–85.

15. This elimination picks up the idea of the latrine drain that carried away the portion of food that does not provide nourishment.

16. Davies and Allison, *Matthew*, 2:536.

17. *Jub.* 16:5; 20:3, 5; 23.14, 17; 25.1; 33.10–14, 19–20; 41.25–26.

18. *Jub.* 1.9; 20.7; 2 Bar 60.1–2; 66.2; *As. Mos.* 5.3; *Pss. Sol.* 1.8; 2.3; 8.13; *m. Šebu.* 1.4–5; *t. Šebu.* 1.3; *t. Mos.* 8.4.

idolatry is addressed at the Jerusalem council through the prohibition of meat contaminated by idols (Acts 15:20, 29).

Mark adds a comment, which Matthew does not include, that Jesus "declared all foods clean" (Mark 7:19). This comment is at least identifying that kosher law is not applicable to Mark's gentile readership, though this may go further and identify that the whole law concerning clean and unclean may not be applicable to Mark's gentile readership. It is important to remember that the food law was bound upon only the Jews of the covenant and the gentiles within the land (Lev 11; Deut 14:3–20; Dan 1:5, 8–16).[19] Those[20] who are inclined to disband the Mosaic law altogether on the basis of this comment must remember, that Mark recorded what Jesus said to the Jewish ruler that everlasting life and kingdom is obtained by complying with the Mosaic law with a generosity that meets the needs of the poor, and follows Christ (Mark 10:17–24). While Mark saw freedom for his gentile readership, he also appreciated that the historical Jesus was more committed to the law for his Jewish audience.

Mark's aside is likely a Petrine explanation because Matthew does not include Jesus' statement "declared all foods clean" (Mark 7:19) and Luke identifies the contributor of this insight is Peter (Acts 10:9–17, 28; 11:3, 7–10). While Peter was staying with Simon the tanner in Joppa, Peter saw a vision of animals let down from heaven,[21] like the sheets above the roof draped over the animal skins to slow the drying process. Peter heard an angel voice encouraging him to kill and eat, because such food should not be considered as unclean when God had "cleansed" all food; an implication for a gentile audience (Acts 9:43; 10:9–17; 11:9 ἐκαθάρισεν; Mark 7:19). While Peter was reflecting on the vision, the Spirit commanded Peter to travel with three men at the gate that were looking for him because god-fearing Cornelius had also seen a vision prompting him to send for Peter. When Peter arrived at Cornelius' house, Cornelius tried to worship Peter, but Peter would not permit it. Being "unlawful" (ἀθέμιτόν),[22] Jews do not associate with and eat with gentiles (Acts 10:28;

---

19. *Esth.* 14.17; *Tob* 1.10–12; Jdt. 10.5; 11.12; 12.1–2; 1 Macc 1.62–63; 2 Macc 6.5–7, 18–28; 7:1–2, 42).

20. Some Lutherans and dispensationalists.

21. Not an allegory like the *Animal Apocalypse* as in *1 En.* 85–90 where different animals stand for nations because the issue is food (Acts 10:12–16; 11:3); Bauckam, "James, Peter, and the Gentiles," 106.

22. Peter uses this term ἀθέμιτόν for gentile food, drunkenness, sensuality, and idolatry, whereas 2 Macc 6.5 refers to sacrificing forbidden animals, 7.1 to eating forbidden pork, and 10.34 to using forbidden words; Bauckam, "James, Peter, and the Gentiles," 108.

11:3; 1 Pet 4:3),[23] Peter explained that beyond the vision about food, God had showed him that he should not consider any person unclean (Acts 10:28–29; 11:11–12).[24] Peter preached the gospel to Cornelius' household and the Spirit fell upon them prompting their praising God, so Peter baptized them. When Peter got back to Jerusalem some circumcised believers took issue with him but he defended that God initiated the acceptance of gentile Christians with the same evidence that had come upon the apostolic band (Acts 11:1–18).

Responding to Jerusalem Jewish-Christians, the issue of kosher was addressed by God's vision (Acts 10:9–17, 28; 11:3, 7–10). In this wake, Peter was generally consistent in discounting kosher with mixed gatherings of gentile and Jewish Christians eating and fellowshiping together (Acts 11:21–26; Gal 2:11). With most of the church in Antioch as gentile Christian, Peter ate and lived as a gentile to express authentic Christianity among them (Gal 2:12, 14).[25] He did not insist upon circumcision, nor obedience to the law. When some Jewish Christians came from James, he once withdrew to eat kosher with the Jewish Christians and thereby showed his inconsistency in this event, having previously fully accepting all believers. At this instance, Paul confronted Peter concerning his inconsistency, since God and Peter previously had fully accepted the gentile believers (Gal 2:11–21).[26]

At the Jerusalem council (AD 50), a more extreme form of this Jewish Christianity claimed that gentile Christians had to become Jews (circumcised and obeying the law) for them to become authentic Christians. Peter stood against this claim by testifying how God accepted Cornelius' household as gentiles, "God made no distinction between us and them, cleansing their hearts by faith, now therefore why do you put God to the test by placing upon the neck of the disciples a yoke which neither our fathers nor we have been able to bear? But we believe that we are saved through the grace of the Lord Jesus, in the same way as they are" (Acts 15:7–11). Richard Bauckham follows Peter Borgen in developing

---

23. Josephus, *War* 2.150, 229; *Ant.* 12.145; 14.285; 1QM 9.8–9; *Ep. Aris.* 139–71, esp. 142 protection of Israel from gentile idolatry, and gentile immorality (151–52, 166); *m. Pesaḥ*; *m. Ṭhar.* 5.8; 7.6; *m. Nid.* 7.3; *t. Nid.* 9.16; *b. Nid.* 69b; *m. Zabim. Par.* 1.1.*t. Zabim.* 2.1; *Sifr. Neg.* par. 1.1; *b. Sabb.* 83a; 127b.

24. Judaism considered gentiles to be morally impure and therefore did not associate with them (*Jub.* 16.5; 20.5, 16; 2 Bar. 82.7; *T. Mos.* 8.4).

25. Hengel, *Saint Peter*.

26. Brown *et al.*, *Peter in the New Testament*, 50–52.

parallels between Peter's argument and that of Paul in Galatians (italics represent exact biblical quotations):[27]

Peter in Acts 15	Paul in Galatians
Gentiles received the Spirit by hearing and believing Gospel (vv. 7–8)	Galatians received the Spirit *by the hearing of faith* (3:2, 5)
God *purified their hearts by faith* (v. 9)	Works of flesh contrast with fruit of the Spirit (5:16–25)
God treated them just as he did us (v. 8) and we will be saved in the same way as they v. 11	We have been justified in the same way as they have (2:15–16)
God *made no distinction between Them, and us* (v. 9)	*There is no longer Jew or Greek . . . for all of you are one in Christ Jesus* (3:28)
[Peter resists circumcised issue with uncircumcision (11:3; 15:1)]	*Neither circumcision nor uncircumcision Counts for anything* (5:6)
The law is *a yoke* (v. 10)	*Do not submit again to a yoke of slavery* (5:1)
Which Jews themselves *have not Been able to bear* (v. 10)	*Even the circumcised do not themselves* obey the law (6:13)
[Implicit is the argument that the law is not the means to moral purity, which rather requires God's purification of the heart.]	If there had been *a law which could make alive, then righteousness would come through the law* (3:12)
	No one will be justified through works of the law (2:16)
Saved through the grace of our Lord Jesus Christ (v. 11)	*the grace of Christ* (1:6; 2:16–21; 6:18)

Bauckham concluded that "it is plausible that Paul first learned this argument from Peter, subsequently saw it confirmed in many other conversions of gentiles who believed and received the Spirit, and of course,

---

27. Borgen, "Jesus Christ," 253–72; Bauckam, "James, Peter, and the Gentiles," 131–32; Kennard added [resistance] comment and Bauckam added [Implicit] comment.

developed it in his own creatively theological way."[28] Following this argument, Paul and Barnabas gave their testimony of gentile ministry conversions with Spirit empirical evidence (Acts 15:12 recounting Acts 13–14). The church leadership pronounced by James, Jesus' brother, that neither circumcision nor the law were required for gentile conversion, while requiring a few proselyte preliminaries to help facilitate a unified church. This trajectory leaves open that when there are only Jewish Christians in a gathering that they could allow kosher to determine their diet (Acts 15:21). So, Mark 7:19 at least declares all food are clean for Mark's gentile readership. This leaves kosher for Jewish Christian practice within the Nazarenes and Ebionites until patristic Christianity attacked them.[29] The patristic church clearly went further, considering Mark 7:19 abrogated kosher for everyone. For Matthew's Jewish Christian audience, Jesus clarified that he was not annulling any feature of the law (Matt 5:17–19). Whereas Luke emphasized that the leadership of the church was of one mind concerning the acceptability of gentile Christians without becoming Jews, so that the church might function as a unified entity (Acts 15:1–31).[30]

Peter addressed "purification" (καθαρισμοῦ) of Christians initiating exodus to kingdom as a "purification from his former sins" (2 Pet 1:9). Thus, all believers have initially been cleansed by Christ's redemptive death, so there is no longer gentile uncleanness, nor Jewish uncleanness for believers benefiting from Christ's atonement. Christ's atonement

---

28. Bauckam, "James, Peter, and the Gentiles," 134.

29. The Patristic attack universalized the law, diminishing specific cultural practices: Klijn, "Study of Jewish Christianity," 419–31; Taylor, "Phenomenon of Early Jewish Christianity," 313–34 and Velasco and Sabourin, "Jewish Christianity of the First Centuries," 5–26; Ignatius, *Phld.* 6; Epiphanius, *Pan.* 2.3–5; 9.3.6; 15.3; 18.7—19.4; 21.1–6; 22.1–11; 30.7.1–7; 30.9.4; Irenaeus, *Haer.* 1.26.2; Hippolytus, *Haer.* 8.18.1–2; Hyppelytus, *Pan.*; Clement of Alexandria, *Strom.* 2.9.45.5; Tertullian, *Adv. Jud.* 4, 6; *Marc.* 4.8; Origen, *Princ.* 4.3.8; *Pseudo-Clementine Homilies* 7.8; *Didascalia Apostolorum* 21; *Pseudo-Clementines Recognitions* 1.28.1–2; 1.32.4; 1.35.2; 1.37.1–4; Chrysostom, *Hom. Act.* 1.11; 32; *Hom. Phil.* 1.13; Cyprian, *Treatises* 12.1.16–17; *The Canons of the Council in Trullo*, canon 55; *Laodicean* Canon 37, "It is not lawful to receive portions sent from the feasts of Jews or heretics, nor to feast together with them," and Canon 38, "It is not lawful to receive unleavened bread from the Jews, nor to be partakers of their impiety"; also 35 raises the issue around angelology; von Hefele, *Histoire des conciles d'après les documents originaux*, 1.2, 989–1028; Rouwhorst, "Jewish Liturgical Traditions," 82; These polemics against the Jewish-Christians are essentially the same polemics made against the Jews (Aphrahat of Persia, *Syriac Demonstrations* 12–16); Skarsaune and Hvalvik, *Jewish Believers in Jesus*, 446, 456, 459, 520–22, 628–31.

30. Brown et al., *Peter in the New Testament*, 50–52.

further identifies that Jesus' atonement cleansing removes all separation between Jewish and gentile believers. This atonement cleansing participates within Jesus' kingdom cleansing as evidenced in unclean lepers, the woman with hemorrhage, and the dead being cleansed through kingdom healing (Mark 1:40, 44; 5:34, 42; Matt 8:2–3; 9:22; 10:8; 11:5; Luke 5:12; 7:15, 22; 17:14, 17; John 11:44). Likewise, the gospel message brings gentiles and Jewish believers in Christ within the way of salvation exodus, extending Jesus' exodus way unto kingdom (2 Pet 1:1–11; Acts 9:2; 13:10; 16:17; 18:25–26; 19:9; 22:4; 24:14, 22).

8

Marriage, Not Divorce

PETER PRESENTS A BROAD command that husbands should "live with your wives in an understanding way" (1 Pet 3:7). It is an expected comment from the house code. However, patriarchy framed the explanation, "as with a weaker vessel,"[1] which is at least a reference to general male physical superiority[2] for tasks of physical exertion (like hunting or labor) but in first-century patriarchy "weaker vessel" could refer to weakness of human nature or morality.[3] Peter does not clarify what kind of weakness he has in mind. In fact, Peter's use of "as" (ὡς) does not make a claim that women are weak but that a husband should try to live with her in an understanding manner "as if" she was weak, that is differentially valuing her perspective. The word "live with" (συνοικοῦντες) often in LXX has reference to sexual intercourse but here it is broader referencing all of

---

1. "Vessel" refers to wife as valued fragile one (like *b. Meg.* 12b; *Midr. Esth.* 1.11) without clarifying what the vessel held, not a reference to "one's own body" as Paul used the word in 1 Thess 4:4 to make a claim that one's wife is one's own body as some might take Paul's argument in Eph 5:28–29. Paul doesn't say that either—he said loving wife is also a love of one's own body, the husband is benefitted by loving his wife.

2. Xenophon, *Lac.* 3.4; Livy, *Hist.* 25.36.9; 28.19.13; Cicero, *Mil.* 21.55; Virgil, *Aen.* 12.52–53; Musonius Rufus, 4, p. 46.8–23; Silius Italicus, *Pun.* 1.445; Dio Chrysostom, *Or.* 2.29; Aulus Gellius, *Att.* 17.21.33; Lucian, *Dial D.* 414; *Lam. Rab.* 4.19.22.

3. Particular female moral or human weakness (1 Tim 2:14; 4 Macc 15:5; Sir 33.20; 4Q416, frag. 2, 4.2–9; PLond. 971.4; Dio Chrysostom, *Or.* 3.70; Clement of Alexandria, *Paed.* 2.10.107; Plutarch, *Bride* 33; *Mor.* 142E; Quintilian, *Decl.* 327.2; *Gen. Rab.* 22.6; *b. Besah* 32b) from human weakness (Rom 5:6; 6:19; Heb 4:15; 5:2; 1 Cor 8:7–13; Plato, *Leg.* 6.781b; *Resp.* 5; 455d; 451c–56a; *Meno* 71c–73c; Philo, *Deus* 80; *Spec.* 1.293–94; Clement of Alexandria, *Strom.* 2.15.62; 2.16.72; 7.3.16; *Paed.* 3.12.86).

life together as is developed in early Jewish wisdom.[4] Such life together is to be informed by knowledge (γνῶσιν), and thus informed sensitivity because she is a woman. Here patriarchy is upended because the husband's informed perspective "should honor his wife as a fellow heir of the grace of life." That is, in Christian marriage a husband should consider his wife an equal heir of God's generous life. This honor goes beyond Roman patriarchy honoring a spouse to avoid infidelity,[5] to include a partner of mutual respect.[6] However, Peter goes further identifying that a Christian husband should consider his wife equal in salvation inheritance (1 Pet 3:7 approaching Paul's sentiment of Gal 3:28).[7] So, the ideal for Christian marriage illustrates the harmonious, sympathetic, compassionate and humble lifestyle that a Christian should excel in society. However, there is an additional benefit for a Christian husband being this way with his wife, because if he is not his prayers may be hindered.

Peter discussed wives framed within his discussion concerning church engagement with society when most of these wives were not married to Christian husbands. In such a house code[8] situation as this, submission and good deeds perform a vital role in providing an overarching canopy which integrates the household of God to the rest of society,[9] since most early believers outside of Israel came from lower classes (slaves and women, Acts 16:11–18; 17:34; 18:1–8; Eph 5:22—6:9; Col 3:18–25).[10] Believers from these vulnerable groups have clear obligations in God's household as she lives in society.

4. Sir 25.8.
5. Plutarch, *Bride* 36, 47; *Mor.* 143, 144F–45A.
6. Porphyry, *Marc.* 2.21; *Sent. Sextus* 238; Ps.-Arist., *Oec.* 3.2.
7. Applegate, "Co-Elect Woman," 587–604.
8. Full treatments include husband/wife, father/children, and master/slave relations much like in early Judaism (Philo, *Decal.* 165–67; *Spec. Laws* 2.225–27; *Hypoth.* 7.14; Josephus, *Ag. Ap.* 2.199–217) and Christianity (Eph 5:22—6:9; Col 3:18—4:1; Titus 2:2–10; *1 Clem.* 1.3; 21.6–89; *Did.* 4.9–11; *Barn.* 19.5–7; Polycarp, *Phil.* 4.2–3; Ignatius, *Pol.* 4.1–3), which reflect Hellenistic house codes (Aristotle, *Pol.* 1.2.1; Musonius Rufus, 8; Arius Didymus, *Epit.* 2.7.11d; Christensen, "Balch/Elliott Debate," 173–93), except Peter completely ignores father/children and master relations, and develops the wife more than the husband, with the focus on inner qualities more than female adornments, thus resisting Hellenism (1 Pet 3:3–4 contra: Clement of Alexandria, *Paed.* 3.11.66; Tertullian, *Or.* 20; *Cor.* 14; *Cult. fem.* 1.6; 2.2.7–14; Cyprian, *Hab. Virg.* 8; Valerius, *Fac. Dict.* 9.1.3; Balch, *Let Wives Be Submissive*; "Early Christian Criticism," 161–73; "Hellenization/Acculturation in 1 Peter," 79–101; Harland, *Associations, Synagogues, and Congregations*, 195).
9. Religion performs this role for any society; Berger et al., *Homeless Mind*, 79.
10. Tertullian, *Apol.* 3; Julian, *Against the Galileans* 206a; Origen, *Cels.* 3.44.

Peter addressed wives to submit to their husbands with a gentle and quiet spirit within a patriarchal culture after the pattern of holy women of old, like Sarah (1 Pet 3:1–5).[11] Peter identifies those Christian wives become the offspring of Sarah by following her habit of doing what is right without fear (1 Pet 3:6). There is no discussion of wives enduring domestic violence as there had been for slaves, because wives enduring domestic violence would not be seen in this patriarchal culture as a virtue.[12] With Christianity present only among such a vulnerable minority, issues of egalitarianism for women and slaves and social justice issues were not championed by Christians of the first century, except on the periphery (such as Philemon or female patrons of a local assembly). The agenda Peter has is the preservation of Christianity unto kingdom and the potential conversion of non-Christians.

Peter provides personal demonstration of his views by traveling missionary journeys with his wife and probably also their children (1 Cor 9:5).[13] Clement of Alexandria presents Peter and his wife as an example of blessed Christian marriage, each collaborating on the mission, controlling their feelings even in deeply emotional settings, such as martyrdom.[14] Ignatius and Clement of Alexandria discussed that during Peter's travels,

---

11. Sarah called Abraham "lord" in Gen 18:12 and *T. Abr.* 224–38, with a pattern of obedience (Gen 16:2, 6; 21:12; Josephus, *Ag. Ap.* 2.200–201). In Roman patriarchal culture female submission to the patriarch was expected (Plutarch, *Advice* 140.19) and often taught by pointing to an ideal role model as Peter has done (Xenophon, *Oeconomicus* 7.1—10.13; Plutarch, *Advice* 48), countered only by a few Isis advocates defending egalitarianism (*Poxy.* 1380.145–48; Meeks, *First Urban Christians*, 25). A "gentle" or "meek" wife is valued in patriarchal culture (1 Tim 2:9, 15; Musonius Rufus, 3, p. 40.17–18, 20; 3, p. 42.26; 4, p. 44.16–18, 22; Dio Chrysostom, *Or.* 32.56; Lucian, *Hall* 7; *Sent. Sextus* 237; Libanius, *Speech* 18.3; *Thesis* 1.13.26–27; *Narr.* 37; Euripides, *Oed.* frag. 545; *1 Clem.* 21.7), but meekness also describes Jesus (Matt 11:29; 21:5; 2 Cor 10:1) and is a male virtue (Ps 36:11; Matt 5:5; Gal 5:23; Eph 4:2; Col. 3:12; Titus 3:2). A quiet wife is valued in a patriarchal culture (1 Tim 2:11; Sir 26.14; Philo, *Spec. Laws* 3.174; Sophocles, *Aj.* 293; Aristotle, *Pol.* 1.5.8. 1260a; Val. Max., *Fac. Dict.* 3.8.6; Plutarch, *Lyc. Num.* 3.5), but quiet is also a virtue for males in a feudal culture (2 Thess 3:12; 1 Tim 2:2). Often the virtues of gentleness and quiet are combined (1 Pet 3:4; 1 Tim 2:2, 11; *1 Clem.* 13.4; *Barn.* 19.4; Hermes, *Mand.* 5.2.3; 6.2.3; 11.8; funerary descriptions from Lefkowitz and Fant, *Womens' Life in Greece and Rome*, 104–5, 209).

12. DeSilva, "1 Peter," 33–52, esp. 39; Jobes, *1 Peter*, 206.

13. Clement of Alexandria, *Strom.* 3.52.1–2, 4; 3.52.5 = Eusebius, *Hist. eccl.* 3.30.1; *Acts of Peter* 7; *Acts of Philip*; *Pseudo-Clementine Recognitions* 7.25.3; 7.36.1; 9.38; *Homiline* 13.1.1; 13.11.2; Hengel, *Saint Peter*, 125–27.

14. Clement of Alexandria, *Strom.* 3.53.3; 7.11; Hengel, *Saint Peter*, 125–27.

Peter's wife was led to martyrdom, and Peter encouraged her to resign to her martyrdom and anticipate kingdom.[15]

In a very different direction, Mark provides a narrative within Israeli Judaism (removing the temporary resident church evangelism context of 1 Pet), where Pharisees test Jesus concerning the law of divorce (Mark 10:1–12). Deuteronomy permitted the husband to divorce his wife if he found some "indecency" ('rwt) in her (Deut 24:1–4). Within the Pentateuch, this indecency is best understood as "indecent exposure or public nakedness" (Gen 9:22–23; 42:9, 12; Exod 20:26; 28:42). Even in the near context, the word is used of "indecent public exposure" (that is, excrement needs to be buried and not left "exposed," Deut 23:13–14). In this Deuteronomy instance, 'rwt cannot mean "sexual immorality," for the punishment of sexual immorality was not being sent away in divorce but rather capital punishment (Lev 18:6–19; 20:11–21). In this Deuteronomy discussion, legal dissolution of marriage is permitted for indecency.

This legal framework was taken in divergent views in Jesus' day. Qumran judged that divorce and remarriage was illicit in all circumstances because "God made them male and female" and "they became one flesh."[16] In mainstream Judaism, opinion was divided among the school of Shammai, which permitted divorce with the possibility of remarriage to another for gross indecency,[17] while Hillel permitted divorce for real or imagined offenses, including an improperly cooked meal. For example, the Hillelite rabbi Aiba permitted divorce and remarriage to another even for a case of a roving eye for pretty women,[18] the sin Jesus had just condemned in the Sermon on the Mount discussion (Matt 5:28–29). Josephus even permitted divorce "for any cause whatsoever."[19] Others tried to diminish divorce as a practice because they saw its abuse to be devastating.[20]

---

15. Ignatius, *Phil* 4; Clement of Alexandria, *Strom.* 7.11.

16. CD 4:21 justifies no divorce on the basis of original design, the pattern in the ark during the flood, and the command for the king not to multiply wives in Deut 17:17 which is interpreted as no second marriage while one's wife is still alive, because the ensuing defilement of another in intimate sexual union would separate the previous marriage partner (1QApGen. 20.15, Abraham's prayer against loosing Sarah to Pharaoh), thus an argument against polygamy in 11QTemple 57:17–19; Tosato, "Law of Leviticus 18:18," 199–214.

17. Philo, *Spec. Laws* 3.30; Josephus, *Ant.* 4.253; *Sipre* on Deut. 24:1.

18. *M. Gittin* 9:10 or 90b.

19. Josephus, *Ant.* 8.23.

20. *M. Gittim* 9.10; *b. Gittim* 90b; *Sifre Deut.* 269.

The discussion of divorce was conducted from a male perspective in all the Gospel texts except perhaps Mark 10:12 where there is some concession to non-Palestinian circumstances where a woman could more easily initiate divorcing her husband.[21] Divorce was envisioned as a possibility for Jewish women to initiate for those living at Elephantine in Egypt in the fifth century BC, because a number of Aramaic marriage contracts mention it explicitly,[22] but the evidence for such a practice in Israel itself is almost nonexistent.[23]

Jesus stands out starkly, perhaps closest to Qumran, as he extends the law in a new covenant manner. Jesus continues his discussion in the sermon on the mount with Matt 5:31 beginning with δέ, implying that the preceding argument continues; divorce is the moral equivalent to adultery. So, Jesus' response to the Pharisees draws upon this ban because for Jesus, God's design sets the priority: therefore, do not divorce or try any other form of separation because God has joined the two together (Gen 2:24; Mark 10:5–9; Matt 19:3–6).[24] Jesus admits that the Mosaic process of divorce was permitted for those who have hardness of heart. Jesus was not annulling the law as some of the divergent views in the first-century context evidence that they annulled the law. That is, Jesus permits those who are willfully rebellious from God's design to have a legal loophole which permits divorce, but such an option is precarious at best. However, Jesus transcends the issue of legal and permissible, to a higher order of what is right by God's design. The remainder of Jesus' teaching on divorce reflects a moral problem which is comparable to adultery.

The statements in Mark 10 and Matt 19 are roughly equivalent in emphasizing design priority over legal permission. The statements in Matt 5:32 and Luke 16:18 come in contexts that emphasize the binding nature of the law. Three passages make it clear that the husband commits adultery (μοιχεύσεις) if he remarries after divorce (Mark 10:11; Matt 19:9). Mark 10:12 clarifies that the wife also commits adultery (μοιχεύσεις) if she remarries after divorce. Furthermore, if anyone happened to marry a divorced

---

21. *Elephantine* papyri in Bammel, "Markus 10:11f," 95–101; and Philo, *Spec. Laws* 3.30 in Treggiari, *Roman Marriage*, 441–46.

22. Cowley, *Aramaic Papyri*, 15.9–39 (p. 45); Fitzmyer, "Matthean Divorce Texts," 205; "Re-Study," 137–68; Kraeling, *BMAP* 2:9, 7:25; cf. *AP* 9.8 (p. 27).

23. There is only one instance, Josephus, *Ant.* 15.7.10.

24. CD 4:21; 1QApGen. 20.15; Some claim that Jesus' absolute prohibition echoes the view of Tob 6:18 "she was destined for you [to be with in marriage] from eternity," however, Jesus' rationale merely goes back to the design of creation (Gen 1:27; 2:24); Fitzmyer, "Matthean Divorce Texts," 203.

woman, then even this previously unmarried individual would commit adultery (μοιχεύσεις) in marrying a divorcee (Matt 5:32; Luke 16:18).

The word πορνείας includes every kind of unlawful sexual intercourse including the complete semantic field of μοιχεύσεις.[25] For anyone who is married, the two words are synonymous; a married person who does πορνείας does μοιχεύσεις and a person who does μοιχεύσεις does πορνείας. These words of illicit sexual act speak of a deed, not a characteristic of life (such as being a perpetual adulterer or prostitute). However, acts described by these words are sexual immorality in which the law required the participants to be executed under capital punishment (Lev 18:6–19; 20:11–21). That is, the sin in the law's exception clause (indecency or public nakedness) is not as grave a sin as sexual immorality (πορνείας), since divorce is permitted instead of a death sentence.

Unlike the Mark and Luke passages which have no exception clauses, the two Matthew passages have exception clauses to the effect of "except for the cause of unchastity" (πορνείας). For example, Matt 5:32 says that a husband who divorces his wife except for the cause of unchastity (πορνείας) makes her commit adultery (μοιχεύσεις). The exception clauses in Matthew do not render divorce acceptable. Remember that the whole discussion of divorce and remarriage has been rendered equal to adultery (by the δέ; Matt 5:31), and rebellious by the disregard for God's design and involvement in making the couple one flesh (Mark 10:5–9; Matt 19:3–6). There is no substantial reason for Matthew's exception clause to be read into Mark or Luke, since they are themselves Scripture and clear in what they say. Mark and Luke have not included an exception clause, and their texts are understandable without any exception clause. Therefore, any remarriage of a divorced person is an act of adultery for both persons being married (Mark 10:10–12; Luke 16:18). Thus, the exception clause in Matt 5:32 and 19:9 does not prevent adultery in a remarriage situation if the divorce was motivated by immorality. Remember Jesus' ethic on this point of the law is more restrictive than the law in its appeal.[26] Therefore, Jesus' exception clause cannot be softening and expanding the law's exception clause. If Jesus is saying that it is acceptable to divorce a wife for her sexual immorality, then he is denying several commands of the law that required capital punishment (Lev 18:6–19; 20:11–21) and

25. In Mark 7:21 and Matt 15:19 these words are synonyms; BDB, 528, 699.

26. Jesus appeals to God's design, God's involvement in making the couple one flesh, and Moses' permission to accommodate moral hardness of heart (Mark 10:6–9; Matt 19:4–8).

rendering himself under his own declaration to be least in the kingdom and therefore self-contradictory (Mark 10:11–12; Matt 5:18–19; Luke 16:16–18). Not only does the prior context call for a higher ethic but the subsequent context shows that the disciples got the point that a higher ethical order was demanded, as evidenced by their statement, "if the relationship of the man with his wife is like this, it is better not to marry" (Matt 19:10). Furthermore, Jesus affirmed the disciples in their conclusion, that some for various reasons will prefer celibacy. Those who prefer celibacy have it as a gift (Matt 19:11) even though it might have been a condition from birth or a condition of employment or a condition for kingdom service (Matt 19:12). Jesus concluded his discussion of celibacy by urging those able to accept the preference of a celibate life to accept such a life. So that this higher ethic is not encouraging divorce, but rather warning that a person does an adultery deed if he divorces and remarries (Matt 5:32; 19:9). That is, one who remarries after divorce does the deed of sexual immorality (πορνείας). Therefore, the exception clause describes that a divorcee commits sexual immorality (μοιχεύσεις) in the act of remarriage, except in the case that they have done so previously, in which case an additional act of sexual immorality does not render them immoral for they are already in an immoral condition. This interpretation permits the passages without the exception clause to declare that remarriage is sexual immorality (μοιχεύσεις; Mark 10:11–12; Luke 16:18), and the whole travesty of divorce and remarriage to be a violation of sexual immorality (μοιχεύσεις), unless they have already violated sexual immorality (πορνείας; Matt 5:32; 19:9). In English the phrase is, "Anyone who divorces his wife makes her commit adultery [μοιχεύσεις] provided she has not already committed adultery [πορνείας]." The verbal construction of the consequences of the divorce force the divorced wife into the act of adultery (μοιχεύσεις). This does not mean that a divorced wife becomes a prostitute and starts taking in clients. The grammatical description of the consequences are an act of adultery and not necessarily a characteristic lifestyle of being an adulteress. In this first-century context, for the average divorced woman to make her way virtually requires her to remarry (unless she has significant wealth) in order to deal with her vulnerability and come within the oversight of a man in a male-dominated society (Ruth 1:20–21; Isa 1:23; 10:2; 54:4; Jas 1:27). The act of remarriage would be an act of adultery (Mark 10:12). Or perhaps this making her commit adultery (μοιχεύσεις) builds off preceding verses in the Sermon on the Mount, which discuss the committing of adultery (μοιχεύσεις) through the process of internalized lust (Matt 5:28). That is, in the same way that a man may lust after a woman, prompted by the visual stimulation, so a divorced woman might lust after a man, prompted by the previous experience of the sexual intimacy which marriage brought and divorce removed. The exception clause fits, in that if she has already done the deed of adultery (πορνείας) in mind or body then she is not somehow in her divorce being forced to do adultery (μοιχεύσεις) by the divorce; she already did adultery (πορνείας) by her own choice.

Mark has Jesus conclude this discussion of divorce by permitting children to come to him, taking them in his arms and blessing them (Mark 10:13–16). Jesus encourages his disciples to do the same to enable them to enter kingdom, because the humility of children demonstrates that the kingdom belongs to such as these (Mark 10:13; Matt 18:1–10; 19:13–15).

9

Mark 10:17–31: Standard and Poor[1]

THE ACCOUNTS OF THE rich young man are punctuated with an enigmatic statement saying, "the last will be first and the first will be last." This statement runs counter to the view that material abundance was a sign of divine blessing on one's life.[2] This concern is timely in a context where the wealthy get richer and the poor fall through the cracks because these texts warn that if those with ability do not help the poor where they can then they are likely to miss Jesus' kingdom. Kingdom life is centered in the standard of loving one's neighbor as one loves oneself. To the extent that a person has resources then he should generously meet needs.

Jesus' standard ethical pattern is to love God and love one's neighbor as one loves oneself (Mark 12:29–34; Matt 22:36–40; Luke 10:26–27). Jesus responded to a lawyer that the greatest commandment is "You shall love the Lord your God with all your heart, and with all your soul, and with all your mind," but he quickly followed with a second command, "You shall love your neighbor as yourself." These two commands set a standard ethic for heading toward the kingdom of God" (Mark 12:34).[3]

Whereas some operate as though they could love God and money at the same time. Jesus said that such a love and pursuit of money is mutually exclusive of a legitimate love for God (Matt 6:24; Luke 16:13). Mark 10:17–31 (and its parallels) argues that such a love and pursuit of money

---

1. This chapter is from Markan perspective, reworked from Matthew's perspective in Kennard, *Gospel*, 77–94.

2. Davids, "Rich and Poor," 701–10.

3. Akiva, *Sipre* on Lev 19:18; *T. Iss.* 5.2; 7.6; *T. Dan.* 5.3; Aristeas, *Ep.* 229; Philo, *De virt.* 51; 95; *Spec.* 2.63; *Abr.* 208; *T. Naph.* 8.9–10; *Jub.* 7.20; 20.2; 36.7–8; Josephus, *War* 2.139.

excluded both a love for God and love for one's neighbor, thus worthy of damnation. Kingdom-oriented Christianity calls the disciple back to the standard of loving God and loving one's neighbor as one loves oneself. Such a love must be expressed in a practical manner.

Jesus addressed issues of wealth and kingdom in a context in which he urged God's designed best option in contrast to a Pharisaic concern for a less ideal but legally permitted option (Mark 10:2–12 and Matt 19:3–12, commitment in marriage in contrast to divorce). Jesus emphasized that disciples need to buy into kingdom whatever it costs as evident by the parables of treasure and pearl (Matt 13:44–46). Such zealous alignment with kingdom should define the disciple.

In the context, Jesus showed his sensitivity to vulnerable children who appropriately fit within the kingdom and are blessed by him (Mark 10:13–16; Matt 19:13–15; Luke 18:15–17). Jesus' kingdom concern also extends to meeting the needs of the poor (Mark 12:42–43; Matt 11:5; Luke 4:18; 6:20; 7:22; 14:13, 21; 16:19–31). Additionally, all the Synoptics regularly show Jesus' healing those in need.

The structure of the account of the rich young man begins with an alternating conversation between the rich young ruler and Jesus. Then there is a shift to Jesus alternating with the disciples. Finally, there is a personal alternating interchange between Peter and Jesus.

It is in this light that Jesus comments to the rich young man that he supports practically what has been taught in the Sermon on the Mount (Mark 10:17–30; Matt 19:16–26; Luke 18:18–30).[4] The rich young man addressed Jesus as "teacher."[5] Jesus is asked "What good thing shall I do that I may obtain everlasting life?" Here obtaining everlasting life is analogous to entering the kingdom and being saved (Mark 10:17; Matt 19:16, 23, 24, 25; Luke 18:18, 24–25).[6] Jesus' answer for this Jewish ruler[7] is the

---

4. Also corroborated by *Gos Nazareans* 1, as recounted by Origen, *Comm. Matt.* 15.14; John Chrysostom, *Hom. Matt.* 63.2.

5. After early and good Alexandrian and Western texts leave ἀγαθέ absent, later texts add "good" to teacher in Matt 19:16–17, "Why do you call me good?" following Mark 10:17–18 and Luke 18:18–19.

6. Early Jewish sources support this point as well (1QS4.6–8; CD3.20; 4Q1811.3–4; *1 En.* 37.4; 40.9; 58.3; 4 Macc 15.3; *Ps. Sol.* 3.12).

7. Luke alone adds that the rich man is a "ruler" (ἄρχων; Luke 18:18) but Matt 19:20 calls him "young" (νεανίσκος, perhaps twenty-something, Philo, *Migr.* 105; Josephus, *Ant.* 6.179), which would indicate that he is not likely a ruler in a synagogue, for then he would be an elder, so he has likely inherited a position with his wealth within one of the local councils at Jerusalem, Gadara, Amathus, Jericho, or Sepphoris originally arranged by Syrian governor Gabinis in 57 BC and continuing to provide governance through

covenant nomist option to keep the commandments of the law, so that he might continue in blessing unto kingdom. Jesus does not say to try to do the law until you find out you can't and then throw yourself on the mercy of God; Jesus says keep the law. N. T. Wright identifies, "The Torah was the boundary marker of the covenant people: those who kept it would share the life of the coming age."[8] This should not surprise us because it is what Jews repeatedly expected and Christian Jews for several centuries tried to live.[9] Since God alone is good (Matt 19:17),[10] Jesus' answer points to God's commands. Judaism affirmed that the law is by extension also good.[11] Even Mark and Luke (who do not emphasize the keeping of the law as does Matthew) declare on Jesus' lips that keeping the law is the way to everlasting life (Mark 10:17–19; Luke 10:25, 28; 18:18–20). Or as N. T. Wright described it, the kingdom is obtained by following "Jesus in finding a new and radicalized version of Torah observance" which fits within early Jewish expectations.[12] Jesus further clarifies that the command-

---

the Jewish War in AD 67 (Josephus, *Ant.* 14.90–91; *War* 1.170; Meyers, *Galilee Through the Centuries*, 113; Freyne, *Jesus Movement and Its Expansion*, 50).

8. Wright, *Jesus and the Victory of God*, 301.

9. Kennard, *Messiah Jesus*, 107–52; Jer 31:31–34 and Ezek 36:24—37:28; Jdt 5:17–21; 8:18–23; 10:5; 12:2, 9–19; 13:8; Pr Azar 6–14; *Jub.* 1:22–25; 2:17–33; 15:11–34; 1Q3 4, 5; 1QH 4, 5, 18; 4QShirShalb; Tob 1.10–12; 4:12–13; 1 Macc 1:48; 2:15–28; 2 Macc 6:18–31; 7:1–42; 3 Macc 3.4–7; 4 Macc 5:1—6:30; *T. Jud.* 26; *Jos. Asen.*; Josephus, *War* 1.145–47, 157–60, 651–55; 2.169–74; *Ant.* 13.252; 14.237; 17.149–67; 18.55–59, 261–64, 267, and 271; *mek. Bachodesh* 5.81–82; Augustine, *Serm.* 35.1; Wright, *Jesus and the Victory of God*, 301; Sanders, *Paul and Palestinian Judaism*; *Paul, the Law*; *Jewish Law*; and *Judaism: Practice and Belief*; and Dunn, *Jesus, Paul and the Law*; *Jews and Christians*; and *Paul and the Mosaic Law*—especially interesting is Wright's chapter "The Law in Romans 2," 131–50. Furthermore, Biblical texts like Jas, Matt, and Acts indicate that Jews and Jewish Christians were zealous for the law. However, especially at focus is Matt 5:17–48 and 19:16–22; Saldarini, *Matthew's Christian-Jewish Community* and Kennard, *Biblical Covenantalism*, 3:15–160; Klijn, "Study of Jewish Christianity," 419–31; Taylor, "Phenomenon of Early Jewish Christianity," 313–34 and Velasco and Sabourin, "Jewish Christianity of the First Centuries," 5–26; Klijn and Reinink, *Patristic Evidence*; Strecker, "Appendix 1," 257; Strecker, "Kerygmata Petrou," 2:102–27, esp. 210–22 and 270–71; Strecker, *Das Judenchristentum in den Pseudoklementinen*; Schoeps, *Theologie und Geschichte*; *Jewish Christianity*; van Voorst, *Ascents of James*.

10. Philo, *Mut.* 7; *m. Ber.* 9.2; *b. Ber.* 45b, 46a, 48b, 49a, 59b, 60b; *Pesaḥ.* 50a; *p. Ta'an*, 2.1, 10; 4.5, 10; *Gen. Rab.* 13.15; 57.2; Justin, *Dial.* 101; 1 *Apol.* 16; Irenaeus, *Haer.* 1.20.2. Some Jewish texts permit human teachers to be referred to as good (*m. Ber.* 9.2; *B. Menaḥ.* 53b; Abrahams, *Studies in Pharisaism and the Gospels*, 2:186).

11. 1 Chr 16:34; Pss 34:8; 73:1; 86:5; 119:30, 68; Rom 7:12, 13, 16; Philo, *Leg.* 1.47; Josephus, *Ant.* 9.1; *m. 'Abot* 6.2; *m. Ber.* 9.2; *b. Ber.* 28b.

12. Wright, *Jesus and the Victory of God*, 307; Consistent with early Judaism: *T. Jos.* 18.1; *Jub.* 5.10; 10.17; 22.22; 2 Bar. 14.12; 48.22b; 51.7; Wis 5.15; 6.18; *Pss. Sol.* 9.3–5; 1QS 3–4; CD 3.11–16, 20–21; 7.5, 9; 13.11; 20.17–20, 25–27; 4Q228 frag. 1 1.9; 4Q266,

ments he has in mind are those like the fifth, sixth, seventh, eighth, and ninth of the Ten Commandments, all of which have financial overtones.[13] Jesus' statement of the ninth command omits that the bearing of false witness was "against your neighbor" (Exod 20:16; Deut 5:20) but adds a restatement, "Do not defraud," which accentuates the issue of suffering as a result of abuse by false witness (Mark 10:19, 34).[14] This addition to the commandments may raise the issue that the wealthy are often the abusers of common people by defrauding them, and these wealthy should be especially known for generosity, not abuse. Jesus recognized that the law has its primary focus on the loyalty relationship to the Lord (Mark 12:29–30), however, Jesus' focuses on the human side of the law here emphasizing the love relationship to others as demonstrating practically whether one truly loves the Lord (Mark 12:31). Practicing this radical love commitment identifies one's inheritance of everlasting life and kingdom (Mark 12:29–34; Matt 5:45; 12:34; Luke 10:25, 28). Jesus' citation of commands has in mind here particularly those commandments that others can see and benefit from or at least not suffer under their violation. The young man affirmed that under a legally tight reading of the law, he had kept all these commands (Mark 10:20), which is not atypical in early Judaism.[15] Jesus declared that the rich young ruler still lacks (Mark 10:21; Luke 18:22).[16] Giving up wealth for the welfare of the poor is required

---

frag. 11; 4QMMT C; 1QS 3.7–12; 4 *Ezra* 6.5; 7.34–36, 77; 8.33, 36; 13.39–40; *Hymn Scroll* 19.12–14; Bird, "Salvation in Paul's Judaism?," 16.

13. These commandments are from the broadly Protestant numbering of the Decalogue. All the Synoptic Gospels list the fifth command last after the others, however, Luke 18:20 reverses the first two (giving the order as: seventh, sixth, eighth, ninth and fifth, and Mark inserts "do not defraud" after the ninth and before the fifth command. Neither Mark nor Luke has Lev 19:18 as does Matthew, bringing an emphasis of love one's neighbor, which is also developed in rabbinic teaching (*Sifra Qed.* 4.200.3.7; *Gen. Rab.* 24.7; *b. Šabb.* 31a).

14. Other OT and early Jewish texts that concur: Exod 23:4–5; 1 Sam 24:17–19; 2 Sam 19:6 LXX; 1 Kgs 3:11; Job 31:29 (Eusebius, *Dem. ev.* 1.6); Ps 7:3–5; Prov 24:17–18 (*m. 'Abot* 4.19); 24:29; 25:21–22; Jer 29:7; Jonah 4:10–11; *T. Iss.* 7.6; *Jub.*7.20; 20.2; 36.4; Philo, *Decal.*108–10.

15. SB 1:814; *b. Sanh.*101a; Phil 3:6.

16. Matt 19:20 indicated that the young man realized he was still lacking on his own with a similar question as in *b. Soṭah* 22b. In Matt 19:21, Jesus offers the young man "maturity" (1 Kgs 11:4; Tob 3.14; *Jub.* 23.10; 27.17; Pr Man 8; 11QPsDavComp 1.3; *T. Iss.* 7.1–7; *T. Abr.* A 10.13–14; 2 Bar. 9.1; *T. Mos.* 9.4; *t. Sanh.* 13.3; *b. Qidd.* 40b), commanded in Matt 5:48, as a radical extension of Lev 19:18 love for neighbor (Rabbi Chiyah identifies that the righteous come into kingdom by loving others with practical good deeds [*Semachot de Rabbi Chiyah* 3.2]; Tob 4.5–11; *b. B. Bat.* 10a; Origen, *Comm. Matt.* 15.14; Augustine, *Serm.* 35.1; 36; John Chrysostom, *Hom. Matt.* 63.1).

to fulfill the law.[17] Jesus does not develop the attitude of being willing to give to the poor; his emphasis is on doing: keeping the commandments, selling and giving to the poor (Mark 10:19, 21).

Perhaps behind Jesus' sentiment lies Prov 10:2, "treasuries of wickedness," as understood by Waltke, meaning accumulating wealth for personal use as opposed to giving it away to those in need; "the wicked... store up physical assets for themselves and lose their lives, and the righteous use their resources to serve others and store up life for themselves."[18] This sentiment is echoed by Sir 5.8a, "Do not trust in wealth that lies." Furthermore, Sir 31.1–11 warns about the different effect of pursuing wealth by rich and poor, damning the wealthy who are not generous benefactors of the needy.

> A rich man loses weight by wakeful nights,
> When the cares of wealth drive sleep away;
> Sleepless worry keeps him wide awake,
> just as serious illness banishes sleep.
> A rich man toils to amass a fortune,
> and when he relaxes he enjoys every luxury.
> A poor man toils to make a slender living,
> And when he relaxes he finds himself in need.
> Passion for gold can never be right;
> The pursuit of money leads a man astray.
> Many a man has come to ruin for the sake of gold
> And found disaster staring him in the face.
> [They cannot be saved from evil
> Nor delivered on a day of wrath.][19]
> Gold is a pitfall to those who are infatuated with it,
> And every fool is caught by it.
> Happy the rich man who has remained free of its taint
> And has not made gold his aim!
> Show us that man, and we will congratulate him;
> He has performed a miracle among his people.
> Has anyone ever had it in his power to sin and refrained,
> Or to do wrong and has not done it?
> Then he shall be condemned in his prosperity,
> And the whole people will hail him as a benefactor.

---

17. Tob 4.5–11; *b. B. Bat.* 10a; Origen, *Comm. Matt.* 15.14; Augustine, *Serm.* 35.1; 36; John Chrysostom, *Hom. Matt.* 63.1.

18. Waltke, *The Book of Proverbs*, 1:453; also echoed by Prov 11:4. 9 and *T. Jud.* 25.4.

19. Anderson, *Charity*, 58–59 pointed out the textual addition added by a later scribe.

Individual and corporate greed to increase personal or corporate wealth at the neglect of others is damnable, and a characteristic of false teachers (Mark 10:21–22; 2 Pet 2:3–6, 9, 15–17).

Generosity of the benefactor reflects the core beatitude virtue of showing mercy which Jesus oriented his disciples toward, "Blessed are the merciful for they shall receive mercy" (Matt 5:7). Jesus' teaching reflects the sentiment of rabbis elsewhere.[20] The merciful are the benefactors who attempt to meet other's needs.[21] The dominant expression of mercy in the Synoptics is the Son of David's healing others in need (Mark 5:19; 10:47–48; Matt 9:27; 15:22; 17:15; 20:30–31; Luke 1:58; 17:13; 18:38–39).[22] Whereas, in Jewish tradition, the primarily merciful One is God (1 Sam 23:21; Ps 72:13; Prov 14:21; Mic 6:8; continued in 1 Pet 1:3).[23] According to Jesus, mercy (as one of the weightier matters of the law) was unfortunately neglected by the scribes and Pharisees (Matt 23:23). One form of the Jewish neglect of mercy was their restrictiveness to their own Jewish group.[24] Jesus' disciples must have mercy in ministering to sinners and forgiving others without judging them (Mark 11:25; Matt 6:12–15; 7:1–5; 9:13; 12:7; 18:21–35). The good Samaritan exemplifies mercy in meeting his neighbor's and even enemy's needs (Matt 5:44–47; Luke 10:37). This sentiment of showing mercy universally was also a factor in some forms of Jewish tradition.[25] The merciful shall receive mercy (Matt 5:7).[26] The future mercy to be received could be in this life or the kingdom beyond.[27]

---

20. This is parallel in *b. Šabb.* 151b, "He who has mercy on people obtains mercy from heaven;" also *t. B. Qam.* 9.30, "As long as you are merciful, the Merciful One is merciful to you"; *T. Sim.* 4.4; Josephus, *Ant.* 10.41. Additionally, the rabbis identified that God judged the world by two measures: justice and mercy (*Lev. R.* 29.3), so that following a verse about righteousness it is appropriate to develop the theme of mercy. This sentiment continues in early Christendom (*1 Clem.* 13.2; Polycarp, *Ep.* 2.3; Tertulian, *Or.* 4.2; 5.1; *Paen.* 6.4; *Exh. Cast.* 2.3; *Marc.* 2.6.7; 4.31.1; Cyprian, *Eleem.* 1, 2.5; Rhee, *Loving the Poor*, 73–102).

21. *T. Jud.* 18.3–4; Epictetus, *Diatr.* 1.18.4.

22. Kennard, *Messiah Jesus*, 23–67.

23. *T. Zeb.* 5.1, 3; 7.1–8.6; Philo, *Spec. Laws* 4.72, 76–77.

24. For example, Qumran, the Essenes and other Jews maintained mercy within the community but urged hate to outsiders (1QS 1.4, 10–11; 2.4–9; 9:21–23; 1QM 4.1–2; 15.6; 1QH 5.4; *b. Ber.* 33a; *b. Sanh.* 92a; Josephus, *War* 2.139).

25. A commitment to universal mercy is present in rabbinic Judaism (*Sipra on Lev.* 19:18 and *Mek. on Ex.* 21:35) and outside the Jewish tradition (Polybius 18.37.7; Hesiod, *Op.* 342–43, Solon, frag. 1.3–5; Plato, *Tim.* 17d–18a; *Resp.* 375c; *Meno* 71e; Tacitus, *Hist.* 5.5–6).

26. This theme is echoed salvifically by Leo the Great, *Sermon* 10.

27. 2 Tim 1:18; Jude 21; *1 Clem.* 28.1.

Jesus commanded the rich man to sell his possessions and give to the poor (Mark 10:21; Matt 19:21). Such giving away all wealth to the poor went against rabbinic teaching.[28] However, Jesus had some followers who as patrons supported his ministry while not giving all their money to the poor (Matt 27:38–42, 57; Luke 8:1–3; 10:38–42; John 3:1). Among these patrons there was a concern for generous restitution and the hosting of sinners so that they might have access to Jesus (Mark 2:14–17; Matt 9:9–13; Luke 5:27–32; 19:5–10). Such generous restitution and hosting evidenced that salvation included these patrons (Luke 19:9). Furthermore, those who had wealth and wished to itinerantly follow Jesus, such as Matthew, left his wealth and tax collection franchise to others to follow Jesus (Mark 2:14–22; Matt 9:9–17; Luke 5:27–39). Matthew has himself accomplished what the rich man rejects for his future. This rich man had many possessions (Mark 10:22). Jesus expressed what rabbinics conclude, "where your treasure is, there will be your heart also" (Matt 6:21; Luke 12:34).[29] "In fact it is impossible to serve both God and money" (Matt 6:24; Luke 16:13).[30]

Giving up these possessions would enable the young man to follow Jesus in his itinerant ministry as Peter and the disciples had done (Mark 10:21, 29). Perhaps Mark includes Jesus' statements of giving to the poor for purposes of the itinerant ministry, to address issues in his readers' lives such as poverty from famine, or dispersion as persecuted Jewish Christians. If the young man had complied, he would have had kingdom treasure as the disciples were to receive (Mark 10:21, 29). Unfortunately, the young man was unwilling to pay the price of Jesus' radical law demands. His departure provided an opportunity to instruct the disciples in the near impossibility of a rich person pursuing the kingdom. The primary focus of the law is evident as serving God, rather than money (Matt 6:24). The fact that the young man went away with his riches shows that ultimately he was unwilling to serve God and love his neighbor as he loved himself. In this case the kingdom is missed for failure to keep the law, namely, loving one's neighbor as oneself.

28. B. Ketub. 50a; Hagner, *Matthew*, 2:558.

29. B. Ber. 61b.

30. *T. Job* 33.4–5; Tob 4.8–9; Sir 29.10–13; 31.7; *Pss. Sol.* 5.2, 11; 9.5, 9; 10.6–7; 15.1; 18.2; 2 Bar 14.12; 24.1; 44.8; *T. Levi* 13.5; *1 En.* 94.6–8; 95.4–7; 96.4–8; 97.7–8; 98.9–16; 99.1–16; 100.4, 9; 1QS 4.3–11; Philo, *Praem.* 104; 4 Ezra 7.77; *m. Pe'a* 1.1; *b. B. Bat.* 11a; *Tosefta Peah* 4.18; *Gos. Thom.* 47, 64, 76. From this perspective Clement of Alexandria considers that the rich man is damned and the generous are saved (*Who Is the Rich Man*, 1.6–7; 16.5). Hoag, *Wealth in Ancient Ephesus*, 100–130.

There is no evidence that the rich young man enters kingdom, for he does not follow Jesus but instead leaves grieving (Mark 10:22). Jesus responds that it is hard for a rich man to enter the kingdom of heaven, illustrating it by a rabbinic hyperbolic simile of the largest animal in Israel, namely, a camel going through the eye of a sewing needle as being easier than for a rich man to enter the kingdom.[31] The disciples recognize the impossibility of this and wonder "then who can be saved?" (Mark 10:23-24; Matt 19:25). Such impossibility (Mark 10:27) makes it clear that a sewing needle is in view instead of a small wicket gate requiring unloading a burdened animal.[32] Furthermore, there is no early Jewish evidence that such human-sized gates were called needles, or even existed by a larger gate, so that is a later interpretive conjecture. Wealthy humans trying to save themselves cannot be successful no matter what else their money can buy. The wealthy show by their excess wealth that they do not really love God or their neighbor, thus they will not be saved.[33]

In recognizing the impossibility of wealthy being saved, the disciples respond, "then who can be saved?" (Mark 10:26). Such "salvation" is seen as eschatological salvation, realized at the last judgment (Mark 10:23-24; Matt 1:21; 10:22; 16:25; 18:11). Jesus corrects them by saying that such salvation by humans is impossible, but with God all things are possible (Mark 10:27). So that the impression the context brings is not that the rich will necessarily be reduced to a low position in the kingdom, but that they tend to not even make it into the kingdom in the first place

---

31. Later Greek texts read "rope" but earlier texts present "camel" with strong textual support. Both words would sound alike so it is easy to imagine a scribe writing the slight misspelling he thought he heard. Rabbinic parallels are consistent with Jesus' statement: *b. Ber.* 55b and *b. B. Mes.* 38b portray the impossible by the largest animal of Babylon (an elephant) going through a sewing needle, and *b. Yebam.* 45a describes the impossibility of a camel dancing in a tiny area. So these might identify Jesus' statement as an existing proverbial statement. Augustine, *Serm.* 35.2 and John Chrysostom, *Hom. Matt.* 63.2 recognize that Jesus discusses the impossibility of a camel going through a sewing needle.

32. The view that a "needle" is a small wicket gate is very common among exegetes (Barclay, *Matthew*, 217) since the fifteenth-century when forts and castles utilized human-sized doors (restricting how many could enter) within a larger door or next to a larger door that would pass riders and wagons, but there is no ancient Near Eastern archeological evidence for such a gate. Chalmers utilized this as an example of an illusory truth effect that occurs when an in-group bias confirms a view through a false consensus within a group with no archeological evidence (Chalmers, "Influence of Cognitive Biases," 477).

33. Origen, *Comm. Matt.* 15.14; Clement of Alexandria, *Who Is the Rich Man*; Commodianus, *Instruction* 29; Augustine, *Serm.* 35.5 damns the wealthy and 35.4 calls all to be rich in good works.

and are thus damned. Mark 10:29 and Luke 13:30 do not have a subsequent parable and reiteration of the idea of the last being first, so they tend to reinforce that this text is emphasizing that the disciples will gain great place and the rich will be last. The Luke 13:30 enigmatic statement is removed from the rich young man (Luke 18:18–30) but reflective of the narrow way to eschatological judgment (Luke 13:23–30). The word "last" (ἔσχατοι) in Luke 13:30 is best seen in that context as those Jesus casts away as damned evildoers who weep and gnash their teeth (Luke 13:23–30). Subsequently, Mark 10 identifies that Jesus fulfills his own standard by leaving everything for his kingdom ministry and heading toward his death. Therein, Jesus' teaching in Mark 10 is spun for the disciples to follow in this narrow kingdom way. Only those who enter by the narrow door gain entrance into the kingdom, though others may try and be damned (Matt 7:13–14).

At this point in Matthew, Peter chimes in and says, "Behold, we have left everything and followed you," perhaps desiring reassurance that the disciples will gain kingdom (Mark 10:28, without an express concern for their gain as in Matt 19:27). Jesus reassures the disciples that they have complied with this radical paying the cost of the law, and that they will have a unique role of judging Israel (Matt 19:28). In fact, everyone who has left house and family members[34] for Christ's sake will receive many times as much[35] and will inherit everlasting life (Mark 10:30). For most of the disciples, this is a modest loss of time away from family, and perhaps giving up house, fishnet, and boat (Matt 4:18–22; 8:14–15). For tax-collector-turned-disciple Matthew there was more wealth than the other disciples have described of them (Mark 2:14–15; Matt 9:9–13; Luke 5:27–29; 19:2–9 similar pattern with tax collector Zaccheus). So, when Matthew becomes a disciple, he hosts Jesus, the disciples, and many sinners as a patron of Jesus' ministry. This Matthean response was like what Jesus asked the wealthier ruler to do (Mark 1:21). Jesus reassures the disciples in their giving up family, houses, and farms that they will be truly rewarded with responsibilities and benefits in the kingdom. Mark also adds that part of one's loss might be through increased persecutions in identifying with Jesus (Mark 10:30). Perhaps, part of the reason for

---

34. The text sandwiches family members between houses and lands. Some later texts add "wife" γυναῖκα after "mother" but this is likely a scribal assimilation to the Lukan parallel 18:29.

35. Mark 10:30 reads "hundredfold" and Luke 18:30 reads either "manifold" or "sevenfold" but these are all comparable and reflect dissimilarity among multiple attestation.

this Petrine/Markan account is a warning recognition that the wealthy are more likely to oppress Jesus' disciples actively or passively. Matthew adds, when the regeneration phase of kingdom has the Son of Man sitting on his throne, then the disciples will also sit upon twelve thrones, judging the twelve tribes of Israel, which is an extreme privilege for them (Matt 19:24, 28).[36] The kingdom is described as of heaven and of God and salvation and where Christ reigns (Matt 19:23–25, 28). Within this kingdom, the disciples also have the benefits of everlasting life and many times more reward than the cost of those things and family, which they left to follow Jesus.

Jesus summarized the relation to others in service identifies eschatological outcome, "the first will be last; and the last first" (Mark 10:31; Matt 19:30; 20:16).[37] In this context, the disciples are the last who will be first, encouraging them (Mark 10:31; Matt 19:24, 28; Luke 13:30). There is no extended kingdom ministry of the prophets in the context so that this phrase might grow out of the preceding issue and events, meaning that the wealthy (first) will be last place in the kingdom and those who have given up everything (last) will be first place in the kingdom with responsibilities and benefits; which further encourages the disciples.[38] Jesus' enigmatic statement is echoed by rabbinic and popular Jewish eschatological reversal identifying that those who present themselves as last place in humble poverty will be eschatologically elevated to first place in kingdom (Luke 1:51–52; 6:20–26).[39] Such a view of damning the wealthy and encouraging generous disciples was how the phrase "first will be last and last will be first" was taken in the parallel Synoptic Gospel accounts (Mark 10:31; Matt 19:30; Luke 13:30 which concludes with Jesus' narrow way teaching). The young ruler was called to the same kingdom standard that Jesus disciples were "Love your neighbor as yourself."

---

36. Such judging of the twelve tribes is also apparent in: *Pss. Sol.* 17.26, 29; Philo, *QE* 1, 2.114; *T. Jud.* 25.

37. Matt 20:16 adds a few more words than 19:30 but with the same meaning following strong textual support.

38. Like: Luke 16:19–31; *Ruth Rab.* 3.3; *Eccl. Rab.* 1.16.1; *y. Ber.* 2.5c, 15.

39. *1 En.* 104.6; *2 En.* 50.5; 1QpHab 6.1; 9.4–6; *T. Jud.* 25.4; *Jos. Asen.* 12.12; *B. Bat.* 10a; Rabbinic parallel, "Some obtain and enter kingdom in an hour, while others reach it only after a lifetime" (*b. 'Abod. Zar.*17a; *Ebel Rabbati* 3); Schmidt, *Hostility to Wealth*, 46–47; Carter, *Households and Discipleship*, 127, 138; Talbert, *Matthew*, 238–39; Eubank, *Wages of Cross-Bearing*, 95–96.

10

Jesus' Historical Death and Resurrection[1]

PETER DEVELOPS THAT JESUS predicts his death and resurrection as historical events. For example, Jesus predicts that he must suffer many things from the elders, chief priests, and scribes, and be condemned to death (Acts 2:23; 4:10, 27; Mark 8:31; 9:12, 31; Matt 16:21; 17:12, 22–23; 20:18; Luke 9:22, 44; 17:25; 18:31; 22:22).[2] In the Synoptics, Jesus does not explain why this must happen; He just said it must take place. In the Synoptics, these wicked religious leaders were simply following the foolish way of killing a righteous man who showed up their evil ways.[3] Peter's presentation in Acts develops that the sovereign's plan includes these leaders culpably rejecting and killing Christ, while God vindicates Christ through resurrection (Acts 2:23–24; 3:13–18; 4:10, 24–27; 10:39–41). Jesus predicts that his death would be by crucifixion and that he would resurrect on the third day (Mark 9:31; Matt 16:21; 17:9, 23; 20:19; Luke 9:22). At times the disciples did not understand what Jesus was saying (Luke 9:44). Eventually, Peter becomes a witness of Christ's sufferings (1 Pet 5:1; Acts 10:30).

Jesus sets his resolve like flint to suffer (Isa 50:6–7) because he realized that the kingdom is only obtainable by going through the messianic woes (Dan 9:24–27). These Messianic woes begin his martyrdom and the

---

1. Kennard, *Messiah Jesus*, 269–92, 333–53.

2. Additional texts utilized beyond Mark and other Petrine statements further supports Mark's case for historicity of these events through multiple attestation.

3. This fits the Jewish pattern spoken by Wis 2.12–20.

potential martyrdom of his disciples. Albert Schweitzer developed this briefly as follows:

> In order to understand Jesus' resolve to suffer, we must first recognize that the mystery of this suffering is involved in the mystery of the kingdom of God, since the kingdom cannot come until the [tribulation] *peirasmos* has taken place. . . . The novelty lies in the form in which [the sufferings] are conceived. The tribulation, so far as Jesus is concerned, is now connected with an historical event: He will go to Jerusalem, there to suffer death at the hands of the authorities. . . . In the secret of his passion which Jesus reveals to the disciples at Caesarea Philippi the pre-Messianic tribulation is . . . concentrated upon himself alone, and that in the form that they are fulfilled in his own passion and death at Jerusalem. That was the new conviction that had dawned upon him. He must suffer for others . . . that the kingdom might come.[4]

These predictions of Jesus' crucifixion, provide a call to the cost of discipleship in mimetic atonement and a reassurance that the death and resurrection were God's plan. The main contextual implication for Jesus' death in these predictive comments is an undergirding of the cost of discipleship; since Jesus is heading for crucifixion, the true disciple must follow him by taking up their cross in impending martyrdom as well (Mark 8:34–37; Matt 10:38–39; 16:24–26; Luke 9:23–26; 14:27).[5] That is, they must be ready for the live possibility that those who will kill Christ, may kill them as well (Acts 7:54–60; 12:1–6).[6] This mimetic atonement view was common in Jewish,[7] Greek, and Roman literature.[8] Hellenistic biography presents the "supreme indicator" of a person's character to be

4. Schweitzer, *Quest for the Historical Jesus*, 384–90; for an expansion of this perspective see Pate and Kennard, *Deliverance Now and Not Yet*.

5. This emphasis is in line with that of scholarly commentators on these verses. Davies and Allison, *Matthew*, 2:222–23, 670–671; Senior, *Passion of Jesus in Matthew*, 40–45; Gundry, *Mark*, 452–54; Bock, *Luke*, 1:850–57; 2:1286–87; Beck, "'Imiatio Christi'," 28–47.

6. Nero's persecution of Christians: Tacitus, *Ann.* 15.44; *1 Clem.* 6; *Did.* 16.3–5.

7. 1 Macc 2.27–28; 2 Macc 6.12–17.42; 4 Macc 1.8–11; 6.27–30; 7.8–9; 9.23–24; 10.10; 11.12–27; 12.16–18; 16.16, 24–25; 17.2, 11–22; 18.1–5; Wis 2.12–20; 3.5–6; 4.18—15.14; 7.14; 11.19; 12.22; *T. Mos.* 9–10.10; Pate and Kennard, *Deliverance Now and Not Yet*, 29–71; Seeley, *Noble Death*; Green, *Death of Jesus*, 168.

8. Seneca, *Ad Lucilium Epistulae Morales*, 24.4–7; 98.12–14; Silius Italicus, *Punica* 6.531–38; Tacitus, *Ann.* 15.62; 16.35; *Epictetus* 4.1.168–72; Pate and Kennard, *Deliverance Now and Not Yet*, 19–28; Seeley, *Noble Death*; Talbert, *Learning Through Suffering*, 17–29.

the way he faces his own death,[9] which shows why the Gospel of Mark ends with Jesus' martyrdom, and underscores mimetic atonement.

Most of these predictive statements about Jesus' death and resurrection are removed some distance from the passion narrative, showing that especially Mark and Matthew's narrative of Jesus' death and resurrection does not set up an evidential demonstration. Of course, when the events of Jesus life in history are considered, they show that they were within Jesus' and God's plan. However, only in John's Gospel is the retelling of Jesus' death and resurrection emphasizing a fulfillment theme by punctuating it with fulfilled prophecy statements. Mark's narrative of Jesus' death retells what historically happened.

The primary predictions that are close to the crucifixion narrative are predictions about Judas' betrayal, Peter's denials, and the disciples scattering. All three of these predictions occur at the celebration of Passover. Jesus identifies that one of his disciples would betray him, the one who dips his hand in a bowl with Jesus and to whom Jesus gives a bread piece (Mark 14:18–21; Matt 26:23–25; Luke 22:21–22). This identifies Judas as the betrayer. Regarding this betrayal, there are several details itemized as fulfilling OT prophecy, namely that 1) the betrayal money was thirty pieces of silver and it bought a potter's field, and that 2) Judas forfeited his apostolic portion and position through this betrayal (Mark 14:49; Acts 1:20; Pss 69:25; 109:8; Zech 11:12–13; Matt 26:54–56; 27:9–10). Jesus does not develop his own death here but rather the horrible consequences of dishonor and damnation that await Judas, since he is described as "lost" as "the son of perdition" (John 17:12; Acts 1:20).[10] The potential damnation is also hinted at by 1) Jesus' statement that "it would have been better for him to have never been born," (Mark 14:21; Matt 26:24),[11] 2) Luke's description that Satan enters Judas (Luke 22:3), and 3) that Peter mentioned that Judas goes "to his own place" (Acts 1:25).[12] The disciples are clearly upset about such a revelation and repeatedly claim that they will be loyal.

In contrast, Jesus predicts that the disciples will all scatter (Mark 14:27; Zech 13:7; Matt 26:31–32). The disciples are not as loyal as they think when brought face to face with their impending martyrdom. Peter's

---

9. Bond, *First Biography of Jesus*, 68.

10. Brown, *John*, 760; this is the more damning evidence against Judas, but the other two notes to follow speak in this direction.

11. Cf. Matt 18:6–9; 2 Pet 2:20; 1 *En.* 38.2; 1 *Clem.* 46.8; *Herm. Vis.* 4.2; *m. Ḥag.* 2.1.

12. Lightfoot, *Commentary on the New Testament*, 4:19.

denials (which Jesus predicts) are a special example undercutting this overconfidence (Mark 14:29-31; Matt 26:33-35; Luke 22:31-34). Jesus disorients Peter with the claim that Satan will sift them, which sifting results in Peter denying Jesus three times. Jesus reassured Peter that he will strengthen the disciples after his denials. The passion narrative alludes to this prediction very softly by recounting that after Peter denied Jesus and the cock crowed, then Peter remembered Jesus' statement that he would deny him.

Luke is unique among the Synoptics in developing two resurrection appearances in which Jesus recounts from OT prophecy why Christ had to suffer these things to enter glory (Luke 24:26-27, 44-46). These two accounts probably provide Peter's sermonic rationale for why Jesus must resurrect (Acts 2:24-33; 3:15).

JESUS' PASSION

The historicity of the passion accounts unpacks an event on the eve of Passover between AD 30-34.[13] Mark and the Synoptics present Jesus' death in a streamlined historical narrative recounting of what took place in Christ's passion, without embellishments of fulfilling prophecy or explaining their theological significance. If there is an emphasis beyond this historical witness, it is that Jesus is the king of the Jews.

Judas betrays Jesus with a kiss (Mark 14:42-45; Matt 26:47-50; Luke 22:47-48). As the mob closes in, Peter cuts off the ear of Malchus, the servant (Mark 14:49; Matt 26:50-56; Luke 22:49-53). Jesus heals the ear and tells everyone to put up their weapons for he has twelve legions of angels available to him if he desired their aid (Matt 26:53). He asked the mob why they came to him in secret with weapons as for a thief. They seize Jesus, so the disciples fled. One young man[14] escaped naked (Mark 14:51-52).

Jesus had a hearing before Caiphas where conflicting false testimony could not convict him (Mark 14:55-66; Matt 26:57-68; Luke 22:63-71;

---

13. Passover eve (Mark 15:25; Matt 27:45-46; *Jub.* 49.10; Josephus, *Ant.* 14.65; *War* 6.423; Philo, *Spec. Laws* 2; *m. Pesaḥ.* 5.1), no earlier than AD 30 (with Jesus' ministry beginning around AD 28 [Luke 3:1-2; Tacitus, *Ann.* 1] and at least three Passovers within Jesus' ministry [First Passover: John 2:13, 23; Second: John 6:4; Third: Mark 14:1-2; Matt 26:2, 5; Luke 22:1-2; *Gos. Pet.* 5; *m. Sanh.* 6; *b. Sanh.* 43a; *Sifre Deut.* 221]) and no later than AD 34 when Pilate is entangled putting down a Samaritan rebellion for which he was recalled by the Roman Senate (Josephus, *Ant.* 18.85); McKnight, *Jesus and His Death.*

14. The young man might be John Mark since his is the only account of this event.

Acts 4:6).[15] The witnesses testified that Jesus claimed to be able to destroy the temple and rebuild it in three days. Harkening in this direction, Jesus had begun to be a real annoyance in running the money changers out of the temple possibly three times, maybe twice in one week (Mark 11:11, 15–18; John 2:14–20; Matt 21:12–13; Luke 19:44–46). However, one of the primary charges is that Jesus claimed to be the temple rebuilder, which role was understood at that time to be primarily a messianic role (Mark 14:58; Matt 26:61).[16] Later the *Babylonian Talmud* claimed the charges to be "because he practiced sorcery and enticed and led Israel astray."[17] However, the conflicting testimony at this hearing did not allow any of these charges to stick. N. T. Wright sums up the reason the Jewish authorities had Jesus killed as a fivefold answer[18] and I add a sixth.

1. Because many (not least many Pharisees, but also, probably, the chief priests) saw him as "a false prophet, leading Israel astray";[19]

2. because, as one aspect of this, they saw his temple action as a blow against the central symbol not only of national life but also of YHWH's presence with his people;[20]

3. because, though he was clearly not leading a real or organized military revolt, he saw himself as in some sense messiah, and could thus become a focus of serious revolutionary activity;

4. because, as the pragmatic focus of these three points, they saw him as a dangerous political nuisance, whose actions might well call down the wrath of Rome upon temple and nation alike;[21]

---

15. There are abundant irregularities of what becomes Jewish *mishnaic* judicial regulation: Sus 44–59; 11QTemp 61:9; *m. Sanh.* 4.1 prohibits night trials, 4.5; 7.5, a capital verdict cannot be passed against a blasphemer unless his blaspheme includes the divine name; Juel, *Messiah and the Temple*, 59–64; Gundry, *Mark*, 893–94.

16. God is portrayed to be the builder of the temple (1 *En.* 90.28–29; *Jub.* 1.17; 11QTemp 29.8–10; 4QFlor. 1.3, 6; *Midr. Ps.* 90.17; *Mek.* of R. Ishmael 3). Messiah is also claimed to be the temple builder (2 Sam 7:13; 1 Chr 17:12; Zech 4:7–10; Acts 6:13–14; *Sib. Or.* 5.420–33).

17. *B. Sanh.* 43a and 107b.

18. Wright, *Jesus and the Victory of God*, 551–52; Kennard added the following notes.

19. Point one is supported by *b. Sanh.* 43a and 107b.

20. Point two is supported by Jer 26:11 and Josephus, *War* 6.300–309.

21. Points three and four are virtually the same except point three fears Jewish abuse (as in Matt 26:5) and point four fears Roman abuse (as emphasized in John 11:48–50).

5. because, at the crucial moment in the hearing, he not only (as far as they were concerned) pleaded guilty to the above charges, but also did so in such a way as to place himself, blasphemously, alongside the god of Israel;[22]

6. because Jesus was seen as a royal messianic pretender, which rendered the death sentence legal as an act of the Roman governor.[23]

Jesus was silent and did not defend himself before his accusers and the Sanhedrin (Mark 14:61; 1 Pet 2:21–24).[24]

Wright mentioned in his fifth reason and I in the sixth reason, the high priest put Jesus under oath to truthfully tell whether he is the Christ (anointed as the king of the Jews), the Son of God (Mark 15:2; Matt 26:63; 27:11; Luke 20:20; 22:67, 70; 23:2–3; John 18:29–33; 19:7–9).[25] Jesus answers "yes" to these appellations and then identifies himself as Daniel's Son of Man who will come in the clouds to judge all and reign. This statement combines phrases from Psalm 110:1 and Daniel 7:13 like early Jewish eschatological texts had done.[26] On this basis, Caiphas accuses Jesus of blasphemy for identifying himself as the messiah and sentences Jesus to death. Such a death sentence in the context of Jesus' claims renders these religious leaders sentencing themselves to utter defeat and destruction under the conquest of the Son of Man. Ignorant of this, the other Sanhedrin participants[27] mock and beat Him.

22. The biblical text has the religious leaders claim Jesus blasphemes in his claim to be Daniel's Son of Man (Mark 14:62–64; Matt 26:64–65; Luke 22:69–71).

23. Tacitus, *Ann.* 15.44.3; Harvey, *Jesus and the Constraints*, ch. 2.

24. Isa 53:7; Acts 8:32–33; *Barn.* 5.2, 14; *Sib. Or.* 8.288–93; *Odes of Sol.* 31.10–11; *Gos. Pet.* 4.10; *Mart. Pol.* 8.3.

25. *Gos. Pet.* 3.6–9; 4.7, 11; 11.45–46; 15.32; around AD 200 Serapion discovered that the greater part of the *Gos. Pet.* was in accordance with the historical Jesus, but he rejected its authority, pointing out that there were heretical additions.

26. *1 En.* 62.5; *T. Benj.* 10.6; *T. Job* 33.3–9; *Apoc. El.* 1.8; Peter claims that the Psalm 110:1 claim is already realizable in Christ's ascension to be seated at God's right hand (Acts 2:33–36; Heb 1:3, 13; 10:13).

27. Sanders ("Pharisees in Luke-Acts," 148) argued that unlike Matthew and Mark which place the Pharisees as active opponents of Jesus to bring about Jesus' death, Luke does not develop the Pharisees in this negative light. Sanders argues that the Pharisees' only problems with Jesus in Luke is the repeated affirmation of his messiahship and his claims to forgive sins (pp. 153–54). However, in this context surrounding Jesus' death, Mark 12:13 and Matt 22:34, 41; 23:2, 13, 15, 23, 25, 27, 29 merely place the Pharisees as opponents to Jesus' teaching. Matt 27:62 includes the Pharisees as concerned to secure Jesus' tomb, as though they were concerned that Jesus' followers would not co-op the Pharisaic inclination to believe in resurrection. Perhaps the Pharisees saw Jesus and his disciples as a rival Pharisaic sect. Regarding the death of Christ, the trial account

Meanwhile Peter, who was warming himself in the courtyard, denies Jesus three times, even to a slave girl with an oath (Mark 14:66–72; Matt 26:69–75; Luke 22:54–62).[28] Those around Peter could tell by his accent (probably the dropping of his H's)[29] that he was a Galilean and accused him further of being one of Jesus' disciples. Peter denied her accusation with an oath. The cock crowed. Peter remembered Jesus' statement and noticed Jesus' glance at him, so he ran away weeping.

After Jewish sentencing, the Romans had to grant permission for carrying out the death sentence (Acts 2:23 "lawless men;" 4:26–27; John 18:31; 19:7).[30] With this in mind, Pilate questioned Jesus in the Praetorium of the Herodian palace and tried to release him (Mark 15:1–15; Matt 27:11–26; Luke 23:1–5, 13–25; John 18:38–40). Jesus was silent before Pilate and Herod as the chief priests and scribes accused him vehemently (1 Pet 2:22–23; Mark 15:4–5).[31] Herod and his soldiers treated Jesus with contempt, mocking him (Acts 4:11, 27; Luke 23:11). Herod sent Jesus back to Pilate declaring him innocent and having Jesus dressed in a gorgeous robe of royalty.[32] Pilate now wished to release Jesus referring to him in his crown of thorns as "the man" (John 19:5). Pilate even offered to punish and release Jesus instead of capital punishment (Luke 23:16). However, the mob asked for Barabbas instead, and demanded Jesus be

---

describes the involvement to be especially the: chief priests, scribes, Sadducees, and the elders (Mark 14:53, 55, 60, 63; 15:1; Matt 26:14, 47, 59, 62–65; 27:1, 6, 20, 41; Luke 22:2, 66; 23:1, 13). None of the synoptic accounts place the Pharisees as particularly culpable for Jesus' death, though all Synoptics recognize the Pharisees as opponents to Jesus' teaching during his lifetime. Luke presents less Pharisaic rejection of Jesus' teaching than is found in Matt and Mark.

28. Peter's oath could have been using the oath phrase, "I neither know nor understand what you're saying;" *m. Šebu.* 8.3, 6.

29. Vermes, *Jesus the Jew*, 52–53 explains the Galilean tendency to drop Hs from pronunciation and cites a *Talmud* text *b. ʿErub.* 53b to example this with a purchase of something in Aramaic called *ʿamar* as follows, "You stupid Galilean, do you want something to ride on [a donkey = *hamār*]? Or something to drink [wine = *hamar*]? Or something for clothing [wool = *ʿamar*]? Or something for a sacrifice [lamb = *immar*]?"

30. Josephus, *War* 6.126; *y. Sanh.* 18a, 24b; However, the described stoning that happened to Stephen (Acts 6–7) and James (Josephus, *Ant.* 20.200) do not include this feature. On the other hand, Acts 12:1–2 describes Herod as actively having James killed under his authority.

31. Isa 53:7; Acts 8:32–33; *Barn.* 5.2, 14; *Sib. Or.* 8.288–93; *Odes of Sol.* 31.10–11; *Gos. Pet.* 4.10; *Mart. Pol.* 8.3.

32. *Gos. Pet.* 1.2 and 2.5 has Herod deliver Jesus over to the Jewish people to be killed. However, the *Gos. Pet.* 11.47–48 identifies that Pilate has governance over Jesus' death and tomb.

crucified, claiming that to not kill a pretender to kingship is disloyalty to Caesar (Luke 23:2; John 19:12). Pilate was vulnerable to this insistence because he was a brute who bullied and took bribes.[33] The Jews pressed Pilate that if he did not kill Jesus then he was no "friend of Caesar" for letting a publicly proclaimed king not be condemned.[34] The Jews already had amassed a series of charges against Pilate but within four years after this trial, when Pilate killed a mob of Jews and violently put down a rebellion in Samaria, a Jewish delegation was sent to Rome. In response, Tiberius recalled Pilate to have him executed. At this point in the passion narrative, Pilate washed his hands in a play for innocence[35] but he still retained the power to thwart Jesus' death and thus remained culpable as buckling to the Jewish leadership (Acts 2:23; 4:27). However, the mob claimed that Jesus' blood was on them and their children, thus affirming their greater culpability. Pilate had Jesus scourged and delivered over to be crucified (Mark 15:15; Matt 27:24-26; Luke 23:24; John 19:16-21).[36] Mark and Matthew identify that the death of Christ was performed by the Praetorian Guard from the Roman cohort, specifically indicating their culpability (Mark 15:16; Matt 27:27). In this, Jesus was mocked by Pilate's Roman soldiers as the king of the Jews in the same manner as Herod's soldiers had done (Mark 15:16-20; Matt 27:27-31; John 19:2-3). In this mockery, the Romans gave Jesus the accoutrements of royalty: robes, crown and a reed scepter. Lagrange argued that in contrast to this account by Matthew and Mark, by leaving the scourging account out Luke states that the Jewish leadership and presumably their guard carried out the crucifixion (Luke 23:25-26).[37] However, John specifically states that Pilate had Jesus scourged (John 19:1). Additionally, Luke recounting Petrine statements

33. Philo, *Leg.* 302-3.

34. Tiberius policy was to not disturb the Jewish customs (Philo, *Leg.* 161, 304-5), so the Jewish leadership had leverage to press Pilate (who was vulnerable by this time because of the record of his abuses) to do their bidding.

35. Corroboration also implied by the beginning to *Gos. Pet.* 1. Like: Pss. 26:6; 73:13; Aristeas, *Ep.* 305-6; Herodotus 1.35; Sophocles, *Ajax* 654; Ovid, *Fast.* 2.45-46; Virgil, *Aen.* 2.719.

36. Mara bar Serapion; Josephus, *Ant.* 18.3.3; Agapius, *Book of the Title*; Tacitus, *Ann.* 15.44; *b. Sanh.* 43a; Bock, *Luke*, 2:1843 for texts.

37. Isa 50:6; Zech 12:10; *Epis. Barn.* 5.14; 7.6-11; *Sib. Or.* 8.285-309; *Gos. Pet.* 3.6-9; Crossan, *Cross That Spoke*, 114-59; Lagrange, *Evangile selon Saint Luc*, 548; Sanders, *Jews in Luke-Acts*, 9.

in Acts shows additional Roman culpability for Jesus' death (Acts 2:23, "Lawless men"; 4:25–27, "Gentiles," Pontus Pilate, and Herod).[38]

While normal crucifixion had the criminal tied by rope to the crossbeam (*patibulum*), so that he would walk with it to the execution site and then be lifted by forked poles into the notch of the stationary upright,[39] Jesus is presented as possibly carrying the whole cross, and then Simon the Cyrene (the father of Alexander and Rufus) is pressed into service to carry the whole cross (σταυρὸν; Mark 15:21; Matt 27:32; Luke 23:26; John 19:17). While ropes were normally used to hold the crucified in place, Peter mentions that Jesus had been nailed to the cross and then raised into place (Acts 2:23; John 20:25, 27; Col 2:14).[40]

Jesus was crucified at the place of the skull under the charge "The King of the Jews" (Mark 15:21–39; Matt 27:32–54; Luke 23:33–49).[41] In Mark there are six times Jesus is called "king," which challenges the legitimacy of other kings in the book (Mark 15:2–32).[42] John especially emphasizes this charge by mentioning that it was in Hebrew, Latin, and Greek and that the religious leaders took issue with its text, for it actually claimed him to be the king of the Jews, rather than as Jewish leadership desired, that Jesus had wrongly claimed to be such a king (John 19:19–21). However, Pilate kept the text how he wrote it as a slam against the Jews.

Jesus was taunted by mob and Jewish leadership with such statements as: "Ha! You who were going to destroy the temple and rebuild it in three days, save yourself, and come down from the cross!" and "He trusts in God: let Him deliver now, if he takes pleasure in him; for he said, 'I am the Son of God'" and "He saved others; let him save himself if this is the messiah of God, his chosen one" (1 Pet 2:6; Mark 15:29–32; Matt 27:42–43; Luke 23:35). Jesus was mocked by the mob and the robbers (based on the plural: λῃσταὶ). The mocking demanded Jesus come down off the cross so that they might believe in him. The robbers on their crosses chimed in, also "bring us down too." When one robber repented

---

38. Josephus, *Ant.* 18.63–64; Ignatius, *Smyr.* 1.2; *Trall.* 9.1; Justin, *1 Apol.* 40.5–7; *Dial.* 103.3–4; Irenaeus, *Epid.* 74; 77; Melito of Sardis, *Homily on the Passion* 93; Tertullian, *Res.* 20.4; *Didascalia Apostolorum* 5.19.4–5; *Dialogue of Adamantius* 5.1; Tacitus, *Ann.* 15.44.

39. Pliny, *Nat. Hist.* 28.11.

40. Lucan, *Civil War* 6.547; *m. Šabb.* 6.10; Hewit, "Use of Nails in the Crucifixion"; Brown, *Death of the Messiah*, 949–51.

41. *Gos. Pet.* 4.2.

42. Herod is called "king" five times (Mark 6:14–27) and plural kings are mentioned once (Mark 13:9); Gelardini, "Contest for a Royal Title," 93–106.

and defended Jesus, Jesus reassured him that today he would join him in paradise (Mark 15:31; Matt 27:42, 44; Luke 23:39-44).⁴³ Jesus asked the Father to forgive them for they do not know what they are doing (Acts 3:17; Luke 23:34). The Romans tried to give Jesus wine mixed with myrrh, to dull his senses (Mark 15:23; Matt 27:34; John 19:29).⁴⁴ The Roman soldiers divided Jesus' clothes between them, gambling with lots for his seamless robe (Mark 15:24; Matt 27:35; Luke 23:34; John 19:23-24).⁴⁵

There was darkness in the land (Mark 15:33; Matt 27:45; Luke 23:44-45).⁴⁶ The *Gospel of Peter* 5.15 describes that the people were afraid that the sun might set in such darkness while Jesus was on the cross, which would render the land unclean (Deut 21:23). In the darkness, Jesus called out, "My God, my God, why have you forsaken me" and then Jesus prayed to his Father yielding up his spirit (Mark 15:34-37; Matt 27:46-50; Luke 23:46).

The temple veil was torn without explaining its meaning.⁴⁷ An earthquake split rocks but the account does not identify which ones,

---

43. *Gos. Pet.* 4.4 has one of the dying criminals defend Jesus as innocent.

44. This was a usual offer based on Prov 31:6; *b. Sanh.* 43a; *Barn.* 7.3, 5; *Gos. Pet.* 5.16.

45. Ps 22.18; *Gos. Pet.* 4.12; *Barn.* 6.6; Justin Martyr, *1 Apol.* 35.5-8. This results in Jesus probably wearing only a loincloth, in the execution pattern of *Jub.* 3.30-31; 7.20.

46. *Gos. Pet.* 5.15.

47. Some commentators (Josephus, *War* 5.212-14; 6.288-309; *b. Yoma* 39b; *y. Yoma* 6.43c; Tertullian, *Marc.* 4.42; Chrysostom, *Hom. on Mt.* 88.2; Davies and Allison, *Matthew*, 3:631) hold that this veil is the outer veil and it thus symbolizes the destruction of the temple in AD 70 as had been predicted by Habakkuk (*Liv. Proph. Hab.* 12; *2 Bar.* 6.7-9) and *T. Levi* 10.3 predicts that the curtain of the temple will be torn so that Israel's sins would no longer be concealed. Notice that no Gospel account develops that the outside veil looked like the starry sky (*b. B. Mes.* 59a), even though Allison (*End of the Ages Has Come*, 33) suggested that it represented the rending of the heavens on the Day of the Lord (Job 14:12 LXX; Ps 102:26; Isa 34:4; 63:19; Hag 2:6, 21; Matt 24:29; Luke 21:25; 2 Pet 3:10; Rev 6:14; *Sib. Or.* 3.82; 8.233, 413). Corroborating this, the tractate *Yoma* 6.3 recounts repeated miraculous opening of the temple gate at night around 40 years before AD 70, which "Rabban Yohanan ben Zakkai said, 'O Temple, why do you frighten us? We know that you will end up destroyed. For it has been said, "Open your doors, O Lebanon, that the fire may devour your cedars!"'" (Zech 11:1). Other commentators (Toussaint, *Behold the King*) interpret this to be the inner veil and symbolizing the sacrificial system is obsolete. Such a view would have limited communication value for there would be no way for the populous to know if the inner veil had torn unless priests officiating at the incense altar or Levites replacing the holy oil or bread spoke of these things, and there is no mention of this. Additionally, such an anti-law rational doesn't fit Jewish-Christian practice in Jerusalem, which continued to offer sacrifices until the destruction of the temple (Matt 5:23-24; Acts 21:21-28). Note that Heb 10:20-22, with its tabernacle description, is probably where the modern view emerges of splitting the

except that tombs are also opened by the earthquake. In response, a centurion pronounced that Jesus was innocent and truly a son of God, indicating Jesus' kingly role (Mark 15:39; Matt 27:54; Luke 23:47).

The legs of the thieves on their crosses were broken as usual to speed their death, but Jesus' did not have his legs broken because he had already died in the realm of his flesh (1 Pet 3:18; John 19:32–36).[48] To further confirm Jesus' death, the guard thrust a spear into Jesus' side, showing the death separation of water and blood pouring from Jesus' side (John 19:34–37).[49]

In contrast to this synoptic and Acts sermon emphasis of the historical events and culpability, the Petrine epistles apply Jesus' death toward vicarious atonement, while continuing to develop synoptic mimetic atonement.[50]

---

inner veil, so that Christians might draw near in intimacy to God, but in this context there is no discussion of a temple veil; rather Jesus' flesh is pictured as a veil, and the heavenly Holy of Holies remains only accessed by Jesus operating as the high priest (Heb 9:21, 23–25), so not describing the splitting of a temple veil.

48. *Gos. Pet.* 4.13–14; 4.4–5 claims that Jesus' legs would not be broken because when dying criminals claimed Jesus was innocent, the soldiers plotted to increase Jesus' agony; *Martyrium Andreae alterum* 1.13–16. Jesus died during the time that the Passover lambs were being killed, afternoon until evening (Exod 29:39; *Jub.* 49.10, 19; Philo, *Leg.* 2.145; R. Natan in *Mek. Bo* 5; *m. Pesaḥ.* 5.1; Josephus, *War* 6.423; *Ant.* 14.65). Such timing fits nicely with Paul identifying Jesus as the Passover Lamb (1 Cor 5:7), and Peter considering Jesus' death as a redemption to initiate a new exodus (1 Pet 1:2, 18; 2 Pet 2:1) but none of the biblical authors explain the meaning of this allusion or timing. Some commentators suggest that Jesus' legs not being broken to identify him as the Paschal Offering, which was not to have a bone broken (Exod 12:46; Num 9:12). None of the Gospels develop Jesus as the Paschal sacrifice, nor develop the meaning of this time or lack of bone breaking under a Passover metaphor, despite there being some apotropaic tendencies to develop the non-breaking of the bones of the Paschal sacrifice as a metaphor for Israel's bones to not be broken (*Jub.* 49.13). The timing of Passover only affects the Gospel accounts in that the Jewish leadership desired the execution to be complete before the Passover begins, so that the nation would not riot (Mark 14:2) and perhaps also not be rendered unclean (Deut 21:22–23). So, I conclude that the mention of Jesus' bones not breaking simply indicates that he was already dead.

49. This is likely a natural phenomenon of separation of fluid from dark red fluid, rather than a lance breaking his heart or a miracle as Catholic tradition maintains (Brown, *John*, 946–47).

50. These atonement themes are developed in Kennard, *Petrine Theology*, the chapter on atonement and redemption.

JESUS' BURIAL AND RESURRECTION

The concept of resurrection in the OT is marginal at best.[51] For example, the Pentateuch occasionally states that the heroes of the faith are gathered to their forefathers. However, when there is no family tomb, such a reference is a very ambiguous comfort (Num 20:24, 26). In a vague event, the witch of Endor conjured up Samuel bodily from the grave (1 Sam 28:14–20). While he vanished when the conjuring was over, he must have been available from *sheol* to temporarily bodily resurrect. Additionally, Ezekiel's vision of the valley of dry bones is better understood as a metaphor describing Israel's national resurrection and reunion, rather than a personal resurrection of individuals (Ezek 37).[52] Perhaps the only clear mention of personal resurrection in the OT is that of Dan 12:2–3 where the dead will awake from their sleep among the dust to either everlasting life or everlasting contempt.[53] This sort of resurrection hope is much more common in early Judaism.[54] That is, when the Mosaic covenant faithful

---

51. Von Rad, *Old Testament Theology*, 1:470–71, 2:350; Brueggemann, *Theology of the Old Testament*, 483–84; Wright, *Resurrection*, 85–128.

52. Zimmerli, *Ezekiel*, 2:256–57.

53. Baldwin, *Daniel*, 204–6; Wright, *Resurrection*, 108–10.

54. *1 En.* 58.3; 62.14–16; 91.10; 92.2; 108.11–14; *2 Bar.* [Syriac] 30.1–5; 2 Macc 7.9–14, 22–23; 14.43–46; 4 Macc 7.19; 16.25; *4 Ezra* 7.32; *Sib. Or.* 4.180; *T. Ben.* 10.6–8; *T. Levi* 18; *T. Jud.* 24; *T. Hos.* 6:2 interpret this text to be resurrection whereas the text speaks of the reviving of Israel on the third day; *Tg. Jon.* on Isa 27:12–13 describes salvation as being accomplished on the third day; *b. Sanh.* 90b where Gamaliel claims that God would give the resurrected patriarchs land, not merely their descendants, and *Johanan Numbers* 18:28 the portion of YHWH given to Aaron is taken that he will be alive again, likewise Num 15:31 is claimed that the remaining guilt of the offender will be accountable in the world to come; 91b–92a; *B. Ta'an.* 2a; *B. Ketub.* 111; *m. Sanh.* 10.1, 3; *T. Mos.* 10.8–10; *Gen. Rab.* 14.5; 28.3; *Lev. Rab.* 14.9; *Messianic Apocalypse* adds resurrection to a modification of Ps 146:5–9 as a Messianic expectation to be done to others; *T. Jud.* 25.4 claims this Messianic resurrection would begin with Abraham, Isaac, and Jacob; *T. Benj.* claims that after these are raised the whole of Israel will be raised; *Pss. Sol.* 3.11–12; 4Q521 frag. 2, col. 2.1–13; frags. 7 and 5, col. 2.1–7; 1QH 14.29–35; 19.10–14; *Targum Songs* 8.5; the benediction in the *Amidah*, the *Shemoneh Esre*. However, Wis 3.1; 8.19–20; 9.15 and Josephus' description of the Pharisees (*Ant.* 17.152–54; 18.1.3–5; *War* 2.151–53; 2.8.14; *Ap.* 2.217–18) follow more a Platonic immortality of the soul view, but even here, departing from Platonism, the soul eventually is given a body to match (Wis 9.15; Josephus, *War* 2.163). Also, the biblical authors (Mark 12:18–27; Matt 22:23–33; Acts 23:6–7) and the *Eighteen Benedictions* present the Pharisees as believing the bodily resurrection of the dead; Gillman, *Death of Death*, 101–42; Wright, *Resurrection*, 129–206 for the post-biblical Jewish view. The early church from patristic through medieval eras embraced bodily resurrection instead of Platonic immortality of the soul with regard to personal eschatology (Bynum, *Resurrection of the Body*; Wright, *Resurrection*, 480–552).

die, they are still blessed in the afterlife with bodily resurrection unto Paradise. For example, some Qumran manuscripts speak of an afterlife as everlasting life,[55] and possibly others even intimate bodily resurrection for the faithful.[56]

In a precarious time, David prayed the lament Ps 16, with its bold confession of trust in the protecting relationship with Yahweh for this life and beyond (Ps 16:1, 8–11; Acts 2:25). David's confidence is that Yahweh would "not abandon my life to *sheol*; neither will Thy holy one to undergo decay" (Ps 16:10). The synonymous parallelism indicates that David is confident that he will not suffer a premature death.[57] Whereas, Luke records Peter as fusing this psalm with 2 Sam 7:12 to proclaim the necessity that David's greatest son reigning on David's throne, thus Jesus must have risen (Acts 2:25–32).[58] The rationale[59] is built on the confidence that David remained in his tomb in Peter's day and that Jesus has evidentially been identified by this resurrection to be the Davidic King, thus as Davidic King Jesus must have raised so that he could be seated on the Davidic throne as king (Acts 2:29–32). Furthermore, since Jesus was the prince of life (Acts 3:15), Jesus resurrected, to which Peter was a witness. Peter is a witness to Jesus' resurrection such that it becomes a feature of his gospel.

Jesus was buried by Joseph of Arimathea in a recently carved family tomb (Mark 15:42–47; Matt 27:57–66; Luke 23:50–56). Pilate gave the priests a guard to seal the tomb but early on the first day of the week a severe earthquake and a shining angel moved the stone away (Mark 16:1–8; Matt 28:1–17; Luke 24:1–11). The guards fell down catatonic and then reported to the chief priests what had happened.[60] The chief priests set up the conspiracy theory that while the guards slept, the disciples

---

55. 1QS 4.6–8; CD 3.20; 4Q181 3–4; *1 En.* 37.4; 40.4; 58.3; 4 Macc 15.3; *Ps. Sol.* 3.12; *Sib. Or.* 3.49 frag. 3.

56. 1QH 3.10–22; 6.34; 11.12; 1QM 12.1–4.

57. Anderson, *Psalms*, 1:145–46; Eichrodt, *Theology of the Old Testament*, 1:524; von Rad, *Old Testament Theology*, 1:405; Wright, *Resurrection*, 104–5.

58. Bock (*Proclamation*) developed that OT quotes are used by Luke for their proclamation value in these sermons; Marshall (*Acts*, 77–78) claims that like Ps 132 and 2 Sam 7:10–16 (present in Acts 2:30) being interpreted by 4QFlor as Messianic, so to Peter takes Ps 16 as referring to the Messiah.

59. This line of argument reflects a similar fusion of Ps 132 and 2 Sam 7:10–16, which 4QFlor interprets to be messianic.

60. While the canonical Gospels report Jesus' resurrection as having occurred without observers except the guards, *Gos. Pet.* 34–39 presents a crowd of observers watching the angel's role to move the stone away in compliance to a divine voice.

stole the body. This would mean a death sentence for the Roman guards for sleeping on duty. However, the guards were paid and protected.

Two angels (looking like men) announced to the women at the grave that Jesus had arisen, but that they should not be afraid (Mark 16:1–8; Matt 28:5–17; Luke 24:1–12; John 20:1–18). The angel showed the women where Jesus had been laid, and then told them to tell Peter and the disciples. The women departed quickly with fear and great joy to tell the disciples. Mark does not recount the disciples' experiences with the resurrected Jesus, as other Gospels do. John and Peter ran to the tomb. When Peter arrived and went into the tomb and beheld the linen wrappings lying there and face cloth rolled up by itself.[61] No one would have taken the body and left the wrappings, so they conclude Jesus must have resurrected!

Jesus appeared to some of them, including Simon, on the Emmaus Road. Was this Simon Peter who Paul records as seeing the risen Christ before the twelve (1 Cor 15:5) or is this Simon the Zealot, and Cephas had another resurrection appearance? The two walking to Emmaus were sad because they viewed Jesus as a prophet empowered by God to bring in the kingdom, but their hopes for this were dashed with Jesus' death (Luke 24:13–35). Then they recounted that they were troubled earlier in the day by the testimony of some women that that tomb was empty, and Jesus was alive. On the road to Emmaus with a couple of disciples, Jesus explained from the Scriptures why the anointed king must suffer these things before entering glory.[62] Then Jesus vanished from their sight. Jesus' miraculous appearing and disappearing through walls may reflect that he is divine rather than being normative for our resurrection bodies. This group of disciples with Jesus at Emmaus then quickly returned to Jerusalem and told the other disciples of these things.

Peter was present as a witness when resurrected Jesus appeared in their midst saying, "Peace be with you" (Luke 24:36–46; John 20:11–23; Acts 2:32; 3:15; 4:10; 10:41; 1 Cor 15:5). The disciples were startled and frightened thinking they were seeing a spirit. Jesus urged them to not be troubled but to touch him because a spirit does not have flesh and bones

---

61. The concept of description of the linen wrappings in John 20:6–7 probably does not give credence to the view that Jesus in his resurrection passed through the burial clothes, leaving them undisturbed. He may have, but if he had, one would expect the face cloth to be lying where the head had been. In fact, it was rolled up in a place by itself. The one thing that can be certainly said is that it was extremely unlikely that someone had taken the body and left all these wrappings. Brown, *John*, 1007–8.

62. This claim is justifiable from the perspective of early Jewish targum evidence and the NT quotes of OT texts concerning resurrection.

as Jesus has. While they were marveling, Jesus asked for some broiled fish, and he ate before them. Jesus opened the disciples' minds to understand that he had predicted his death and resurrection, and so had Moses, the prophets and the Psalms, which all must be fulfilled (Luke 24:44; 1 Cor 15:4). Jesus then reminded them that he will send them to preach repentance and remission of sins in Christ's name, as the Father had sent him (Luke 24:47–49; Acts 1:8). He breathed on them and said, "Receive the Holy Spirit." Jesus then reiterated their scribal role, "If you forgive the sins of any, their sins will be forgiven; if you retain the sins of any, they will be retained."

Thomas had not been with them during this visit, so they told him that they had seen the Lord (John 20:24–31). He responded that unless he saw and placed his finger in the nail prints, that he would not believe. After eight days, with the doors shut, Jesus stood in their midst. Jesus greeted them again with "Peace be with you." Then he said to Thomas, "Reach here with your finger and see My hands; and reach here your hand and put it into My side; and be not unbelieving but believing." Thomas answered, "My Lord and my God." Jesus recognized that Thomas had now believed because he had seen the resurrected evidence, but he blessed those who do not see and yet believe. At this point John reflects on the repeated miraculous evidence that Jesus had provided to foster an ongoing faith in Jesus as the Christ, the Son of God.

Jesus then met up with the disciples in Galilee, by the Sea of Tiberias (Luke 24:36–46; John 21:1–25). At the third instance where Jesus manifested himself to them, Peter and the fishermen had gone fishing but had caught nothing. Jesus urged them to cast their net on the right side of the boat, which probably means for them to fish the very water that they had cast their net in from the left side. The catch was too great to haul into the boat with one hundred and fifty-three fish (John 21:3–6, 11).[63] At that point John recognized that it was Jesus who had made the request. Peter jumped overboard and swam the hundred yards to shore. The rest rowed the catch in behind the boat. When they got ashore, Jesus had a charcoal fire with some fish on it and some bread, but he requested some more fish from them. So, Peter drew the net into shore and John remembered the count of the number of the fish. Jesus fed them breakfast.

After breakfast Jesus questioned Peter to help him articulate his supreme love (John 21:15–17). Jesus repeated Simon's name in a very formal

---

63. This account has eyewitness evidence.

pattern reiterating that what followed was significant. The question was aimed at discerning Peter's supreme loyalty.[64] This question was asked three times. Each time Peter answered in the affirmative. Jesus responded to each answer with a command reiterating Peter's responsibility to care for the flock owned by Jesus, the Great Shepherd.[65] Jesus did not give the flock over to Peter, but he delegated to Peter the task of shepherding his flock.

Jesus attempted to end the conversation with the pointed exhortation ringing in Peter's ears, "Follow Me!" In this context this exhortation calls for a commitment of loyalty to Christ all the way to death, with Christ being Peter's example. Christ brings the focus back to Peter, "You follow me!" (John 21:22).

These Galilee resurrection appearances continued to occur because in one instance only seven were present, while another instance may have had the eleven, and another had five hundred at one time (Matt 28:7–20; John 20:24–26; 21:2; Acts 1:2–13; 1 Cor 15:6). Resurrected Jesus was seen also by James, Mathias, and Justus (Acts 1:22–23; 1 Cor 15:5, 7). Jesus claimed all authority in heaven and earth, commissioning the disciples with the coming Spirit empowerment to be witnesses proclaiming the kingdom message of repentance for forgiveness of sins to all nations beginning in Jerusalem and to make disciples of all people groups baptizing and teaching them to observe all that Jesus commanded them (Matt 28:18–20; Luke 24:47–53; Acts 1:5–8). After reassuring them that he would be with them until the end of the age Jesus lifted his hands to bless them and then bodily ascended into heaven (Acts 1:9–11). Two angels told the disciples that Jesus would return in the same manner as

---

64. The question "Do you love Me more than these?" has three possible meanings. Perhaps, because Peter had previously professed a greater loyalty than the others (Matt 26:33; Mark 14:29; John 13:37; 15:12), Jesus asked "Are you more loyal than they?" Maybe Jesus asked if Peter loved Jesus more than he loved these other disciples. That is, Peter had remained with his friends when they all forsook Christ. Perhaps Jesus asked Peter if he was more loyal to Jesus than to these things of fishing (his old occupation). The text appears to be ambiguous in discerning between these, but the commonality between them all is a discernment of Peter's supreme loyalty for Christ (Morris, *John*, 870–71).

65. The different ways of speaking in this passage are probably not significant. For example, Jesus asks whether Peter loves him with ἀγαπᾷς the first two times and φιλεῖς the third time. To each of the questions Peter answered "Yes" and then added that he loved (φιλῶ) Jesus. The result of this is that Peter loves Jesus with both ἀγαπαω and φιλενω. Likewise, the reiteration of "feed" or "tend" and "lambs" or "sheep" is also not significant except that Peter is given the shepherding responsibility over Jesus' whole flock (Brown, *John*, 1102–6).

you have watched him go. They returned to Jerusalem with great joy and continued to praise God in the temple.

The Gospel accounts of Jesus' resurrection do not develop great soteriological work but are narrative accounts of witnesses telling what they saw and providing prophetic rationale why Jesus must have been resurrected. Both the OT and Jesus predicted several of these events but the Synoptics play down an evidential perspective surrounding his death and resurrection, unlike Peter's Acts sermons which evidentially build from the fact that Peter is an eyewitness of Jesus' resurrection.

The most emphasized feature of Jesus' through the narratives of his death and resurrection is that Jesus is king (Acts 2:24–36).[66] The fact that Jesus is already king, seated at the right hand of God, identifies that he will judge and rule all forever, when he returns on the clouds. Prior to then he shows his kingdom greatness by leaving a pattern of service for all disciples to follow epitomized by his martyrdom. Jesus' resurrection and ascension vindicates Jesus as King and identifies him with the authority to commission and empower the disciples to 1) be witnesses of these things, 2) proclaim the kingdom message, and 3) make disciples.

First Peter 1:3–5 identifies Christ's resurrection into kingdom as grounding the believer's hope in their joining in kingdom resurrection. The initiation of faith toward resurrection is a work of the Father causing the believer to be born again, as reflected in his baptism pledge (1 Pet 1:3; 3:21; Acts 2:38; 10:43, 47). Christ's resurrection guarantees the born again with an imperishable kingdom inheritance reserved for them. The Christian's resurrection reflects Christ's resurrection.

---

66. Acts 2:34–36 may defend that Christ is also God. Künneth (*Theology of the Resurrection*, 114–15) even claims that through the resurrection his divinity was conferred upon him. However, Christ's pre-incarnate divinity would indicate that resurrection would not be a conferral but possibly could be a recognition of his divinity.

Select Bibliography

Abbot, Edwin. *Flatland: A Romance of Many Dimensions*. London: Seeley, 1884.

Abegg, Martin G. "The Covenant of the Qumran Sectarians." In *The Concept of the Covenant in the Second Temple Period*, edited by Stanley Porter and Jacqueline deRoo, 81–98. Leiden: Brill, 2003.

Abraham, William J. "The Epistemology of Jesus: An Initial Investigation." In *Jesus and Philosophy: New Essays*, edited by Paul Moser, 149–68. Cambridge: Cambridge University Press, 2009.

Abrahams, Israel. *Studies in Pharisaism and the Gospels*. 1st Series. Cambridge: Cambridge University Press, 1917.

———. *Studies in Pharisaism and the Gospels*. 2nd Series. Cambridge: Cambridge University Press, 1924.

Achtemeier, Paul. *1 Peter*. Hermenia. Minneapolis, MN: Fortress, 1996.

Adams, Edward. "The Coming of the Son of Man in Mark's Gospel." *TynBul* 56.2 (2005) 39–61.

———. *Constructing the World: A Study in Paul's Cosmological Language*. Edinburgh: T. & T. Clark, 2000.

Adams, Robert. "The Problem of Total Devotion." In *Rationality, Religious Belief, and Moral Commitment*, edited by Robert Audi and William Wainwright, 169–94. Ithaca: Cornell University Press, 1986.

Aland, Barbara, et al. *The Greek New Testament*. Stuttgart: Deutsche Bibelgesellschaft, 2014.

Aland, Kurt. *The Authorship and Integrity of the New Testament: Some Recent Studies*. Theological Collections 4. London: SPCK, 1965.

Allison, D. C. *The End of the Ages Has Come*. Philadelphia, PA: Fortress, 1985.

Alston, William. *Perceiving God: The Epistemology of Religious Experience*. Ithaca: Cornell University Press, 1991.

Althaus, Paul. *The Theology of Martin Luther*. Minneapolis, MN: Fortress, 1966.

Anderson, A. A. *The Book of Psalms. Volume 1 Psalms 1–72*. Grand Rapids: Eerdmans, 1972.

Anderson, Gary. *Charity: The Place of the Poor in the Biblical Tradition*. New Haven: Yale University Press, 2013.

Anderson, Hugh. *The Gospel According to Mark*. Edinburgh: Oliphants, 1976.
Anderson, R. Dean. *Glossary of Greek Rhetorical Terms Connected to Methods of Argumentation, Figures and Tropes from Anaximenes to Quintilian*. Leuven: Peeters, 2000.
Anderson, Ray S. "On Being Human: The Spiritual Saga of a Creaturely Soul." In *Whatever Happened to the Soul? Scientific and Theological Portraits of Human Nature*, edited by Warren Brown et al., 40–73. Minneapolis, MN: Fortress, 1998.
Anselm. "Foreknowledge and Freechoice." In *Readings in Medieval Philosophy*, edited by Andrew Schoedinger, 203–8. New York: Oxford University Press, 1996.
Applegate, J. K. "The Co-Elect Woman of 1 Peter." *NTS* 38 (1992) 587–604.
Aquinas, Thomas. "Summa Theologica." In *Aquinas: Great Books of the Western World*, 19:1–826; 20:1–1085. Chicago: Encyclopaedia Britannica, 1952.
Assmann, Jan. *Das kulturelle Gedächtnis: Schrift, Erinnerung und politische Identität in frühen Hochkulturen*. Munich: C. H. Beck, 1992.
Augustine. *Great Books of the Western World*. Vol. 18, *Augustine*. Chicago: Encyclopaedia Britannica, 1952.
Aulén, Gustav. *Christus Victor: An Historical Study of the Three Main Types of the Idea of Atonement*. New York: Macmillan, 1969.
Aune, David. "The Forgiveness Petition in the Lord's Prayer: First Century Literary, Liturgical and Cultural Contexts." In *Jesus, Gospel Tradition and Paul in the Context of Jewish and Greco-Roman Antiquity*, 66–71. Tübingen: Mohr Siebeck, 2013.
———. "Magic in Early Christianity." *Principat 23/2; vorkonstantinisches Christentum. Vchaeltnis zu roemischem Staat und heidischer Religion. Aufstieg und Niedergang der Roemischen Welt: 2*, edited by Wolfgang Haase, 1507–57. New York: Walter de Gruyter, 1980.
Austin, John. *How To Do Things with Words*. Oxford: Oxford University Press, 1976.
Avi-Yonah, Michael. *Hellenism and the East: Contacts and Interrelations from Alexander to the Roman Conquest*. Jerusalem: Institute of Languages, Literature and the Arts, Hebrew University, University Microfilms International, 1978.
Ayayo, Karelynne. "Magical Exectations and the Two-Stage Healing of Mark 8." *BBR* 24.3 (2014) 379–91.
Bahr, G. J. "The Seder of Passover and the Eucharistic Words." *NovT* 12 (1970) 181–202.
Bailey, K. E. "Informal Controlled Oral Tradition and the Synoptic Gospels." *AJT* 5 (1991) 34–54.
———. "Middle Eastern Oral Tradition and the Synoptic Gospels." *ExpTim* 106 (1995) 363–67.
Balch, David. "Early Christian Criticism of Patriarchal Authority: 1 Peter 2:11—3:12." *USQR* 39 (1984–85) 161–73.
———. "Hellenization/Acculturation in 1 Peter." In *Perspectives on First Peter*, edited by Charles Talbert, 79–101. Macon, GA: Mercer University Press, 1986.
———. *Let Wives Be Submissive: The Domestic Code in 1 Peter*. SBLMS 26. Chico: Scholars, 1981.
Baldwin, Joyce. *Daniel: An Introduction & Commentary*. Downers Grove: InterVarsity, 1978.
Balentine, Samuel. *Leviticus: Interpretation*. Louisville: Westminster John Knox, 2002.
Baley, Daniel. "Our Suffering and Crucified Messiah' [*Dial*. 111.2]: Justin Martyr's Allusions to Isaiah 53 in His Dialogue with Trypho with Special Reference to the New Edition of Marcovich." In *The Suffering Servant: Isaiah 53 in Jewish and*

Christian Sources, edited by Bernd Janowski and Peter Stuhlmacher, 324–417. Grand Rapids: Eerdmans, 2004.

Baltzer, Klaus. *The Covenant Formulary in the Old Testament*. Philadelphia, PA: Fortress, 1971.

———. *Das Bundesformular. Seine Ursprung und Seine Verwendung im A.T. Wiss. Monograph 2. A. und N.T. 4*. Neukirchen: Neukirchen-Vluyn, 1964.

Bammel, Ernst. "Markus 10:11f und das jüdische Eherecht." *ZNW* 61 (1970) 95–101.

Barclay, William. *The Gospel of Matthew*. Philadelphia, PA: Westminster, 1975.

Barnett, P. W. "The Jewish Sign Prophets." *NTS* 27 (1980) 679–97.

Barr, James. *The Semantics of Biblical Language*. London: Oxford University Press, 1961.

Barrett, C. K. *A Critical and Exegetical Commentary on the Acts of the Apostles*. 2 vols. London: T. & T. Clark, 1994.

Barth, Karl. *Church Dogmatics*. Edinburgh: T. & T. Clark, 1956.

Barton, Stephen. *Discipleship and Family Ties in Mark and Matthew*. Cambridge: Cambridge University Press, 1994.

———. "Memory and Remembrance in Paul." In *Memory in the Bible and Antiquity: The Fifth Durham-Tubingen Research Symposium (Durham, September 2004)*, edited by Stephen Barton et al., 333–34. Tübingen: Mohr Siebeck, 2007.

Bauckham, Richard. "The Gospel of John and the Synoptic Problem." In *New Studies in the Synoptic Problem, Oxford Conference, April 2008*, edited by P. Foster et al., 658–85. Leuven: Uitgeverij Peeters, 2011.

———. "James, Peter, and the Gentiles." In *The Missions of James, Peter, and Paul: Tensions in Early Christianity*, edited by Bruce Chilton and Craig Evans, 91–142. Leiden: Brill, 2005.

———. *Jesus and the Eyewitnesses: The Gospels as Eyewitness Testimony*. Grand Rapids: Eerdmans, 2006.

———. *Jude, 2 Peter*. WBC 50. Waco: Word, 1983.

———. "Markan Christology According to Richard Hays: Some Addenda." *Journal of Theological Interpretation* 2.1 (2017) 21–36.

———. "The Martyrdom of Peter." *ANRW* 2.26.1 (1992) 539–95.

Bauer, Walter. *Orthodoxy and Heresy in Earliest Christianity*. Minneapolis, MN: Fortress, 1971.

Bauman-Martin, Betsy. "Speaking Jewish: Postcolonial Aliens and Strangers in First Peter." In *Reading First Peter with New Eyes: Methodological Reassessments of the Letter of First Peter*, edited by Robert Webb and Betsy Bauman-Martin, 144–77. London: T. & T. Clark, 2007.

Bauman-Martin, Betsy, and Robert L. Webb. "Reading First Peter with New Eyes." In *Reading First Peter with New Eyes: Methodological Reassessments of the Letter of First Peter*, edited by Robert Webb and Betsy Bauman-Martin, 1–40. London: T. & T. Clark, 2007.

Baur, Ferdinand. "Die Chrisuspartei in der korinthischen Gemeinde, der Gegensatz des paulinischen und petrinischen Christentums in der altesten Kirche, der Apostel Petrus in Rom." In *Tübinger Zeitschrift für Theologie*, 61–206. Tübingen: Friedrich Fucs, Fahrgang, 1831.

———. *Kritische Untersuchungen über die kanonischen Evangelien, ihr Verhältniss zu einander, ihren Charakter und Ursprung*. Boston: Wentworth, 2018.

Beale, G. K. *A New Testament Biblical Theology: The Unfolding of the Old Testament in the New*. Grand Rapids: Baker, 2011.

Beare, Francis. *First Epistle of Peter*. Oxford: Basil Blackwell, 1970.
Beasley-Murray, G. R. *Baptism in the New Testament*. London: Macmillan, 1963.
Beck, Brian E. "*Imiatio Christi* and the Lucan Passion Narrative." In *Suffering and Martyrdom in the New Testament*, edited by William Horbury and Brian McNeil, 28–47. London: Cambridge University Press, 1981.
Beckman, Gary A., and Harry A. Hoffner. *Hittite Diplomatic Texts*. 2nd ed. Writings from the Ancient World 7. Atlanta, GA: Society of Biblical Literature, 1999.
Bede the Venerable. *Commentary on the Seven Catholic Epistles*. Translated by David Hurst. Kalamazoo, MI: Cistercian, 1985.
Beiringer, Reimund, and Didier Pollefeyt. *Paul and Judaism: Crosscurrents in Pauline Exegesis and the Study of Jewish-Christian Relations*. Library of New Testament Studies 463. London: T. & T. Clark, 2012.
Bell, Harold. *Jews and Christians in Egypt: The Jewish Troubles in Alexandria and the Athanasian Controversy, Illustrated by Texts from Greek Papyri*. London: British Museum, 1924.
Bellinger, William, and William R. Farmer. *Jesus and the Suffering Servant: Isaiah 53 and Christian Origins*. Atlanta, GA: Trinity, 1998.
Bengel, J. A. *Gnomon of the New Testament*. Philadelphia, PA: Sheldon & Co., 1864.
Ber, Yitzhaq ben Arye Yosef. *Seder 'Avodat Yisrael*. New York: Schocken, 1937.
Berding, Kenneth. *Polycarp and Paul: An Analysis of Their Literary and Theological Relationship in Light of Polycarp's Use of Biblical and Extra-biblical Literature*. Boston: Brill, 2002.
Berger, Adolf. *Encyclopedic Dictionary of Roman Law*. 2 vols. in 1. Philadelphia, PA: American Philosophical Society, 1953.
Berger, Peter. *The Social Reality of Religion*. London: Faber & Faber, 1969.
Berger, Peter, and Thomas Luckmann. *The Social Construction of Reality: A Treatise in the Sociology of Knowledge*. London: Penguin, 1967.
Berger, Peter, et al. *The Homeless Mind: Modernization and Consciousness*. New York: Vintage, 1973.
Berkeley, George. "Principles of Human Knowledge." In *The Great Books of the Western World*, edited by John Locke et al., 35:403–50. Chicago: Encyclopaedia Britannica, 1952.
Berkowitz, Luci, et al. *Thesaurus Linguae Graecae Canon of Greek Authors and Works*. New York: Oxford, 1990.
Bermejo-Rubio, Fernando. "Did Jesus the Galilean Redefine the Concept of Kingship? Apologetic Agendas from Ancient Texts to Modern Scholarship." *Annali di Storia dell'Esegesi* 35.1 (2018) 51–82.
Best, Ernest. *1 Peter*. NCB. Grand Rapids: Eerdmans, 1971.
———. "1 Peter II 4–10—A Reconsideration." *Nov Test* 11.4 (1969) 270–93.
———. *Following Jesus: Discipleship in the Gospel of Mark*. Sheffield: JSOT, 1981.
Bettenson, Henry, and Chris Maunder. *Documents of the Christian Church*. Oxford: Oxford University Press, 1999.
Betz, Hans Dieter. *Nachfolge und Nachahmung Jesu Christi im Neuen Testament*. BHT 37. Tübingen: Mohr/Siebeck, 1967.
Bigg, Charles. *A Critical and Exegetical Commentary on the Epistles of St. Peter and St. Jude*. Edinburgh: T. & T. Clark, 1978.
Bird, Michael F. "Salvation in Paul's Judaism?" In *Paul and Judaism Paul and Judaism: Crosscurrents in Pauline Exegesis and the Study of Jewish-Christian Relations*, edited

by Reimund Beiringer and Didier Pollefeyt, 15–40. Library of New Testament Studies 463. London: T. & T. Clark, 2012.

Blaising, Craig. "Gethsemane a Prayer of Faith." *JETS* 22 (1979) 333–43.

Blakley, J. Ted. "Incomprehension or Resistance? The Markan Disciples and the Narrative Logic of Mark 4:1—8:30." PhD diss., University of St. Andrews, 2008.

Blass, Fredrich, et al. *A Greek Grammar of the New Testament and Other Early Christian Literature*. Chicago: University of Chicago Press, 1961.

Blenkin, G. W. *The First Epistle General of Peter*. Cambridge: Cambridge University Press, 1914.

Blinzler, Josef. "ΙΕΡΑΤΕΥΜΑ, Zur Exegese von 1 Peter 2,5 u. 9." In *Episcopus: Studien über das Bischofsamt. Festschrift für Kardinal Michael von Faulhaber*, edited by the Theologische Fakultät der Universität München, 49–59. Regensburg: Gregorius, 1949.

Blue, Bradley. "Architecture, Early Church." In *Dictionary of the Later New Testament and Its Developments*, edited by Ralph P. Martin and Peter H. Davids, 91–95. Downers Grove, IL: InterVarsity, 1997.

Blum, Edwin A. "1 Peter." In *The Expositor's Bible Commentary*, edited by Frank Gaebelein, 12:209–56. Grand Rapids: Zondervan, 1981.

———. "2 Peter." In *The Expositor's Bible Commentary*, edited by Frank Gaebelein, 12:257–92. Grand Rapids: Zondervan, 1981

Bock, Darrell. *Acts*. BECNT. Grand Rapids: Baker, 2007.

———. *Blasphemy and Exaltation in Judaism: The Charge Against Jesus in Mark 14:53–65*. Grand Rapids: Baker, 2000.

———. *Luke*. Grand Rapids: Baker, 1996.

———. *Proclamation from Prophecy and Pattern: Lucan Old Testament Christology*. JSNTSup 12. Sheffield: JSOT, 1987.

———. *A Theology of Luke and Acts*. Grand Rapids: Zondervan, 2012.

Böckh, August, and Johannes Franz, eds. *Corpus Inscriptionum Graecarum*, Vol. 2. Olms: Hilgesheim, 1977.

Bockmuehl, Markus. *The Remembered Peter in Ancient Reception and Modern Debate*. Tübingen: Mohr Siebeck, 2010.

———. "Simon Peter and Bethsaida." In *The Missions of James, Peter, and Paul: Tensions in Early Christianity*, edited by Bruce Chilton and Craig Evans, 53–90. Leiden: Brill, 2005.

———. *Simon Peter in Scripture and Memory*. Grand Rapids: Baker, 2012.

Boda, Mark. *A Severe Mercy: Sin and Its Remedy in the Old Testament*. Winona Lake, IN: Eisenbrauns, 2009.

Boismard, M. E. *Quatre Hymns baptismales dans la Première Epître de Pierre*. Paris: Latour-Maubourg, 1982.

———. "Une liturgie baptismale dans la Prima Petri." *RevBib* 63 (1946) 182–208; 64 (1957) 161–83.

Bond, Helen. *The First Biography of Jesus: Genre and Meaning in Mark's Gospel*. Grand Rapids: Eerdmans, 2020.

Bond, Helen, and Larry Hurtado. *Peter in Early Christianity*. Grand Rapids: Eerdmans, 2015.

Bonhoeffer, Dietrich. *The Cost of Discipleship*. New York: Macmillan, 1963.

Bonner, Campbell. "The Violence of Departing Demons." *HTR* 37 (1944) 334–36.

Bonsirven, Joseph. *Palestinian Judaism in the Time of Jesus*. New York: Holt, Rinehart & Winston, 1964.

Bonz, Marianne. *The Past as Legacy: Luke-Acts.* Minneapolis, MN: Fortress, 2000.

Boobyer, G. H. "The Indebtedness of 2 Peter to 1 Peter." In *New Testament Essays: Studies in Memory of Thomas Walter Manson 1893–1958*, edited by A. J. B. Higgins, 34–53. Manchester: Manchester University Press, n.d.

Boomershine, Thomas. "Jesus of Nazareth and the Watershed of Ancient Orality and Literacy" In *Orality and Textuality in Early Christian Literature*, edited by Joanna Dewey, 7–17. Atlanta, GA: Society of Biblical Literature, 1995.

Booth, R. P. *Jesus and the Laws of Purity.* JSNTSup 13. Sheffield: Sheffield Academic, 1986.

Borg, Marcus. *Conflict, Holiness and Politics in the Teaching of Jesus.* Lewiston: Edwin Mellen, 1984.

———. *Jesus: A New Vision.* London: SPCK, 1993.

Borgen, P. "Jesus Christ, the Reception of the Spirit and a Cross-National Community." In *Early Christianity and Hellenistic Judaism*, edited by P. Borgen, 253–72. Edinburgh: T. & T. Clark, 1996.

Boring, M. Eugene. "Narrative Dynamics in First Peter: The Function of Narrative World." In *Reading First Peter with New Eyes: Methodological Reassessments of the Letter of First Peter*, edited by Robert Webb and Betsy Bauman-Martin, 7–40. London: T. & T. Clark, 2007.

Bornemann, W. "Der erste Petrusbrief–eine Taufrede des Silvanus?" *ZNW* 19 (1919–20) 143–65.

Bornkamm, Günther. "The Authority to 'Bind' and 'Loose' in the Church in Matthew's Gospel." In *The Interpretation of Matthew*, edited by Graham Stanton, 83–97. IRT 3. Philadelphia, PA: Fortress, 1983.

Borrell, Agustí. *The Good News of Peter's Denial: A Narrative and Rhetorical Reading of Mark 14:54.66–72.* Atlanta, GA: Scholars, 1998.

Botterweck, Johannes, and Helmer Ringgren. *Theological Dictionary of the Old Testament.* 17 vols. Grand Rapids: Eerdmans, 1974–2021.

Bourke, M. M. "Peter in the Gospel of Luke." In *Peter in the New Testament: A Collaborative Assessment by Protestant and Roman Catholic Scholars*, edited by Raymond Brown et al., 109–28. Minneapolis, MN: Augsburg, 1973.

Bowes, William B. "Faith-Language, Jesus's Disciples, and Narrative Fulfillment in Luke-Acts." *JETS* 64.4 (2021) 767–84.

Boyarin, Daniel. "Beyond Judaisms: Metatron and the Divine Polymorphy of Ancient Judaism." *JSJ* 41.3 (2010) 323–65.

Bradley, K. R. *Slaves and Masters in the Roman Empire: A Study in Social Control.* Oxford: Oxford University Press, 1987.

Brettler, Marc. *God Is King: Understanding an Israelite Metaphor.* Sheffield: Sheffield Academic, 1989.

Brichto, Herbert Chanan. "On Slaughter and Sacrifice, Blood and Atonement." *HUCA* 47 (1976) 19–55.

Broadhead, Edwin. *Naming Jesus: Titular Christology in the Gospel of Mark.* Sheffield: Sheffield Academic, 1999.

Brooke, George. "Isaiah 40:3 and the Wilderness Community." In *New Qumran Texts and Studies: Proceedings of the First Meeting of the International Organization for Qumran Studies, Paris 1992*, edited by George Brooke, 117–32. Leiden: Brill, 1994.

Broughton, T. R. S. "Roman Asia Minor." In *An Economic Survey of Ancient Rome*, edited by Frank Tenney, 4:631–840. Paterson, NJ: Pageant, 1933.

Brown, Colin. *New International Dictionary of New Testament Theology*. 3 vols. Grand Rapids: Zondervan, 1977.
Brown, Jeannine. *The Gospel as Stories: A Narrative Approach to Matthew, Mark, Luke, and John*. Grand Rapids: Baker, 2020.
Brown, Raymond. *The Death of the Messiah from Gethsemane to the Grave: A Commentary on the Passion Narratives in the Four Gospels*. New York: Doubleday, 1994.
———. *The Gospel According to John xiii–xxi*. The Anchor Bible 29A. Garden City, NY: Doubleday, 1970.
Brown, Raymond, and John Meier. *Antioch and Rome: New Testament Cradles of Catholic Christianity*. New York: Paulist, 1983.
Brown, Raymond, et al. *Peter in the New Testament*. Minneapolis, MN: Augsburg, 1973.
Brown, Warren, et al. *Whatever Happened to the Soul? Scientific and Theological Portraits of Human Nature*. Minneapolis, MN: Fortress, 1998.
Brownlee, W. H. "Biblical Interpretation Among the Secretaries of the Dead Sea Scrolls." *BA* 14 (1951) 54–76.
———. *The Midrash Pesher of Habakkuk*. Missoula, MT: Society of Biblical Literature, 1979.
Bruce, F. F. *Commentary on the Book of Acts*. Grand Rapids: Eerdmans, 1979.
———. *Peter, Stephen, James, and John: Studies in Early Non-Pauline Christianity*. Grand Rapids: Eerdmans, 1980.
———. *The Speeches in the Book of Acts of the Apostles*. London: Tyndale, 1942.
———. "The Speeches in Acts—Thirty Years After." In *Reconciliation and Hope: New Testament Essays on Atonement and Eschatology Presented to L. L. Morris on his 60th Birthday*, edited by Robert Banks, 53–68. Carlisle: Paternoster, 1974.
Brueggemann, Walter. *A Pathway of Interpretation: The Old Testament for Pastors and Students*. Eugene, OR: Cascade, 2008.
———. *Theology of the Old Testament: Testimony, Dispute, Advocacy*. Minneapolis, MN: Fortress, 1997.
Büchler, Adolf. *Studies in Sin and Atonement: In the Rabbinic Literature of the First Century*. New York: KTAV, 1967.
Bultmann, Rudolf. "Bekenntris-und Lied fragmente im ersten Petrusbrief." In *Coniectanea Neotestamentica 11: In honorem Antonii Fridrichsen sexagenarii*, 1–14. Lund: Gleerup, 1947.
———. *Jesus Christ and Mythology*. New York: Scribner, 1958.
———. *History of the Synoptic Tradition*. New York: Harper & Row, 1963.
———. *Theology of the New Testament*. New York: Scribner, 1951.
Bultmann, Rudolf, et al. *Kerygma and Myth: A Theological Debate*. New York: Harper & Row, 1961.
Burkett, Delbert. *Theologie des Neuen Testaments*. Tübingen: Mohr-Paul Siebeck, 1948.
———. "The Transfiguration of Jesus (Mark 9:2–8): Epiphany or Apotheosis?" *JBL* 138.2 (2019) 413–32.
———. *The Son of Man Debate: A History and Evaluation*. SNTSMS 107. Cambridge: Cambridge University Press, 1999.
Butts, James. "The *Progymnasmata* of Theon the Sophist: A New Text with Translation and Commentary." PhD diss., Claremont Graduate School, 1987.
Bynum, Caroline Walker. *The Resurrection of the Body in Western Christianity, 200–1336*. New York: Columbia University Press, 1995.
Byrskog, Samuel. *Story as History-History as Story: The Gospel Tradition in the Context of Ancient Oral History*. Tübingen: Mohr, 2000.

Cadbury, Henry. "Acts and Eschatology." In *The Background of the New Testament and Its Eschatology*, edited by W. D. Davies and D. Daube, 300–321. Cambridge: Cambridge University Press, 1964.

———. "The Speeches in Acts." In *The Beginnings of Christianity: Part I, The Acts of the Apostles*, edited by J. Foakes Jackson and Kirsopp Lake, 1:402–26. 5 vols. Grand Rapids: Baker, 1979.

Callan, Terrance. "The Syntax of 2 Peter 1:1–7." *CBQ* 67.4 (2005) 632–40.

Calvin, John. *Calvin's Commentaries*. Grand Rapids: Baker, 1979.

———. *Institutes of the Christian Religion*. Philadelphia, PA: Presbyterian Board of Christian Education, 1936.

———. *Sermons on Deuteronomy*. Edinburgh: Banner of Truth, 1987.

Campbell, Barth. *Honor, Shame, and the Rhetoric of 1 Peter*. SBLDS 160. Atlanta, GA: Scholars, 1998.

Campbell, John K. *Honour, Family, and Patronage: A Study of Institutions and Moral Values in a Greek Mountain Community*. Oxford: Clarendon, 1964.

Caragounis, Chrys. *Peter and the Rock*. Berlin: Walter de Gruyter, 1990.

"The Decree of Stratonicae" in Caria, Asia Minor In *Corpus Inscriptionarum Graecarum*, 2:2715

Carrington, Philip. *The Primitive Christian Catechism: A Study in the Epistles*. Cambridge: Cambridge University Press, 1940.

Carter, Warren. "Going All the Way? Honoring the Emperor and Sacrificing Wives and Slaves in 1 Peter 2.13–13.6." In *A Feminist Companion to the Catholic Epistles*, edited by Amy-Jill Levine and Maria Mayo Robbins, 14–33. London: T. & T. Clark, 2004.

———. *Households and Discipleship: A Study of Matthew 19–20*. Sheffield: JSOT, 1994.

Casel, Odo. "Die λογικὴ θυσία der antiken Mystik in christlichliturgischer umdeutung." *JLW* 4 (1924) 37–47.

Casey, Maurice. "Aramaic Idiom and the Son of Man Problem: A Response to Owen and Shepherd." *JSNT* 25 (2002) 3–32.

———. *Aramaic Sources of Mark's Gospel*. SNTSMS 102. Cambridge: Cambridge University Press, 1998.

———. *The Solution to the "Son of Man" Problem*. London: T. & T. Clark, 2007.

———. *Son of Man: The Interpretation and Influence of Daniel 7*. London: SPCK, 1979.

A Century of Lawmaking for a New Nation: US Congressional Documents and Debates 1774–1875. Washington, DC: Congress, 1875.

Cerfaux, L. "Vestiges d'un florilège dans 1 Cor 1:18—3:24." *RHE* 27 (1931) 24–25.

Chalmers, Aaron. "Influence of Cognitive Biases on Biblical Interpretation." *BBR* 26.4 (2016) 467–80.

Chang, Andrew. "Second Peter 2:1 and the Extent of the Atonement." *BSac* 142 (1985) 55–56.

Charles, J. Daryl. *Virtue amidst Vice: The Catalog of Virtues in 2 Peter 1*. JSNTSup 150. Sheffield: Sheffield Academic, 1997.

Charlesworth, James. "Intertextuality: Isaiah 40:3 and the Serek ha-Yahad." In *The Quest for Context and Meaning: Studies in Biblical Intertextuality in Honor of James A. Sanders*, edited by Craig Evans and Shemaryahu Talmon, 197–224. Leiden: Brill, 1997.

Charue, A. *Les Epitres Catholiques*. Paris: La Sainte Bible. 1938.

Chase, Francis. "2 Peter." In *Hastings' Dictionary of the Bible*, edited by James Hastings, 3:809. 5 vols. Grand Rapids: Baker, 1994.

Chernus, Ira. "Visions of God in Merkabah Mysticism." *JSJ* 13 (1982) 123–46.
Chester, A., and R. P. Martin. *The Theology of the Letters of James, Peter and Jude*. Cambridge: Cambridge University Press, 1994.
Chilton, Bruce, and Craig Evans. *The Missions of James, Peter, and Paul: Tensions in Early Christianity*. Leiden: Brill, 2005.
Chilton, Bruce, and Jacob Neusner. *Classical Christianity and Rabbinic Judaism: Comparing Theologies*. Grand Rapids: Baker, 2004.
Chilton, Bruce, et al. *The Missing Jesus: Rabbinic Judaism and the New Testament*. Boston: Brill, 2002.
Christensen, Sean. "The Balch/Elliott Debate and the Hermeneutics of the Household Code." *TrinJ* 37 (2016) 173–93.
———. "Solidarity in Suffering and Glory: The Unifying Role of Psalm 34 in 1 Peter 3:10–12." *JETS* 58.2 (2015) 335–52.
Clerc, Michel. *De la condition des étrangers domiciles dans les cites grecques*. Toulouse: Universitaires du Midi Press, 2007.
Collins, John. *The Scepter and the Star: The Messiahs of the Dead Sea Scrolls and Other Ancient Literature*. New York: Doubleday, 1995.
———. "The Son of Man in First-Century Judaism." *NTS* 38 (1992) 448–66.
Conzelmann, Hans. *Acts of the Apostles*. Hermenia. Philadelphia, PA: Fortress, 1972.
———. *Die Kleineren Briefe des Apostels Paulus*. Edited by H. W. Beyer et al. Göttingen, Vandenhoeck & Ruprecht, 1962.
———. "History and Theology in the Passion Narratives." *Int* 24.2 (1970) 178–82.
———. *The Theology of St. Luke*. Philadelphia, PA: Fortress, 1961.
Cooper, Craig. *Politics of Orality*. Vol. 6, *Orality and Literacy in Ancient Greece*. Leiden: Brill, 2007.
Cooper, John. *Body, Soul, & Life Everlasting*. Grand Rapids: Eerdmans, 1989.
Corbo, Virgil. "The House at Capernaum." In *New Memoirs of Saint Peter by the Sea of Galilee*, edited by Virgil Corbo and Stanislaus Loffredda, 23–27. Jerusalem: Franciscan, 1969.
Cothenet, Edward. "Imitation du Christ." In *Dictionnaire de Spiritualité*, edited by Edward Cothenet et al., 7:1536–1601. Paris: Beaucresne, 1971.
Coults, John. "Ephesians 1:3–14 and 1 Peter 1:3–12." *NTS* 3 (1957) 115–27.
Cowley, A. E. *Aramaic Papyri of the Fifth Century B.C. Edited with Translation and Notes*. Oxford: Clarendon, 1923.
Cranfield, C. E. B. *The Gospel According to St. Mark*. Cambridge: Cambridge University Press, 1974.
Crawford, Matthew. "'Confessing God from a Good Conscience': 1 Peter 3:21 and Early Christian Baptismal Theology." *JTS* 67.1 (2016) 23–37.
Creed, J. M. *The Gospel According to St. Luke*. New York: Macmillan, 1930.
Crosby, Michael. *House of Disciples: Church, Economics and Justice in Matthew*. New York: Orbis, 1988.
Cross, Frank L. *1 Peter: A Paschal Liturgy*. London: A. R. Mowbray, 1954.
Crossan, John Dominic. *The Cross That Spoke*. San Francisco: Harper & Row, 1988.
Crouzel, Henri. "L'imitation et la 'suite' de Dieu et du Christ dans les premiers siècles chrétiens, ansi que leurs sources gréco-romaines et hébraiques." *JAC* 21 (1978) 7–41.
Crum, J. M. C. *St. Mark's Gospel*. Cambridge: Heffer, 1936.
Cullmann, Oscar. *Christ and Time*. Philadelphia, PA: Westminster, 1964.

———. *The Christology of the New Testament*. London: SCM, 1963.
———. *Peter: Disciple, Apostle, Martyr*. Philadelphia, PA: Westminster, 1953.
Dahl, M. E. *The Resurrection of the Body*. London: SCM, 1962.
Dalton, W. J. *Christ's Proclamation to the Spirits: A Study of 1 Peter 3:18—4:6*. Rome: Pontifical Biblical Institute, 1989.
Daly, Robert. "The Soteriological Significant of the Sacrifice of Isaac." *CBQ* 39 (1977) 45–75.
Damgaard, Finn. *Rewriting Peter as an Intertextual Character in the Canonical Gospels*. London: Routledge, 2015.
Danker, F. *Benefactor Epigraphic Study of a Graeco-Roman and New Testament Semantic Field*. St. Louis: Clayton, 1982.
———. "1 Peter 1:24—2:17–A Consolatory Pericope." *ZNW* 58 (1967) 93–102.
———. "2 Peter 1: A Solemn Decree." *CBQ* 40 (1978) 65–72.
Daube, David. *The New Testament and Rabbinic Judaism*. London: University of London, 1956.
———. "Public Pronouncement and Private Explanation in the Gospels." *ExpTim* 57 (1945–46) 175–77.
———. "Rabbinic Methods of Interpretation and Hellenistic Rhetoric." *HUCA* 22 (1949) 239–64.
David, Carl Judson. *The Name and Way of the Lord: Old Testament Themes*. New Testament Christology. Sheffield: Sheffield, 1996.
Davids, Peter. *The First Epistle of Peter*. NICNT. Grand Rapids: Eerdmans, 1990.
———. "James." In *A Theology of James, Peter, and Jude: : A Biblical Theology of the New Testament*, 31–91. Grand Rapids: Zondervan, 2014.
———. *The Letters of 2 Peter and Jude*. The Pillar New Testament Commentary. Grand Rapids: Eerdmans, 2006.
———. "Rich and Poor." In *Dictionary of Jesus and the Gospel*, edited by Joel Green and Scot McKnight, 701–10. Downers Grove: InterVarsity, 1992.
———. "Textual Criticism of 1 Peter 3:10." Paper presented at Institute for Biblical Research, March, 2014.
———. *A Theology of James, Peter, and Jude: A Biblical Theology of the New Testament*. Grand Rapids: Zondervan, 2014.
Davies, Paul E. "Primitive Christology in 1 Peter." In *Festschrift to Honor F. Wilbur Gingrich*, edited by Eugene Barth and Ronald Cocroft, 115–22. Leiden: Brill, 1972.
Davies, W. D., and Dale C. Allison Jr. *The First Epistle of Peter*. NICNT. Grand Rapids: Eerdmans, 1990.
———. *The Gospel of Matthew*. 3 vols. ICC. Edinburgh: T. & T. Clark, 1991.
Dawsey, James. *Peter's Last Sermon: Identity and Discipleship in the Gospel of Mark*. Macon: Mercer University Press, 2010.
Dean-Otting, Mary. *Heavenly Journeys: A Study of the Motif in Hellenistic Jewish Literature*. New York: Lang, 1984.
De Boer, Willis P. *The Imitation of Paul: An Exegetical Study*. Kampen: J. H. Kok, 1962.
De Campos, Mateus. "Markan Epistemology and the Problem of Incomprehension." *JETS* 64.4 (2021) 74–66.
———. "The 'Sign from Heaven' (Mark 8,10–13)." *Bib* 98.2 (2017) 234–56.
Deissmann, Adolf. *Bible Studies*. Edinburgh: T. & T. Clark, 1901.
———. *Light from the Ancient East: The New Testament Illustrated by Recently Discovered Texts of the Graeco-Roman World*. Translated by Lionel Strachan, New York: Daron, 1927.

Demosthenes. *Demosthenes.* 7 vols. Translated by J. H. Vince *et al.* London: Heinemann, 1926–49.
De Saussure, Ferdinand. *Cours de linguistique Générale.* Paris: Payot, 1969.
Descartes, René. "Meditations on First Philosophy." In *Great Books of the Western World: Descartes, Spinoza*, edited by Robert Maynard Hutchins and Mortimer J. Adler, 31:69–103. Chicago: Encyclopaedia Britannica, 1952.
DeSilva, David. "1 Peter: Strategies for Counseling Individuals on the Way to a New Heritage." *ATJ* 32 (2000) 33–52.
Deterding, Paul. "Exodus Motifs in First Peter." *Concordia Journal* 7 (1981) 58–65.
deVilliers, J. L. "Joy in Suffering in 1 Peter." *Neot* 9 (1975) 70–80.
Dewey, Arthur. "A Re-Hearing of Romans 10:1–15." In *Orality and Textuality in Early Christian Literature*, edited by Joanna Dewey, 109–27. Atlanta, GA: Society of Biblical Literature, 1995.
Dewey, Joanna. *Orality and Textuality in Early Christian Literature.* Semia Studies. Atlanta, GA: Scholars, 1995.
Dibelius, Martin. *A Fresh Approach to the New Testament and Early Christian Literature.* London: Nicholson & Watson, 1937.
———. "The Speeches in Acts and Ancient Historiography." In *Studies in the Acts of the Apostles*, edited by H. Greeven, 138–85. New York: Scribner's, 1956.
Dihle, Albrecht. "The Gospels and Greek Biography." In *The Gospel and the Gospels*, edited by Peter Stuhlmacher, 361–86. Grand Rapids: Eerdmans, 1991.
Dill, Samuel. *Roman Society from Nero to Marcus Aurelius.* London: Macmillan, 1925.
Diodorus of Sicily. *The Library of History.* 12 vols. Cambridge: Harvard University Press, 1933–67.
Dix, Dom Gregory. *Jew and Greek: A Study in the Primitive Church.* London: Dacre, 1967.
Dodd, C. H. *According to the Scriptures.* London: Nisbet, 1952.
———. *The Apostolic Preaching and Its Developments.* New York: Harper, 1936.
———. "The Framework of the Gospel Narrative." *ExpTim* 43 (1931–32) 396–400.
Doering, Lutz. "Schwerpunkte und Tendenzen der neueren Petrus-Forschung." *BTZ* 19 (2002) 203–23.
Domeris, W. R. "The Office of Holy One." *Journal of Theology for Southern Africa* 54 (1968) 35–38.
Dossey, Lesley. "Wife Beating and Manliness in Late Antiquity." *Past and Present* 199 (2008) 3–40.
Douglas, J. D. *The New International Dictionary of the Christian Church.* Rev. ed. Grand Rapids: Zondervan, 1978.
Draper, Jonathan. *Orality, Literacy, and Colonialism in Antiquity.* Semia Studies. Atlanta, GA: Society of Biblical Literature, 2004.
Dubis, Mark. *Messianic Woes in First Peter: Suffering and Eschatology in 1 Peter 4:12–19.* Studies in Biblical Literature 33. New York: Lang, 2002.
Duchesne, Louis. *Histire ancienne de l'Englise.* Paris: A. Fontemoing et cie, 1910.
Dunn, James D. G. *Christianity in the Making.* Vol. 2, *Beginning from Jerusalem.* Grand Rapids: Eerdmans, 2009.
———. "Has the Canon a Continuing Function?" In *The Canon Debate*, edited by L. M. McDonald and J. A. Sanders, 558–79. Peabody, MA: Hendrickson, 2002.
———. *Jesus' Call to Discipleship.* Cambridge: Cambridge University Press, 1992.
———. *Jesus, Paul, and the Law: Studies in Mark and Galatians.* Louisville: Westminster/John Knox Press, 1990.

———. *Jesus Remembered*. Grand Rapids: Eerdmans, 2003.
———. *Jews and Christians: The Parting of the Ways, A.D. 70 to 135*. Grand Rapids: Eerdmans, 1992.
———. "The Messianic Secret in Mark." *TynBul* 21 (1970) 92–117.
———. *Paul and the Mosaic Law*. Grand Rapids: Eerdmans, 1996.
———. "Pharisees, Sinners, and Jesus." In *Jesus, Paul, and the Law: Studies in Mark and Galatians*, 61–88. Louisville: Westminster/John Knox, 1990.
———. "Q as Oral Tradition." In *The Written Gospel*, edited by Markus Bockmuehl and Donald A. Hagner, 45–69. Cambridge: Cambridge University Press, 2005.
———. *The Theology of Paul the Apostle*. Grand Rapids: Eerdmans, 1998.
———. *Unity and Diversity in the New Testament: An Inquiry into the Character of Earliest Christianity*. London: SCM, 1977.
Durham, John. *Exodus*. WBC 3. Waco: Word, 1987.
Ebright, Charles R. *The Petrine Epistles: A Critical Study of Authorship*. Cincinnati: Methodist Book Concern, 1917.
Edwards, Jonathan. *Freedom of the Will*. New Haven: Yale University Press, 1957.
———. *A Treatise Concerning Religious Affections*. New Haven: Yale University Press, 1959.
Ehrman, Bart. *Lost Scriptures: Books That Did Not Make It into the New Testament*. Oxford: Oxford University Press, 2005.
Eichrodt, Walter. *Theology of the Old Testament*. Philadelphia, PA: Westminster, 1961.
Eidersheim, Alfred. *Sketches of Jewish Social Life*. London: Religious Tract Society, 1876.
Eisenman, Robert. *James the Brother of Jesus*. New York: Viking, 1996.
Eisler, Robert. *The Messiah Jesus and John the Baptist: According to Flavius Josephus' Recently Rediscovered 'Capture of Jerusalem' and the Other Jewish and Christian Sources*. London: Methuen, 1931.
Elliger, Karl. *Leviticus*. HAT 4. Tübingen: Mohr, 1966.
Elliott, John. *1 Peter: A New Translation with Introduction and Commentary*. AB. New York: Doubleday, 2000.
———. "1 Peter, Its Situation and Strategy: A Discussion with David Balch." In *Perspectives on First Peter*, edited by Charles Talbert, 61–78. Macron: Mercer University, 1986.
———. *Conflict, Community, and Honor: 1 Peter in Social-Scientific Perspective*. Eugene, OR: Cascade, 2007.
———. "Elders as Leaders in 1 Peter and the Early Church." *CurTM* 28.6 (2001) 549–59.
———. *The Elect and the Holy: An Exegetical Examination of 1 Peter 2:4–10 and the Phrase βασίλειον ἱεράτευμα*. NovTSup 12. Leiden: Brill, 1966.
———. *A Home for the Homeless: A Sociological Exegesis of 1 Peter, Its Situation and Strategy*. Philadelphia, PA: Fortress, 1981.
———. "Ministry and Church Order in the NT: A Traditio-Historical Analysis (1 Pt 5, 1–5 & plls.)." *CBQ* 32.3 (1970) 367–91.
———. "The Rehabilitation of an Exegetical Step-Child: 1 Peter in Recent Research." *JBL* 95 (1976) 243–54.
Ellis, E. E. *The Gospel of Luke*. NCB. Grand Rapids: Eerdmans, 1974.
Ellul, Danielle. "Un exemple de cheminement rhétorique: 1 Pierre." *Revue d'hiustoire et de philosophie religieuses* 70 (1990/91) 17–34.
Eubank, Nathan. *Wages of Cross-Bearing and Debt of Sin: The Economy of Heaven in Matthew's Gospel*. Berlin: DeGruyter, 2013.

Evans, Craig. "A Fishing Boat, a House, and an Ossuary: What Can We Learn from the Artifacts?" In *The Missions of James, Peter, and Paul: Tensions in Early Christianity*, edited by Bruce Chilton and Craig Evans, 211–31. Leiden: Brill, 2005.

Farrar, Austin. *A Study in St. Mark*. London: Dacre, 1951.

Fay, Greg. "Introduction to Incomprehension: The Literary Structure of Mark 4:1–34." *CBQ* 51.1 (1989) 65–81

Feder, Yitzhaq. "On *Kuppuru, Kippēr* and Etymological Sins that Cannot be Wiped Away." *VT* 60 (2010) 535–45.

Feldmeier, Rinhard. *The First Letter of Peter: A Commentary on the Greek Text*. Waco: Baylor University Press, 2008.

Felix, Paul. "Penal Substitution in the New Testament: A Focused Look at First Peter." *TMSJ* 20.2 (2009) 171–97.

Ferda, Tucker. "The Ending of Mark and the Faithfulness of God: An Apocalyptic Resolution to Mark 16:8." *Journal of Theological Interpretation* 13.1 (2019) 36–52.

Fernadez, Pérez. "Rabbinic Text in the Exegesis of the New Testament." *The Review of Rabbinic Judaism* 7 (2004) 95–120.

Feuillict, A. "La coupe et le baptême de la passion (Mc, x, 35–40; Mt. xx, 20–23; Lc., xxii, 50)." *RB* 74 (1967) 356–91.

Filium, C. Gerald. *Corpus Scriptorum Ecclesiasticorum Latinorum*. New York: Johnson, 1972.

Filson, Floyd. "Partakers with Christ, Suffering in First Peter." *Int* 9 (1955) 410.

Finkel, Asher. *The Pharisees & the Teacher of Nazareth*. Leiden: Brill, 1964.

Finlan, Stephen. *The Background and Content of Paul's Cultic Atonement Metaphors*. Leiden: Brill, 2004.

Fiore, Benjamin. *The Function of Personal Example in the Socratic and Pastoral Epistles*. An. Bib. 105. Rome: Biblical Institute Press, 1986.

Fitzmyer, Joseph. "The Aramaic Qorban Inscription from Jebel Hallet et-Tûrî and Mk7:11/Mt 15:5." *JBL* 78 (1959) 60–65.

———. *The Gospel According to Luke (I–IX)*. Anchor Bible 28. New York: Doubleday, 1982.

———. "The Matthean Divorce Texts and Some New Palestinian Evidence." *Theological Studies* 37 (1976) 197–226.

———. "A Re-Study of an Elephantine Aramaic Marriage Contract (AP 15)." In *Near Eastern Studies in Honor of William Foxwell Albright*, edited by H. Goedicke, 137–68. Baltimore: Johns Hopkins University Press, 1971.

Flusser, David. *Jesus*. Jerusalem: Varda, 2014.

———. *Jesus' Jerusalem*. Jerusalem: Varda, 2013.

Foakes-Jackson, F. J. *Peter: Prince of Apostles*. London: Hodder & Stoughton, 1927.

Foakes-Jackson, F. J., and Kirsopp Lake, eds. *The Acts of the Apostles*. 5 vols. Grand Rapids: Baker, 1979.

Foley, John Miles. "Indigenous Poems, Colonialist Texts." In *Orality, Literacy, and Colonialism in Antiquity*, edited by Jonathan Draper, 28–31. Atlanta, GA: Society of Biblical Literature, 2004.

Ford, David F. "Paul Ricoeur: A Biblical Philosopher on Jesus." In *Jesus and Philosophy: New Essays*, edited by Paul Moser, 169–93. Cambridge: Cambridge University Press, 2009.

Fornara, Charles William. *The Nature of History in Ancient Greece and Rome*. Eidos Studies in Classical Kinds. Berkeley: University of California, 1983.

Foster, Paul. "Peter in Noncanonical Traditions." In *Peter in Early Christianity*, edited by Helen Bond and Larry Hurtado, 222–62. Grand Rapids: Eerdmans, 2015.

France, R. T. *The Gospel of Mark*. Grand Rapids: Eerdmans, 2002.

Francis, Fred. "The Form and Function of the Opening and Closing Paragraphs of James and 1 John." *Zeitschrift für die neutestamentliche Wissenschaft und die Kunde des Urchristentums* 61 (1970) 113–25.

Francotte, H. "De la condition des étrangers dans les cites grecques." *Musée* 7 (1903) 350–88.

Freedman, David, and David Miano. "People of the New Covenant." In *The Concept of the Covenant in the Second Temple Period*, edited by Stanley Porter and Jaqueline C. R. de Roo, 7–26. Leiden: Brill, 2003.

Freyne, Seán. *The Jesus Movement and Its Expansion: Meaning and Mission*. Grand Rapids: Eerdmans, 2014.

Funk, R. *A Greek Grammar of the New Testament and Other Early Christian Literature*. Chicago: University of Chicago Press, 1961.

Gammie, John. *Holiness in Israel*. Minneapolis, MN: Fortress, 1989.

Gane, Roy. *Cult and Character: Purification Offerings, Day of Atonement, and Theodicy*. Winona Lake, IN: Eisenbrauns, 2005.

———. "Private Preposition מן in Purification Offering Pericopes and the Changing Face of 'Dorian Gray.'" *JBL* 127 (2008) 209–22.

Garland, David. *Mark*. NIV Application Commentary. Downers Grove: InterVarsity, 1996.

Geddert, Timothy. "The Implied YHWH Christology of Mark's Gospel: Mark's Challenge to the Reader to 'Connect the Dots.'" *BBR* 25.3 (2015) 325–40.

Gelardini, Gabriella. "The Contest for a Royal Title: Herod Versus Jesus in the Gospel According to Mark (6,14–29; 15,6–15)." *Annali di Storia dell' Esegesi* 28.2 (2011) 93–106.

Gerhardsson, Bernard. *The Gospel Tradition*. Lund: Gleerup, 1986.

———. *Memory and Manuscript: Oral Tradition and the Written Transmission in Rabbinic Judaism and Early Christianity*. Lund: Gleerup, 1998.

Gese, Hartmut. "The Atonement." In *Essays on Biblical Theology*, 93–116. Minneapolis, MN: Fortress, 1981.

———. "Die Sühne." In *Zur biblischen Theologie Alttestamentliche Vorträge*, 85–106. Munich: Verlag, 1977.

Gibson, Craig. "Learning Greek History in the Ancient Classroom: The Evidence from the Treatises on Progymnasmata." *CP* 99 (2004) 103–29.

Gillman, Neil. *The Death of Death: Resurrection and Immortality in Jewish Thought*. Woodstock, VT: Jewish Lights Publishing, 2000.

Goguel, Maurice. *The Birth of Christianity*. Crows Nest, Australia: George Allen & Unwin, 1953.

Goldingay, John. *The Message of Isaiah 40–55: A Literary-Theological Commentary*. London: T. & T. Clark, 2005.

———. *Psalms*. Grand Rapids: Baker, 2008.

Goldingay, John, and David Payne. *Isaiah 40–55: A Critical and Exegetical Commentary*. London: Bloomsbury, 2014.

Goodspeed, E. J. "Enoch in 1 Peter 3:19." *JBL* 73 (1954) 84–92.

Goppelt, Leonhard. *A Commentary on 1 Peter*. Grand Rapids: Eerdmans, 1993.

———. *Der erste Petrusbrief*. Göttingen: Vandenhoeck & Ruprecht, 1978.

Goulder, Michael. *St. Paul versus St. Peter: A Tale of Two Missions*. Louisville: Westminster John Knox, 1994.
Grappe, Christian. *Images de Pierre aux deux premiers siècles*. Vol. 75, *Etudes d'historie et de philosophie religieuses*. Paris: Universitaires de France, 1995.
Grässer, Erich. "Der Hebräerbrief, 1938–63." *TRu* 30 (1964–65) 138–236.
Green, Edward Michael Banks. *2 Peter Reconsidered*. London: Tyndale, 1961.
———. *The Second Epistle of Peter and the Epistle of Jude*. Grand Rapids: Eerdmans, 1968.
Green, Gene. "'As for Prophecies, They will Come to an End': 2 Peter, Paul and Plutarch on 'the Obsolescence of Oracles.'" *JSNT* 82 (2002) 107–22.
———. *Jude, 2 Peter*. BECNT. Grand Rapids: Baker, 2008.
———. *Vox Petri: A Theology of Peter*. Eugene, OR: Cascade, 2020.
Green, Joel. *The Death of Jesus: Tradition and Interpretation in the Passion Narrative*. WUNT 2/33. Tübingen: J. C. B. Mohr, 1988.
———. "Embodying the Gospel: Two Exemplary Practices." *Journal of Spiritual Formation and Soul Care* 7 (2014) 11–21.
Green, Michael. *Saint Peter: A Biography*. New York: Scribner, 1995.
Greeven, H., ed. *Studies in the Acts of the Apostles*. New York: Scribner's, 1956.
Gregerman, Adam. "Critique of *Short Stories by Jesus*." A paper presented at the Society for Biblical Literature, November 22, 2015.
Grice, H. Paul. "Meaning." *Philosophical Review* 66 (1957) 377–88.
———. "Utterer's Meaning and Intentions." *Philosophical Review* 78 (1969) 147–77.
———. "Utterer's Meaning, Sentence-Meaning, Word-Meaning." In *The Philosophy of Language*, edited by J. R. Searle, 54–70. Oxford: Oxford University Press, 1977.
Grindheim, Sigurd. "Biblical Authority: What Is It Good For? Why the Apostles Insisted on a High View of Scripture." *JETS* 59.4 (2016) 791–803.
Gruenwald, Itamar. *Apocalyptic and Merkavah Mysticism*. Leiden: Brill, 1980.
Guarducci, Margherita. *La tomba di San Pietro: Une straordinario vicenda*. Milano: Saggi Boupiani, 2000.
Gubler, Marie-Louise. *Die Frühesten Deutungen des Todes Jesu: Eine motifgeschichtliche Darstellung aufrung der neuen exegetischen Forschung*. Orbis Biblicus et Orientalis 15. Freiburg: Universtatsverlag, 1977.
Guilbert, P. "The Message of Salvation in the Acts of the Apostles: Composition and Structure." *Lumen-Vitoria* 12 (1957) 406–17.
Gundry, Robert. *Mark: A Commentary on His Apology for the Cross*. Grand Rapids: Eerdmans, 1993.
———. *Peter: False Disciple and Apostate According to Saint Matthew*. Grand Rapids: Eerdmans, 2015.
———. *Soma in Biblical Theology: With Emphasis on Anthropology*. Grand Rapids: Zondervan, 1987.
———. *A Survey of the New Testament*. 4th ed. Grand Rapids: Zondervan, 2003.
Gurney, O. R. *Some Aspects of Hittite Religion*. London: Oxford University Press, 1977.
Guthrie, Donald. "The Development of the Idea of Canonical Pseudepigrapha in New Testament Criticism." In *The Authorship and Integrity of the New Testament: Some Recent Studies*, by Kurt Aland, 14–39. Theological Collections 4. London: SPCK, 1965.
———. *New Testament Introduction*. Downers Grove: InterVarsity, 1970.
———. "Tertullian and Pseudonymity." *EvT* 67 (1956) 341.
Gutiérrez, Gustavo. *A Theology of Liberation*. Maryknoll: Orbis, 1973.

Gutierrez, Pedro. *La Paternité spirituelle selon S. Paul.* Paris: Gabalda, 1968.
Hafemann, Scott. "'Divine Nature' in 2 Pet 1,4 within its Eschatological Context." *Bib* 94.1 (2013) 80–99.
———. "Salvation in Jude 5 and the Argument of 2 Peter 1:3–11." In *The Catholic Epistles and Apostolic Tradition*, edited by K. W. Niebuhr and R. W. Wall, 339–42, 480–82. Waco: Baylor, 2009.
Hägerland, Tobias. "Prophetic Forgiveness in Josephus and Mark." *Svensk exegetisk arsbok* 79 (2014) 125–39.
Hagner, Donald. *Matthew 14–28.* WBC 33B. Dallas: Word, 1995.
Halbwachs, Maurice. *Les cadres sociaux de la mémoire.* Paris: Alcan, 1925.
———. *On Collective Memory.* Edited by Lewis Coser, Chicago: University of Chicago Press, 1992.
Hallo, William, ed. *The Context of Scripture.* 3 vols. Leiden: Brill, 1997–2002.
Hanneken, Todd. "Moses Has His Interpreters: Understanding the Legal Exegesis in Acts 15 from the Precedent in Jubilees." *CBQ* 77.4 (2015) 686–706.
Harland, Philip A. *Associations, Synagogues, and Congregations: Claiming a Place in Ancient Mediterranean Society.* Minneapolis, MN: Fortress, 2003.
Harnack, *Die Chronologie der altchristlichen Literatur bis Eusebius.* Leipzig: J. C. Hinrichs, 1897.
Harris, J. Rendel. "A Further Note on the Use of Enoch in 1 Peter." *Expositor* 6 (1901) 346–49.
———. *Testimonies.* Cambridge: Cambridge University Press, 1916–20.
Harris, Laird, et al. *Theological Wordbook of the Old Testament.* Chicago: Moody, 1980.
Harris, Murray. *Jesus as God: The New Testament Use of Theos in Reference to Jesus.* Grand Rapids: Baker, 1992.
Harrison, James. "The Persecution of Christians from Nero to Hadrian." In *Into All the World: Emergent Christianity in its Jewish and Greco-Roman Context*, edited by Mark Harding and Alanna Nobbs, 266–300. Grand Rapids: Eerdmans, 2017.
Hartman, L. "Some Unorthodox Thoughts on the 'Household-Code Form.'" In *The Social World of Formative Christianity and Judaism*, edited by J. Neusner et al., 219–34. Philadelphia, PA: Fortress, 1988.
Harvey, A. E. *Jesus and the Constraints of History.* London: Duckworth, 1982.
Hastings, James, ed. *Hastings' Dictionary of the Bible.* Grand Rapids: Baker, 1994.
Hawthorne, Gerald, et al. *Dictionary of Paul and His Letters.* Downers Grove: InterVarsity, 1993.
Hauck, F. *Die Katholischen Briefe.* Göttingen: Vandenhoeck & Ruprecht, 1933.
Hayes, Richard. *Echoes of Scripture in the Gospels.* Waco: Baylor, 2017.
Helyer, Larry. *The Life and Witness of Peter.* Downers Grove: InterVarsity, 2012.
———. "The Necessity, Problems, and Promise of Second Temple Judaism for Discussions of New Testament Eschatology." *JETS* 47 (2004) 606–9.
Hemer, Colin J. *The Book of Acts in the Setting of Hellenistic History.* Winona Lake, IN: Eisenbrauns, 1990.
———. "The Speeches in Acts II: The Areopagus Address." *TynBul* 40 (1989) 239–59.
Hengel, Martin. *The Charismatic Leader and His Followers.* New York: Crossroad, 1981.
———. "Eye-Witness Memory and the Writing of the Gospels." In *The Written Gospel*, edited by Markus Bockmuehl and Donald A. Hagner, 70–96. Cambridge: Cambridge University Press, 2005.
———. *Saint Peter: The Underestimated Apostle.* Grand Rapids: Eerdmans, 2010.

———. *The Son of God: The Origin of Christology and the History of Jewish Hellenistic Religion*. London: SCM, 1976.
Hengel, Martin, and Daniel P. Bailey. "Effective History of Isaiah 53." In *The Suffering Servant: Isaiah 53 in Jewish and Christian Sources*, edited by Bernd Janowski and Peter Stuhlmacher, 75–146. Grand Rapids: Eerdmans, 2004.
Hennecke, Edgar. *New Testament Apocrypha*. 2 vols. Philadelphia, PA: Westminster, 1963–66.
Hermann, Johannes. *Die Idee der Sühne im Alten Testament: eine Ubersuchung über Gebrauch und Bedeutung des Wortes kipper*. Leipzig: Hinrichs, 1905.
Hewit, J. W. "The Use of Nails in the Crucifixion." *HTR* 25 (1932) 29–45.
Hicks, Robert. *Epicurus Principle Doctrines*. http://Classics.mit.edu/Epicurus/princdoc.html.
Hiebert, D. Edmund. "The Prophetic Foundation for the Christian Life: An Exposition of 2 Peter 1:19–21." *BSac* 141 (1984) 166.
Hillyer, Norman. *1 and 2 Peter, Jude*. New International Biblical Commentary 16. Peabody, MA: Hendrickson, 1992.
Himes, Paul. "Why Did Peter Change the Septuagint? A Reexamination of the Significance of the Use of τίθημι in 1 Peter 2:6." *BBR* 26.2 (2016) 227–44.
Hines, Paul. "Peter and the Prophetic Word: The Theology of Prophecy Traced through Peter's Sermons and Epistles." *BBR* 21 (2011) 227–41.
Hoag, Gary. *Wealth in Ancient Ephesus and the First Letter to Timothy: Fresh Insights from Ephesiaca by Xenophon of Ephesus*. Winona Lake, IN: Eisenbrauns, 2015.
Hobbes, Thomas. "Leviathan." In *The Great Books of the Western World: Machiavelli, Hobbes*, 23:39–283. Chicago: Encyclopaedia Britannica, 1952.
Hoffner, Harry A., Jr. "Hittite-Israelite Cultural Parallels." In *The Context of Scripture: Archival Documents from the Biblical World*, edited by William Hallo, xxix–xxxiv. Leiden: Brill, 2002.
Holdsworth, John. "The Sufferings in 1 Peter and 'Missionary Apocalyptic.'" *StudBib* 3 (1978) 226–31.
Hollaz, David. *Acromaticum Universam Theologiam Thetico-Polemicam Complectens*. Lipsiae: B.C. Breitkopfii, 1763.
Hollenbach, Paul. "Jesus, Demoniacs, and Public Authorities: A Socio-Historical Study." *JAAR* 49 (1981) 567–88.
Holtzmann, H. J. *Die Apostelgeschte. Hand-Commentar zum Neuen Testament* ½. Tübingen: J. C. B. Mohr, 1901.
Holzmeister, U. *Commentarius in Epistles SS. Petri et Iudae, Apostolorum. Cursus Scripturae Sacrae 3/13*. Paris: Lethielleux, 1937.
Hooker, Morna. *From Adam to Christ*. Cambridge: Cambridge University, 1990.
———. *Jesus and the Servant: The Influence of the Servant Concept of Deutero-Isaiah in the New Testament*. London: SPCK, 1959.
———. *The Son of Man in Mark: A Study of the Background of the Term "Son of Man" and Its Use in St. Mark's Gospel*. Montreal: McGill University, 1967.
———. "'Who Can This Be?' The Christology of Mark's Gospel." In *Contours of Christology in the New Testament*, edited by Richard Longenecker, 79–99. Grand Rapids: Eerdmans, 2005.
Horrell, David. "Between Conformity and Resistance: Beyond the Balch-Elliott Debate Towards a Postcolonial Reading of First Peter." In *Reading First Peter With New Eyes: Methodical Reassessments of the Letter of First Peter*, edited by Robert L. Webb and Betsy Bauman-Martin, 111–43. London: T. & T. Clark, 2007.

———. "The Label Χριστιανός: 1 Peter 4:16 and the Formation of Christian Identity." *JBL* 126.2 (2007) 361–81.

———. *The Social Ethos of the Corinthian Correspondence: Interests and Ideology from 1 Corinthians to 1 Clement*. Edinburgh: T. & T. Clark, 1996.

Horrell, David, et al. "Visuality, Vivid Description, and the Message of 1 Peter: The Significance of the Roaring Lion (1 Peter 5:8)." *JBL* 132.3 (2013) 697–716.

Horsley, G. H. R. "Speeches and Dialogue in Acts." *NTS* 32 (1986) 609–14.

Horsley, Richard. *Oral Performance, Popular Tradition, and Hidden Transcript in Q*. Semia Studies. Atlanta, GA: Society of Biblical Literature, 2007.

Horsley, Richard, et al. *Performing the Gospel: Orality, Memory, and Mark*. Minneapolis, MN: Fortress, 2006.

Hort, F. J. A. *The First Epistle of St. Peter 1:1—2:17*. London: Macmillan, 1898.

———. "A Note on the Words κοφίνους, σπυρίς, sarganh." *JTS* 10 (1909) 567–71.

Howard, V. "Did Jesus Speak About His Own Death?" *CBQ* 39 (1977) 515–27.

Howe, Bonie. "Review of *Reading First Peter with New Eyes: Methodological Reassessments of the Letter of First Peter*, edited by Robert Webb and Betsy Bauman-Martin, New York: T & T Clark, 2007." *RBL* 5 (2009) 3–4.

Huck, Albert. *Synopsis of the First Three Gospels*. Los Angeles: Hard, 2014.

Hugh of St. Victor. *On the Sacraments of the Christian Faith*. Translated by Roy Defarrari. Cambridge: The Catholic University of America, 1951.

Hughes, P. E. "The Blood of Jesus and His Heavenly Priesthood in Hebrews." *BSac* 131 (1973) 99–109.

Hummel, Reinhart. *Die Auseinandersetzung zwischen Kirche und Judentum im Matthäusevangelium*. BEvT 33. Munich: Kaiser, 1963.

Hunter, Archibald. *The Gospel according to John*. Cambridge Bible Commentary. Cambridge: Cambridge University Press, 1965.

Hurst, L. D. *The Epistle to the Hebrews: Its Background of Thought*. Cambridge: Cambridge University Press, 1990.

Hurtado, Larry. "Apostle Peter in Protestant Scholarship: Cullmann, Hengel, and Bockmuehl." In *Peter in Early Christianity*, edited by Helen Bond and Larry Hurtado, 1–15. Grand Rapids: Eerdmans, 2015.

———. "Christology in Acts: Jesus in Early Christian Belief and Early Christian Belief and Practice." In *Issues in Luke-Acts*, edited by Sean Adams and Michael Pahl, 217–37, Piscataway: Gorias, 2012.

———. *Lord Jesus Christ: Devotion to Jesus in Earliest Christianity*. Grand Rapids: Eerdmans, 2003.

Hurtado, Larry, and Paul Owen. *"Who Is the Son of Man?" The Latest Scholarship on a Puzzling Expression of the Historical Jesus*. London: T. & T. Clark, 2011.

Hutchison, John. "Servanthood: Jesus' Countercultural Call to Christian Leaders." *BSac* 166.1 (2009) 53–68.

Isaacs, Marie. *Sacred Space: An Approach to the Theology of the Epistle to the Hebrews*. Sheffield: Sheffield Academic, 1992.

Jacobs, Paul, and Hartmut Krienke. "Foreknowledge, Providence, Predestination." In *NIDNTT*, edited by Colin Brown, 1:693. Grand Rapids, 1975.

Jaffee, Martin. "The Oral-Cultural Context of the Talmud Yerushalmi: Greco-Roman Rhetorical Paedeia, Discipleship, and the Concept of Oral Torah." In *Transmitting Jewish Traditions: Orality, Textuality, and Cultural Diffusion*, edited by Yaakov Elman and Israel Gershoni, 27–73. New Haven: Yale University Press, 2000.

Janowski, Bernd. *Sühne als Heilsgeschehen: Stidien zur Sühnetheologie der Priesterschrift und zur Wurzel KPR im Alten Testament*. Neukirchen-Vluyn, Germany: Neukirchener Verlag, 1982.
Janowski, Bernd, and Peter Stuhlmacher. *The Suffering Servant: Isaiah 53 in Jewish and Christian Sources*. Grand Rapids: Eerdmans, 2004.
Jeremias, Jeremias. *The Eucharistic Words of Jesus*. London: SCM, 1966.
Jewett, Robert. *Romans*. Minneapolis, MN: Fortress, 2007.
Jobes, Karen. *1 Peter*. BECNT. Grand Rapids: Baker, 2005.
———. "Got Milk? Septuagint Psalm 33 and the Interpretation of 1 Peter 2:1–3." *WTJ* 63 (2002) 1–14.
———. "'O Taste and See': Septuagint Psalm 33 in 1 Peter." *Stone-Campbell Journal* 18 (2015) 241–51.
Johnson, Andrew. "Error and Epistemological Process in the Pentateuch and Mark's Gospel: A Biblical Theology of Knowing from Foundational Texts." PhD diss., University of St. Andrews, 2011.
Johnson, Luke Timothy. *Constructing Paul*. Grand Rapids: Eerdmans, 2020.
———. "Critique of *Short Stories by Jesus*." Paper presented at the Society for Biblical Literature, November 22, 2015.
———. "The Jesus of the Gospels and Philosophy." In *Jesus and Philosophy: New Essays*, edited by Paul Moser, 63–83. Cambridge: Cambridge University Press, 2009.
Jones, D. L. "The Christology of the Missionary Speeches in the Acts of the Apostles." PhD diss., Duke University, 1966.
Jones, M. R. *New Testament Apocrypha*. Berkeley: Apocryphile, 2004.
Juel, D. *Messiah and the Temple*. SBLDS 31. Missoula, MT: Scholars, 1977.
Julicher, Adolf. *Einleitung in das Neue Testament*. Tübingen: Mohr, 1894.
Justin Martyr. *Saint Justin Martyr: The First Apology, The Second Apology, Dialogue with Trypho, Exhortation to the Greeks, Discourse to the Greeks, The Monarchy; or the Rule of God*. Edited by Thomas B. Falls. New York: Christian Heritage, 1949.
Juza, Ryan. "Echoes of Sodom and Gomorrah on the Day of the Lord: Intertextuality and Tradition in 2 Peter 3:7–13." *BBR* 24.2 (2014) 227–45.
Kähler, "Zur Form- und Traditionsgeschichte von Matth. xvi. 17–19." *NTS* 23.1 (1974) 36–58.
Kalluveettil, P. *Declaration and Covenant: A Comprehensive Review of Covenant Formula from the Old Testament and Ancient Near East*. Rome: Pontifical Biblical Institute, 1982.
Kaminsky, Joel. "Israel's Election and the Other in Biblical, Second Temple, and Rabbinic Thought." In *The "Other" in Second Temple Judaism*, edited by Daniel Harlow et al., 17–30. Grand Rapids: Eerdmans, 2011.
Kant, Immanuel. "Critique of Practical Reason." In *Great Books of the Western World: Kant*, 42:291–364. Chicago: Encyclopaedia Britannica, 1952.
———. "Critique of Pure Reason." In *Great Books of the Western World: Kant*, 42:1–252. Chicago: Encyclopaedia Britannica, 1952.
———. *Religion within the Boundaries of Mere Reason*. Cambridge: Cambridge University Press, 1998.
Käsemann, Ernst. "An Apologia for Primitive Christian Eschatology." In *Essays on New Testament*, 169–95. London: Allenson, 1964.
———. "Eine Apologie der urchristlichen Eschatologie." *ZST* 49 (1952) 272–96.
Kautzsch, E., and A. E. Cowley. *Gesenius' Hebrew Grammar*. Oxford: Clarendon, 1976.

Keck, Leander. "Mark 3:7–12 and Mark's Christology." *JBL* 84 (1965) 349–59.
Keener, Craig. *1 Peter*. Grand Rapids: Baker, 2021.
———. *Acts: An Exegetical Commentary*. Grand Rapids: Baker, 2013.
———. *The Gospel of John: A Commentary*. Peabody, MA: Hendrickson, 2003.
———. *The Gospel of Matthew: A Socio-Rhetorical Commentary*. Grand Rapids: Eerdmans, 2009.
———. "Miracle Reports and the Argument from Analogy." *BBR* 25.4 (2015) 475–95.
———. *Miracles: The Credibility of the New Testament Accounts*. 2 vols. Grand Rapids: Baker, 2011.
Kelber, Werner. "The Case of the Gospels: Memory's Desire and the Limits of Historical Criticism." *Oral Tradition* 17 (2002) 55–86.
———. "The Generative Force of Memory: Early Christian Tradition as a Process of Remembering." *BTB* 36 (2006) 15–22.
Kelber, Werner, and Samuel Byrsog. *Jesus in Memory: Traditions in Oral and Scribal Perspectives*. Waco: Baylor University Press, 2009.
Kelly, J. N. D. *A Commentary on the Epistles of Peter and Jude*. Grand Rapids: Baker, 1969.
———. *Early Christian Doctrines*. San Francisco: HarperSanFrancisco, 1958.
Kennard, Douglas. *Biblical Covenantalism*. 3 vols. Eugene, OR: Wipf & Stock, 2015.
———. *A Biblical Theology of Hebrews*. Eugene, OR: Wipf & Stock, 2018.
———. *A Biblical Theology of the Book of Isaiah*. Eugene, OR: Wipf & Stock, 2020.
———. *The Classical Christian God*. Toronto Studies in Theology 86. Lewiston: Edwin Mellen, 2002.
———. "Covenant Pneumaticism." In *Biblical Covenantalism*, 3:30–161. Eugene, OR: Wipf & Stock, 2015.
———. *A Critical Realist's Theological Method: Returning the Bible and Biblical Theology to be the Framer for Theology and Science*. Eugene, OR: Wipf & Stock, 2013.
———. "The Doctrine of God in Petrine Theology." ThD diss., Dallas Theological Seminary, 1986.
———. *Epistemology and Logic in the New Testament*. Eugene, OR: Wipf & Stock, 2016.
———. *The Gospel*. Eugene, OR: Wipf & Stock, 2017.
———. *Messiah Jesus: Christology in His Day and Ours*. New York: Lang, 2008.
———. "Petrine Redemption: Its Meaning and Extent." *JETS* 30.4 (1987) 399–405.
———. *Petrine Studies*. Eugene, OR: Wipf & Stock, 2022.
———. *Petrine Theology*. Eugene, OR: Wipf & Stock, 2022.
———. "The Reef of the O.T.: A Method for Doing Biblical Theology that Makes Sense for Wisdom Literature." *SwJT* 56 (2013) 227–57.
———. *The Relationship Between Epistemology, Hermeneutics, Biblical Theology and Contextualization*. Lewiston: Mellen, 1999.
Kennedy, George. *New Testament Interpretation through Rhetorical Criticism*. Chapel Hill: University of North Carolina Press, 1984.
Kertelege, Karl. *Die Wunder Jesu im Markusevangelium: Eine redaktionsgesgeschichtliche Untersuchung*. Munich: Kösel, 1970.
Kierkegaard, Søren. *Fear and Trembling*. Princeton: Princeton University Press, 1983.
Kim, Seyoon. "Jesus—The Son of God, the Stone, the Son of Man, and the Servant: The Role of Zechariah in the Self-Identification of Jesus." In *Tradition and Interpretation in the New Testament*, edited by Gerald Hawthorne with Otto Betz, 134–48. Grand Rapids: Eerdmans, 1987.
Kingsbury, Jack. *The Christology of Mark's Gospel*. Philadelphia, PA: Fortress, 1983.

Kirk, Alan. "Social and Cultural Memory." In *Memory, Tradition, and Text: Uses of the Past in Early Christianity*, edited by Alan Kirk and Tom Thatcher, 1–24. Semeia Studies 52. Atlanta, GA: Society of Biblical Literature, 2005.

Kirk, Alan, and Tom Thatcher. "Jesus Tradition as Social Memory." In *Memory, Tradition, and Text: Uses of the Past in Early Christianity*, edited by Alan Kirk and Tom Thatcher, 25–42. Semeia Studies 52. Atlanta, GA: Society of Biblical Literature, 2005.

———. *Memory, Tradition, and Text: Uses of the Past in Early Christianity*. Semeia Studies 52. Atlanta, GA: Society of Biblical Literature, 2005.

Kirk, J. R., and Stephen Young. "'I Will Set His Hand to the Sea': Psalm 88:26 LXX and Christology in Mark." *JBL* 133.2 (2014) 333–40.

Kistemaker, Simon. *Exposition of the Acts of the Apostles*. Grand Rapids: Baker, 1990.

———. *New Testament Commentary: Exposition of the Epistles of Peter and of the Epistle of Jude*. Grand Rapids: Baker, 1987.

Kittel, Gerhard, and Gerhard Friedrich. *Theological Dictionary of the New Testament*. 10 vols. Grand Rapids: Eerdmans, 1964–76.

Klassen, William. "The Sacred Kiss in the New Testament: An Example of Social Boundary Lines." *NTS* 39 (1993) 122–35.

Klauck, Hans-Josepf. *Ancient Letters and the New Testament: A Guide to Context and Exegesis*. Waco: Baylor University Press, 2006.

Klawans, Jonathan. *Impurity and Sin in Ancient Judaism*. Oxford: Oxford University Press, 2000.

Klijn, A. F. J. "The Study of Jewish Christianity." *NTS* 20 (1973–74) 419–31.

Klijn, A. F. J., and G. J. Reinink. *Patristic Evidence for Jewish-Christian Sects*. Leiden: Brill, 1973.

Knopf, R. *Die Briefe Petri und Judae*. Göttingen: Vandenhoeck & Ruprecht, 1912.

Koch, Dietrich-Alex. "The Quotations of Isaiah 8,14 and 28,16 in Romans 9,33 and 1Peter 2,6.8 as Test Case for Old Testament Quotations in the New Testament." *ZNW* 101.2 (2010) 223–40.

Kochenash, "Cornelius's Obeisance to Peter (Acts 10:25–26) and Judaea Capta Coins." *CBQ* 81.4 (2019) 627–40.

Koester, Craig R. *Hebrews: A New Translation with Introduction and Commentary*. Anchor Bible 36. New York: Doubleday, 2001.

Kolenkow, Bingham. "The Genre Testament and Forecasts of the Future in the Hellenistic Jewish Milieu." *JSJ* 6 (1975) 57–71.

Kraeling, E. G. *The Brooklyn Museum Aramaic Papyri: New Documents of the Fifth Century B.C. from the Jewish Colony at Elephantine*. New Haven: Yale University Press, 1953.

Kuhn, Karl. "The Kingdom Story through Speech and Theme in Luke 24 and the Acts of the Apostles" In *The Kingdom according to Luke and Acts: A Social, Literary, and Theological Introduction*, 147–78. Grand Rapids: Baker, 2015.

Kümmel, H. M. "Ersatzkönig und Sündenbock." *ZAW* 80 (1968) 289–318.

Künneth, Walter. *Theology of the Resurrection*. London: SCM, 1965.

Kurtz, Johann Heinrich. *Sacrificial Worship of the Old Testament*. Edinburgh: T. & T. Clark, 1863.

Kurz, William. "Narrative Models for Imitation in Luke-Acts." In *Greeks, Romans, and Christians*, edited by D. L. Balch, 171–89. Minneapolis, MN: Fortress, 1990.

Lacey, W. K. *The Family in Classical Greece*. London: Thames & Hudson, 1968.

Lackey, Jennifer, and Ernest Sosa. *The Epistemology of Testimony*. Oxford: Clarendon, 2006.
Lagrange, M. J. *Evangile selon Saint Luc*. Paris: Gabalda, 1948.
Lampe, G. W. H. "The Lucan Portrait of Christ." *NTS* 2 (1955/56) 160–75.
Lanzinger, Daniel. "Petrus und der Sigende Hahn: Eine Zeitgeschichtliche Anspielung in der markinischen Verlengnungsperikope (Mk 14,54. 66–72)." *ZNW* 109.1 (2018) 32–50.
Lapham, F. *Peter: The Myth, the Man and the Writings: A Study of Early Petrine Text and Tradition*. Sheffield: Sheffield Academic, 2003.
Lea, Thomas. "The Early Christian View of Pseudepigraphic Writings." *JETS* 27 (1984) 65–75.
Leaney, A. R. C. "1 Peter and the Passover: An Interpretation." *NTS* 10 (1964) 238–51.
———. *The Gospel According to St. Luke*. Black's New Testament Commentaries. London: A. & C. Black, 1967.
Lefkowitz, M., and M. Fant. *Womens' Life in Greece and Rome: A Source Book in Translation*. Baltimore: John Hopkins University, 1982.
Leitzmann, Hans. "Die Anfange des Glaubensbekenntnisses." In *Kleine Schriften*, 3:163–81. New York: Wentworth, 2019.
"Letter of the Emperor Claudius to the Alexandrians." https://www.csun.edu/~hcfll004/claualex.html.
Levine, Amy-Jill. *Short Stories by Jesus: The Enigmatic Parables of a Controversial Rabbi*. New York: HarperOne, 2014.
Levine, Baruch A. *In the Presence of the Lord: A Study of Cult and Some Terms in Ancient Israel*. Leiden: Brill, 1974.
———. *Leviticus*. JPS Torah Commentary. Philadelphia, PA: Jewish Publication Society, 1989.
Levine, Lee. *The Ancient Synagogue: The First Thousand Years*. New Haven: Yale University Press, 2000.
Liebengood, Kelley. *The Eschatology of 1 Peter: Considering the Influence of Zechariah 9–14*. New York: Cambridge University Press, 2014.
Lightfoot, John. *Apostolic Fathers*. Grand Rapids: Baker, 1981.
———. *A Commentary on the New Testament from the Talmud and Hebraica, Matthew—1 Corinthians*. 4 vols. Grand Rapids: Baker, 1979.
———. *St. Paul's Epistle to the Philippians*. London: Macmillan, 1881.
Lightfoot, Robert. *History and Interpretation in the Gospels*. London: Hodder & Stoughton, 1935.
Lim, Timothy. *Pesharim*. London: Sheffield, 2002.
Lincoln, Andrew T. *Paradise Now and Not Yet: Studies in the Role of the Heavenly Dimensions in Paul's Thought with Special Reference to His Eschatology*. Society for New Testament Studies Monograph 43. Cambridge: Cambridge University Press, 1981.
Lindars, Bernard. *New Testament Apologetic*. Philadelphia, PA: Westminster, 1961.
Lo, Jonathan. "Did Peter Really Say That? Revisiting the Petrine Speeches in Acts." In *Peter in Early Christianity*, edited by Helen Bond and Larry Hurtado, 62–75. Grand Rapids: Eerdmans, 2015.
Locke, John. "Concerning Human Understanding." In *Great Books of the Western World: Locke, Berkely, and Hume*, 20:85–402. Chicago: Encyclopaedia Britannica, 1952.
———. "A Discourse of Miracles." In *The Works of John Locke*, 9:256–65. London: C. & J. Rivington, 1824.

———. "The Reasonableness of Christianity." In *The Works of John Locke*, 6:21–71. London: C. & J. Rivington, 1824.

Lohse, Eduard. *Märtyrer und Gottesknecht: Untersuchungen zur urchistlichen Verkündigung vom sühntod Jesu Christi*. Forschungen zur Religion und Literature des Alten und Neuen Testaments 49. Göttingengen: Vandenhoeck & Ruprecht, 1963.

Longenecker, Richard N. *The Christology of Early Jewish Christianity Studies in Biblical Theology*. London: SCM, 1970.

Lossky, Vladimir. *In the Image and Likeness of God*. New York: St Vladimir's Seminary, 1974.

———. "Redemption and Deification." In *In the Image and Likeness of God*, 97–110. New York: St Vladimir's Seminary, 1974.

Love, Julian. "The First Epistle of Peter." *Int* 8 (1954) 82–83.

Luce, H. K. *The Gospel According to S. Luke*. Cambridge: Cambridge University Press, 1933.

Lund, Allan. "Zur Verbrennung der sogenanten *Chrestiani* (Tac. Ann. 15,44)." *ZRGG* 60.3 (2008) 253–61.

Lund, Oystein. *Way Metaphors and Way Topics in Isaiah 40–66*. Tübingen: Mohr Siebeck, 2007.

Luther, Martin. *Luther's Works*. Edited by E. Theodore Bachman. Philadelphia, PA: Fortress, 1960.

———. *Luther's Works*. Edited by Jaroslav Pelikan and Helmut Lehmann. Saint Louis: Concordia, 1955–2015.

Luz, Ulrich. "Das Geheimnismotiv und die markinische Christologie." *ZNW* 56 (1965) 9–30.

MacDonald, Dennis Ronald. "The Synoptic Problem and Literary Mimesis: The Case of the Frothing Demoniac." In *New Studies in the Synoptic Problem*, edited by P. Foster et al., 509–21. Leuven: Uitgeverij Peeters, 2011.

MacDonald, William. *True Discipleship*. Kansas City: Walterick, 1962.

Mackay, E. Anne. *Signs of Orality: The Oral Tradition and Its Influence in the Greek and Roman World*. Leiden: Brill, 1999.

Magness, J. Lee. *Sense and Absence: Structure and Suspicion in the Ending of Mark's Gospel*. Atlanta, GA: Scholars, 1981.

Maimonides, Moses. *Thirteen Principles of the Faith*. Brooklyn: Kol Menachem, 2008.

Manson, T. W. "The Life of Jesus: Some Tendencies in Present-Day Research." In *The Background of the New Testament and Its Eschatology: In Honor of C. H. Dodds*, edited by W. D. Davies and D. Daube, 211–21. New York: Cambridge University Press, 1956.

Marcus, Joel. "Mark 4:10–12 and Marcan Epistemology." *JBL* 103.4 (1984) 557–74.

———. *The Way of the Lord: Christological Exegesis of the Old Testament in the Gospel of Mark*. Louisville: Westminster/John Knox Press, 1992.

Marger, Martin N. *Race and Ethnic Relations: American and Global Perspectives*. Belmont, Wadsworth, 1991.

Markschies, Christoph. "Jesus Christ as a Man before God: Two Interpretive Models for Isaiah 53 in the Patristic Literature and Their Development." In *The Suffering Servant: Isaiah 53 in Jewish and Christian Sources*, edited by Bernd Janowski and Peter Stuhlmacher, 225–323. Grand Rapids: Eerdmans, 2004.

Marshall, I. H. *The Acts of the Apostles: An Introduction and Commentary.* Grand Rapids: Eerdmans, 1980.
———. *The Gospel of Luke: A Commentary on the Greek Text.* NIGTC. Grand Rapids: Eerdmans, 1978.
———. *The Pastoral Epistles.* ICC. Edinburgh: T. & T. Clark, 1999.
Martin, Martina. "It's My Perogative: Jesus Authority to Grant Forgiveness and Healing on Earth." *The Journal of Religious Thought* 59.1 (2006) 67–74.
Martin, Ralph P. "Aspects of Worship in the New Testament Church." In *Vox Evangelica II*, 6–32. London: Epworth, 1963.
———. *Mark, Evangelist and Theologian.* Grand Rapids: Zondervan, 1986.
———. *Vox Evangelica II: Biblical and Historical Essays.* London: Epworth, 1963.
Martin, Ralph, and Peter Davids. *Dictionary of the Later New Testament & Its Developments.* Downers Grove: InterVarsity, 1997.
Martin, Troy. *Metaphor and Composition in 1 Peter.* Society of Biblical Literature Dissertations Series 131. Atlanta, GA: Scholars, 1992.
———. "The Rehabilitation of a Rhetorical Step-Child: First Peter and Classical Rhetorical Criticism." In *Reading First Peter with New Eyes*, edited by Robert Webb and Betsy Bauman-Martin, 41–71. London: T. & T. Clark, 2007.
Martínez, Garcia, and J. Trebolle Barrera. *The People of the Dead Sea Scrolls.* Leiden: Brill, 1995.
Martyn, Louis. *Theological Issues in the Letters of Paul.* Edinburgh: T. & T. Clark, 1997.
Masterman, J. Howard. *The First Epistle of St. Peter.* London: Macmillan, 1900.
Mathetes. *Epistle to Diognetus.* Leiden: E. J. Brill, 1964.
Mayor, Joseph. *The Epistles of St. James: The Greek Text with Introduction, Notes and Comments.* Grand Rapids: Baker, 1978.
———. *The Epistles of St. Jude and the Second Epistle of St. Peter.* Minneapolis, MN: Klock & Klock, 1978.
McArthur, Harvey, and Robert Johnston. *They Also Taught in Parables.* Grand Rapids: Zondervan, 1990.
McCarthy, Dennis J. *Treaty and Covenant: A Study in Form in the Ancient Oriental Documents and in the Old Testament.* AnBib 21. Rome: Biblical Institute, 1981.
McCartney, Dan G. "Atonement in James, Peter and Jude." In *The Glory of the Atonement: Biblical, Historical & Practical Perspectives*, edited by Charles Hill and Frank James, 176–89. Downers Grove: InterVarsity, 2004.
McDonald, H. D. *The Christian View of Man.* Westchester: Crossway, 1981.
McDonald, L. M., and J. A. Sanders. *The Canon Debate.* Peabody, MA: Hendrickson, 2002.
McGrath, Alister E. *Iustitia Dei: A History of the Christian Doctrine of Justification.* Cambridge: Cambridge University Press, 1998.
McKenzie, John A. *Dictionary of the Bible.* New York: Macmillan, 1965.
McKnight, Scot. *Jesus and His Death: Historiography, the Historical Jesus, and Atonement Theory.* Waco: Baylor University Press, 2005.
———. *The King Jesus Gospel: The Original Good News Revisited.* Grand Rapids: Zondervan, 2011.
McNeile, Alan Hugh, and C. S. C. Williams. *An Introduction to the Study of the New Testament.* Oxford: Oxford University Press, 1953.
McPhee, Brian. "Walk, Don't Run: Jesus Water Walking Is Unparalleled in Greco-Roman Mythology." *JBL* 135.4 (2016) 763–77.

Meeks, Wayne. *The First Urban Christians: The Social World of the Apostle Paul.* New Haven: Yale University Press, 2003.
Meier, John. *A Marginal Jew: Rethinking the Historical Jesus.* Vol. 1, *The Roots of the Problem and the Person.* New York: Doubleday, 1991.
———. *A Marginal Jew: Rethinking the Historical Jesus.* Vol. 2, *Mentor, Message, and Miracles.* New Haven: Yale University Press, 1994.
———. *A Marginal Jew: Rethinking the Historical Jesus.* Vol. 5, *Parables.* New Haven: Yale University Press, 2016.
Melanchthon, Philip. *Corpus Reformatorum.* Vol. 21, *Loci Communes.* Edited by Karl Gottlieb Bretschneider. Berlin: C. A. Schwetschke, 1834.
Menard, Jacques E. "*Pais Theou* as a Messianic Title in the Book of Acts." *CBQ* 19 (1957) 83–92.
Mendenhahall, G. E. "Covenant Forms in Israelite Tradition." *BA* 17.3 (1954) 50–76.
———. *Law and Covenant in Israel and the Ancient Near East.* Pittsburgh: The Biblical Colloquium, 1955.
Merkle, Benjamin L. *The Elder and Overseer: One Office in the Early Church.* New York: Peter Lang, 2003.
Metzger, Bruce. *A Textual Commentary on the Greek New Testament.* 2nd ed. Stuttgart: Deutsche Bibelgesellschaft, 2002.
Meye, Robert. *Jesus and the Twelve: Discipleship and Revelation in Mark's Gospel.* Grand Rapids: Eerdmans, 1968.
Meyendorff, John, et al. *The Primacy of Peter.* Leighton Buzzard, Bedfordshire: Faith, 1973.
Meyer, Eduard. *Ursprung und Anfänge des Christentums.* 3 vols. Sydney: Wentworth, 2018.
Meyers, Eric. *Galilee Through the Centuries: Confluence of Cultures.* Winona Lake, IN: Eisenbrauns, 1999.
Meyers, Eric, and Mark Chancey. *Alexander to Constantine.* Vol. 3, *Archeology of the Land of the Bible.* New Haven: Yale University Press, 2012.
Michaels, J. Ramsey. *1 Peter.* WBC 49. Waco: Word Biblical, 1988.
Miegge, Giovanni. *Gospel and Myth in the Thought of Rudolf Bultmann.* Richmond: John Knox Press, 1960.
Migne, J.-P. *Patrologiae cursus completus: Series Latina.* 221 vols. Paris: Imprimerie Catholique, 1844–64.
———. *Patrologiae cursus completus: Series Graeca.* 161 vols. Paris: Imprimerie Catholique, 1857–66.
Milgrom, Jacob. "Israel's Sanctuary: 'The Priestly Picture of Dorian Gray.'" *RB* 83 (1976) 390–99.
———. *Leviticus 1–16.* The Anchor Bible 3. New York: Doubleday, 1991.
———. *Numbers.* The JPS Torah Commentary. Philadelphia, PA: The Jewish Publication Society, 1990.
———. "The Preposition מִן in the חַטָּאת Pericopes." *JBL* 126 (2007) 161–63.
———. *Studies in Levitical Terminology: The Encroacher and the Levite: The Term 'Aboda.* Berkeley: University of California, 1970.
Milik, Józef T. *Ten Years of Discovery in the Wilderness of Judea.* London: SCM, 1959.
Millauer, Helmut. *Leiden als Gnade: Eine Traditionsgeschichtliche Untersuchung zur Leidenstheologie des ersten Petrusbriefes.* Europäische Hochschulschriften. Reihe 23. Frankfurt: Lang, 1976.

Moffatt, James. *Introduction to the Literature of the New Testament*. New York: Scribner's, 1918.

Molina, Bruce, and Jerome Neyrey. *Calling Jesus Names: The Social Value of Labels in Matthew*. Foundations and Facets: Social Facets. Salem, OR: Polebridge, 1988.

Moloney, F. J. *The Johannine Son of Man*. Biblioteca di Scienze Religiose 14. Rome: LAS, 1976.

———. "The Johannine Son of Man Revisited." In *Theology and Christology in the Fourth Gospel: Essays by the Members of the SNTS Johannine Writing Seminar*, edited by G. Van Belle et al., 177–202. Biblotheca Ephemeridum Theologicarium Lovaniensium 434. Leuven: Leuven University, 2005.

Moo, Douglas. *A Biblical Theology of Paul and His Letters: The Gift of the New Realm in Christ*. Grand Rapids: Zondervan, 2021.

Moore, George F. "The Am Ha-ares (the People of the Land) and the Haberim (Associates)." In *The Beginnings of Christianity: Part I, The Acts of the Apostles*, edited by F. J. Foakes-Jackson and Kirsopp Lake, 1:439–45. 5 vols. Grand Rapids: Baker, 1979.

Morris, Leon. *The Gospel According to John*. Grand Rapids: Eerdmans, 1971.

———. *The Gospel According to St. Luke: An Introduction and Commentary*. Tyndale New Testament Commentaries. Grand Rapids: Eerdmans, 1974.

Moscicke, Hans. "The Gerasene Exorcism and Jesus' Eschatological Expulsion of Cosmic Powers: Echoes of Second Temple Scapegoat Traditions in Mark 5:1–20." *JSNT* 41.3 (2019) 363–83.

Moser, Paul. *The Elusive God: Reorienting Religious Epistemology*. Cambridge: Cambridge University Press, 2008.

———, ed. *Jesus and Philosophy: New Essays*. Cambridge: Cambridge University Press, 2009.

Moule, C. F. D. "The Nature and Purpose of 1 Peter." *NTS* 3 (1956–57) 1–11.

Moulton, James Hope, and George Milligan. *The Vocabulary of the Greek Testament: Illustrated from Papyri and Other Non-Literary Sources*. Peabody, MA: Hendrickson, 1997.

Mowinckel, Sigmund. *La décalogue*. Paris: Felix Alcan, 1927.

Müller, Morgens. *The Expression "Son of Man" and Development of Christology: A History of Interpretation*. London: Equinox, 2008.

Munck, J. "Discours d'adieu dans le Nouveau Testament et dans la Littérature biblique." In *Aux Sources de la Tradition Chrétienne*, edited by M. Maurice Goguel, 155–70. Neuchatel: Delachaux & Niestlé, 1959.

Murphy, Nancey. *Bodies and Souls, or Spiritual Bodies?* Cambridge: Cambridge University Press, 2006.

———. "Human Nature: Historical, Scientific, and Religious Issues." In *Whatever Happened to the Soul? Scientific and Theological Portraits of Human Nature*, edited by Warren Brown et al., 19–39. Minneapolis, MN: Fortress, 1998.

———. "Reductionism: How Did We Fall Into It and Can We Emerge From It?" In *Evolution and Emergence: Systems, Organisms, Persons*, edited by Nancey Murphy and William Stoeger, 19–39. Oxford: Oxford University Press, 2007.

Murphy, Nancey, and William Stoeger. *Evolution and Emergence: Systems, Organisms, Persons*. Oxford: Oxford University Press, 2007.

Mussner, Franz. "Ein Wortspiel in Mk 1,24?" *BZNF* 4 (1960) 285–86.

Myers, Alicia. *Characterizing Jesus: A Rhetorical Analysis on the Fourth Gospel's Use of Scripture in Its Presentation of Jesus*. London: T. & T. Clark, 2012.
Nagel, Norman. "Luther and the Priesthood of All Believers." *CTQ* 61.4 (1997) 283–84.
Neil, William. *The Acts of the Apostles*. NCB. Edinburgh: Oliphants, 1973.
Neusner, Jacob. *The Idea of Purity in Ancient Judaism*. Leiden: Brill, 1973.
———. *Sifre to Numbers: An American Translation and Explanation*. 2 vols. Brown Judaic Studies 118 and 119. Atlanta, GA: Scholars, 1986.
Neusner, Jacob, and Bruce Chilton. "Sanders Misunderstanding of Purity: Uncleanness as an Ontological, Not Moral-Eeschatological Category." In *Judaic Law from Jesus to the Mishnah*, edited by Jacob Neusner, 205–30. Atlanta, GA: Scholars, 1993.
Newton, M. *The Concept of Purity at Qumran and in the Letters of Paul*. Cambridge: Cambridge University Press, 1985.
Neyrey, Jerome. *2 Peter, Jude: A New Translation with Introduction and Commentary*. Anchor Bible 37C. New York: Doubleday, 1993.
———. "The Form and Background of the Polemic in 2 Peter." *JBL* 99 (1980) 407–31.
———. *The Social World of Luke-Acts: Models for Interpretation*. Peabody, MA: Hendrickson, 1991.
Nickelsburg, George. *Jewish Literature between the Bible and the Mishnah. A Historical and Literary Introduction*. Philadelphia, PA: Fortress, 1981.
———. *Resurrection, Immortality, and Eternal Life in Intertestamental Judaism*. Cambridge: Harvard University Press, 1972.
Niebecker, E. *Das allgemeine Priestertum der Gläubigen*. Paderborn: Schöningh, 1936.
Niebuhr, H. Richard. *Christ and Culture*. New York: Harper & Row, 1975.
Nineham, D. E. *Studies in the Gospels: Essays in Memory of R. H. Lightfoot*. Oxford: Basil Blackwell, 1955.
Noland, "Salvation-History and Eschatology." In *Witness to the Gospel: The Theology of Acts*, edited by I Howard Marshall and David Peterson, 63–82. Grand Rapids: Eerdmans, 1998.
Noonan, Benjamin. "On the Efficacy of the Atoning Sacrifices: A Biblical Theology of Sacrifice from Leviticus." *BBR* 31.3 (2021) 285–318.
Norden, Edward. *Die antike Kunstprosa vom Vi. Jahrhunddert V. Chr. Bis im Die Zeit Der Renaissance*. Sydney: Wentworth, 2018.
Novenson, Matthew V. "Why Are There Some Petrine Epistles Rather Than None?" In *Peter in Early Christianity*, edited by Helen Bond and Larry Hurtado, 146–57. Grand Rapids: Eerdmans, 2015.
Nygren, Anders. *Agape and Eros*. London: SCPK, 1957.
O'Brien, P. T. "Letters, Letter Forms." In *Dictionary of Paul and His Letters*, edited by Hawthorne et al., 550–53. Downers Grove: InterVarsity, 1993.
O'Conner, Daniel William. *Peter in Rome: The Literary, Liturgical, and the Archeological Evidence*. New York: Columbia University Press, 1969.
Oden, Thomas. *The Justification Reader*. Grand Rapids: Eerdmans, 2002.
Oliver, Nicholas. "The Fisherman as Expositor." *ExpTim* 28 (1917) 230.
Ortlund, Dane. "The Old Testament Background and Eschatological Significance of Jesus Walking on the Sea (Mark 6:45–52)." *Neot* 46.2 (2012) 325–26.
Oss, Douglas. "The Interpretation of the 'Stone' Passages by Peter and Paul: A Comparative Study." *JETS* 32.2 (1989) 181–200.
Oswalt, John. *The Book of Isaiah*. Grand Rapids: Eerdmans, 1988.
Otto, Rudolf. *The Idea of the Holy: An Inquiry into the Non-Rational Factor in the Idea of the Divine and Its Relation to the Rational*. Hamondsworth: Penguin, 1959.

Padilla, Osvaldo. "The Speeches in Acts: Historicity, Theology, and Genre." In *Issues in Luke-Acts: Selected Essays*, edited by Sean Adams and Michael Pahl, 171-94. Piscataway, NJ: Gorgias, 2012.
Pannenberg, Wolfhart. *Anthropology in Theological Perspective*. Philadelphia, PA: Westminster, 1985.
———. *Systematic Theology*. Grand Rapids: Eerdmanns, 1988.
Pao, David. *Acts and the Isaianic New Exodus*. Grand Rapids: Baker, 2000.
Parvis, Paul. "When Did Peter Become Bishop of Antioch?" In *Peter in Early Christianity*, edited by Helen Bond and Larry Hurtado, 263-72. Grand Rapids: Eerdmans, 2015.
Paschke, Boris A. "The Roman ad bestias Execution as a Possible Historical Background for 1 Peter 5.8." *JSNT* 28 (2006) 489-500.
Patai, Raphael. *The Messiah Texts: Jewish Legends of Three Thousand Years*. Detroit: Wayne State, 1979.
Pate, C. Marvin. *Communities of the Last Days: The Dead Sea Scrolls, the New Testament and the Story of Israel*. Downers Grove: InterVarsity, 2000.
Pate, C. Marvin, and Douglas Kennard. *Deliverance Now and Not Yet: The New Testament and the Great Tribulation*. New York: Lang, 2003.
Perdelwitz, R. *Die Mysterienreligion und das Problem des 1 Petrusbriefes*. Giessen: Alfred Töpelmann, 1911.
Perkins, Pheme. *Peter: Apostle for the Whole Church*. Minneapolis, MN: Fortress, 2000.
Perkins, William. *The Workes of That Famous and Worthy Minister of Christ in the University of Cambridge, Mr. William Perkins*. London: Legat, 1635.
Pierce, C. A. *Conscience in the New Testament*. London: SCM, 1955.
Pierce, Chad. *Spirits and the Proclamation of Christ: 1 Peter 3:18-22 in Light of Sin and Punishment Traditions in Early Jewish and Christian Literature*. Tübingen: Mohr Siebeck, 2011.
Pierce, Charles Sanders. *The Collected Papers of Charles Sanders Pierce*. Edited by Charles Hartshorne and Paul Weiss. Cambridge: Harvard University Press, 1966.
———. "The Fixation of Belief." *Popular Science Monthly* 12 (1877) 1-15.
———. "How to Make Our Ideas Clear." *Popular Science Monthly* 12 (1878) 286-302.
Pitre, Brant. *Jesus, the Tribulation, and the End of the Exile: Restoration Eschatology and the Origin of the Atonement*. Tübingen: Mohr Siebeck, 2005.
Plantinga, Alvin. *Knowledge and Christian Belief*. Grand Rapids: Eerdmans, 2015.
———. "Reason and Basic Belief in God." In *Faith and Rationality: Reason and Belief in God*, edited by Alvin Plantinga and Nicholas Woltersdorff, 16-93. Notre Dame: University of Notre Dame, 1983.
———. *Warrant and Proper Function*. New York: Oxford, 1993.
Plato. "Meno." In *Great Books of the Western World: Plato*, 7:115-41. Chicago: Encyclopaedia Britannica, 1952.
———. "Phaedo." In *Great Books of the Western World: Plato*, 7:174-90. Chicago: Encyclopaedia Britannica, 1952.
———. "Phaedrus." In *Great Books of the Western World: Plato*, 7:220-51. Chicago: Encyclopaedia Britannica, 1952.
———. "Timaeus." In *Great Books of the Western World: Plato*, 7:442-77. Chicago: Encyclopaedia Britannica, 1952.
Plummer, Alfred. *A Critical and Exegetical Commentary on the Gospel According to St. Luke*. ICC. Edinburgh: T. & T. Clark, 1896.

———. *The General Epistles of St. James and St. Jude*. The Expositor's Bible. London: Hodder & Stoughton, 1899.
Poland, Franz. *Geschichte des griechischen Vereinswesens*. Preis-schriften... der fürstlich Jablonowkischen Gesellschaft 38. Leipzig: Teubner, 1909.
Porten, Bezalel. *Archives from Elephantine*. Berkley, CA: University of California, 1968.
Porter, Stanley. "Thucydides 1.22.1 and Speeches in Acts: Is There a Thucydidean View?" *NovT* 2 (1990) 121–42.
———. "τοῦτο πρῶτον γινώσκοντες ὅτι in 2 Peter 1:20 and Hellenistic Epistolary Convention." *JBL* 127.1 (2008) 156–71.
Puech, Émile. "Une apocalypse messianique (4Q521)." *Revue de Qumrân* 15.4 (1992) 475–522.
Quenstedt, Johann Andreas. *Theologia didactio-polemica Polemica*. Wittenberg: Johanne Ludolph Quenstedt, 1685.
Raackam, Richard. *The Book of Acts in Its First Century Setting*. Grand Rapids: Eerdmans, 1995.
Rahner, Karl, and Herbert Vorgrimler. *Theological Dictionary*. New York: Herder & Herder, 1965.
Räisänen, Heikki. *Das "Messiasgheimnis" im Markusevangelium*. Helsinki: Länsi-Suomi, 1976.
Reeder, Caryn. "1 Peter 3:1–6: Biblical Authority and Battered Wives." *BBR* 25.4 (2015) 519–39.
Reese, Ruth A. *2 Peter & Jude*. Two Horizons New Testament Commentary. Grand Rapids: Eerdmans, 2007.
Reicke, Bo Ivar. *The Disobedient Spirits and Christian Baptism: A Study of 1 Pet. iii.19 and Its Context*. Kobenhaun: Ejnar Munksgaard, 1946.
———. *The Epistles of James, Peter and Jude*. Bijbel 37. Garden City, NY: Doubleday, 1964.
Reid, Thomas. *Thomas Reid: An Inquiry into the Human Mind on the Principles of Common Mind*. Edited by Derek Brookes. Edinburgh: Edinburgh University Press, 1997.
Reuschling, Wyndy. "The Means and End in 2 Peter 1:3–11: The Theological and Moral Significance of Theosis." *Journal of Theological Interpretation* 8.2 (2014) 275–86.
Reynolds, B. E. "The 'One Like a Son of Man' According to the Old Greek of Daniel 7.13–14." *Bib* 89 (2008) 70–80.
Rhee, Helen. *Loving the Poor, Saving the Rich: Wealth, Poverty, and Early Christian Formation*. Grand Rapids: Baker, 2012.
Rhetorica ad Herennium. Translated by H. Rackham. Cambridge: Harvard University Press, 1957.
Richards, G. C. "1 Peter 3:21." *JTS* 32 (1931) 77.
Richards, E. Randolf. "Silvanus Was Not Peter's Secretary: Theological Bias in Reading Bias in Interpreting διὰ Σιλουανοῦ ἔγραψα in 1 Pet 5:12." *JETS* 43 (2000) 417–32.
Richards E. Randolf, and Kevin Boyle. "Did Ancients Know the Testaments Were Pseudepigraphic? Implications for 2 Peter." *BBR* 30.3 (2020) 403–23.
Ricoeur, Paul. *Essays on Biblical Interpretation*. Minneapolis: Fortress, 1980.
———. *Memory, History, Forgetting*. Chicago: University of Chicago Press, 2004.
———. *Oneself as Another*. Chicago: The University of Chicago Press, 1992.
———. "Toward a Hermeneutic of the Idea of Revelation." In *Essays on Biblical Interpretation*, 73–118. Minneapolis: Fortress, 1980.

Ridderbos, Herman. *The Speeches of Peter in the Acts of the Apostles.* London: Tyndale, 1956.
Ridlehoover, Charles. "The Matthean Peter: as Archetype and Antitype." *JETS* 64.4 (2021) 729–44.
Riesenfeld, Herald. *Jesus Transfiguré: l'arriére-plan récit évangélique de la transfiguration de Notre-Seigneur.* Kobenhaven: Munksgaard, 1947.
Rigaux, Beda. *The Testimony of St. Mark.* Chicago: Franciscan Herald, 1966.
Robbins, Vernon. *Exploring the Texture of Texts: A Guide to Socio-Rhetorical Interpretation.* Valley Forge: Trinity, 1996.
———. *The Tapestry of Early Christian Discourse: Rhetoric, Society and Ideology.* London: Routledge, 1996.
Roberts, Alexander, and James Donaldson. *The Ante-Nicene Christian Library: Translations of the Fathers Down to A.D. 325.* 24 vols. Edinburgh: T. & T. Clark, 1866–72.
Roberts, R. C., and W. Jay Wood. *Intellectual Virtues: An Essay in Regulative Epistemology.* Oxford: Clarendon, 2007.
Robertson, A. T. *Grammar of the Greek New Testament in Light of Recent Research.* Nashville: Broadman Press, 1934.
———. "The Greek Article and the Deity of Christ." *The Expositor* 21 (1921) 185.
Robinson, J. A. T. *The Body: A Study in Pauline Theology.* London: SCM, 1952.
———. "The Most Primitive Christology of All?" *JThS* 97 (1956) 181–83.
Rogers, Richard. *Seven Treatises Leading and Guiding to True Happiness.* London: Man, 1610.
Rohrbaugh, Richard L. "The Pre-industrial City in Luke-Acts: Urban Social Relations." In *Social World of Luke-Acts: Models for Interpretation*, edited by Jerome Neyrey, 125–50. Peabody, MA: Hendrickson, 1991.
Rood, T. "Thucydides." In *Narrators, Narratees, and Narratives in Ancient Greek Literature*, edited by Irene de Jonge et al., 115–28. Leiden: Brill, 2004.
Rosenberg, Roy A. "Jesus, Isaac and the Suffering Servant." *JBL* 84 (1965) 381–88.
Roth, Martha. *Law Collections from Mesopotamia and Asia Minor.* Atlanta, GA: Society of Biblical Literature, 1997.
Rouwhorst, G. "Jewish Liturgical Traditions in Early Syriac Christianity." *VC* 51 (1997) 72–93.
Ruether, Rosemary Radford. *Introducing Redemption in Christian Feminism.* Sheffield: Sheffield Academic, 1998.
Russell, D. S. *Method and Message of Jewish Apocalyptic: 200 BC-AD 100.* Philadelphia, PA: Westminster, 1980.
Ryan, Jordon. *The Role of the Synagogue in the Aims of Jesus.* Minneapolis, MN: Fortress, 2017.
Sabourin, Leopold. "The Biblical Cloud." *BTB* 4 (1974) 290–311.
Saldarini, Anthony. *Matthew's Christian-Jewish Community.* Chicago: University of Chicago Press, 1994.
Saller, Richard. *Patriarchy, Property and Death in the Roman Family.* Cambridge: Cambridge University Press, 1994.
Sanday, William, and Arthur Headlam. *A Critical and Exegetical Commentary on the Epistle to the Romans.* Edinburgh: T. & T. Clark, 1902.
Sanders, E. P. *Jesus and Judaism.* Philadelphia, PA: Fortress, 1985.
———. *Jewish Law from Jesus to the Mishnah.* London: SCM, 1990.
———. *Judaism: Practice and Belief 63 B.C.E.-66 C.E.* London: SCM, 1992.

―――. *Paul and Palestinian Judaism*. Philadelphia, PA: Fortress, 1977.
―――. *Paul, the Law, and the Jewish People*. Minneapolis, MN: Fortress, 1983.
Sanders, Jack T. *The Jews in Luke-Acts*. Philadelphia, PA: Fortress, 1987.
―――. "The Pharisees in Luke-Acts." In *The Living Text: Essays in Honor of Ernest W. Saunders*, edited by Dennis E. Groh and Robert Jewett, 141–88. Lanham: University Press, 1985.
Sandmel, David. "Critique of *Short Stories by Jesus*." Paper presented at the Society for Biblical Literature, November 22, 2015.
Santos, Narry. "The New Family of Jesus and the Relativization of the Natural Family: An Exposition on Honor and Shame (Mark 1:16–20; 2:13–14; 3:13–35)." *RevExp* 115.4 (2018) 542–601.
Sapp, David A. "LXX, 1QIsa, and MT Versions of Isaiah 53 and the Christian Doctrine of Atonement." In *Jesus and the Suffering Servant: Isaiah 53 and Christian Origins*, by William Bellinger and William R. Farmer, 170–92. Atlanta, GA: Trinity, 1998.
Sawyer, John. *The Fifth Gospel: Isaiah in the History of Christianity*. Cambridge: Cambridge University Press, 2000.
Schafer, Peter. *Kehhalot-Studien*. Tübingen: Mohr Siebeck, 1988.
Schaff, Philip. *History of the Christian Church*. Peabody, MA: Hendrickson, 1996.
―――. *A Select Library of the Nicene and Post-Nicene Fathers of the Christian Church*. Grand Rapids: Eerdmans, 1994.
Schenker, Adrian. "*kōper* et expiation." *Bib* 63 (1982) 32–46.
Schlatter, Adolf. *New Testament Theology*. Grand Rapids: Baker, 1997.
Schleiermacher, Fredrich. *The Life of Jesus*. Philadelphia, PA: Fortress, 1975.
―――. "Uber die Zeugnisse des Papias." In *Theologisches Studien U. Kritiken*. Philadelphia, PA: Sunday School Times, 1887.
Schmidt, Thomas. *Hostility to Wealth in the Synoptic Gospels*. Ottawa: UNKNO, 1987.
Schnelle, Udo. *Theology of the New Testament*. Grand Rapids: Baker, 2007.
Schoedinger, Andrew. *Readings in Medieval Philosophy*. New York: Oxford University Press, 1996.
Schoeps, Hans-Joachim. *Jewish Christianity: Factual Disputes in the Early Church*. Philadelphia, PA: Fortress, 1969.
―――. *Paul: The Theology of the Apostle in the Light of Jewish Religious History*. Translated by Harold Knight. Philadelphia, PA: Westminster, 1961.
―――. *Theologie und Geschichte des Judenchristentums*. Tübingen: Mohr, 1949.
Schrange, W. "Zur Ethik der NT Haustafeln." *NTS* 21 (1974) 1–22.
Schreiner, Thomas. *1, 2 Peter, Jude*. NAC 37. Nashville: Broadman & Holman, 2003.
Schreuer, Adiel. "Midrash, Theology, and History: Two Powers in Heaven Revisited." *JSJ* 39 (2008) 230–54.
Schubert, Paul. "The Final Cycle of Speeches in the Book of Acts." *JBL* 87 (1968) 1–16.
Schultz, Anselm. *Nachfolgen und Nachahmen. Studien über das Verhältnis der neutestamentlichen Jüngerschaft zur ur christlichen Vorbildethink*. SANT 6. Munich: Kösel-Verlag, 1962.
Schürer, Emil. *The History of the Jewish People in the Age of Jesus Christ (175 BC–AD 135)*. Revised and edited by M. Black et al. 1973. Rev. ed. Edinburgh: T. & T. Clark, 1987.
Schürmann, Heinz. *Das Lukasevangelium*, Vol. 1. Herders theologischer Kommentar zum Neuen Testament 3. Freiberg: Herder, 1969.
Schutter, W. L. "1 Peter 4.17, Ezekiel 9.6, and Apocalyptic Hermeneutics." In *SBL Seminar Papers*, 276–84. SBLSP 26. Atlanta, GA: Scholars, 1987.

———. *Hermeneutic and Composition in First Peter*. WUNT 2. Tübingen: Mohr [Siebeck], 1989.

Schweitzer, Albert. *Quest for the Historical Jesus: A Critical Study of its Progress from Reimarus to Wrede*. London: A. & C. Black, 1906, 1954.

Schweizer, Eduard. "Concerning the Speeches in Acts." In *Studies in Luke–Acts*, edited by L. E. Keck and J. L. Martyn, 208–16. London: SPCK, 1968.

———. *The Good News According to Mark*. Richmond: Knox, 1970.

———. *Lordship and Discipleship*. SBT 28. London: SCM Press, 1960.

Scott, James C. *Domination and the Arts of Resistance: Hidden Transcripts*. New Haven: Yale University Press, 1990.

———. *Weapons of the Weak: Everyday Forms of Peasant Resistance*. New Haven: Yale University Press, 1985.

Searle, John. *Speech Acts*. Cambridge: Cambridge University Press, 1970.

Seeley, David. *The Noble Death: Greco-Roman Martyrology and Paul's Concept of Salvation*. JSNTSup 28. Sheffield: JSOT, 1990.

Segal, Alan. "Hellinistic Magic: Some Questions of Definition." In *Studies in Gnosticism and Hellenistic Religions: Giles Quispel Festschrift*, edited by R. van den Broek and M. J. Vermaseren, 349–75. Leiden: Brill, 1981.

———. *The Two Powers in Heaven: Early Rabbinic Reports about Christianity and Gnosticism*. Leiden: Brill, 1977.

Segovia, Fernando. *Discipleship in the New Testament: 1982 Marquette University Symposium "Call and Discipleship: New Testament Perspectives."* Philadelphia, PA: Fortress, 1985.

Selwyn, Edward G. "Eschatology in 1 Peter." In *The Background of the New Testament and Its Eschatology*, edited by W. D. Davies and D. Daube, 394–401. Cambridge: Cambridge University Press, 1964.

———. *The First Epistle of St. Peter*. Grand Rapids: Baker, 1981.

———. "The Problem of the Authorship of 1 Peter." *ExpTim* 60 (1948) 257–58.

Seneca. *Ad Lucilium Epistulae Morales*. Translated by R. M. Gummere. LCL. Cambridge: Harvard University Press, 1947.

Senior, Donald. *The Passion of Jesus in Matthew*. Wilmington: Michael Glazier, 1985.

Sevenster, J. N. *Paul and Seneca*. NovTSup 4. Leiden: Brill, 1961.

Sheeley, Steven. *Narrative Asides in Luke-Acts*. Sheffield: Sheffield Academic, 1992.

Sh'muel, Y'huda Ibn. *Midr'she G'ula*. Jerusalem: Mosad Bialik-Massada, 1954.

Sholem, Gershom. *Jewish Gnosticism, Merkabah Mysticism, and Talmudic Tradition*. New York: Jewish Publication Society of America, 1960.

Sibley, Jim. "You Talkin' to Me? 1 Peter 2:4–10 and a Theology of Israel." *SwJT* 59.1 (2016) 59–75.

Silberman, Lou. *Orality, Aurality and Biblical Narrative*. Semia Studies. Atlanta, GA: Scholars, 1987.

Silius Italicus. *Punica*. LCL. Translated by J. D. Duff. Cambridge: Harvard University Press, 1949.

Simon, Ulrich. *A Theology of Salvation: A Commentary on Isaiah 40–55*. London: SPCK, 1953.

Sjöberg, Erik. *Der Menschensohn im ältiopischen Henochbuch*. Lund: Gleerup, 1946.

Skarsaune, Oskar, and Reidar Hvalvik. *Jewish Believers in Jesus: The Early Centuries*. Peabody, MA: Hendrickson, 2007.

Skehan, P. W. "A Note on 2 Peter 2,13." *Bib* 41 (1960) 69–71.

Sklar, Jay. "Sin and Atonement: Lessons from the Pentateuch." *BBR* 22 (2012) 472–89.

———. "Sin and Atonement: What the Pentateuch Teaches Us." Paper presented for Institute for Biblical Research, November 20, 2010.
———. *Sin, Impurity, Sacrifice, Atonement: The Priestly Conceptions*. Sheffield: Sheffield Phoenix, 2005.
Slater, T. B. "One Like a Son of Man in First Century CE Judaism." *NTS* 41 (1995) 183–98.
Sleeper, Freeman. "Political Responsibility According to 1 Peter." *NovT* 10 (1968) 281–85.
Smith, Clyde. "Laodicea, Canons of." In *The New International Dictionary of the Christian Church*, edited by J. D. Douglas, 578. Grand Rapids: Zondervan, 1978.
Smith, Morton. *Jesus the Magician*. San Francisco: Harper & Row, 1978.
Smith, Terence. *Petrine Controversies in Early Christianity: Attitudes towards Peter in Christian Writings of the First Two Centuries*. Tübingen: J. C. B. Mohr, 1985.
Snodgrass, Klyne. "From Allegorizing to Allegorizing: A History of the Interpretation of the Parables of Jesus." In *The Historical Jesus in Recent Research*, edited by James Dunn and Scot McKnight, 248–68. Winona Lake, IN: Eisenbrauns, 2005.
Snyder, John Ivan. *The Promise of His Coming: The Eschatology of 2 Peter*. San Mateo, CA: Western, 1986.
Snyder, Graydon F. "Survey and 'New' Thesis on the Bones of Peter." *BA* 32.1 (1969) 1–24.
Soards, Marion L. *The Speeches in Acts: Their Content, Context, and Concerns*. Louisville: Westminster, 1994.
Soden, Herman von. *Urchristliche Literaturgeschichte in Die Schriften des Neuen Testaments*. Berlin: Alexander Duncker, 1905.
Spicq, Ceslas. *L'Epitre aux Hebreux*. Paris: Gabalda, 1952.
Stamm, Johann Jakob. *Erlösen und Vergeben im alten Testament: Eine begriffsgeschichtliche Untersuchung*. Bern: Francke, 1940.
Stanley, David. "The Conception of Salvation in Primitive Christian Preaching." *CBQ* 18 (1956) 231–54.
Starr, James. *Sharers in Divine Nature: 2 Peter 1:4 in Its Hellenistic Context*. ConB 33. Stockholm: Almqvist & Wiksell, 2000.
Stauffer, Ethelbert. *Jesus and His Story*. Translated by Richard and Clara Winston. New York: Knopf, 1960.
Stegman, Thomas. "'The Spirit of Wisdom and Understanding': Epistemology in Luke-Acts." In *The Bible and Epistemology: Biblical Soundings on the Knowledge of God*, edited by Mary Healy and Robin Parry, 90–94. Milton Keynes: Paternoster, 2007.
Stendahl, Krister. *The School of St. Matthew & Its Use of the Old Testament*. Lund: C. W. K. Gleerup, 1954.
Stern, Ephraim. *New Encyclopedia of Archeological Excavations in the Holy Land*. Jerusalem: Carta, 1993.
Stibbs, Alan M. *The First Epistle General of Peter*. TNTC. Grand Rapids: Eerdmans, 1959.
Stobel, Albert. "Das Aposteldekratt als Folge des antiechenischen Strettes." In *Kontinutat und Erdenherit*, edited by G. Muller and H. Strenger, 81–104. Freeberg: Verlag Herder GmbH, 1981,
Stock, Augustine. "Is Matthew's Presentation of Peter Ironic?" *BTB* 17.2 (1987) 64–69.
———. *The Way in the Wilderness: Wilderness and Moses Themes in Old Testament and New*. Collegeville: Liturgical, 1969.

Strack, Herman L., and Paul Billerbeck. *Kommentar zum Neuen Testament aus Talmud und Midrash*. München: Beck, 1978–83.

Strack, Max. "Die Müllerinnung in Alexandrien." *ZNW* 4 (1903) 213–34.

Strange, James. "Ancient Texts, Archeology as Text, and the Problem of the First Century Synagogue." In *Evolution of the Synagogue: Problems and Progress*, edited by Howard Clark Kee and Lynn Cohick, 27–45. Harrisburg: Brill, 1999.

Strange, James, and Hershel Shanks. "Has the House Where Jesus Stayed in Capernaum Been Found?" *BAR* 8 (1982) 30–32.

Strauss, David. *The Life of Jesus Critically Examined*. London: Chapman, 1846.

Strecker, Georg. "Appendix 1: On the Problem of Jewish Christianity." In *Orthodoxy and Heresy in Earliest Christianity*, by Walter Bauer, 241–85. Minneapolis, MN: Fortress, 1971.

———. *Das Judenchristentum in den Pseudoklementinen*. TU 70, no. 2. Berlin: Akademie, 1981.

———. "The Kerygmata Petrou." In *The New Testament Apocrypha*, edited by Edward Hennecke and Wilhelm Schneemelcher, 2:102–27. Philadelphia, PA: Westminster, 1965.

Streeter, Burnett H. *The Primitive Church*. New York: Macmillan, 1929.

Stuhlmacher, Peter. *The Gospel and the Gospels*. Grand Rapids: Eerdmans, 1991.

Stuhlmueller, Carroll. "Yahweh-King and Deutero-Isaiah." *BR* 15 (1970) 32–45.

Swinburne, Richard. *The Evolution of the Soul*. Oxford: Clarendon, 1986.

Tacitus. *Ann.* Translated by John Jackson. LCL. Cambridge: Harvard University Press, 1951.

Talbert, Charles. *Matthew*. Grand Rapids: Baker, 2010.

———. *Perspectives on First Peter*. Macon: Mercer University Press, 1986.

Talbert, G. W. "Biographies of Philosophers and Rulers as Instruments of Religious Propaganda in Mediterranean Antiquity." *ANRW* 2.16.2 (1978) 1619–51.

———. *Learning Through Suffering. The Educational Value of Suffering in the New Testament and Its Milieu*. Collegeville: Liturgical Press, 1991.

Taylor, J. E. "The Phenomenon of Early Jewish Christianity: Reality or Scholarly Invention." *VC* 44 (1990) 313–34.

Taylor, R. O. P. *The Groundwork of the Gospels*. Oxford: Basil Blackwell, 1946.

Tenney, Merrill. "Some Possible Parallels Between 1 Peter and John." In *New Dimensions in New Testament Study*, edited by Richard Longenecker and Merrill Tenney, 370–77. Grand Rapids: Zondervan, 1974.

Tertullian. *The Writings of Quintus Sept. Flor. Tertullianus*. Edited by Richard Ellmann. Kila: Kessinger, 1869–70.

Teugels, Lieve M. "Consolation and Composition in a Rabbinic Homily on Isaiah 40: *Pesiqta' de Rav Kahana'* 16." In *Studies in the Book of Isaiah*, edited by J. Van Ruiten and M. Vervenne, 433–46. Leuven: Leuven University Press, 1997.

Thatcher, Tom. *Jesus, the Voice, and the Text: Beyond the Oral and Written Gospel*. Waco: Baylor University Press, 2008.

———. "Why John Wrote a Gospel: Memory and History in an Early Christian Community." In *Memory, Tradition, and Text: Uses of the Past in Early Christianity*, edited by Alan Kirk and Tom Thatcher, 79–98. Semeia Studies 52. Atlanta, GA: Society of Biblical Literature, 2005.

Thayer, Joseph. *A Greek-English Lexicon of the New Testament: Coded with Strong's Concordance Numbers*. Carol Stream: Tyndale, 1995.

Theissen, Gerd. *Lokalkolorit und Zeitgeschichte in den Evangelien*. NTOA 8. Göttingen: Universitatsverlag Freiburg Vandenhoeck Ruprecht, 1989.

Theissen, Gerd, and Annette Merz. *The Historical Jesus: A Comprehensive Guide*. Minneapolis, MN: Fortress, 1998.

Thiselton, Anthony. *The First Epistle to the Corinthians*. Grand Rapids: Eerdmans, 2000.

Thomas, John. *Footwashing in John 13 and the Johannine Community*. JSNTSup 61. Sheffield: Sheffield Academic Press, 1991.

Thornton, T. D. G. "1 Peter, a Pascal Liturgy?" *JTS* 12 (1961) 17–26.

Thurén, Lauri. *Argument and Theology in 1 Peter: The Origins of Christian Paraenesis*, Sheffield: Sheffield Academic, 1995.

———. *The Rhetorical Strategy of 1 Peter, with Special Regard to Ambiguous Expressions*. Åbo, Findland: Åbo Academy Press, 1990.

Tillich, Paul. *Systematic Theology*. Chicago: University of Chicago, 1963.

Tite, Philip. "The Compositional Function of the Petrine Prescript: A Look at 1 Pet 1:1–3." *JETS* 39 (1996) 47–56.

———. "Nurslings, Milk and Moral Development in Greco-Roman Context: A Reappraisal of the Paraenetic Utilization of Metaphor in 1 Peter 2.1–3." *JSNT* 31.4 (2009) 371–400.

Tödt, H. E. *The Son of Man in the Synoptic Tradition*. Translated by D. M. Barton, London: SCM, 1965.

Torrance, T. F. *The Royal Priesthood*. Edinburgh: T. & T. Clark, 1993.

Tosato, Angelo. "The Law of Leviticus 18:18: A Reexamination." *CBQ* 46 (1984) 199–214.

Toussaint, Stanley. *Behold the King: A Study of Matthew*. Portland: Multnomah, 1980.

Towner, Philip H. "Households and Household Codes." In *Dictionary of Paul and His Letters*, edited by Gerald Hawthorne et al., 417–19. Downers Grove: InterVarsity, 1993.

Tracy, Steven. "Domestic Violence in the Church and Redemptive Suffering in 1 Peter." *CTJ* 41 (2006) 279–96.

Treggiari, Susan. *Roman Marriage: Iusti coniures from the Time of Cicero to the Time of Ulpian*. Oxford: Clarendon, 1991.

Trites, Allison. *The New Testament Concept of Witness*. Cambridge: Cambridge University Press, 1977.

Trompf, G. W. *The Idea of Historical Recurrence in Western Thought: From Antiquity to the Reformation*. Berkeley: University of California Press, 1979.

Tuckett, C. M. *The Messianic Secret*. Issues in Religion and Theology 1. London: SPCK, 1983.

Twelftree, Graham. *The Miracle Worker*. Downers Grove: InterVarsity, 1999.

Tyson, Joseph B. "Blindness of the Disciples in Mark." *JBL* 80.3 (1961) 261–68.

Tzaferis, Vassilios. "Capernaum." In *New Encyclopedia of Archeological Excavations in the Holy Land*, edited by Ephraim Stern, 1:201–95. 4 vols. Jerusalem: Carta, 1993.

Van Brock, N. "Substitution rituelle." *RHA* 17.65 (1959) 117–46.

VanderKam, James, and Peter Flint. *The Meaning of the Dead Sea Scrolls: Their Significance for Understanding the Bible, Judaism, Jesus, and Christianity*. San Francisco: HarperSanFrancisco, 2002.

VanGemeren, Willem. *New International Dictionary of Old Testament Theology and Exegesis*. 5 vols. Grand Rapids: Zondervan, 1997.

Van Gulick, Robert. "Reduction, Emergence, and the Mind/Body Problem: A Philosophic Overview." In *Evolution and Emergence: Systems, Organisms, Persons*, edited by Nancey Murphy and William Stoeger, 40–73. Oxford: Oxford University Press, 2007.

Van Kooten, George. *Paul's Anthropology in Context: The Image of God, and Tripartite Man in Ancient Judaism, Ancient Philosophy and Early Christianity*. Tübingen: Mohr Siebeck, 2008.

Van Unnik, W. C. "Christianity According to Peter." *ExpTim* 68 (1956) 79–83.

———. "The Teaching of Good Works in 1 Peter." *NTS* 1 (1954) 95–109.

Van Voorst, Robert E. *The Ascents of James: History and Theology of a Jewish-Christian Community*. SBLDS 112. Atlanta, GA: Scholars, 1989.

Varma, Ashish. "Jews and Gentiles Together in Christ? The Jerusalem Council on Racial Reconciliation." *ExAud* 33 (2017) 153–74.

Velasco, Jesus Maria, and Leopold Sabourin. "Jewish Christianity of the First Centuries." *BTB* 6 (1976) 5–26.

Vermes, Geza. *Jesus the Jew: A Historian's Reading of the Gospels*. Philadelphia, PA: Fortress, 1981.

———. "Qumran Forum Miscellanea I." *JJS* 43 (1992) 303–4.

———. *Scripture and Tradition in Judaism: Haggadic Studies in Studia Post-Biblica*. Leiden: Brill, 1961.

Verner, David. *The Household of God: The Social World of the Pastoral Epistles*. Chico: Scholars, 1983.

Volf, Miraoslav. "Soft Difference: Theological Reflections on the Relation between Church and Culture in 1 Peter." *ExAud* 10 (1994) 16–21.

Von Harnack, Adolf. *Die Chronologie der altchristlichen literatur bis Eusebius*. Leipzig: J. C. Hinrichs, 1904.

———. *Die Chronologie der altchristlichen Litteratur bis Irenäus*. Leipzig: Hinrichs, 1897.

Von Hefele, Karl. *Histoire des concilesd'après les documents originaux: 755–870*. Charleston, SC: Nabu, 2011.

Von Rad, Gerhard. *Old Testament Theology*. New York: Harper & Row, 1962–65.

Von Soden, Herman. *Die Brief des Petrus, Jakobus, Judas*. Freiburg: J. C. B. Mohr, 1891.

Vrba, Carl Franz, and Joseph Zycha. *Sanct Aureli Augustini De peccatorum meritis et remissione et de baptismo parvulorum ad Marcellinum libri tres*. Vindobonae: F. Tempsky, 1913.

Wachsman, Shelley. "The Galilee Boat 2,000 Year-Old Hull Recovered Intact." *BAR* 14.5 (1988) 18–33.

Wainwright, William. "Obedience and Responsibility." In *The Wisdom of the Christian Faith*, edited by Paul Moser and Michael McFall, 58–76. Cambridge: Cambridge University Press, 2012.

Waldis, Joseph. *Sprache und stil der grossen Griechischen Inschrift von Nemrud-Dagh in Kommagen*. Zürich: Koine-Forschung, 1920.

Wallace, Daniel. *Greek Grammar Beyond the Basics: An Exegetical Syntax of the New Testament*. Grand Rapids: Zondervan, 1996.

Walls, Andrew. "The Canon of the New Testament." In *The Expositor's Bible Commentary*, edited by Frank Gaebelein, 1:631–44. Grand Rapids: Zondervan, 1979.

———. "Papias and Oral Tradition." *VC* 21 (1967) 137–40.

Waltke, Bruce. *The Book of Proverbs*. Grand Rapids: Eerdmans, 2004.

Waltke, Bruce, and M. O'Connar. *An Introduction to Biblical Hebrew Syntax*. Winona Lake, IN: Eisenbrauns, 1990.

Walton, John, and Brent Sandy. *The Lost World of Scripture: Ancient Literary Culture and Biblical Authority*. Downers Grove: InterVarsity, 2013.
Wand, J. W. C. *The General Epistles of St. Peter and St. Jude*. London: Methuen, 1934.
Watson, D. E. *Invention, Arrangement, and Style: Rhetorical Criticism of Jude and 2 Peter*. Atlanta, GA: Scholars, 1988.
Watts, John. *Isaiah 1–33*. WBC 24. Nashville: Thomas Nelson, 2000.
———. *Isaiah 34–66*. WBC 25. Nashville: Thomas Nelson, 2005.
Webb, Robert. "Intertexture and Rhetorical Strategy in First Peter's Apocalyptic Discourse: A Study in Sociorhetorical Interpretation." In *Reading First Peter with New Eyes*, edited by Robert Webb and Betsy Bauman-Martin, 72–110. London: T. & T. Clark, 2007.
Webb, Robert, and Betsy Bauman-Martin. *Reading First Peter with New Eyes: Methodological Reassessments of the Letter of First Peter*. London: T. & T. Clark, 2007.
Weidinger, Karl. *Die Haustetafeld, ein Stück urchristlicher Paränese*. Leipzig: Hinrichs, 1928.
Weidner, E. F. *Politische Dokumente aus Kleinasien: Die Staatsverträge in akkadischer Sprache aus dem Archiv von Boghazköi-Studien 8–9*. Leipzig: Hinrichs, 1923.
Weinfeld, Moshe. "The Covenant Grant in the Old Testament and in the Ancient Near East." In *Essential Papers on Israel and the Ancient Near East*, edited by F. E. Greenspahn, 69–102. New York: New York University Press, 1991.
Weiss, Johannes. *Das Alteste Evangelium, ein Beitrag zum Verstandis des Markusevangeliums und der altesten evangelischen Uberleiferung*. Whitefish, MT: Kessinger, 2010.
———. *Das Urchristentum*. Sydney: Wentworth, 2016.
———. *Die Predigt Jesu vom Reiche Gottes*. Göttingen: Vandenhoeck & Ruprecht, 1892.
———. *Jesus' Proclamation of the Kingdom of God*. Translated and edited by R. H. Hiers and D. L. Holland. London: SCM, 1971.
Wendling, Emil. *Ur-Marcus, Versuch einer Wiederherstueling der altesten Mitteilungen uber das Leben Jesus, und Die Enstehung des Marcusevangeliums, philogische Untersuchunger*. Tubingen: Mohr, 1905.
Westphal, Merold. "Taking St. Paul Seriously: Sin as an Epistemological Category" In *Christian Philosophy*, edited by Thomas Flint, 200–226. Notre Dame: University of Notre Dame Press, 1990.
White, Aaron. "The Apostolic Preaching of the Lord Jesus: Seeing the Speeches in Acts as a Coherent Series of Sermons." *Presbyterian* 44.2 (2018) 33–51.
Wilde, Oscar. *The Picture of Dorian Gray*. Philadelphia, PA: Ivers, 1890.
Wilken, Robert. *The Christians as the Romans Saw Them*. New Haven: Yale, 1984.
Willard, Dallas. *The Spirit of the Disciplines: Understanding How God Changes Lives*. San Francisco: HarperSanFrancisco, 1988.
Williams, Margaret H. "From Shimon to Petros: Petrine Nomenclature in the Light of Contemporary Onomastic Practices." In *Peter in Early Christianity*, edited by Helen Bond and Larry Hurtado, 30–45. Grand Rapids: Eerdmans, 2015.
Williams, David J. *Acts*. NIBCNT. Peabody, MA: Hendrickson, 1990.
Williams, Jocelyn. "A Case Study in Intertextuality: The Place of Isaiah in the 'Stone' Sayings of 1 Peter 2." *RTR* 66.1 (2007) 37–55.
Williams, Prescott. "The Poems About Incomparable Yahweh's Servant in Isaiah 40–55." *SwJT* 11 (1968) 73–87.

Williams, Travis. "The Divinity and Humanity of Caesar in 1 Peter 2,13." *ZNW* 105.1 (2014) 131–47.
Wilson, B. R. *Magic and the Millennium: A Sociological Study of Religious Movements of Protest Among Tribal and Third-World Peoples*. London: Heinemann, 1973.
Wilson, Jan. *Mesopotamia*. Herstellung: Verlag Butzon & Bercker Kevelaer, 1994.
Windisch, Hans, and H. Preisker. *Die katholische Briefe*. Tübingen: J. C. B. Mohr-Paul Siebeck, 1951.
Witherington, Ben, III. *The Acts of the Apostles: A Socio-Rhetorical Commentary*. Grand Rapids: Eerdmans, 1998.
———. *The Indelible Image: The Theological and Ethical Thought World of the New Testament*. Vol. 1, *The Individual Witnesses*. Downers Grove: InterVarsity, 2009.
Woan, Sue. "The Psalms in 1 Peter." In *The Psalms in the New Testament*, edited by Steve Moyise and Maarten Menken, 213–29. London: T. & T. Clark, 2004.
Wolff, Hans Walter. *Anthropology of the Old Testament*. Philadelphia, PA: Fortress, 1974.
Wolters, Al. "'Partners of the Deity': A Covenantal Reading of 2 Peter 1:4." *CTJ* 25 (1990) 28–46.
———. "Postscript to 'Partners of the Deity.'" *CTJ* 26 (1990) 418–20.
———. "Worldview and Textual Criticism in 2 Peter 3:10." *WTJ* 49 (1987) 405–13.
Wood, Jay. *Epistemology: Becoming Intellectually Virtuous*. Downers Grove: InterVarsity, 1998.
Wood, J. Edwin. "Isaac Typology in the New Testament." *NTS* 14 (1968) 583–89.
Wrede, William. *The Messianic Secret*. London: Clarke, 1971.
Wright, David P. *The Disposal of Impurity: Elimination Rites in the Bible and in Hittite and Mesopotamian Literature*. SBLDS 101. Atlanta, GA: Scholars, 1987.
Wright, N. T. *Following Jesus: Biblical Reflections on Discipleship*. Grand Rapids: Eerdmans, 1994.
———. *Jesus and the Victory of God*. Minneapolis, MN: Fortress, 1996.
———. *The New Testament and the People of God*. Minneapolis, MN: Fortress, 1992.
———. *Paul and the Faithfulness of God*. Minneapolis: Fortress, 2013.
———. *The Resurrection of the Son of God*. Minneapolis, MN: Fortress, 2003.
———. *What Saint Paul Really Said: Was Paul of Tarsus the Real Founder of Christianity?* Grand Rapids: Eerdmans, 1997.
Young, Edward. *The Book of Isaiah: The English Text, with Introduction, Exposition, and Notes*. Grand Rapids: Eerdmans, 1969–72.
Zacharias, Daniel. "Old Greek Daniel 7:13–14 and Matthew's Son of Man." *BBR* 21 (2011) 454–55.
Zehnle, R. F. *Peter's Pentecost Discourse: Tradition and Lukan Reinterpretation in Peter's Speeches of Acts 2 and 3*. Nashville: Abingdon, 1971.
Ziegler, Joseph, and Oliver Munnich. *Susanna-Daniel-Bel et Draco. Editio secunda: Versionis juxta LXX interpretes textum plane novum constituit Oliver Munnich*. Vetus Testamentum Graecum 16/2. Göttingham: Vandenhoeck & Ruprecht, 1999.
Zimmerli, Walter. *Ezekiel 2: A Commentary on the Book of the Prophet Ezekiel Chapters 25–48*. Hermeneia. Philadelphia, PA: Fortress, 1983.
Zzaan, J. de. "The Use of the Greek Language in Acts." In *The Beginnings of Christianity: Part I, The Acts of the Apostles: Prolegomena II: Criticism*, edited by F. J. Foakes-Jackson and Kirsopp Lake, 2:30–65. 5 vols. London: Macmillan, 1922.

Subject Index

Authorship, 11–24, 27–35

Babylon, 53

Call to Discipleship, 59–60

Discipleship, 60–72

Epistemology, 86–106
Epistle form, 47–56

Gentile conversion, 107–15

Hymn, 48–49

Jesus' Death, 134–50
Jesus' Divinity, 66–67
Jesus Resurrection, 145–50
Jew/Gentile Relation, 41–42, 44–46, 81–84, 107–15
Jewish Tradition, 107–15

Kiss, 53

Marriage, not Divorce, 116–23
Mimetic Atonement, 69, 72, 135–36
Miracles, 59–71, 73–77, 81

Persecution, 15–17
Peter as Rock, 68
Peter as Scribe, 68
Peter's Biography, 57–85
Peter's Call to Love and Shepherd, 75–77
Peter's Confession, 65–69
Peter described Physically, 58
Peter's House, 59–60
Peter's Temptation, 71–72
Prayer, 49
Provinces of 1 Pet, 36–38
Pseudepigrapha, 14–15, 33–34

Recipients, 36–46
Rhetorical criticism, 49–50, 55–56

Salvation/Healing, 62
Simon name, 57
Sources, 11–35
Source criticism, 47–49, 54–55

Temporary residents, 36–44
Trade Guilds, 41–42

Vocations, 43

Wealth, 124–33
Witness to Resurrection, 74–78

Author Index

Abraham, W, 100
Abrahams, I, 126
Achtemeier, P, 16
Adams, R, 94
Adams, S, 25
Agapius, 141
Akiva, 124
Allison, D, 58, 66, 68, 90–91, 107, 110, 135, 143
Alston, W, 91
Anderson, A, 146
Anderson, H, 30, 105, 128
Aphrahat of Persia, 114
Aphthonius, 101
Applegate, J, 117
Aristeas, 141
Aristides, 66, 112, 124
Aristotle, 5, 26, 49, 55, 95, 100–102, 105, 117
Artapanus, 70
Arrian, 70
Assman, J, 7, 97
Athenaeus, 59
Augustine, 126–28, 131
Austin, J, 49, 89, 95, 103
Ayayo, K, 65

Bahr, G, 103
Bailey, K, 7, 97
Balch, D, 117
Baldwin, J, 145

Baltzer, K, 54
Bammel, E, 120
Barclay, W, 131
Barrera, J, 110
Barrett, C, 25
Barton, S, 87–88, 103
Bauckham, R, 6–7, 54, 85, 92, 96–99, 110–14
Bauman-Martin, 8
Bauer, F, 81
Baur, F, 4–5, 82–83, 85
Beale, G, 3
Beare, F, 3, 12, 15, 37–38, 48
Beck, B, 135
Berding, K, 12
Berger, A, 43–44
Berger, P, 117
Berkowitz, L, 11, 36–37, 52
Best, E, 16, 37, 49, 87
Bietenhard, 88
Bigg, C, 14, 18, 20–21, 37, 53
Bird, M, 127
Blakley, J, 91
Blenkin, G, 14
Blum, E, 22
Bock, D, 8, 74, 88–89, 103, 135, 141, 146
Böckh, A, 21
Bockmuehl, M, 5, 7, 11, 53, 58, 66, 81–83, 85
Boismard, M, 48
Bond, H, 136

Bonz, M, 27
Boomershine, 7, 97, 106
Booth, R, 58, 107
Borgen, P, 112-13
Boring, M, 8
Bornemann, W, 48
Bornkamm, G, 68
Borrell, A, 72
Bourke, M, 71
Boyle, K, 54
Brown, J, 32-33
Brown, R, 12, 74, 76, 82-83, 112, 114, 136, 142, 147, 149
Bruce, F, 57
Brueggemann, W, 87, 94, 145
Bultmann, R, 3, 48, 92, 100
Burkett, D, 70
Bynum, C, 145
Byrsog, S, 7, 97, 99

Campbell, J, 50
Caragounis, 68
Carrington, P, 48
Carter, W, 133
Chalmers, A, 131
Charue, A, 13
Chase, F, 21
Chilton, B, 89
Chiyah, Rabbi, 127
Christensen, S, 117
Chrysostom, J, 1, 98, 114, 116, 118, 125, 127-29, 131
Cicero, 21, 49, 55-56, 98, 101, 116
Clement Alexandria, 7, 28, 60, 71, 80, 84-85, 92, 97, 114, 116, 118-19, 130-31
Clement Rome, 1, 12, 23, 52, 89-90, 118, 135
Clerc, M, 44
Commodians, 131
Conzelmann, H, 99
Cooper, C, 6, 96
Corbo, V, 59
Coults, J, 49
Council of Trullo, 114
Couthenet, E, 101
Cowley, A, 120
Cranfield, C, 29

Creed, J, 60
Crosby, M, 87
Cross, F, 48
Crossan, J, 141
Crouzel, H, 101
Crum, J, 32
Cullmann, O, 68, 74, 81, 88
Cyprian, 1, 85, 114, 117, 129
Cyril Alex, 1

Danker, F, 54
Daube, D, 90
Davids, P, 3-4, 8, 36-37, 52-53, 124
Davies, W, 58, 66, 68, 90-91, 107, 110, 135, 143
Dawsey, J, 73
De Boer, W, 101
De Campos, M, 65, 91
Deissmann, A, 21, 52-53, 88
Demetrius, 49, 56
Demosthenes, 6, 96
Detering, P, 48
Dewey, A, 6-7, 96-97
Dibelius, M, 48
Didymus, A, 2, 117
Dio, Cassius, 65, 84
Diodorus Sicily, 100-101
Diognetus, 40
Dionysius of Corinth, 85
Dionysius of Halicarnassus, 26, 100-101
Dodd, C, 49, 60
Doering, L, 5, 83
Donfried, K, 82
Donaldson, J, 14, 46, 76, 84
Draper, J, 7, 97
Duchesne, L, 85
Dunn, J, 5, 7-8, 12, 58, 86, 92, 97, 107, 126

Ebright, C, 13, 19
Ehrman, B, 106
Eichrodt, W, 146
Eidersheim, A, 58
Eisenmann, R, 8
Eisler, R, 57
Elliott, J, 3-4, 8, 11, 16, 18, 36-39, 42-44, 49-51, 89, 92, 94, 117
Ellis, E, 60

Ellul, D, 50
Epictetus, 129
Epiphanius, 1, 114
Eubank, N, 133
Euripides, 100, 118
Eusebius, 6–7, 12, 18, 23, 26, 28, 33–34, 53, 60, 70, 76, 80, 84–85, 92, 96–97, 99–101, 118, 127
Evans, C, 110

Fant, M, 118
Farrar, A, 28
Feldmeier, R, 12, 17
Ferda, T, 29
Fernadez, P, 89
Finkel, A, 58, 107
Fiore, B, 101
Fitzmyer, J, 61, 110, 120
Flusser, D, 60–61
Foakes-Jackson, 2
Foley, J, 103
Ford, D, 87
Fornara, C, 101
Foster, B, 33–34
France, R, 29, 65
Francotte, H, 44
Franz, J, 21
Freyne, S, 126

Gaius, 85
Garland, D, 65
Gelardini, G, 142
Gellius, A, 116
Gerhardsson, 7, 97
Gibson, C, 100
Gilchrist, 86
Gillman, N, 145
Goetzmann, 86
Goppelt, L, 3
Gorgias, 6
Goulder, M, 5, 82
Grappe, C, 5, 82–83
Green, G, 3–4, 8–10, 19–22, 29–30, 32, 55–56, 59
Green, J, 87–88, 103–5
Gregerman, A, 105
Gregory of Nazianus, 98
Gregory the Great, 82

Grice, H, 95
Grindheim, S, 89
Guarducci, M, 85
Gundry, R, 23, 58, 69, 72, 107, 135, 138
Guthrie, D, 13–15, 17, 19–21, 23
Gurierrez, G, 101

Hagner, D, 130
Halbwachs, M, 7, 92, 97
Hanneken, 83
Harland, P, 16, 40–42, 117
Harris, J, 49
Harrison, J, 17
Hauck, F, 48
Hegel, G, 4–5
Helyer, L, 2, 4, 9, 59
Hengel, M, 2, 8, 46, 82–85, 97, 112, 118
Hennecke, E, 33
Heraclitus, 6, 96
Hermes, 118
Herodotus, 71, 141
Hesiod, 129
Hewit, J, 142
Hiebert, D, 89
Hillyer, L, 52
Hines, P, 89
Hippolytus, 14, 46, 48, 76, 80, 84, 114
Hoag, G, 130
Homer, 66
Horsley, G, 6, 96
Howe, B, 8
Huck, A, 29
Hurtado, L, 2, 25, 32, 85
Hvalvik, R, 114
Hyppelytus, 114

Ignatius, 2, 12, 28, 75, 81, 85, 89, 98, 114, 119
Irenaeus, 6, 12, 18, 26, 28, 80, 85, 89, 92, 96, 98–99, 101, 114, 126, 142
Ishmael, Rabbi, 138

Jaffee, M, 7, 97
Jeremias, J, 103
Jerome, 14, 20, 23, 46, 81–82, 84
Jobes, K, 14, 38, 52–53
John of Sardis, 100
Johnson, A, 91

Johnson, L, 8, 95, 105
Johnston, R, 105
Josephus, 5, 41, 54, 61, 63, 69–70, 73,
    80, 88, 95, 99–101, 108, 112,
    118–20, 124–26, 129, 137–38,
    140–42, 144–45
Juel, D, 138
Julian, 117
Julicher, A, 15
Justin Martyr, 12, 17, 80, 89–90, 98, 126,
    142–43

Käsemann, E, 55
Kelber, W, 6–7, 92, 96–97
Kelly, J, 1, 14
Keener, C, 12, 15, 17–18, 25, 32, 87,
    92, 99
Kennard, D, 5, 8–10, 25, 27, 50, 52, 55–
    56, 86, 95, 101, 105–7, 110, 113,
    124, 126, 129, 134–35, 138, 144
Kierkegaard, S, 94
Kirk, A, 7, 97, 100
Kirk, J, 66–67
Kistemacher, 26, 52, 102
Klassen, W, 104
Klawans, J, 58, 107
Klijn, A, 114, 126
Knopf, R, 15, 54
Kochenash, 81
Kolenkow, B, 54
Kraeling, E, 120
Künneth, W, 150
Kurz, J, 101

Lackey, J, 100
Lactantius, 17, 65, 85, 87
Lagrange, M, 141
Lanzinger, D, 72
Laodicean Canon, 114
Lapham, F, 86
Lea, T, 15
Leany, A, 48, 60
Leitzmann, H, 48
Lefkowitz, M, 118
Leo the Great, 129
Levine, A, 105
Libanius, 118
Lightfoot, J, 58, 65, 68, 72, 85, 136
Lim, T, 88

Lo, J, 25, 27, 32
Locke, J, 87, 92
Lucan, 142
Lucian of Samosata, 95, 99–100, 116, 118
Lund, A, 17
Luther, M, 3

Mackay, E, 6, 96
Magness, J, 29
Maklas, 57–58
Marger, M, 41
Marcus, J, 89, 91
Marshal, I, 60, 74, 79, 103, 146
Martin, R, 28
Martin, T, 50–51
Maritnez, G, 110
Maximus the Confessor, 1
Mayor, J, 17, 19, 22, 24–25
McArthur, H, 105
McDonald, H, 86, 100
McKnight, S, 137
McNeile, A, 15
McPhee, B, 67
Meeks, W, 118
Meier, J, 12, 71, 105
Melito of Sardis, 42, 48, 142
Meyendorf, 2
Meyer, E, 32
Meyers, E, 126
Michaels, J, 52
Miegge, G, 92
Moffatt, J, 19
Moo, D, 8
Moore, G, 58
Morris, L, 60, 76, 149
Moser, P, 87, 93
Moule, C, 51
Munck, J, 19
Myers, A, 100

Nathan, Rabbi, 144
Newton, M, 108, 110
Neyrey, J, 55
Nineham, D, 60
Noland, 99
Norden, E, 21
Novenson, M, 34
Nygren, A, 94

AUTHOR INDEX 195

O'Conner, D, 85
Oliver, N, 59
Origen, 12, 19, 23, 28, 34, 65, 74, 82, 98, 114, 117, 125, 127–28, 131
Orosius, P, 84
Ortlund, D, 66–67
Ovid, 141

Pahl, M, 25
Palamas, 2
Papias, 6, 12, 81, 85, 92, 96
Pate, M, 50, 101, 135
Perdelwitz, R, 47–48
Perkins, P, 2, 7, 79
Peter Deacon, 59
Philo, 5, 42, 69, 88, 95, 99, 101, 110, 116–20, 124–27, 129–30, 133, 137, 141
Photius, 2, 23
Pierce, C, 91, 94
Pindar, 6, 96
Plantinga, A, 87, 93, 100
Plato, 5–6, 95–96, 116, 129
Plautus, 59
Pliny, 12, 17, 90, 142
Plummer, A, 103
Plutarch, 6, 55, 70, 96, 99, 101, 116–18
Polybius, 99, 129
Polycarp, 12, 18, 52, 117, 129
Porphyry, 117
Porter, S, 54
Preisker, H, 48–49

Quintilion, 21, 26, 100–102, 116

Reicke, B, 54
Reid, T, 94, 100
Reinink, G, 126
Reumann, J, 82
Rhee, H, 129
Richards, E, 11–12, 36–37, 52, 54
Ricoeur, P, 7, 87, 92, 95, 97
Ridderbos, H, 27
Ridlehoover, C, 69, 72
Rigaux, B, 32
Roberts, A, 14, 46, 84, 94
Roberts, R, 93
Robertson, A, 25, 76
Robbins, V, 51

Rood, T, 26, 101
Rouwhorst, G, 114
Rufus, M, 116–18

Sabourin, L, 114, 126
Saldarini, A, 126
Sanders, J, 126, 139, 141
Sandmel, D, 105
Sandy, B, 7, 97
Santos, N, 88
Schaff, P, 2
Schillebeeckx, 7
Schlatter, A, 3
Schleiermacher, 32
Schmidt, 38–39, 133
Schnelle, U, 3
Schoeps, H, 126
Schürer, E, 17
Schweitzer, A, 135
Schweizer, E, 67
Searle, J, 49
Seeley, D, 135
Selwyn, E, 16–17, 26, 45, 48, 50, 102
Seneca, 6, 92, 94–96, 135
Senior, D, 135
Serapion, 141
Shanks, H, 59
Sheeley, S, 26, 101
Silberman, L, 7, 97
Silius Italicus, 100, 116, 135
Skarsaune, O, 114
Smith, C, 23
Smith, T, 71
Snodgrass, K, 105
Snyder, G, 85
Soden, H, 15, 32
Sophocles, 6, 96, 118, 141
Sosa, E, 100
Spicq, C, 13
Stegman, T, 99
Stobel, A, 81
Stock, A, 69, 72
Strabo, 90
Strange, J, 59
Strecker, G, 126
Streeter, B, 48
Suetonius, 17, 43, 65, 80, 84, 88

Tacitus, 17, 57, 65, 85, 100–101, 129, 135, 137, 139, 141–42
Talbert, G, 101, 133, 135
Taylor, J, 114, 126
Tenney, M, 14
Tertullian, 12, 17, 41–42, 66, 85, 98, 114, 117, 142–43
Thatcher, T, 7, 97, 100
Thaumaturgus, G, 85
Theodoret, 1
Theon of Alexandria, 100–101
Theophrastus, 90
Thiselton, A, 74
Thornton, T, 48
Thucydides, 26, 99–100, 102
Thurén, L, 49–50
Tosato, A, 119
Treggiari, S, 120
Trites, A, 5, 95
Trompf, G, 101
Tyson, J, 91
Tzaferis, V, 59

Valerius Maximus, 118
Van Voorst, R, 126
Van Unnik, 16–17
Varma, A, 83
Varro, 90
Velasco, J, 114, 126
Vermes, G, 72, 140
Virgil, 27, 116, 141
Von Harnack, 14, 47, 85

Von Hefele, K, 114
Von Rad, G, 145

Wachsman, S, 66
Wainwright, W, 94
Waldis, J, 21
Walls, A, 23, 28, 34
Waltke, B, 128
Walton, J, 7, 97
Wand, J, 14
Watson, D, 55
Webb, R, 8, 51
Wendling, E, 32
Westphal, M, 94
Williams, C, 15
Williams, D, 26, 102
Williams, M, 57
Wilson, 86
Windisch, H, 48–49
Wood, J, 93–94
Wrede, W, 32
Wright, N, 8, 74, 126, 138, 145–46

Xenophon, 99, 116, 118

Yohanan ben Zakkai, 143
Young, S, 66–67

Zacchai, J, 90
Zimmerli, W, 145
Zzaan, J, 25

Scripture Index

OLD TESTAMENT

Genesis

1:27	120
2:24	120
9:22–23	119
15:13	39
16:2–6	118
21:12	118
23:4	38
42:9–12	119
47–49	54
47:30	62

Exodus

2:15–22	39
3:14	67
12:3	78
12:45–46	39, 144
14:10—15:21	67
16:14–22	63
18:3	39
19:1	78
19:6	4
20:16	127
20:26	119
24:8	104
28:42	119
29:39	144
30:11–21	70, 108–9

Leviticus

11	111
15:1–12	61
15:11	108
15:19–31	61
15:27	61
16:30	110
18:6–19	119, 121
18:20	110
19:18	127
19:31	110
20:1–3	110
20:11–21	119, 121
22:10	39
25:6–47	39
25:23	40

Numbers

9:12	144
15:38–41	61
19:11	62
20:24–26	145
32:41	62
35:15	39

Deuteronomy

	54
5:16	109
5:20	5, 95, 127
14:3–20	111

Deuteronomy (cont.)

14:21	39
17:6	5, 95
17:17	119
19:15–18	5, 95
21:22–23	143–44
22:12	61
23:7	39
23:13–14	119
24:2–4	119
28:25	38
29:17–19	79

Judges

7:19–26	78
10:3–4	62

1 Samuel

12	54
23:21	129
28:14–20	145

2 Samuel

7:12–13	88, 138, 146

1 Kings

1:1:21	62
2:10	62
4:1–44	63
11:21–43	62
13:1–10	61
17:8–16	63

2 Kings

4:42–44	63

1 Chronicles

5:10	39
17:11	62
17:12	138
20:5	62
29:15	40

2 Chronicles

9:31	62
16:13	62
21:1	62
23:19	110
26::2–23	62
27:9	62
28:27	62
32:33	62
33:20	62
36:8	62
36:14	110

Ruth

1:20–21	122

Esther

2:5	62

Job

9:8	67
22:26	63
38:17	68
38:25	66

Psalms

2	89
9:13	68
16	146
32:18	143
33:7	66
39:12	38, 40
51:2–11	110
65:7	66
69:22–28	77, 136
72:13	129
77:16	66
88:26	66
89:8–25	66
93:3–4	66
106:8–9	66
107:18	68
107:23–32	66–67
109:6–29	77, 136
110:1	88–89, 139
118:22	89
119:19	40

Proverbs

10:2	128
14:21	129
20:9	110
30:4	66
31:6	143

Ecclesiastes

7:20	110

Isaiah

1:16	110
1:25	122
6:5	110
6:9–10	91
9:1	13
10:2	122
38:10	68
40:3–5	69
50:6–7	134, 141
51:9–10	66
53:7	139–40
53:12	104
54:4	122
58:6	79
66:17	110

Jeremiah

2:23	110
7:30	110
14:8	39
31:12	64
31:31	104
32:34	110
33:8	110

Lamentations

4:14–15	110

Ezekiel

5:11	110
9:7	110
20:7–31	110
22:3–24	110
23:7–38	110
36:18	110
37	145
37:23	110
43:6–9	110

Daniel

1:5–16	111
4:31	70
7:13	72, 139
9:24–27	134
12:2–3	62, 145

Hosea

1:6–10	46
2:22	64
5:3	110
6:10	110

Joel

2:19	64

Amos

4:13	66

Jonah

1:1–16	67

Micah

6:8	129

Zechariah

4:7–10	138
11:1	143
11:12–13	136
12:10	141
13:7	71, 136
14:6	69

Malachi

1:11–12	110

NEW TESTAMENT

Matthew

	99
1:21	99, 131
4:18–22	132
4:19	60
4:21–23	13, 101
5–7	102
5:7	129
5:14–15	91
5:17–19	114, 122
5:23–24	143
5:28–29	119, 123
5:31–32	120–22
5:44–47	129
5:45	127
6:12–15	129
6:21	130
6:24	124, 130
7:1–5	129
7:13–14	132
7:17–18	90
8:2–3	110, 115
8:4	5, 95
8:14–15	59–60
8:18	65
8:23–27	65
9:2–8	61
9:9–10	98
9:9–17	130, 132
9:13	129
9:18–19	62
9:20–22	61–62, 115
9:23–26	62
9:27	129
9:35	101
10:2–4	1, 98
10:5–6	7
10:8	110, 115
10:22	131
10:33	72
10:38–39	135
11:5	110, 115, 125
11:6	90
11:25	58
12:7	129
12:34	127
12:48–50	88
13:1–9	89
13:13–16	91
13:16	67
13:18–23	89
13:41–42	90
13:44–46	125
13:47	59
14:14–21	63
14:24–33	66
14:28	1
15:3–10	109
15:11–20	110
15:15	1
15:19	110, 121
15:22	129
15:32–39	64
16:1–12	64
16:4	57, 65, 67
16:15–20	1, 57, 65, 67–69
16:21–28	69, 134–35
16:25	131
16:28—17:9	69
17:1	1
17:5	20
17:9	134
17:12	134
17:15	129
17:22–23	134
17:24–27	70
18:1–10	123
18:6–9	90, 136
18:11	131
18:12–13	105
18:14–15	132
18:16	5, 95
18:18	68
18:21	1
18:21–35	129
19:3–6	120–21, 125
19:7–8	121, 125
19:9	120, 122, 125
19:10–12	122, 125
19:13–15	123, 125
19:16	125
19:17	126
19:20	125

19:21	130
19:23–25	125, 131, 133
19:27–28	132–33
20:16	133
20:18–19	134
20:30–31	129, 133
21:12–13	138
22:23–33	145
22:34	139
22:36–40	124
22:41	139
23:2–29	139
23:23	129
23:25–26	109
25:1–13	23
26:5	138
26:14—27:41	140
26:17	73
26:20–29	72, 103, 136
26:29–75	72
26:31–32	71, 136
26:33	75, 149
26:33–35	137, 139
26:35–40	1
26:47–50	137
26:50–56	137
26:53	137
26:54–56	136
26:57–68	137
26:61	138
26:62–64	139
26:69–75	93, 140
27:9–10	136
27:11–26	139–41
27:27–31	141
27:32–54	142–43
27:38–43	130, 142
27:50	62
27:51–54	73, 144
27:52	62
27:57–61	73
27:62	139
28:1–17	73, 146
28:5–17	147
28:7–20	77, 149
28:18–20	77, 81, 149

Mark

	27–33
1:1	26, 32, 100–102
1:2–4	69, 102
1:11	32
1:12–13	89
1:14	57, 101
1:15	26, 57, 100–101
1:16–20	30, 57
1:17	60
1:19–20	13, 59
1:21	59, 132
1:25–34	87
1:29	59, 61
1:29–39	30, 58, 60
1:40–42	87, 110, 115
1:44	110, 115
2:1	59
2:1–12	61
2:4–12	87
2:14–22	130
3:1–6	61
3:5–15	87
3:11	32
3:13–19	1
3:22–30	87
3:25	87
3:33–35	88
4:1–34	26, 105
4:3–20	89
4:11	91, 100
4:12	91
4:21	91
4:21–25	91
5:15	87
5:19	129
5:22–24	62
5:25–34	61–62
5:35–43	62
5:37	1, 30
6:14–27	142
6:34–44	63
6:39	64
6:45–52	66
6:53–56	87
6:56	61
7:2	58, 108

Mark (*cont.*)

7:3-4	108
7:6-7	109
7:8-13	109-10
7:15-23	110
7:19	81, 111, 114
7:21	121
7:24-37	87
7:26	108
8:1-9	64
8:1-21	64
8:15-18	65
8:22-26	1, 65
8:27-30	65, 67
8:29	32
8:31	134
8:33-38	69, 135
8:35	101
9:1-10	69
9:2	1, 30
9:2-13	30
9:5	1
9:7	70
9:12	134
9:14-29	87
9:31	134
9:42-49	90
10:1-13	26, 119, 125
10:5-9	120-21
10:10-12	120-22
10:13	123
10:13-16	123, 125
10:17-24	111, 125-26
10:17-31	124-33
10:19-21	127-28
10:21-22	129-31
10:23-24	131
10:26-27	131
10:28	1, 59
10:29	87, 130
10:31	133
10:34	127
10:42-43	125
10:47-48	129
11:11	138
11:15-18	138
11:25	129
12:13	139
12:18-27	145
12:29-34	124, 127
12:31	127
12:35	32
13:3	1, 30
13:9	142
13:10	101
14:2	144
14:9	101
14:12-25	73
14:17-31	103, 136
14:22-25	71
14:26-31	33, 71, 137
14:29	75, 149
14:32-42	30, 89
14:42-45	137
14:49	136-37
14:51-52	99, 137
14:53-66	137, 140
14:58	138
14:61-62	72, 139
14:62-64	139
14:66-72	72, 140
14:68	93
14:70	72
14:71	93
14:72	72, 86
15	72
15:1	140
15:1-15	140
15:2	139
15:2-32	142
15:4-5	140
15:15-20	141
15:21	30, 73, 142
15:21-39	142-43
15:29-32	142-43
15:34-37	143
15:38-39	32, 73, 144
16:1-8	73, 146-47
16:8	29
16:9	74
16:15	101
16:17-19	30

Luke

	99
1:1–4	95, 99–100, 102
1:21–22	99
1:51–52	86, 133
1:58	129
1:79	62
2:14–29	62
3:1–2	57
4:18	15
4:38	59–60
5:1–11	30, 60
5:5–10	59, 66
5:10	13
5:12	110, 115
5:18–26	61
5:27–29	132
6:6–10	61
6:13–16	1
6:20–23	101, 125
6:20–26	133
7:15	115
7:22	110, 115, 125
7:50	62
8:1–3	130
8:5–15	89
8:10	91
8:14	90
8:16–18	91
8:21	88
8:22–25	66
8:41–42	62
8:43–48	61, 66
8:49–56	62
8:49—9:9	101
9:20	67
9:20–27	69, 134–35
9:27–36	69
9:28	1
9:31	58
9:33–49	66, 134
9:57–58	69
10:5–6	62
10:7	98
10:23	67
10:25	126–27
10:26–27	124, 127
10:28	126–27
10:37	129
10:38–42	130
11:32–41	108
11:33	91
12:34	130
13:23–30	132
13:30	132–33
14:1–6	61
14:13	125
14:15	64
14:21	125
14:27	135
15:2–32	105
16:13	124, 130
16:16–18	122
16:18	120–21
16:19–31	125, 133
17:13	66, 129
17:14–17	110, 115
17:25	134
18:15–17	125
18:18–30	125–26, 132
18:22	127
18:24–25	125
18:31	134
18:38–39	129
19:2–9	132
19:5–10	130
19:12–17	63
19:38–42	62
19:44–49	138
20:9–47	101
20:20	139
22:2—23:13	140
22:3	136
22:7	73
22:14–34	103
22:16	64
22:20	104
22:21–22	134, 136
22:31–34	71, 93, 137
22:44–46	137
22:47–48	137
22:49–53	137
22:54–72	72, 140
22:57	93
22:60	93

Luke (cont.)

22:61–72	72, 137, 139
23:1–5	140
23:2–3	139, 141
23:11–25	140
23:24–26	141–42
23:33–49	142–43
23:46–47	62, 144
23:50–56	73
24:1–12	73, 146–47
24:13–35	147
24:36	62, 77
24:36–46	75, 77, 147
24:47–53	5, 75, 77, 81, 149
24:48	95

John

1:34–42	57, 60
1:44	58
2:14–20	138
3:1	130
6:5–13	63
6:10	64
6:14–15	64
6:16–21	59, 66
6:20–23	101
6:31	22
6:68	1
7:35	39
11:43–47	101, 115
11:48–50	138
13–17	54, 103
13:37	75, 149
14:27	62
15:12	75, 149
15:26–27	99
16:33	62
17:12	136
18:12	76
18:17–18	76
18:24	76
18:25–27	72, 76
18:29–33	139
18:31	140
18:38–40	140
19:1–3	141
19:5	140
19:7–9	139–40
19:12–21	141–42
19:23–24	143
19:32–37	144
20:1–18	73, 147
20:6–7	73
20:11–18	74–75, 147
20:13–35	147
20:19–26	62, 68
20:24–27	77, 142, 148–49
20:27–31	75, 148
20:29	67
21:1–25	75, 148
21:2	77, 149
21:7	59
21:15–17	75, 148
21:18	76
21:20–23	23, 77, 149

Acts

	102
1:1	95, 102
1:2	99
1:3	98
1:2–13	23, 77, 149
1:8	5, 77, 81, 95, 148–49
1:13–15	1
1:16	77
1:17	93
1:20	136
1:21–23	77–78, 99, 149
1:25	136
2	12, 14, 27, 88–89
2–4	26
2:4	87
2:9	45–46
2:14	1
2:14–39	31, 92
2:15	69
2:17–21	87
2:22–23	25–26, 87, 101, 103, 134, 140–41
2:24–36	78, 134, 137, 150
2:25–32	46, 146
2:30	88
2:31	92
2:32	78, 92, 147
2:33	88

2:33–36	139, 150	7:6	39, 42
2:34	88–89	7:29	39, 42
2:36	25, 88	7:54–60	135
2:38	16, 150	7:59	62
2:42–47	78, 101	8:4	39
2:47	26, 100	8:14–25	79
3–4	79	8:20	1, 79
3:4	1	8:20–23	79
3:6	16, 25	8:25	81
3:7–9	87, 98	8:32–33	139–40
3:11	87	9:2	115
3:11–26	31, 92	9:14	16
3:12	1	9:15	7, 82
3:13	46	9:16	16
3:13–18	134	9:18	98
3:15	78, 92, 137, 146–47	9:21	16
		9:25	63
3:16	26, 102	9:27–30	16, 82
3:17	87, 92, 143	9:31	26, 101
3:21–26	46	9:32–43	79, 81, 98, 111
4:8	1	10	81
4:8–12	80, 92	10:9–17	81, 111–12
4:10	25, 78, 134, 147	10:9—11:18	1, 20, 27, 111–12
4:11	140	10:28–29	81, 111–12
4:12	16	10:30–37	26, 62, 134
4:13	13, 51, 58	10:34–43	31, 92
4:17	16	10:36–37	87, 102
4:19	80	10:37–39	25, 79, 134
4:24–30	101, 134	10:40	134
4:25–26	89, 140, 142	10:41	78, 92, 134, 147
4:27	140, 142	10:42	27, 92, 103
4:30	16	10:43–47	87, 150
4:32–37	78, 101	10:48	16
4:43	16	11:1–18	81, 111–12
4:47	141	11:3	113
5:1–11	78	11:15	87
5:3–8	1	11:16	25
5:12	79	11:19–22	39, 81
5:15–16	79	11:21–26	81
5:29–32	80	12:1–6	17, 140
5:33–42	80	12:1–11	27, 80, 135
5:40	17	12:12	30
5:41	16	12:18–19	27
5:42—6:7	101	12:20–23	80
6–7	140	12:24	26, 101
6:1–7	79	13–14	14, 37, 114
6:7	26, 101	13:10–11	98, 115
6:8—8:3	17	13:14–46	82
6:13–14	138	13:13—14:20	46

Acts (*cont.*)

13:17	39, 42
13:43	45
13:48–49	45
13:50–51	45
14:1–4	82
14:4–20	17, 45
15:1	113
15:1–31	114
15:7	1, 113
15:7–11	82, 112–13
15:8	87
15:12	114
15:13–21	80
15:14	57
15:20	111
15:21	114
15:22–40	15
15:29	111
15:41—16:8	45
16:1–10	14, 46
16:5	26, 101
16:10–18	98–100, 115, 117
16:13–15	82
16:14	41
16:19–29	15, 17
17:1–4	82
17:4–15	15
17:34	117
18:1–2	41
18:1–11	84, 117
18:5	15
18:19–21	46
18:23–41	45–46
18:24	83
18:25–26	115
19:1	83
19:9	115
19:12	61
19:20	26, 101
19:23–41	17
20:3	86
20:5—21:18	46, 98–99
20:10	62
20:17–28	54
21:13	16
21:21–28	143
22:4	115
22:16	16
22:21	7
23:6–7	145
23:11–21	17
24:14–22	115
24:27	98
26:17–18	7, 82
27:1—28:66	98–99
28:1–10	98
28:22	86
28:30–31	26, 98, 101

Romans

5:6	116
6:19	116
9:5	22
9:25–26	46
11:26–29	4
16:16	53

1 Corinthians

1:10	86
1:12–13	83–84
1:12—2:6	83
2:1–5	83
3:4–6	83
3:10–15	84
3:22	83–84
4:6	83
4:15	84
5:7	144
7:25–40	86
8:7–13	116
9:5	60, 81, 84, 118
10:16	103
11:23–26	103
11:25	99–100
15:4	148
15:5	74, 77, 147
15:5–7	101, 149
15:6	62, 77
16:12	83
16:20	53, 104

2 Corinthians

1:19	15
13:12	53, 104

Galatians

1:2	37
1:6	113
1:18–24	80
1:18—2:21	84
1:19	80
2:1–12	83
2:6	1
2:7	5, 82
2:9	83
2:11	81, 83
2:11–21	82, 112–13
2:12	82
2:13–28	83
2:14	82
3:2–5	113
3:12	113
3:28	113, 117
5:1	113
5:6	113
5:16–25	113
6:13–18	113

Ephesians

1:18	86
2:19	40
5:14	62
5:22—6:9	117

Colossians

2:14	142
3:18–25	117
4:14	98

1 Thessalonians

1:1	15
4:4	116
5:26	53, 104

2 Thessalonians

1:1	15
2:1–4	23
3:12	118

1 Timothy

1:4	100
2:1–2	41, 118
2:11	118
5:17	98

2 Timothy

	54
1:18	129
4:11	98

Titus

3:13	83

Philemon

24	98

Hebrews

1:1	22
1:7–13	139
4:12	86
4:15	116
5:2	116
9:21	144
9:23–25	144
9:28	23
10:13	139
10:20–22	143
11:8–13	38

James

1:1	39
1:27	122

1 Peter

	11–18, 22, 47–52
1:1	11, 14, 36, 38–39, 46, 51–52, 83–84, 86, 104
1:2	13, 21, 26, 51–52, 103, 144
1:3–5	92–93, 129, 150
1:3–12	51–52
1:3—2:10	52

1 Peter (cont.)

1:6–7	16–17, 21
1:7	94
1:8	94
1:11	89
1:12–14	86
1:14	13, 45, 92
1:17	37, 39, 42, 104
1:18	21, 45, 87, 93, 144
1:19	17, 21
1:20	13, 17, 103
1:22	51–52, 104
1:23	17
1:24	17
1:25	13
2:4	13
2:4–10	3
2:5	42, 87
2:6–8	25, 32, 142
2:7	89
2:9	13
2:10	46
2:11	37, 39, 42, 53, 104
2:11—3:13	42
2:11—5:11	52
2:12	16, 94
2:14	13
2:15	93–94
2:17	42, 104
2:17–20	42
2:18	42, 94
2:21	51, 94
2:21–24	139–40
2:22	94, 140
2:23	72, 140
3:1	13, 94
3:1–5	118
3:2	86
3:3	13
3:4	42, 62, 94, 188
3:6	42, 118
3:7	52, 116–17
3:8	87, 104
3:9–12	42
3:13–17	16, 42, 94
3:14	13
3:15	94
3:16	16, 94
3:17	13
3:18	13, 51, 63, 92, 144
3:20	13
3:21	150
4:1	87
4:3	45, 112
4:4	16, 45
4:5	27, 42, 103
4:6	13, 42, 63
4:8	104
4:10	52
4:11	26, 102
4:12	16–17, 53
4:12—5:11	51
4:13	17
4:14	13, 15–17
4:15	16
4:16	15–16
4:17	42
4:18	42
4:19	16, 42
5:1	11, 13–15, 134
5:4	13
5:5	52
5:9	104
5:10	52
5:12	11–12, 36, 52, 104
5:13	11–12, 28, 30, 53
5:14	52, 53, 104

2 Peter

18–24, 51–56

1	54
1:1	17–18, 21, 25, 32, 53, 57, 86, 92–93
1:1–11	19, 24, 88, 115
1:2	21, 24–25, 32, 54, 89, 92–93
1:3	21, 92–93
1:4	21, 89, 93
1:5	92–93
1:6	92–93
1:7	93
1:8	94
1:9	94, 114
1:10	94
1:11	69–70, 94
1:12	20, 24, 46, 54, 83, 86, 88

1:13	46, 54, 83, 86
1:14	19, 23–24, 46, 54, 83, 86
1:15	19, 46, 83
1:16	46, 53, 83, 92, 95, 99–100
1:16–18	19, 21, 69, 86
1:17	20, 86, 92, 95
1:18	92
1:19	86
1:20	89
1:21	20
2:1	19–21, 23, 93, 144
2:1–4	20, 24
2:1–22	54, 94
2:2	93
2:3–6	129
2:4–9	93, 129
2:6–7	22, 24
2:11–12	24, 93
2:15–16	20, 22, 24, 129
2:17–18	24, 129
2:19–22	21
2:20	89, 136
2:21	93
3:1	18, 20, 36, 53–54, 83
3:2–3	24, 54, 86
3:4	22, 54
3:5–6	22, 26, 102
3:10	54, 143
3:14–18	54
3:16	20, 91
3:17	91
3:18	89, 91
3:19	91

1 John

1:1	95
5:20	86

2 John

1	14

3 John

1	14

Jude

	24–25
2	24
3	24
4–13	24
10	24
17–18	24
21	129

Revelation

14:8	11
16:19	11
17–18	11
17:13–17	86
19:9	64

www.ingramcontent.com/pod-product-compliance
Lightning Source LLC
Chambersburg PA
CBHW062022220426
43662CB00010B/1430